THE
ROYAL NAVY

Below: In 1959 the last of the wartime-designed cruisers, the 'Minotaur' class was finally completed, having lain uncompleted since 1945. The three cruisers (the *Lion* is seen here in 1961) were redesigned and completed to mount new 6in and 3in guns. The rate of fire of the new 3in was so high that with the magazine space available the rate of fire had to be reduced in order not to risk running out of ammunition at a crucial moment in an engagement. (ACPL)

THE
ROYAL NAVY
An Illustrated History

ANTHONY J. WATTS

ARMS AND
ARMOUR

Arms and Armour Press
A Cassell Imprint
Wellington House,125 Strand London WC2R 0BB

First paperback edition published 1995

Distributed in Australia by Capricorn Link (Australia) Pty. Ltd,
2/13 Carrington Road, Castle Hill, NSW 2154.

British Library Cataloguing-in-Publication Data: a catalogue
record for this book is available from the British Library

ISBN 1-85409-324-X

Designed and edited by DAG Publications Ltd. Designed by
David Gibbons; layout by Anthony A. Evans; edited by Philip
Jarrett; printed and bound in Great Britain.

Contents

Introduction

The aim of this book is to present the reader with a pictorial and textual survey of the technological and military development of the Royal Navy from the time of the Industrial Revolution, overlaid by political changes which have impacted on that development. Within the confines of the space available it is impossible to cover every change, neither is it possible to cover in great depth all the factors affecting a particular change. This book must, therefore, be considered as a primer, leading those interested in particular aspects of the Royal Navy's history to study those areas in greater depth using other sources.

There will doubtless be some who will be disappointed at not seeing their favourite topic referred to, or covered in the depth they feel necessary, while others may feel that the wrong topics have been chosen to illustrate a point. The responsibility for inclusion or exclusion of subject matter and the depth of coverage has been entirely my own responsibility.

By the time the story begins to unfold in the 1850s-60s, the navy had remained virtually unchanged in every way for well over a century. But within a few decades the navy was to change almost out of all recognition. New technologies and materials were introduced from which new weapons were developed, which demanded radical changes in ship design, completely new fighting tactics, and new methods of training.

It is no wonder that men who had been brought up in the tradition of the old sailing navy found themselves incapable of comprehending or even grasping a vision of what such changes could offer. They were not attuned to accepting such change. Fortunately for the navy, there were men who did understand these technologies, realised their importance and were able to ensure that they could be introduced and the navy maintain its hard-won supremacy.

But it was not enough to develop new materials, ships and weapons. The navy had also to develop new fighting tactics. In a long period of peace it was not easy to develop new fighting skills to take advantage of the developing technologies. At that time many of the leading officers responsible for the conduct of naval war had themselves never seen action before. Within the short space of just a few decades an enormous learning curve had to be overcome.

As the turn of the century approached the situation improved and it was time to reorganise the navy's Order of Battle, consider various priorities and start to formulate plans to fight the next war, for there were unmistakable signs that the international scene was changing. The navy has always been an instrument of the nation's foreign policy and as such is so shaped and structured to provide the power, and if necessary force, to ensure that national interests overseas are not interfered with in any way. The Government gave the navy its full support, and was able to call on the navy for its full assistance in pursuance of its political agenda on the international scene. Fortunately the navy was ready - it was trained, it had the ships, it had the weapons and it had the men. And these were shortly to be tested in the First World War.

The story of the First World War is primarily one of containing the German Fleet - which was largely successful, even if it was not totally destroyed as had been hoped might have been achieved at Jutland; and the countering of the submarine campaign. In spite of criticism, the navy emerged from its first real conflict since 1815 with a sense of a task having been reasonably well accomplished, and as the most powerful force afloat.

But forces were at work which were soon to spell yet more major changes for the navy, and not all for the good. Previously it had been technology which had dictated changes within the navy. This time, however, a horrendous war with its huge losses in men, public apathy, a Treasury scraping the bottom of the barrel to meet the cost of the war, a waning importance of the British Empire and growing naval forces in other regions of the world were to impose other far reaching changes. On top of this the country was about to go through a period of political instability and no clearly defined foreign policy was being laid down to meet the changing international situations as they developed through the 1920s and 1930s.

The end result was continuous cutbacks in defence spending and restrictive arms limitations treaties. This resulted in new technologies and equipment entering service behind time or in small quantities, a potentially disastrous battle with the RAF over control of naval air assets, and cutbacks in planned fleet growth and strengthening defences of overseas bases.

The navy was more or less ready when war broke out in September 1939. New technology, new tactics, even new types of ship such as the aircraft carrier, were put to the test and not found wanting. What the navy lacked, however, was numbers. The legacy of the inter-war years and political parsimony left the navy woefully short in numbers in almost all categories of warship.

The story of the Second World War is one largely of technological resources and industrial might being put to the test to meet a major world threat within the short space of just a few years. The strain on the British economy was overwhelming, and was almost more than British industry could bear. However, the navy did receive the numbers of ships it required and the new technology to combat the enemy, and in the process new tactics were quickly developed to put these to maximum use for the defeat of the enemy. It was a close run battle, but it was won, as much by the hard efforts of the men themselves, as by the ships and equipment which they manned and worked.

The usual run-down in naval strength occurred at the end of the war, but it was hoped that the navy would stand resplendent among other navies with its new force of aircraft carriers. But the situation was not to last for long. Soon after, the Warsaw Pact came into being and its western counter, NATO. Within the framework of the new Alliance the navy was given the primary task of anti-submarine warfare, a role it had carried out with consummate skill in the massive convoy battles during the late war. Emphasis was therefore placed on developing ASW skills, ships and equipment, considerations on the development of a carrier-based fleet soon being allowed to wane. With the demise of the Empire, and the reliance

and involvement with NATO it was almost inevitable that foreign policy makers should see the primary function of the navy as supporting NATO allies, rather than pursuing any national foreign policy goals. Hence, the navy was gradually restructured as an ASW force. Apart from various minor skirmishes on the international scene, and usual arguments over defence spending, the navy during the Cold War era managed to maintain its strength and develop its capability in ASW without too much trouble.

Apart from being a period of political restriction the Cold-War era was marked in the Royal Navy by two major technological developments — the introduction of nuclear power for submarines — technology initially imported from America — and the development of missiles.

It is over the last three years that the navy has begun to face a problem of major proportions - one which reaches down to the very roots of the reason for its existence. With the collapse of the Warsaw Pact there is now a requirement for a more general purpose force rather than one dedicated to ASW. But any attempt to define a new role for the navy in the post-Cold War era has been bedevilled by the inability of the government to define any long term strategy regarding its foreign policy. And so the navy is being left to wither, not sure what type of ships or armaments to develop to meet what type of situation or scenario.

Below: In the mid-1960s the carrier *Eagle* underwent a major refit, during which she was given a fully angled deck and the Type 984 fighter direction radar. (ACPL)

Chapter 1

The Royal Navy and Pax Britannica

As the Napoleonic Wars came to an end, Britain began to look forward to an era of peace and stability, and the Government began to change and formulate new policies and attitudes. The role of the Royal Navy, the main instrument of the Government's foreign policy, also began to change, almost imperceptibly. During the previous two centuries Britain had been busily engaged in expanding her trading interests overseas, pursuing a policy of mercantile trade (a trade in which goods were just sold, not purchased). This policy gave rise to Napoleon's famous quip that Britain was 'a nation of shopkeepers'. However, the pursuance of such a policy meant that at some time Britain would come into competition with other nations with similar aims and objectives. Where these interests clashed it was inevitable that there would be incidents and even, possibly, conflict. To ensure that British trading interests were protected and that the country retained its monopoly in this area, the navy had previously been called upon to engage the forces of France, Holland, Portugal and Spain.

After 1815 the Government began to change its policy of mercantile trade. With the fall of the Napoleonic Empire, Britain was now the pre-eminent force in Europe, and possessed the strongest navy and largest merchant fleet in the world. Being in the dominant trading position, and with a powerful navy ready to back up foreign policy objectives, the British Government decided that their interests could henceforth best be served by a policy of free trade, rather than a policy of mercantile trade. Instead of having to fight to gain a monopoly of mercantile trade, the Government could afford to be at peace and trade with everyone – the Pax Britannica. With Great Britain thus leading the world in trade and wealth, and with the strongest military forces available to ensure that this position was maintained, it was more profitable for former enemies to trade with Britain than to fight her.

In the light of this major shift in policy, the role of the Royal Navy changed. No longer would it be necessary for the navy's ships to be constantly on the offensive, ready to engage the ships of competitors to prevent them from interfering with the free passage of British merchant ships in order to maintain the nation's trading position. Instead, the navy's ships could now turn to the more defensive task of protecting merchant ships engaged in legitimate free trade throughout the world and ensuring the freedom of the seas for all. Woe betide those, however, who sought to prevent others from freely using the seas, or engaged in illicit trading enterprises.

Not only did the role of the navy change, but its ships and men changed too. Before long a new kind of sailor was walking the decks of the men-of-war. The changes were to be so dramatic that, by the end of the 19th century, the only remaining vestige of the old navy would be its tradition. The strict adherence to tradition, however, held many disadvantages.

It was a long time before living conditions for the ordinary seaman began to undergo major changes. The ordinary seaman's life in the navy of 1815 was abominable. The Royal Navy may have been the most powerful navy in the world, with undisputed command of the seas, but the men lived and worked under much the same conditions that had prevailed at the beginning of the 18th century. On a first rate ship of the line, up to 170 sweating men would be crammed below in the steaming mess decks, where the bulkheads dripped with water. These humid conditions were ideal for spreading diseases such as scurvy and tuberculosis. The problem lay in the fact that the design of ships had changed little during the preceding century — they were slightly larger and carried more guns, but still relied on sail for movement.

Working conditions, too, were harsh in the extreme. The press gang remained the only real method of making up a ship's complement. As soon as a ship was due to commission, notices requesting volunteers were posted in various public places in its home port. But the rough conditions on board and the meagre pay meant that few were willing to volunteer for duty which would probably end in their being dismissed as a result of injury (hernias, ruptures and limbs amputated or, at best, badly healed from breakages, resulting in a major handicap) or madness. Even if a man survived all of this, he could certainly look forward to a greatly reduced life expectancy from the hardships suffered. Consequently there were never enough volunteers, and the press gang was relied upon to fill the numerous gaps in the crew list.

The first targets for the press gangs were the merchant vessels returning home after long voyages from abroad; then the waterfronts, where many seafaring men could be found; and lastly the town centres. Anyone offering resistance was usually clubbed over the head and carried aboard senseless. It was no use beating the man too hard, however, or he would not be fit for duty the next morning. As a means of recruitment, though, the press gang was reaching the end of its days.

On board Royal Navy vessels the cat-o'-nine-tails was king and the captain was God. The discipline was probably the harshest of any seafaring nation. Even the most

Right: The main armament of the wooden sailing ship-of-the-line up to the middle of the 19th century was the 32pdr. (ACPL)

Lower right: Types of elongating round fired from the 32pdr cannon. (ACPL)

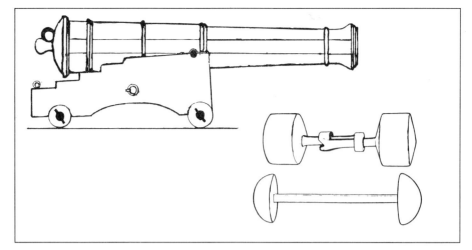

minor offences could result in a man being flogged, the normal punishment being from three to six dozen lashes. 'If we do not use the cat the crew will mutiny,' was a cry heard from many an admiral and captain, but it was usually because of the cat and similar cruel punishments that the men mutinied.

The harsh discipline and frequent use of the cat, together with other equally brutal punishments, led to many men being driven insane. The continual knocks and bangs received from the heavy block and tackle and the massive gun carriages, and the large quantities of neat rum consumed to drown sorrows or kill pain (rum was about the only liquid fit to drink on board, each man receiving half a pint a day), were equally to blame for the poor physical state of many of the crews. It was estimated that, in 1815, the Royal Navy had one man in less than a thousand insane, whereas in the country as a whole the figure was only one in 7,000. This led to large numbers of seamen being discharged, with the result that many ships were often undermanned, or manned with unsuitable or unfit men. This in turn meant that those who were fit and trained carried an even greater share of the workload.

Not only were many men driven insane, but many were physically disabled as well, the commonest form of injury being rupture suffered from manhandling the heavy equipment. The 4ft-long, 32-pounder carronade weighed 17cwt and had to be manhandled about the gun deck, while heavy water casks had to be carried everywhere. Lifting tackle was never used. The heavy canvas sails were a further cause of much disablement; in wet weather these became doubly heavy, and the men would lie out on the yards using both hands to haul in the sail and handle the ropes, at anything up to 120ft above the deck, with the vessel often rolling between 20° and 30° in heavy seas.

By 1815 so many men had ruptures and there were so few really fit men ashore (most able-bodied men having been conscripted for the Napoleonic Wars) that the navy was forced to start issuing trusses. The navy's great surgeon, Sir Gilbert Blane, issued about 3,714 trusses between 1808 and 1815.

While the officers did not face the same harsh working regime as that endured by the men, they were beset by worries. Their major concern was promotion. While the ending of the Napoleonic Wars came as a blessed relief for ordinary seamen, for many young officers it spelt disaster. Officers were nearly always drawn from upper-class families, and were usually found a commission by their parents or a friend of the family with a fairly high position in the navy. A young cadet's future was thus assured. For many young officers the Napoleonic Wars had been a godsend. Not being entitled to inherit their family fortunes or titles because they were often younger sons, they relied on the prize money awarded from the capture of enemy ships to amass their personal fortune, and often to purchase a title for themselves.

The system of promotion was archaic in the extreme. During the early part of his career a young officer advanced himself by patronage (the befriendment of a senior officer in the service, usually the one who had found him his first commission). Seniority meant nothing to the up-and-coming young officer. This method of promotion prevailed up to the rank of commander. However, as soon as post (captain) rank was reached the officer quickly found out that seniority was the be-all and end-all. At this point many stagnated in their career, for they could not gain a more senior post while an older man remained in service above them. Neither could the young officer be passed over by a younger man. Owing to the Admiralty's policy of never retiring an officer, even if there were no ship or shore appointment for him, the end of every war and the decommissioning of large numbers of ships meant that large numbers of officers stagnated on the rank they had reached, and 1815 was certainly no exception. As the fleet was quickly run down, large numbers of officers commissioned for the war were simply placed on half pay, and all promotion for more junior officers was blocked until the older ones died.

As a result, the majority of commanding officers were often too old for their sea posts, and few of the junior officers were senior enough in rank or had been given enough responsibility in the past to qualify for command of a ship of the line.

However, in 1815 the Admiralty instituted a policy which regulated the number of cadets entering the navy. Under the new scheme a board had to approve all new applicants for the post of midshipman before they were appointed. This regulation of the numbers entering the commissioned ranks did to some extent alleviate the problem of too many officers in the service. As a side effect it also went part of the way towards sifting out many of those who would have proved unsuitable for positions of authority.

TABLE I. COMMISSIONED OFFICERS IN THE ROYAL NAVY IN DECEMBER 1815

Flag Officers	220
Captains	860
Commanders	870
Lieutenants	over 4,200

TABLE II. SHIPS IN COMMISSION IN 1814 AND 1820

Category	1814	1820
Ships of the line	99	14
Frigates, sloops, brigs etc	505	92

With the conclusion of the Napoleonic Wars the navy began to undertake tasks designed to implement the Government's new free trade policy and ensure the freedom of the seas for all. In February 1815 the Congress of Vienna outlawed the slave trade (the British had already passed an act banning it in 1807), and the navy was called upon to enforce the ban by stopping and searching all vessels suspected of being involved in the illegal trade, irrespective of nationality, and freeing any slaves. Suppressing the slave trade, however, was not an easy matter. The navy suffered heavily from its involvement in what was essentially a very humanitarian task, but which, because of the circumstances of the slaves, was a singularly distasteful job. The bulk of the traffic was centred around the Gulf of Benin in West Africa. This was a most inhospitable coast, with fever-ridden swamps, and some crews in the navy's West Africa Squadron suffered a death rate as high as one in four. The ban was regularly flouted and proved exceedingly difficult to enforce, and not until the end of the American Civil War was there any real reduction in the slave trade from West Africa. Although this then became a mere trickle, a flourishing slave trade continued from the East African coast to the Middle East and beyond.

While the small sloops and frigates of the navy were engaged in the suppression of the slave trade, other warships were sent to break up the bands of Barbary pirates that took a heavy toll of merchant shipping along the North African coast. In this region piracy was organized on a grand scale, and was frequently backed by the ruling body which governed the country from which the pirates operated. To enforce the new freedom of the seas, Admiral Edward Pellew took a squadron of warships to Algiers in 1816 and bombarded the port, where hundreds of Europeans were held in slavery. With *Queen Charlotte* (100 guns) he took with him *Impregnable* (98 guns, flying the flag of Rear-Admiral David Milne), three other ships of the line of 74 guns, one of 50 guns, five frigates, and seven small gunboats. This was a small squadron compared with the 25 ships of the line that Nelson had estimated would be needed to reduce the port.

The force left Plymouth on 28 July 1816 and, after stopping at Gibraltar on 9 August, where it was joined by a small squadron of six Dutch frigates that had requested permission to accompany it, reached Algiers on 27 August. There the Dey had assembled 40,000 men to oppose Admiral Pellew, who on arriving outside the port sent an ultimatum allowing the Dey two hours in which to release all Christian captives and return all plunder taken by the pirates. The Dey declined, and the British force sailed into preselected positions near the city, out of range of about half of the 1,000 guns of the land batteries. The flagship had just anchored about 100 yards from the pier at 1430 when one of the land batteries suddenly opened fire. At once three decks of guns from *Queen Charlotte* replied, sweeping the mole that was dense with troops and killing, it was said, over 500 people. Three broadsides were fired by the British, practically demolishing the town. A small flotilla of Algerian gunboats sallied forth to counterattack, but all were sunk before they could reach the anchored squadron. By 1800 most of the Algerian ships had been set on fire, and by 2200 the enemy batteries had been silenced and Admiral Pellew withdrew his squadron.

The British losses were slight, with 128 killed and 690 wounded, many on *Impregnable*, which had suffered numerous hits. The Algerians lost over 7,000. The Dey surrendered at daybreak, apologizing to the British Consul and releasing over 1,600 European slaves, none of whom proved to be British. For his part in ridding the seas of the pirate menace Admiral Pellew was created Viscount Exmouth. Although a few individual pirates persisted after the action, state-supported piracy virtually disappeared.

Suppression of the slave trade and piracy were just two examples of roles officially performed by the navy in pursuance of the Government's new foreign policy initiatives, which gradually evolved into what became termed 'gunboat diplomacy' during the era of Pax Britannica. Unofficially, the navy became involved in a number of what would now be termed 'low intensity conflicts' around the world, not only in the expansion of the British Empire but also, ironically, championing the self-determination of a number of weaker states against

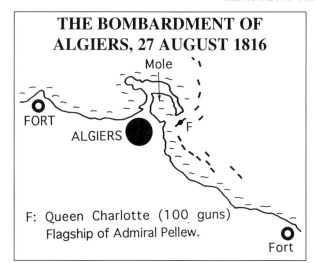

THE BOMBARDMENT OF
ALGIERS, 27 AUGUST 1816

Mole

FORT

ALGIERS

F

F: Queen Charlotte (100 guns)
Flagship of Admiral Pellew.

Fort

Thomas Hurd, in the Admiralty charts, which were then made available to all users of the high seas, and not exclusively to the Royal Navy, as had previously been the case.

Captain Hurd was a man of great skill, and under his guidance the navy undertook many surveys in different parts of the world as far apart as the West Indies, Sicily, Newfoundland and Great Britain itself. He is best remembered for his minutely detailed survey of the coast of Bermuda, a task which took him five years. More glamorous than the straightforward grind of charting currents and coastlines, however, were the Polar expeditions undertaken by the Admiralty during the 19th century. Two Arctic expeditions were fitted out and, although they did not prove very successful, they gave valuable training to future leaders of such explorations.

The first expedition set out in 1817 under Commander John Ross in an attempt to find a North West Passage. In command of the brig *Alexander* was another future leader and hydrographer of the navy, Lieutenant William Edward Parry. The second expedition was under the command of Captain David Buchan, who had with him yet another future explorer — Lieutenant John Franklin — who was in command of *Trent*. Captain Buchan was attempting to reach the North Pole or its near neighbourhood, but both ships in the squadron were severely damaged by the pack ice and failed to reach their objective.

In 1819 two more expeditions were fitted out. The first, under Parry, sailed on 11 May in a further attempt to find a North West Passage. On 4 September Parry, with *Hecla* and *Griper*, passed through 110°W and became entitled to the £5,000 prize offered by the Government to anyone who could penetrate so far to the west within the

the large powers. Warships did not often participate in these struggles, but men unofficially volunteered to serve in the conflicts.

However, the navy was not only responsible for protecting the sea lanes against unlawful attack. It also had to ensure that ships could navigate those sealanes safely. For this it had been given a special commission to chart the oceans and coastlines of the world. The navy's hydrographic department had originally been formed in 1795, but not until the end of the Napoleonic Wars were survey ships really able to set about the enormous task of charting ocean currents, noting hazards such as shoals and wrecks, and surveying multitudinous islands and coastlines. The results of these surveys were subsequently published under the direction of the hydrographer, Captain

Right: A typical 6th rate with reefed sails. Working the heavy canvas sails and rope rigging was hard work, and large numbers of men suffered physically from the heavy work. (ACPL)

Arctic circle. Parry then decided to winter in the Arctic on Melville Island. In May 1820 the ships floated free of the ice and finally broke out on 1 August, having lost only one man out of 94.

The second expedition, led by Franklin, was very different from the one led by Parry. Landing at Hudson Bay, Franklin's force journeyed overland to the mouth of the Coppermine River before taking to their canoes on 21 July 1821. They then began to explore the Arctic coast eastwards, covering 650 miles in atrocious weather conditions and suffering from a constant lack of provisions. Travelling back overland, the party finally reached their base at Hudson Bay in June 1822.

Knighted for his polar expeditions, Sir William Parry succeeded Captain Hurd when he died in 1823. Under his command were twelve vessels which formed the nucleus of the new survey fleet. As his assistants Parry had Francis Beaufort, who took over the office of hydrographer when Parry resigned in 1829, and A.T.E. Vidal. Francis Beaufort, who remained in office for more than 25 years, was knighted for his work, which included a 'Grand Survey of the British Isles' and the invention of the Beaufort wind scale.

Parry, meanwhile, was taking further expeditions north in attempts to find a North West Passage. In 1824 he lost his first vessel, *Fury*, when she was so severely damaged by ice that she had to be abandoned. In April 1827 Parry, by then a captain in the Royal Navy, set out on his last expedition to try and reach the North Pole by sledge from Spitzbergen, taking with him two 20ft flat-bottomed boats. Sailing with Parry was Lieutenant James Clarke Ross, the nephew of Commander John Ross, three other officers and 24 men. After they were checked by ice, the men took to the long boats and, travelling across the floes and on the water, they journeyed for 35 days until the southerly drift of ice forced them to abandon the attempt. They finally planted the British flag in latitude 82° 45' on 26 July 1827.

On his return Lieutenant Ross put forward proposals for an Arctic expedition to discover the North Magnetic Pole. He left England in May 1829 and returned in October 1833, having discovered the North Magnetic Pole on 31 May 1831 and fixed it in latitude 70° 5' 17"N, longitude 96° 46' 45"W.

Below: HMS *Trafalgar*. Originally laid down as a typical first rate two-deck 110-gun ship-of-the-line in 1841, she was subsequently launched as a screw ship in 1859. Apart from the steam plant, the general outline of a sailing ship-of-the-line had changed little during the preceding 100 years. (Imperial War Museum)

Chapter 2

From Sail to Steam

In 1821 an unsuccessful revolt in the Morea area of Greece signalled the start of the Greek War of Independence. Having lived under Turkish rule since the mid-15th century, the Greeks now claimed independence from the Ottoman Empire. They were supported in their fight for freedom by the British and French, who sympathized with the Greek cultural traditions, and by the Russians, who were in sympathy with the Greek Orthodox Church. Fighting continued on and off for six years without any overt support for the Greeks from the European powers. Finally, when Turkey appealed to Egypt for support, the European powers became concerned. However, while Russia was keen to support Greece against Turkey, Britain and France held back, fearing that a destroyed

Turkey would allow Russia greater freedom of movement to entertain ambitions in the Mediterranean region.

Against this uncertain background the three allies sent a combined squadron, under the command of Vice-Admiral Sir Edward Codrington, in an effort to force an armistice between the Greeks and Turks. The Turks declined to accept the recommendation, and the allied squadron sailed in search of the combined Turkish and Egyptian fleets. The allied squadron comprised four British, four French and four Russian ships of the line, one British, one French and four Russian frigates, and a number of smaller vessels. On 11 September 1827 the allied squadron found the Turkish fleet anchored in the harbour at Navarino. The combined Egyptian and Turk-

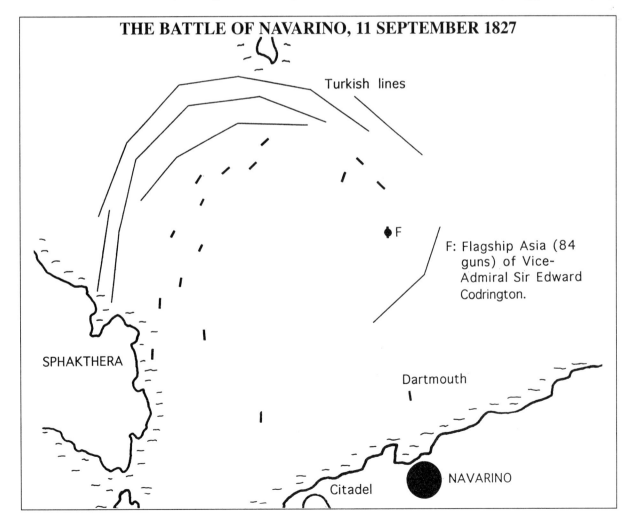

THE BATTLE OF NAVARINO, 11 SEPTEMBER 1827

Turkish lines

F: Flagship Asia (84 guns) of Vice-Admiral Sir Edward Codrington.

SPHAKTHERA

Dartmouth

NAVARINO

Citadel

ish fleet comprised seven ships of the line, fifteen large frigates, twenty-six corvettes and a large number of lesser craft, anchored in a semi-circle in the bay. Vice-Admiral Codrington sailed his squadron into the harbour and moored it on the leeward side of the Turkish-Egyptian fleet, thus preventing any escape to seaward.

As the allied ships took up their positions, the British frigate *Dartmouth* sent a ship's boat away to warn a Turkish fireship to keep its distance. Suddenly the Turks opened fire on ships of the allied squadron, whereupon general action was joined. The Turks were completely annihilated, losing over 50 vessels and about 4,000 men in the 2½hr action. Losses on the allied side were also heavy, totalling 650 men, the main British ships being so severely damaged that they had to return to England for repairs. The battle was notable for two facts. First, it was the last battle between sailing ships of the line fought on traditional lines, in which ships laid themselves alongside each other and blasted away until one of them either surrendered or was sunk. Once action had been joined there was little thought of tactical manoeuvring. Secondly, it was the last time that Great Britain, France and Russia cooperated in a venture until the Dardanelles campaign of 1915.

But momentous changes were already under way for the navy. The advent of steam had begun to have an impact on technological progress, and the navy paid close attention to these developments. However, it was not prepared to rush into a full-scale introduction of the new technology until it had first reached a sensible stage of development. As the world's leading naval power, the navy could not afford to risk its supremacy for the sake of change. Meanwhile, the navy kept itself fully informed of the state of progress concerning steam technology. It could not afford to wait for too long, and risk letting a foreign power take the lead.

The navy had first countenanced steam in 1816, when it ordered some steam-powered dredgers for use in the naval ports. Then, in November 1819, the Admiralty Board ordered the paddle-wheeled steam tug *Comet*. The Admiralty considered that a steam tug with the ability to manoeuvre free of the wind would be invaluable in handling sailing ships in confined spaces such as harbours, where there was a great risk of them grounding and being wrecked. The Navy Board, however, was not at all satisfied with the project and vacillated over the design and construction of the vessel, much to the annoyance of the Admiralty Board. *Comet* (239 tons, 80nhp) was finally launched on 22 May 1822 by Oliver Lang at Deptford. Meanwhile, in December 1821, the Admiralty had ordered two more tugs, *Lightning* and *Echo*.

Steam was in its infancy, however, and the vessels were prone to breakdown. Although it had sanctioned the purchase of *Comet*, the Navy Board under Robert Dundas, the Second Viscount Melville, had little enthusiasm for steam in fighting ships, and its use was restricted to auxiliaries.

A further disadvantage in warships was the use of cumbersome paddles for propulsion, which would have meant a heavy sacrifice in broadside firepower.

Finally, in November 1827, Lord Melville ordered *Dee*, a 700-ton vessel powered by a 200nhp engine and designed to carry two 32-pounders and four carronades. Not for seven years (from 1821 to 1828) was a steam vessel officially entered in the Navy Lists of vessels in commission, and in fact it was not until December 1827 that steam vessels were allowed to use the prefix 'HMS'. Then, in the January 1828 Navy List, the names of steam vessels were published for the first time: the *Lightning* class (*Echo*, *Lightning* and *Meteor*).

In December 1830 a Whig Government replaced the previous Tory administration and at once set about instituting major political and economic changes. One of the immediate priorities of the new administration was to reduce the Navy Estimates, and one proposal was to do away with the the Navy Board. The Navy Board was subordinate to the Admiralty Board, and was responsible for the design and purchase of the navy's ships. It had constantly been at loggerheads with the Admiralty Board, and was finally abolished in April 1832.

In the new administration Sir James Graham was appointed First Lord of the Admiralty, and Sir Thomas Masterman Hardy (Nelson's old Flag Captain) replaced Lord Melville as First Naval Lord of the Navy Board. On assuming office Hardy at once set about redressing some of the navy's shortcomings. One of his most important achievements was to institute important changes in the conditions of service. These concerned the vexed question of promotion for the younger and abler officers. Hardy recognized the cause of the promotion blockage, and as the navy was about to embark on a gradual process of modernization, it was going to be in great need of such men. In spite of the regulations relating to the approval of all new applications for the post of midshipman (see above, page 10), there were still 5,539 commissioned officers in the navy in 1825. Of these, only 550 had active posts; 90 per cent were unemployed. The navy still boasted 205 flag officers (down from 220 in 1815), of which only 10 held active posts, the remaining 95 per cent being unemployed.

Not only were the conditions of service made better, but the ships, too, were steadily improved. One way of improving naval vessels already in service was to increase their mobility. For centuries the main method of fighting at sea was to lay the vessel alongside the enemy, firing broadsides continuously and boarding to capture the vessel. To this end the admirals had called for increasingly heavier broadsides, until a ship of the line in 1830 normally carried between 60 and 74 guns, often had 100, and in some cases even as many as 130. As a start to increasing manoeuvrability and reducing displacement, the batteries on many of the larger ships were removed, converting them into much handier 50-gun frigates. The

46-gun frigates were removed from the fleet or converted into smaller corvettes, while the almost useless sloops and brigs were scrapped altogether. In this way a new navy was slowly created. The heavy broadside was still essential, however, so new ships were designed which would mount new guns in as heavy a broadside as possible while still retaining manoeuvrability.

The ships themselves were not Hardy's only concern. For years the dockyards had been a disgrace. Corruption was rife, especially among the victuallers. These men often supplied food that was unfit even for animals, let alone the hard-working crews of ships. The process of canning had been developed, but even here malpractices occurred. It had been known for a tin of canned meat to contain nothing but a pressed horse's hoof.

Meanwhile, steam continued to advance in the navy. *Dee* had been followed by four *Medea*-type vessels built to a similar design. Then, in 1834, the year that Graham left the Admiralty, ten more steam vessels were ordered. The following year a modified *Medea* design, *Gorgon* (1,610 tons), was ordered, followed by a larger vessel, *Cyclops* (1,960 tons). *Cyclops* carried an armament of two 98-pounder and four 68-pounder cannon, and became the first steam frigate in the navy.

The year 1830 also witnessed a new design of an old invention pioneered by Archimedes, the screw. The few steam vessels bought and built by the Royal Navy had, until 1830, been propelled by paddle wheels. Apart from the fact that their Lordships had reservations about the use of steam in warships, paddle wheels prevented the vessels from fully exploiting the possibilities of broadside fire, as a quarter, and sometimes a third, of their broadside batteries were lost. With the screw placed in the water under the stern of the vessel, the huge encumbrance of the paddle amidships would be eliminated, allowing vessels to regain their full broadside armament and restoring the supremacy the navy had begun to lose. Two great advantages would accrue from the use of the screw — freedom of movement to allow maximum firepower to be brought to bear on any chosen target, and greater protection for the propulsive unit. Paddle wheels were open to destruction from one well aimed shot, but a screw underwater would be practically indestructible.

In 1832 the surveyor of the Royal Navy resigned and was replaced by Captain William Symonds. Symonds had taught himself the mechanics of sailing ship design and construction, but knew little about steam engines. Nor was he really anxious to appraise himself of their capabilities. This was unfortunate, as in 1834, the year that Hardy's term as First Naval Lord came to an end, a certain Edward Berthon presented the Admiralty with a 3ft model of a screw vessel driven by a two-bladed propeller. The Admiralty was not impressed, however, and Captain Symonds continued to build wooden sailing vessels fitted with auxiliary steam engines to drive the paddles. Francis Pettit Smith also tried to convince the Admiralty of the need for screw propulsion, patenting a design in May 1836 which placed an Archimedean screw at the stern of a vessel. Six weeks later the Swede John Ericsson patented a screw propeller model. From this Ericsson developed and built the screw-propelled *Francis B. Ogden*, which was launched on the Thames in April 1837. Their Lordships were then invited to try out the new screw vessel.

To test the capabilities of the new ship it was decided to make her tow the Admiralty Barge down the Thames from Somerset House to Blackwall. The day of the trial dawned, and the most impressive assembly of naval officers ever gathered together to witness a trial duly boarded the Barge at Somerset House. The party included Captain

Right: Frigates were the ideal type of ship to be converted to carry auxiliary steam plant. *Arrogant* (shown here) of 1848 was one of the pioneer wooden steam frigates. (Imperial War Museum)

Left: The first ships to be powered solely by steam were small tugs used to tow the large sailing ships out of harbour, giving the fleet mobility to assemble free of the vagaries of wind and, to a certain degree, tide. Apart from tugs, the only other craft to be powered solely by steam in the early days were smaller, miscellaneous craft used on dispatch duties, etc. All these vessels used the paddle as their prime mover. The picture shows the dispatch vessel *Enchantress* designed by Isaac Watts and built in 1862. She was powered by a 250nhp steam engine to give her a maximum speed of 14kts. (ACPL)

Symonds the surveyor, Captain Francis Beaufort the hydrographer, Rear-Admiral Sir Charles Adam the First Sea Lord, and the Arctic explorer and navigator Captain Sir William Parry. The round trip from Somerset House to Blackwall and back was completed without incident, the Barge being towed along at an average speed of from 9 to 10kts. The man for whose benefit the experiment was really being made, however, was not impressed in the slightest. The only remark he could make at the end of the trip was that, as the screw was at the stern of the vessel, she would be incapable of being steered properly. This after she had just towed the Admiralty Barge down the Thames.

Smith, too, was able to demonstrate his ideas to the Admiralty, partly on the basis of an unofficial suggestion from the Second Secretary to the Admiralty. With the help of a company which he formed in 1838, Smith built a much larger steamer. The new vessel was powered by an 80nhp engine and displaced 232 tons. Named *Archimedes*, she was shown to the Admiralty in 1839 at Sheerness, where she was put through her paces at 9kts. This was not sufficient for the Admiralty, who wanted to see a much more convincing test, especially as all the steamers then in the navy were paddlers. So *Archimedes* was taken to Portsmouth, home of the Royal Navy, and sailed against the navy's fastest paddler, *Vulcan*.

Vulcan was convincingly beaten, but still the admirals were not satisfied. By now there was only one other vessel in Britain against whom *Archimedes* could be matched. This was the merchant paddleship *Widgeon*. As Captain Edward Chappell, appointed to make reports on the tests, noted, there was a marked difference in tonnage between the vessels (*Archimedes* 237 tons, *Widgeon* 192 tons) and also in motive power (*Archimedes* 80nhp, *Widgeon* 90nhp). Naturally *Widgeon* showed up better in the tests, but Captain Chappell emphasized in his report that the power of the screw vessel was at least on a par with that of the paddle steamer, if not superior. However, this was still not the deciding factor.

Following Captain Chappel's report on the trials between *Archimedes* and *Widgeon*, the Admiralty decided to carry out a much fairer trial of strength between the screw and the paddle. To ensure fair conditions, vessels of identical tonnage and horsepower were needed, and it was decided to requisition two sloops for the experiment. The vessels chosen were *Alecto*, a paddle vessel of 200nhp, and a screw vessel, *Rattler*. *Rattler* had originally been laid down by Captain Symonds as a paddle sloop, but her construction had been suspended. Symonds had the plans redraughted, and *Rattler* was completed with a screw and launched in April 1843. In October 1843 she began trials and at once vindicated the screw as a means of propulsion. Although *Rattler* had proved the viability of the screw, the trial with *Alecto* went ahead. On the day of the experiment the two vessels were lashed stern to stern, and when everything was ready they were simultaneously given the signal to steam full ahead. At first nothing happened, but then very gradually *Rattler* began to move ahead, slowly quickening pace until she was towing *Alecto* along at a steady 2.5kts.

In June 1843 the Admiralty had purchased a small iron screw steamer, *Mermaid*, and renamed her *Dwarf*. *Dwarf* was used to carry out further trials with the screw, testing various stern profiles to determine the most effective shape for a stern and propeller, and also testing various propeller configurations, the results subsequently being used in the design of new screw vessels.

Meanwhile, trials with *Rattler* continued, proving beyond doubt the validity of the propeller as an auxiliary method of propulsion. Captain Symonds, however, had reservations concerning the new hull forms being proposed for screw-powered vessels, and believed that they would have an adverse effect on the sailing quality of the ships. In view of this he felt that steam auxiliary would never be suitable for use in major warships.

However, in 1848 the First Lord, Lord Auckland, noted that in the future warships would combine an auxiliary propulsion system with sails. On 21 March 1848 the 516-

ton *Reynard*, a three-masted schooner with a steam-driven auxiliary screw, armed with eight 32-pounders, was launched. The design of *Reynard* was based on experience gained from the experiments with *Rattler* and *Dwarf*, and showed that an increased length-to-beam ratio incorporated in a sailing ship with a steam auxiliary plant would work satisfactorily. In trials *Reynard* proved she could sail as well as a pure sailing vessel, which meant that in future Symonds's wide-beamed sailing vessels could be abandoned for a narrower-beam steam/sail combination. It was found that increased length-to-beam ratio gave better sailing off-wind, and this had always been a problem for sailing ships. Although the new design concept sacrificed manoeuvrability and speed to windward, this could be compensated for by using the steam plant.

The new technology resulted in a revolution in warship design, and leading the world in its introduction gave the Royal Navy an enormous advantage over any potential rival. However, this situation would not last for long.

In 1844 the Admiralty ordered its first screw frigate, *Dauntless*. Whereas paddle steamers were unable to mount the heavy broadside armament of conventional sailing ships, screw-driven vessels could have the full armament. Not only were the ships able to carry a full complement of guns, but the machinery was given added protection by virtue of the fact that it was carried below the waterline, and the screw, being at the stern and below the waterline, was much better protected than the exposed broadside paddle.

Following this, a number of ships of the line were converted to screw propulsion. In the meantime, the French designer Dupuy de Lôme, who had toured British shipyards studying construction methods and techniques, had returned home and was trying to convince Napoleon III that the only answer to British naval supremacy was to construct screw-propelled iron ships protected by armour plate. Napoleon was not fully convinced of the feasibility of the idea, but de Lôme went ahead with an idea of his

Above left: The advent of steam and the development of screw propulsion came at a time when tension between France and Britain was again rising. To build up its steam-powered fleet rapidly, between 1858 and 1859 the navy converted a number of conventional 2-decker wooden sailing ships-of-the-line built in the 1840s to carry auxiliary steam plant. One of the ships so converted was the *St. George*, similar to the ship shown here. (US Naval Historical Center)

Above: The navy's first purpose-designed, screw-propelled battleship was the *Agamemnon*, completed in 1853. The knowledge that the French were building the *Napoleon* spurred the Admiralty to design the *Agamemnon*, which was built on conventional lines with steam auxiliary propulsion. Her armament was typical of the wooden sailing ships of the last hundred years. The *Agamemnon* took part in various operations during the Crimean War and was was present at the bombardment of Sevastopol and the capture of Kinburn. (Imperial War Museum)

own and constructed *Napoleon*, a 92-gun wooden ship of the line, launched in 1850. Her main feature was a 960nhp engine which drove a screw giving her a speed of 12kts. As soon as they received news of the construction of *Napoleon*, the Admiralty lost no time in ordering a British ship of the line specially designed for screw propulsion. Ordered in July 1849 and launched at Woolwich in May 1852, *Agamemnon*, as the new ship was named, had a 600nhp steam engine driving a single screw which gave her a speed of about 12kts. The design proved exceedingly successful, and formed the basis for a new steam battle fleet which the navy forthwith began to build. Apart from her steam plant and an extra 25ft in length, *Agamemnon* was very similar to the classic sailing ship of the line. Steam was still regarded only as an auxiliary to sail, and the navy had not deemed it necessary to review its battle doctrine. In essence this remained the same, with battleships sailing in line-ahead to achieve maximum firepower and then laying themselves alongside the enemy, firing broadside to broadside.

Chapter 3

The Gunnery Revolution and the Ironclad Navy

In the same year as the Battle of Navarino, 1827, a Frenchman by the name of Colonel Henri-Joseph Paixhans produced a new projectile which could be fired from cannon. Called the shell, its incendiary capabilities immediately rendered every British warship a potential fireship. The shell consisted of a hollow canister filled with a charge of 4lb of gunpowder, the whole projectile being the size of an 80lb shot. Having developed the shell, Paixhans, who was determined that the French Navy would not be the losers by it, promptly began experimenting to find a means of defence against it.

The main gun in the navy at the time was the 32-pounder smooth-bore muzzle-loader, so training at first remained fairly straightforward. However, with the advent of the shell a number of 32-pounders were bored out to 8in or 10in to take the new projectile. As it remained spherical for a while, no problems were encountered, and ships normally carried a mixed armament of shot- and shell-firing guns. The usual arrangement was to have the gun deck carrying the shell-firing guns and the batteries above having the 32-pounder shot-firing cannon. It was not until later that gunnery really became complex, when many different sizes and types of guns entered service, with different operational requirements. It was then that the gunners, like the engineers in charge of the steam engines, gained recognition as seaman with their own special training.

In 1830 Paixhans suggested a method by which ships could be defended against his new projectile. Wooden warships, he stated, should be constructed with a belt of iron round the hull which ought to be between seven and eight inches thick. To compensate for this great increase in weight it would be necessary to dispense with one deck of guns.

As a result of the introduction of the new shell and the need for extra protection, the Admiralty began to experiment with new materials. In 1838 they carried out a series of trials at Woolwich with the old three-decker sailing vessel *Prince George*. The trials included a number of tests designed to determine the effect of solid shot against new materials, including a preparation known as kamptulicon. A mixture of cork and india rubber, kamptulicon formed the inside lining of iron plates which were riveted together, the lining being kept in place by wood packing. It was thought, and hoped, that after a shot had passed through the kamptulicon it would close up and form a watertight seal. This it did, but the iron tended to splinter with such adverse effect that its use was discouraged.

William Laird, who had pioneered the construction of iron merchant ships, speculatively built the iron paddle steamer *Nemesis*, launched in 1839. Although Laird had hoped the navy would purchase the vessel, she was finally bought by the East India Company, which used her in China in the Opium War of 1841-43. Her commander, a Royal Navy lieutenant serving in the East India Company, wrote home enthusiastically about the capabilities of *Nemesis*, and this led the Admiralty to give serious consideration to the acquisition of iron ships in 1844-45.

Following the experiments of Paixhans and the tests on the old *Prince George*, the Admiralty began to build vessels of composite construction in which the wooden hulls were protected by iron belts. The next step was to build a vessel completely of iron. This would give the necessary strength to the hull and enable the vessel to mount the more powerful steam engines then being developed, and would also provide extra protection against shellfire.

Like steam, iron was at first used in minor category warships, where it proved successful. This prompted the Admiralty in April 1843 to order a large iron-hulled paddle sloop, the 850-ton *Trident*, which was launched on the Thames at Blackwall in December 1845. Early in 1845, however, even before *Trident* had been launched, the Conservative Government, in its endeavour to capitalize on new technologies and rapidly introduce them into the navy to ensure its supremacy, ordered four large iron-hulled screw frigates.

Captain Symonds, the Surveyor, was not at all happy about these orders. He had had some reservations about accepting steam, which he had overcome, but iron ships and armour plate would, as he pointed out to the Admiralty, 'occupy so much space and involve so enormous an increase of weight as to render the adoption of them entirely out of the question in Her Majesty's steam vessels'. His statement, however, was only based upon the results of the tests that had been carried out by the Admiralty. These results had shown that, when iron was subjected to the fire of solid shot, jagged lengths had been torn off.

Other doubts were voiced about the soundness of iron under fire, and this led to a series of trials between August 1845 and September 1846. The results, however, were inconclusive. In the meantime a Whig government had taken office, and had at once ordered a new series of trials to be conducted using the rusty 73-ton harbour tender *Ruby*. The trials, however, were again rather one-sided. *Ruby* was built of ordinary light iron and contained no armour plate or strengthening of any kind, and was only subjected to the fire of round shot. Inevitably, the results proved inconclusive.

For the trials *Ruby* had been anchored as a stationary target and subjected to carefully directed fire from a 32-pounder and 8in gun at a range of only 450yd. The shot so ruptured the framing and plates of the vessel that, in the official report of Captain Chads (who observed the tests), 'the shot meets with so little resistance that it must inevitably go through the vessel, and should it strike on a rib on the opposite side the effect is terrific, tearing off the iron sheets to a very considerable extent; and even those shot that go clean through the fracture being on the off side, the rough edges are outside the vessel precluding the possibility almost of stopping them'.

The trials continued but the results were still discouraging, the shot causing large holes with extremely irregular and jagged edges, making plugging exceedingly difficult and, if occurring near the waterline, giving rise to a very dangerous situation. As a report in 1849 stated, 'shot of every description in passing through iron makes such large holes that the material is improper for the bottom of ships'. Apart from this there was the possibility of extreme destruction caused to the guns' crews by the disintegration of the shot behind the iron plates. This led Captain Chads to conclude in his report of 1850, 'from these circumstances I am confirmed in the opinion that iron cannot be beneficially employed as a material for the construction of vessels of war'.

Such a damning comment at once sealed the fate of the iron ships. The Admiralty condemned the frigates and, while they were still on the stocks, they were converted to troopships on the orders of the First Lord, the Earl of Auckland — George Eden. One of the iron troopships, *Birkenhead*, gained notoriety when she sank in 1852 off South Africa with the loss of 432 soldiers. Seventeen other iron frigates under construction at the time were scrapped or converted, the largest being *Simoom*, of 2,000 tons.

In October 1853 Turkey declared war on Russia and the Crimean War began. On 30 November a Russian battle fleet comprising six ships of the line and two frigates destroyed a Turkish squadron of seven frigates and three corvettes at the Battle of Sinope. The battle is significant in naval history because it was the first time that the new hollow spherical explosive shell developed by Paixhans was used in action, by the Russians. Despite using the new shell, the Russians took about two hours to annihilate the Turkish squadron, and a further four to demolish the harbour and its fortifications. Although it was of no great significance apart from the use of the new shell, the Battle of Sinope left a legacy which was to have a profound effect on warship development. It finally proved that wooden sailing warships were no longer viable, and that their days were definitely numbered.

The French and British watched the battle with great interest before forming an alliance and declaring war in March 1854, fearing yet again that the main reason for the conflict was Russia's determination to try and gain some sort of access to the Mediterranean. With the Turkish squadron destroyed, and desiring to counter any Russian ambitions to destroy Turkey, the British and French sent a combined squadron to the Dardanelles. The start of the war found the navy wanting in many respects. Only a few ships of the line had been fitted with screw propulsion, and these were all conversions and still carried their sails, while the iron frigates had been converted to troopships. Not a single iron warship was operational in the Royal Navy.

As the Russians possessed no large steam screw warships, and much of their fleet was obsolete, the Allies were left in complete command of the sea. It was soon realized that the primary role for Allied naval forces in the Crimea would be to support the troops ashore, bombarding enemy coastal positions and supporting any amphibious landings that might be planned.

Emperor Napoleon III was so impressed with the outcome of the Battle of Sinope that he told his naval constructor, Dupuy de Lôme, that he could go ahead, with government support, and build an iron-plated vessel. In the meantime Napoleon, who had realized that the wooden sailing ship of the line was finished, proposed a design for a heavily armoured battery for coastal operations that would float very low in the water to minimize the effect of shellfire. The plans for the new battery were sent to the Admiralty, whose chief engineer, Thomas Lloyd, suggested that the French use 4in wrought iron plates for armour protection. Although the French carried out a number of tests with the new armour, the Admiralty desired to carry out their own series of trials before expending vast sums of money on armour plate. The trials were conducted in September 1854 on the orders of the First Lord, Sir James Graham. They involved a 32-pounder gun firing solid shot from a range of 360yd against iron plates 9ft x 15in x 4.5in thick bolted to a wooden backing of fir 4in thick, the whole being fixed to butts. On impact the shot completely disintegrated and the plate was only dented. Even a 68-pounder fired at a range of 900yd failed to damage it significantly. The trials finally showed conclusively that 4in wrought iron plate could withstand the impact of 32-pounder shot.

The success of the trials led to the Admiralty placing an order in October 1854 for four coastal assault vessels (*Aetna*, *Erebus*, *Terror* and *Thunderbolt*). These flat-bottomed craft were protected by 4in wrought iron plates bolted to the hull and bonded together using tongue-and-groove joints. The design did not prove very satisfactory, being slow and difficult to steer. The first, *Aetna*, carrying sixteen 68-pounder guns, was laid down in the naval dockyard at Chatham in November 1855, and her final cost was more than £50,000, as much as a three-deck ship of the line. The other three were ordered from private yards, but before any of them could be completed the Crimean War ended. *Aetna* was commissioned and sent to Sheerness as a police vessel, while a second sailed to Bermuda. The remaining two vessels never commissioned, *Erebus* being used in firing tests in 1858.

Apart from the Battle of Sinope, there were no major fleet actions during the war, operations consisting principally of blockading the Russians in their ports. Odessa was bombarded by frigates in April 1854, and in September of that year a British force of ten ships of the line, two frigates and thirteen armed merchant cruisers began the blockade of Sevastopol, after convoying a Turkish Army for an attack on the port. The Russians refused to sortie and, to avoid being captured, scuttled their fleet in the harbour. The Allied blockade then began with a bombardment of the port which continued sporadically for some weeks. The sailing ships of the line, which were towed into position by steam tugs, became sitting targets for the guns of the fortress and suffered considerable damage. The few vessels that had auxiliary engines fared little better. The few real steam vessels available, however, showed their worth from the start, their complete freedom of movement enabling them to manoeuvre out of range of the Russian batteries. However, the effort was doomed to failure from the start.

Baltic operations during the Crimean War were of little note, although the navy acquitted itself well. Under Admiral Sir Charles Napier a British squadron bombarded Sveaborg and blockaded the Russians behind their strong fortifications at Kronshtadt, from where they floated mines against the British. This was the first time that mines had been used at sea, but they failed to cause any serious material damage to the British ships (*Merlin* suffered some damage), and neither did they force them to raise the blockade. Within a very short time the navy had devised a rudimentary means of sweeping the mines. The mines consisted of 70lb of explosive contained in a spherical casing, from which projected a number of horns containing a glass phial of sulphuric acid. When the horn was struck, the phial broke and the sulphuric acid ignited chlorate of potash, causing the mine to detonate. In spite of the menace of the mines the British squadron continued to bombard Kronshtadt, but with little effect. The Baltic squadron was also bedevilled by a shortage of seamen, many of the crews being supplemented by volunteers from the Scandinavian countries.

It was slowly realized that, as well as the ships being in a materially poor state as a result of being laid up in reserve, they were also the wrong type of ship for these operations. The waters around the Russian ports in the Baltic and Black Sea were very shallow, and the ships of the line could not get near enough to the forts for fear of grounding. What was needed was a large number of boats of very shallow draught, carrying one or two large guns. Admiral Napier had already pointed this out to the First Lord in a letter dated 18 July 1854, in which he said that

the only successful way of attacking Sveaborg was 'by fitting out a great number of gunboats, carrying one gun with a long range'.

The only vessels available were the six wooden-hulled vessels of the *Arrow* class, ordered in March 1854. These were armed with two of the new Lancaster 68-pounder muzzle-loaders. However, even the draught of these vessels proved too great. Because of the pressing need for shallow-draught vessels the Admiralty ordered a new design, the '*Gleaner*' class wooden-hulled gunboats mounting two 68-pounder guns. They were cheap and easy to build, and were ordered in large numbers. The design featured a very shallow draught of only 7ft, and power was provided by a small 60nhp steam engine driving a single screw, but with provision for sails, as there was insufficient bunkerage for the ships to undertake long voyages. The class proved ideal in service, and orders were placed for a further twenty vessels of the '*Dapper*' class of almost similar design. A small flotilla of gunboats was then formed for use in the Sea of Azov, and provided invaluable service attacking depots, troop concentrations and railheads, and generally causing havoc. Others of the new class took part in the second bombardment of Sveaborg in August 1855, with notable success. As a result of these successful operations, the order for the '*Dapper*' class of gunboats was increased to a total of 98. After the war many of these gunboats were taken out of the water and preserved, whilst others served on foreign stations around the world in support of British foreign policy, where their exploits gave rise to the term 'gunboat diplomacy'.

By 1855 the first of Napoleon's batteries was ready for action. Built of wood and protected by 4in armour plate, they displaced 1,400 tons, carried eighteen 50-pounder guns and were manned by 320-man crews. Almost at once the three floating batteries were in action at the Battle of Kinburn on 17 October 1855. During the battle the batteries were floated up to the fortress where, at a range of some 900yd, they suffered numerous hits from 24-pounder guns, one battery having two men killed and thirteen wounded, and a second suffering nine wounded. In spite of being hit more than 137 times, the batteries suffered virtually no material damage whatsoever. However, at the range at which the batteries were struck (at least 900yd), not even wooden-hulled ships would have been penetrated by the small 24-pounder guns. The battle had already been won by mortars and bombardment by ships of the line, but the operation did signal that shallow-draught, flat-bottomed craft such as these might prove extremely effective in amphibious operations.

The war finally came to end at the Congress of Paris, held between 28 February and 30 March 1856, where the preliminary peace conditions agreed to in Vienna on 1 February were finally ratified.

Chapter 4
Gunboat Diplomacy and Conditions of Service

In the same year that the Crimean War ended, trouble broke out again in China, leading to what became known as the Second Opium War, which lasted until 1860. The root of the trouble was the Treaty of Nanking, signed in August 1842, under which China was forced to cede the island of Hong Kong to the British and to grant trading concessions at five other ports, as well as having to pay a heavy indemnity. In October 1856 a series of rebellions broke out over a local dispute at Canton, during which the British ship *Arrow* was seized. In reprisal, a combined Anglo-French naval force under the command of Rear-Admiral Sir Michael Seymour, Commander-in-Chief of the China Station, bombarded Canton in December 1857. Then, in May 1858, a combined Anglo-French force attempted to force a passage through to Peking up the Peiho river. The entrance to the river was guarded by a series of heavily defended forts at Taku. On 20 May 1858 a small force of gunboats bombarded and demolished the forts, which were seized by the allied force. With the Taku

forts in allied hands, the way was open to force a way up to Tientsin. The squadron had by then been reinforced by more gunboats, and their presence outside the walls of Tientsin had a profound effect on the population. In June 1858 the Chinese signed the Treaties of Tientsin, in which they agreed to open more ports to trade and to legalise the importing of opium.

The treaties, however, were soon abrogated, the Chinese refusing to allow foreign diplomats to enter Peking. In April 1859 Rear-Admiral Sir James Hope, who had replaced Admiral Seymour, again tried to force the Peiho river, using a squadron of ten gunboats and a sloop to bombard the forts at Taku which blocked the way. The force became trapped in a narrow channel and suffered severe damage. Admiral Hope was severely wounded, the gunboats *Lee*, *Plover* and *Cormorant* were sunk, and the British landing party was repulsed.

In May 1860 a large combined Anglo-French force of 18,000 troops gathered at Hong Kong and was transported north to carry out an amphibious landing at Pei Tang on 1 August 1860. They travelled overland to take the forts at Taku from the rear on 21 August, assisted by a combined Anglo-French naval squadron of four British and four French gunboats, which carried out a feint attack. The troops then moved up on both sides of the

Below: Under the 1854 Programme, four large frigates were ordered, which capitalized on the new technological developments in iron and steam propulsion. The largest of the four was the *Simoom*, which was subsequently converted into a troopship as pictured here, in which role she served in the Crimean War. (ACPL)

Peiho river, supported by the gunboats, eventually reaching Peking on 26 September. The Summer Palace was assaulted and looted on 6 October, and finally sacked and burnt on 24 October. Meanwhile, on 18 October the Chinese had signed the Treaty of Peking, under which Kowloon was surrendered to the British and a large indemnity paid.

Not long after the end of the Crimean War, Franco-British relations began to deteriorate again, and war was almost declared in January 1858, when an Italian refugee living in London attempted to assassinate Emperor Napoleon III. Matters were serious, as by then the French navy had made up the losses suffered at Trafalgar and the number and quality of their ships equalled those of the Royal Navy (29 steam line-of-battle ships), their steam frigates actually being superior to their British counterparts.

Forced into a compromising position, the Admiralty formed a committee under Lord Derby at the end of 1858, with the commission: 'to consider the very serious increase which had taken place of late years in the Navy Estimates while it represented that the naval force of the country is far inferior to what it ought to be with reference to that of other Powers, and especially France, and that increased efforts and increased expenditure were imperatively called for to place it on a proper footing'.

After due deliberation the committee recommended that eighteen line-of-battle ships should at once be converted into steam vessels, and Sir John Pakington made provision for these in the Spring Estimates of 1859. Plans were made to develop Armstrong's new gun, hoping that this would also help to give the Royal Navy superiority over the French.

Apart from fighting in China, vessels of the Royal Navy were also called upon to intervene on behalf of British citizens in Japan. In September 1862 the Samurai of the Prince of Satsuma killed an Englishman, Charles Richardson. After repeated attempts to negotiate a satisfactory settlement with the assistance of the Shogun, the navy finally sent a squadron of seven ships under the Commander-in-Chief of the China Station, Rear-Admiral Augustus Kuper, to bombard the port of Kagoshima and force the Prince to pay the full indemnity requested. The bombardment was carried out on 15–16 August 1863 by *Argus, Coquette, Euryalus, Havock, Pearl, Perseus* and *Racehorse*. This was the first time that ships had used the new breech-loading gun designed by Armstrong (see page 27) in action. The British ships suffered considerably from the Japanese land-based guns, and returned to Yokohama, where other British warships had arrived from China. Gradually the situation eased and the prestige of the Shogun waned. The British then lent their support for a return to power by the Mikado, a move welcomed by the Prince of Satsuma.

The incident at Kagoshima was followed by action against the Prince of Nagato, an anti-foreigner who wanted to disrupt external trade and who had rebelled against the Shogun. The navy again supported the Shogun, this time forcing the straits of Shimonoseki in September 1864 with *Conqueror*, a ship of the line, and six French, Dutch and American vessels. The Prince of Nagato was forced to accede to the request for unhindered passage through the Straits. This action finally convinced the Prince of Satsuma that he would not be able to defeat the foreigners, and the original indemnity demanded for the murder of the merchant was paid in full.

Across the world, other gunboats of the navy were keeping peace in the Caribbean. Vessels were sent to put down rebellions in Jamaica and Haiti, and to suppress the Fenians in Canada during the mid-1860s. Further small squadrons of gunboats and small vessels were kept hard

Left: The ship-of-the-line *Conqueror*, painted here in a gale, was part of a squadron of British, American, Dutch, and French vessels which forced the Straits of Shimonoseki in September 1864 during the opening up of Japan. (Imperial War Museum)

at work protecting British interests along the west coast of Africa, and stamping out the last of the slave traders off the east and west coasts of the continent.

Meanwhile, the Arctic and Antarctic continued to captivate the minds of the explorers at the Admiralty. In 1839 Ross, by then promoted Captain, had set sail for the southern hemisphere with two ships, *Erebus* and *Terror*, with the object of making a magnetic survey. Knowing that French and American expeditions were engaged in similar explorations, Ross decided to approach the area from an unexpected direction, and, after negotiating severe pack ice, he eventually broke out into open waters in Antarctica. These waters were subsequently named the Ross Sea. Heading southwest from the Ross Sea the explorer discovered new land, which he named South Victoria, and then proceeded to chart some 500 miles of Antarctica's coastline, discovering the Great Ice Barrier. He finally returned to England in September 1843.

On their return, *Erebus* and *Terror* were refitted for a new Polar expedition. As part of the refit they were equipped with auxiliary steam engines taken from railway engines, driving screws. That steam was considered suitable for polar exploration was in part due to the then head of the new naval Department of Steam Machinery, James Ross. Under the command of Captain John Franklin, and with 128 officers and men, the ships set sail in May 1845 in a further attempt to find a North West Passage. This was the last that was seen of the expedition, everyone, as well as the two ships, perishing in the frozen wastes of the north. Recent research in Canada found the graves of some crewmen in which traces of lead poisoning were found. This was one of the first expeditions to carry canned food, and it is possible that lead from the cans contaminated their contents and led to the death of the seamen. The existence of the North West Passage was finally established by Captain Robert McClure.

Conditions of service in the navy remained more or less constant until 1852, when the Admiralty set up a new system of continuous service entry for the lower deck. The scheme was aimed at the younger man, who was invited to volunteer for service at the age of 18, when he would sign on for ten years, after which he could leave the Service if he so wished. The scheme was an immediate success, and the greatly improved organization considerably eased the problem of recruitment. Introduced just before the start of the Crimean War in 1853, the new long-term service engagement was considered to be important, as large numbers of men were required to man the ships. However, although recruiting figures improved, the sudden commissioning of large numbers of ships for the Crimean War still left the navy undermanned, and there was even talk of a return to impressment. The main advantage of the long-term engagement was that it gave the navy time to train a man properly for his job, and when he retired from the Service he formed part of the Fleet Reserve and could be

called up in an emergency. There was still the problem of over-age officers left over from the Napoleonic Wars, who remained on the Navy List, blocking the promotion of younger, more able and more technologically aware officers. There was also a grave shortage of young flag-officers who, in normal circumstances, would have been eligible for overseas commands. With the ending of the Crimean War large numbers of over-age lieutenants with no post and receiving half-pay were placed on the retired list.

In 1855 the Admiralty decided to standardize the seaman's uniform, as many various forms of dress were in use, depending on the whim of each vessel's commanding officer. Rear-Admiral the Hon Henry John Rous was instructed to chair a committee with orders to design a new uniform. After studying all the variations then in use, the committee proposed a uniform of frock white duck with two rows of tape on the collar. Before the idea was accepted, however, it was placed before the Commanders-in-Chief of the two naval bases, Portsmouth and Devonport, who in turn put the proposals before each of the captains under their command. The majority favoured three rows of white tape $^3/_{16}$in wide and spaced $^1/_8$in apart. This was formally accepted, and on 31 January 1857 the Admiralty requested every seaman to modify his dress to comply with the new regulation.

By the late 1860s the whole fabric of the navy had undergone major changes. Warship design and construction had been totally revolutionized, and the conditions of service for the men had seen a significant transformation. The seaman of the 1860s was a much more highly skilled man, but while the press gang was no longer used as a means of recruitment, promotion and length of service remained a bone of contention.

By 1870 the ships had become so complex, with such highly technical equipment, that the old methods of recruitment and training were unsuitable. No longer was a seaman a 'Jack of all Trades', able to turn his hand to any work on board. Many new technical branches had been formed as a result of technological developments, this being particularly so in the engineering and gunnery fields. With the formation of the new branch structures, merchant seamen, who had always formed the reserve of manpower for the fleet, no longer had a place, except as ordinary seamen. So in 1859 a new reserve, called the Royal Naval Reserve, had been formed. This allowed a merchant seaman to volunteer for part-time service with the Royal Navy, and he was then given practical training in the new branches.

Promotion for officers had also improved greatly since Queen Victoria's Order in Council of 1840, which forcibly retired a number of captains from the Service. Another improvement came in 1869, when the regulations further limited the number of nominations a flag officer could put forward for the selection of midshipmen. This restricted a flag officer's patronage to three persons, a

Left: During the middle half of the 19th century, conditions for seamen greatly improved. The picture shows sailors being given their rum ration. (ACPL)

Lower left: Young sailors being instructed by a petty officer. (ACPL)

commodore's to two, and that of a captain of a seagoing ship to one. Furthermore, no officer was allowed to put forward a second candidate within the space of three years.

As the design of ships continued to evolve and improve during the 1870s, so too did the conditions for the men. At the beginning of the decade the last of the old officers remaining from the previous wars were officially retired when the Navy List divided commissioned officers under Active and Retired headings. At long last the way for promotion was clear, the whole process having taken from 1840 to 1870. Apart from better promotion prospects, the man entering the navy had many different branches for which he could be selected, accord-

ing to his talents. This applied not only to ordinary seamen but to officers as well. By the end of the 1870s branches had been formed covering torpedoes, gunnery, signals, navigation, engineering, etc, and all had commissioned officers appointed by commission of the Admiralty, in addition to the warrant officers appointed by Warrant of the Navy Board. Even former civilian posts, such as Paymasters (formerly Pursers), Surgeons, Chaplains and Naval Instructors (formerly Schoolmasters), were now given to commissioned officers. These were given full status of branches in 1864 (with the exception of Chaplains). The highest rank attainable by these many branches was then the rank of Captain, but even this was to change in time.

Chapter 5

The Revolution in Gunnery

With the introduction of Paixhans's new shell, it was only natural that gunnery came to be looked upon as a science rather than an art, as hitherto practised. In 1830 Commander George Smith had commissioned a new establishment for the Royal Navy, the School of Gunnery, which became the navy's first Naval Technical School. It was set up on board the 74-gun ship of the line *Queen Charlotte*, moored in Portsmouth Harbour. Formerly the flagship of Admiral Pellew at the bombardment of Algiers, she was renamed HMS *Excellent*. In Commander Smith's own words, *Excellent* was commissioned to enable 'gunners to learn one general and perfect system of gunnery, not only to be able to give the words of command, but more particularly to see they are executed as they ought to be'.

Once the shell had been introduced, it was not long before the guns themselves underwent major changes. Until the late 1850s naval gunnery was dominated by the smooth-bore, muzzle-loaded cannon. Then, in 1855, a Mr William Armstrong began experiments with a new breech-loading, rifled (BLR) gun that he had developed

from a design prepared by a Mr J. Longridge. The idea was inspired by experience of land operations in the Crimean War. The construction was revolutionary, for instead of the barrel being cast as a single unit, it was made by welding a series of wrought iron tubes spirally wound with wire, and shrinking them on to an inner steel barrel rifled with a number of spiral grooves. This ensured that the inner barrel would be free from the strain caused by whipping when the gun was fired. In addition, instead of being muzzle-loaded, the gun was charged from the breech. The purpose of the rifling was to impart a spin to the projectile which would give it a much straighter and more accurately defined trajectory.

Development of the rifled gun also led to the development of a new shell, which was elongated in shape with a pointed nose, and had a much better aerodynamic profile. Not only did this allow a heavier weight of explosive to be packed into the shell, but it enabled the projectile to maintain a more constant speed for a greater length of time in flight, giving it greater range and far greater accuracy than the conventional spherical projectile. Around the flat base of the shell was a row of studs which engaged with the rifling of the gun barrel, thus imparting spin to the shell as it passed along the length of the barrel.

Below: The first gunnery school for the Royal Navy was set up in 1830 on board the old 74-gun ship-of-the-line *Queen Charlotte* (built in 1810). She was renamed HMS *Excellent* in 1859. (Imperial War Museum)

Left: A 110pdr breech-loading rifled gun on a carriage similar to that which carried the standard 68pdr muzzle loader. (ACPL)

Left: A 110pdr breech-loading rifled gun on a sliding carriage. The screw breech can be seen at the rear of the gun. (ACPL)

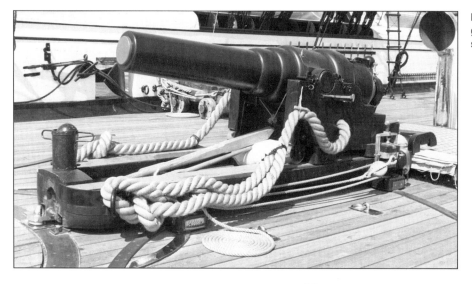

Left: A 110pdr breech-loading rifled gun on a revolving carriage and slide. (ACPL)

The new gun immediately altered the whole course of gunnery, and the race was on between gun and armour. The BLR gun underwent its first test in January 1859, and trials continued throughout the year, using guns of various calibres up to 6in and shells up to 100lb, designed to pierce the new armour plate. Unfortunately the gun did not come up to expectations. It failed to achieve the muzzle velocity necessary to penetrate the 4in wrought-iron plate against which it was tested, even at 50yd (muzzle velocity was measured at between 1,100 and 1,200ft/sec). In fact, the trials proved that the muzzle velocity was less than that of the navy's standard 68-pounder gun. However, in a perverse way the authorities considered that this only proved the ability of the armour plate to withstand shellfire.

Consequently, Armstrong was asked to supply a larger breech-loading gun of 7in calibre, firing a 110lb shell. However, the 110-pounder, as it was called, also failed its trials, being unable to penetrate a test section of *Warrior*'s hull at 200yd. Problems were encountered with the metal used in the breech, which meant that the gun had to use a reduced powder charge, and this resulted in limited penetration against current armour protection. Although the trials did not prove entirely successful, the Army Ordnance Board, which was responsible for ordering all guns used by the army and navy, went ahead and ordered the new gun in 1858 for the ironclad *Warrior*, even before the trials had been completed. While Armstrong's 110-pounder was not a great success, smaller-calibre weapons (40-pounder, 20-pounder, 12-pounder and 6-pounder) manufactured according to his design were found to be acceptable, and were ordered in large numbers for the navy.

At the bombardment of Kagoshima in 1863, Armstrong's new breech-loading guns were in action for the first time. The guns, on which the navy had pinned such great hopes, unfortunately proved a dismal failure, 28 accidents occurring to 21 guns during the firing of a total of 365 rounds. The problem lay primarily with the breech-loading system, which lacked a safety mechanism, there being no means of positively locking the breech lock into position. This allowed the gun to be fired before the breech was properly closed, and led to the vent piece being blown out on numerous occasions. The other major problem lay not in the design, but in the method of manufacture and the materials used,

Right: 100pdr smooth-bore muzzle-loading gun mounted on wooden carriage and slide. (ACPL)

Below: Armstrong 110pdr 7in breech-loading rifled gun mounted on iron carriage and slide. (ACPL)

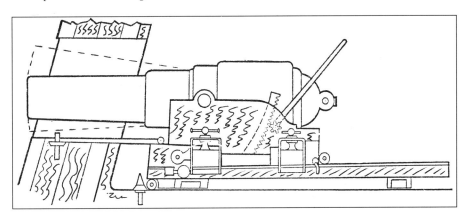

which were found to be unable to withstand the massive pressures that built up in the barrel when the gun was fired.

The faults sealed the fate of the breechloader, and the navy removed it from service. This left the Service without a reliable gun for its warships and so, as a matter of expediency, it was decided to revert to the old muzzle-loader, which continued in service for another twenty years.

Armstrong, however, was not the only engineer experimenting with guns. In April 1856 the engineering works of Mr Whitworth at Manchester received a number of 24-pounder guns from the Woolwich Arsenal, which were bored out and rifled to fire the new Paixhans elongated shell. Whitworth had developed a method for rifling guns which differed from Armstrong's in that spin was imparted by rifled 'surfaces' rather than 'grooves'. Although it was only bored to fire the equivalent of a 9lb shot, the new gun could fire shells of 24lb, 32lb and 48lb, the increased charge being obtained by increasing the length of the shell. Whitworth's gun was tested against Armstrong's in 1863, after which it was decided to adopt the Armstrong gun.

Alongside these new developments the old standard 32-pounder was also improved. By the end of the Crimean War it had been fitted with a flintlock firing mechanism and had a crude sighting arrangement. An attempt was made to improve the truck carriage of the gun, but only a few examples of the Marshall slide carriage, as it was known, were introduced for the stern and bow chasers.

As a result of the experiments with the new types of gun, it was decided to evolve a new system of nomenclature for gun sizes. Instead of referring to a gun by the weight of shot that it fired, it was agreed to size a gun by its calibre.

In 1865, following a long series of trials, a new type of rifled muzzle-loader produced by Royal Gun Factories was introduced into the navy. Basically, the gun was built on the same principle as Armstrong's gun, by shrinking tubes on to one another, the inner tube being rifled. The rifling, referred to as 'Woolwich' rifling after the Royal Arsenal at Woolwich, where the system was developed, had rounded edges rather than sharp angles as in previous rifling. This helped prevent any tendency for the steel to split along the edge of a groove when subjected to intense strain. A number of calibres of muzzle-loading rifled (MLR) gun were manufactured for the navy using this principle.

With steel now replacing the earlier metals used in gun manufacture, and the adoption of slow-burning powders, the advent of the breech-loading gun could not be forestalled any longer. To meet the demands of the new developments the barrels of the guns were continually having to be lengthened until, finally, they could no longer be loaded from the muzzle. A return to breech-loading was therefore inevitable. Furthermore, gun development outstripped the rudimentary methods of fire control then practised in the navy. However, little was achieved in evolving new forms of fire control until the early part of the 20th century. Until then, battleships were forced to prepare for gunnery actions at ranges that were well below the capability of the guns. Not until new fire control systems were developed could capital ships carry out gun engagements at ranges greater than the range of the torpedoes then in service.

Left: The deck of the *Minotaur*, 1868. Note the massive 7in muzzle-loading gun on its sliding carriage in the foreground and the gun crews undergoing instruction and training. The three ships in the class were the largest broadside ironclads in the Navy. (ACPL)

Chapter 6

The Iron Race

Although by 1857 the Crimean War had shown the futility of the continued construction of wooden warships, there were only 58 iron vessels in the Royal Navy, comprising small gunboats, mortar boats and miscellaneous auxiliaries. No iron vessels larger than a gunboat had been built, mainly as a result of the tests carried out on the iron steamer *Ruby* (see page 18). Between 1854 and 1857 only one vessel in five completed was of iron. The backbone of the Royal Navy remained the three-deck sailing vessel, epitomised by *Victoria*. *Victoria* was built to the same design as previous ships of the line, carried 121 guns, and was equipped with auxiliary steam machinery.

Meanwhile, trials with armour plate continued while the navy waited to see what the French would develop before proceeding further with iron warships. By early February 1858 the Surveyor, Sir Baldwin Walker, felt that trials were sufficiently advanced to justify building an experimental wooden-hulled corvette protected by armour plates. Unfortunately, the severe cutbacks in the Estimates following the end of the Crimean War precluded any possibility of building ironclad warships.

However, in May 1858 news reached the Admiralty that an ironclad frigate, the *Gloire*, was under construction at Toulon. Serious doubts about the wisdom of continuing to build more wooden vessels now began to assail the authorities. Alarmed at the French developments, the Queen and Government ordered a Committee of Enquiry to examine the situation. The Surveyor was consulted, and although he thought that the time was not yet right for wooden ships to be totally replaced by ironclads, he felt, nevertheless, that there was an urgent need for Britain to build six armoured ships to match the planned six French frigates.

On 22 June 1858 Walker set out the Admiralty's policy in a statement, in which he said:

> Although I have frequently stated it is not in the interests of Great Britain, possessing as she does so large a Navy, to adopt any important changes in the construction of ships of war which might have the effect of rendering necessary the introduction of a new class of very costly vessels until such a course is forced upon her by the adoption of Foreign Powers of formidable ships of a novel character requiring similar ships to cope with them, yet it then becomes a matter not only of expediency, but of absolute necessity. This time has arrived.

However, a number of factors arose which delayed any plans to implement the call to match the French construction programme. Chief of these was the financial commitment, which the Tory Government, desperate to cut expenditure, was loth to give. Furthermore, there were doubts within the navy itself about the wisdom of embarking upon a major programme of construction involving new technology before it had been fully tried and tested. Two aspects in particular concerned those in charge. Firstly there were the views of the Surveyor himself, who considered that the Armstrong BLR rendered armour obsolete. Secondly, there was no clearly defined role for the ironclad. As a result the Admiralty decided to continue with construction of wooden ships (their decision to some extent was dictated by the fact that the seven Royal Dockyards were not equipped to build iron ships), and were only prepared to sanction the construction of two ironclads. The result was a slow rate of ordering for the new ironclads, and the proving of various designs in ones and twos before any large single class was ordered.

In October 1858 further trials with armour plate were conducted by Captain Hewlett of HMS *Excellent* against the old target *Alfred*, using the Whitworth rifled gun. In these trials the 4in armour plate resisted 68-pounder shot, but was penetrated by the Whitworth gun, the 7in oak side behind also being pierced. However, the gun burst on firing, and the trials were considered inconclusive.

Then, on 27 February 1858, the Secretary to the Admiralty, Henry Thomas Lowry Corry, persuaded the Admiralty to order the first ironclad under the 1859 Estimates. The Admiralty, however, still considered that a wooden hull was essential, although the Surveyor insisted that the ship should be built of iron. Walker had become convinced of the need to build in iron by the need for a vessel superior to the French *Gloire* in all characteristics. This meant that the new vessel would have to have a longer, finer hull, greater speed to enable her to outmanoeuvre hostile ships and to be able to choose her own moment for engagement, and be capable of fighting at a distance such that her armour would be impervious to enemy fire. The Surveyor's views were heavily influenced by Captain Hewlett of HMS *Excellent*.

The design specification was finally issued to the seven Royal Dockyards and eight commercial yards on 27 January 1859. The Chief Constructor, Isaac Watts, selected an in-house design which was approved by the Admiralty Board in April 1859, and a contract was awarded to the Thames Ironworks yard for the construction of the vessel,

which was laid down on 25 May 1859. Watts then proceeded to draw up the detail design for the ship, assisted by Walker and Thomas Lloyd, the Chief Engineer. The ship was named *Warrior* on 5 October 1859, was launched on 29 December 1860, and completed on 24 October 1861. Her sister ship, *Black Prince*, was laid down on 25 October 1859, launched on 27 February 1861, and completed on 12 September 1862.

Warrior had been ordered not a moment too soon, for on 24 November 1859 the French launched the first of their new frigates, *La Gloire*, at Toulon. Basically her hull was that of *Napoleon*, but she was protected by armour plate 5ft x 2ft x 4.5in thick. She was rigged with three masts, as in previous ships, but the area of sail carried was very much reduced. *La Gloire* relied mainly on her steam engines for propulsion, and the sails were carried in case the engines should break down. She carried enough fuel to remain at sea for a month, cruising at 8kts, and her maximum speed was 13kts on a displacement of 5,630 tons.

The Admiralty had staked the whole future of the navy on *Warrior* and her sister ship *Black Prince*, and the policy paid off. Compared to *La Gloire*, *Warrior* was a much larger and superior ship, and was far in advance of any other warship then on the drawing board. *Warrior* was constructed completely of iron and protected by an armour belt 4.5in thick which extended for three-fifths of her length amidships, protecting the ten boilers supplying steam to the 1,250nhp Penn engine which drove the single screw to give a speed of 14.3kts, a speed not bettered until 1875. For the first time steam was the

prime mover. However, the Admiralty still could not bring themselves to do away with sails, so *Warrior* retained a full rig for use as an auxiliary. Sails, however, did give the navy a tremendous advantage, in that the vessels so rigged retained a backup means of propulsion in the event of breakdown of the steam machinery. Furthermore, it made them independent of foreign bases for fuel supplies in the case of long voyages, when it was necessary to conserve coal. Sails therefore remained a standard feature until the navy had established sufficient numbers of coaling stages at strategic points around the world.

Warrior excelled in other ways, too. The fitting of bilge keels resulted in a platform that was much more stable than any previous warship, an essential requirement for accurate gunnery. Although the Admiralty had provided *Warrior* with an armoured belt, there was no armour along the waterline, and her steering gear was vulnerable to a well-aimed shot. There was extra protection, however, in the form of internal subdivisions, there being 92 watertight compartments. As originally designed, *Warrior* was to have mounted 40 68-pounder guns, the only weapon then available which had any effect on armour plate. However, while she was building the Armstrong BLR was adopted, and a number of 110-pounder guns were ordered for her. As completed, *Warrior* mounted 26 68-pounder smooth-bore (SB) guns, of which four forward and four aft were unprotected, and ten 110-pounder BLR and four 70-pounder Armstrong BLR guns. This armament was later altered to 28 7in MLR, four 8in MLR and four 20-pounder BLR guns.

Chapter 7

The Ironclads Develop

With the launching of *Warrior* at Blackwall in 1860, the Royal Navy entered the arms race of the 19th Century. The race was on between the ever increasing size and power of guns and the need to match this with ever thicker and more impenetrable armour. Improvements in equipment were now evolving so rapidly that a new type of ship was obsolete almost before it was launched.

In the same year that *Warrior* was launched, a body of men formed themselves into an association that was to have a profound effect on the design and construction of warships. Under the chairmanship of John Scott Russell, men such as Dr Woolley, headmaster of the school of mathematics and naval construction at Portsmouth, Edward J. Reed (Secretary) and his brother-in-law Nathaniel Barnaby, who were to be responsible for the construction of the new iron navy, and others, created the Institute of Naval Architects.

Left: HMS *Warrior* as completed. (ACPL)

Below: HMS *Warrior* preserved as a museum ship at Portsmouth. (ACPL)

Following the completion of *Warrior* and *Black Prince*, a number of smaller vessels were developed using the concept of *Warrior* as the basis for their design, and out of the gun versus armour race evolved the concept of the central protected battery. The first of the new, smaller ironclads to be ordered under the 1859 Programme and laid down in December 1859 were *Defence* and *Resistance*. These were much smaller than *Warrior* (6,300 tons against 9,210 tons) and carried fourteen of their guns behind the armour belt, the remaining armament being unprotected. Additionally, they were completed with a ram bow, which became the dictum of naval construction in the Victorian era. *Defence* and *Resistance* were followed by *Hector* and *Valiant* (6,710 tons), laid down in March and February 1861 respectively. These two vessels had armour protection for the full length of the gun deck and displaced 6,630 tons, on virtually the same dimensions as the previous two vessels. A third ironclad, *Achilles*, similar to *Warrior*, had been part of the programme which included *Hector* and *Valiant*. However, Edward J. Reed had already observed the lack of armour protection to the steering gear of earlier vessels, and questioned the lack of protection to the steering gear and rudder in the design of *Achilles*. His views were taken note of, and in January 1861 the design was revised to include a complete armour belt running the whole length of the hull from stem to stern along the waterline, surmounted by the same armour belt for the battery as in *Warrior*.

Achilles was laid down in August 1861. Her displacement rose to 9,280 tons, more powerful engines were fitted, and the sail area as completed was the largest ever set in a warship. The design proved most successful, and three other similar vessels of the '*Minotaur*' class — *Agincourt*, *Minotaur* and *Northumberland* — were designed and laid down in September-October 1861. These were designed to carry the heaviest armament then afloat, behind the thickest armour and at the highest speed. They achieved all three requirements, mounting four 9in MLR, 24 7in MLR and eight 24-pounders behind 5.5in armour plate, and having a maximum speed of just over 14kts. On completion they were the largest and most powerful ships afloat, and retained this superiority for the next decade. In their time they were the world's longest, sleekest armoured ships, and marked the zenith of Isaac Watts's design, according to Nathaniel Barnaby.

Having become a member of the Institute of Naval Architects, Reed was encouraged to enter the Admiralty to develop his ideas for armoured vessels. As far back as 1854 he had submitted plans to the Admiralty for a fast

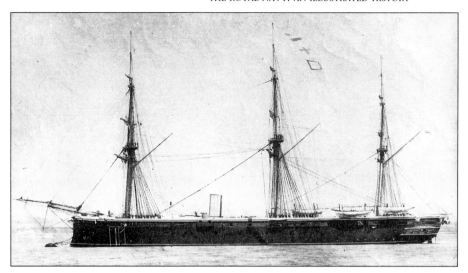

Left: The *Warrior* and *Black Prince* were followed by two smaller ironclads, the *Defence* (shown here) and the *Resistance*. Part of the armament was mounted behind an armour belt, and the ships were referred to as central protected battery ships. (ACPL)

Left: The '*Minotaur*' class (the *Northumberland* is illustrated) was the navy's answer to the French ironclads which followed the *Gloire*. Most of the main armament was fully protected and sited on one deck. The *Northumberland* is seen here as second flagship in the Channel in 1873. (National Maritime Museum)

armoured frigate, but they had been rejected. He now set about developing his ideas for armoured vessels with renewed vigour, and, from a new set of draughts, plans were made to convert three wooden vessels, *Enterprise*, *Favorite* and *Research*, into ironclads with waterline armour belts and their main armament protected by an armoured central citadel. Work on the conversion of the first, *Research*, began in September 1862. The second of the trio, *Enterprise*, was in the very early stages of construction when it was decided to convert her into an ironclad sloop of some 1,350 tons, armed with two 100-pounder SB and two 110-pounder BLR. The final ship of the trio, *Favorite*, was converted into a central battery corvette of 3,232 tons, armed with eight 100-pounder SB. The ships had a narrow 4.5in armoured belt which was carried along the entire length of the waterline, while a central armoured battery protected a reduced number of guns, the increasing size and weight of guns, combined with the thick armour, causing a reduction in the number of guns carried.

The First Lord, the Duke of Somerset, was so impressed with Reed's work and ideas that when Watts, the Chief

Constructor, retired at the beginning of 1863, Reed was appointed to the post. Reed's conception of the ironclad was of a completely new type of vessel whose merits were, 'Possessing great powers of offence and defence, being comparatively short, cheap and handy, and steaming at a high speed... by means of a moderate increase of power on account of the moderate proportions adopted...'.

While these new ironclads were under construction, great efforts were made to build up the effective strength of the Royal Navy by converting wooden ships of the line into ironclads. A number of vessels had their upper decks removed and armour plates fitted round the sides. Ships so converted were *Caledonia* (1860), *Ocean* (1860), *Prince Consort* (1860), *Repulse* (1859), *Royal Alfred* (1859), *Royal Oak* (1860) and *Zealous* (1859). As well as these converted vessels, three other ironclads (*Lord Clyde*, *Lord Warden* and *Pallas*) were laid down in the latter part of 1863 and completed with wooden hulls in an attempt to clear the large stocks of timber stored in the dockyards for the construction of the 'wooden walls'. However, none of the conversions was very successful, and the vessels were soon relegated to minor duties.

In March 1862, during the American Civil War, there occurred the famous battle between *Merrimac* and *Monitor*. Tactically, neither ship gained the advantage, but strategically *Monitor* proved that the the very nature of naval warfare had been altered by the revolutionary carriage of her gun in an armoured revolving turret. However, this was most certainly not the first design of a turret for mounting guns. Captain Cowper Phipps Coles of the Royal Navy had already offered a turret design to the Union, but the *Monitor*'s designer, Ericsson, had managed to have Coles's turret turned down in favour of his own. The main features of the turret were that it protected the gun crew from enemy fire and enabled the gun to fire in any direction irrespective of the position or course of the ship.

Captain Coles had first formulated his ideas concerning gun turrets during the Crimean War. While on service in the Black Sea he had built *Lady Nancy*, a small raft of shallow draught on which he had mounted a 68-pounder gun. Coles had found that it was relatively easy to train the raft as if it were a turntable. Following up his idea after the Crimean War, Coles designed a 32-pounder gun with a shield on a turntable. In 1860 he patented a turret sunk into an armoured breastwork, and then put forward plans to the Admiralty for a ship mounting eight of his turrets, each with two guns and revolving on a series of rollers. After studying the plans the Admiralty ordered an experimental turret with a single gun, which was tested on board *Trusty* at Shoeburyness in 1861. The trials showed that the turret-mounted gun could achieve a rate of fire almost twice that of a broadside-mounted gun. The experimental turret was itself then subjected to fire from 68- and 110-pounder guns, which had no effect on the training mechanism.

In Great Britain the battle between *Monitor* and *Merrimac* had a considerable effect on the public. This was evidenced by a letter to *The Times*, which said, 'Whereas we had available for immediate purposes 149 warships, we now have two, these being the *Warrior* and *Black Prince*. There is not a ship in the English Navy apart from these two that it would not be madness to trust to an engagement with the *Monitor*'.

Apart from the large number of almost useless wooden vessels in the navy, numerous gunboats left over from the Crimean War were also found to be valueless. Many had been completed towards the end of the war and placed straight into reserve. As they had been built in a hurry, unseasoned timber had had to be used. Upon their completion the Admiralty had spent huge sums of money putting the vessels on slips under wooden sheds, but over the years the unpreserved timber had deteriorated and fallen apart with dry rot. In addition to the poor timber, the engines of these gunboats were of an early design, and rapidly wore out. The effective strength of the navy in small vessels was thus greatly reduced.

But even *Warrior* and *Black Prince* had been rendered obsolete by *Monitor*. Equipped with a revolving turret protected by 8in-thick armour, such a vessel could run circles round the British ironclads with their fixed broadside-firing guns protected by a mere 4.5in of armour plate. Not only were the British ironclads made obsolete by the development of the turret, but 40 other ironclads completed or under construction in Europe were similarly affected.

Coles's idea for a turret gun was proven, and the Admiralty accepted the design and ordered Watts to design a coast defence ship, *Prince Albert*, to mount four of Coles's turrets, each carrying a single 9in MLR gun. Ordered in

Right: The battle between the *Monitor* and *Merrimac* in March 1862 in Hampton Roads during the American Civil War proved the value of mounting guns in turrets as opposed to broadside-mounted guns. With her revolving turret the *Monitor* was able to engage the *Merrimac* from any position without having to steam in a specific direction. (US Naval Photographic Center)

February 1862, *Prince Albert* was the Royal Navy's first iron turret ship, and was completed in 1866 with a 4.5in armour belt.

In the meantime, Captain Coles had further developed his ideas on turret-mounted guns, and in April 1862 the Admiralty ordered the conversion of *Royal Sovereign*, a steam-powered three-deck, 131-gun ship of the line, to an armoured turret ship. The top two decks were removed, and the weight thus saved enabled four of Captain Coles's turrets to be fitted. The forward turret carried two 10.5in SB guns, and the other three turrets mounted single 10.5in SB 12.5-ton guns, all the turrets being turned by hand. The turrets were protected by 5.5in iron fixed over 14in of teak, with the face carrying an additional 0.5in of wood surmounted by 4.5in of iron. The conversion was completed in 1864.

While Coles was busy developing his ideas for turret ships, Nathaniel Barnaby had developed a new method for constructing the hull of a warship. Known as the longitudinal bracket frame system, it comprised a series of longitudinal frames which ran the length of the double bottom, which was now extended up beyond the turn of the bilge. The longitudinals joined together two skins of a double bottom, and between these longitudinal ribs were mounted a series of bracket frames to which the plates which formed the double bottom were riveted on the upper and bottom sides. Compared with the trans-verse framing of plates and angle irons used previously, the new method of construction led to a saving in weight of some 180 tons for every 100ft of hull. This method of construction became standard up to the end of the century.

The first warship designed and built using the new construction was *Bellerophon*, designed by Reed and launched in May 1865. The basic design was derived from an earlier plan which Reed had submitted to the Admiralty. The new design incorporated a number of innovative features, including the longitudinal bracket frame construction and a double bottom running the whole length of the ship which gave far greater protection against underwater damage (*Warrior* had a double bottom under the engine spaces only). *Bellerophon* was shorter than *Warrior*, and hence lighter by some 1,000 tons. She proved to be easier to handle, and with a balanced rudder (the first ship to be so fitted) was found to be more manoeuvrable, which greatly facilitated her handling and helped reduce her turning circle. Because she was shorter, it was thought that *Bellerophon* might require greater horsepower than a longer ship, although at that time this was difficult to quantify in precise terms at the design stage. In practice it was found that the power required was not as great as had been anticipated, being 6,521ihp to reach a speed of 14.2kts, compared with the 5,267ihp required by *Warrior* to reach 14.1kts.

Left: In England, Captain Coles convinced the Admiralty to build a ship mounting her guns in turrets. The first ship specifically built for this purpose was the *Prince Albert*. She was followed by a much larger vessel, the *Royal Sovereign* (illustrated here), a 3-deck ship-of-the-line, which was converted to carry four of Coles' turrets. (ACPL)

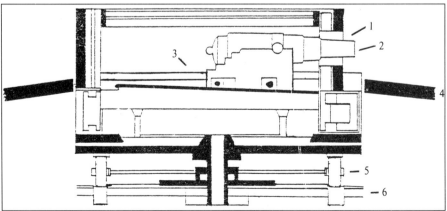

Left: Simplified diagram of Coles' turret. 1, Embrasure; 2, Gun; 3, Gun carriage slide; 4, Main deck; 5, Rollers running on metal circular rail; 6, Lower deck. (ACPL)

Right: The *Bellerophon* was the first ship built using the new longitudinal bracket frame system of construction. (ACPL)

Right: Coles sought to overcome the problem of mounting turrets in ships fitted with sails, the result being the *Captain*. However, although the turrets were so mounted that they could train on either beam, the fact that the ship was fitted with a forecastle and poop and pole masts meant that she was deprived of end-on fire. The Captain is seen here at Plymouth just before sailing on her ill-fated last voyage. (National Maritime Museum)

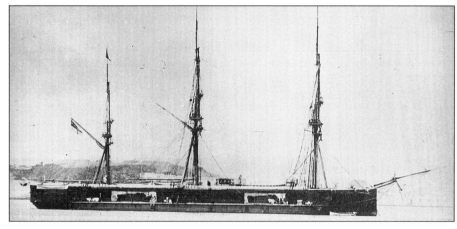

Attempts were made to increase the fighting capability by mounting two 7in MLR guns in a protected position in the bows and three 7in MLR in an unprotected position at the stern, thus developing end-on fire without any sacrifice to the weight of broadside that could be delivered. The concept was not entirely successful, as it hampered movement at sea. The armament comprised ten 9in MLR (*Bellerophon* was the first ship to mount the new 9in MLR) and five 7in MLR guns. Reed was convinced that only high-sided vessels gained full stability, especially when they were fully rigged, as was *Bellerophon*. The citadel protected all the vital parts of the ship, such as the engines and guns, and the armoured belt extended for the whole length of the waterline.

Hercules was the next vessel to be built, designed in 1865 and completed in 1868. She was an enlarged version of *Bellerophon*, carrying eight of the new 10in MLR guns behind 9in armour in a central battery. In addition she mounted a single 9in MLR at either end behind lightly armoured sides, and two 7in MLR were mounted in an unprotected position above the 9in guns.

Meanwhile, the controversy over ships fitted with turrets began to develop. The Admiralty Board dismissed the idea of mounting turrets in seagoing ships as impractical. Both the Controller of the Navy and the Chief Constructor were adamantly opposed to the mounting of turrets in all types of ship unless they were unrigged, low-freeboard vessels which would only be used in a coast defence role, and would under no circumstances be expected to undertake major voyages in open ocean conditions. As a general view it was accepted that ships still could not manage without sails for use on ocean voyages because of the unreliability of the steam engines and their high fuel consumption. Not unnaturally there were some, including Reed, who considered that there would be little value in mounting turrets in ships carrying a full sailing rig, as the rigging would impede the operation of the turrets. Reed remained convinced of the propriety of the central battery concept for rigged ships. The Controller, Sir Spencer Robinson, was also implacably opposed to turret ships, but the First Lord, the Duke of Somerset, was impressed with Coles's ideas.

Captain Coles, however, gathered a large following in his struggle against the gradual evolution of Reed's ideas, sending many letters to the national press in support of his campaign for turret ships. He was convinced that his idea for turning a gun in a turret was better than turning the ship to fire the guns. However, Coles also believed that, for the guns to be effective, the ship should have low sides, which reduced the righting moment of the vessel, and that, in addition to the engines, the ship should be fully rigged. Referring to his plans, he wrote to *The Times* in April 1862, saying, 'I will undertake to prove that on my principle a vessel shall be built nearly 100 feet shorter than the *Warrior*, and in all respects equal to her, with one exception, that I will undertake to disable and capture her within one hour'.

In March 1863 Coles put forward a design which he had drawn up with the assistance of Barnaby, using tripod masts which overcame the need for standing rigging but still allowed a ship to carry a full outfit of sails. Coles heard nothing further regarding these plans, and continued to lobby for his ideas concerning turret ships. Early in 1865, using the plans of *Bellerophon* and *Pallas* as a basis, Coles, aided by Constructor Joseph Scullard from Portsmouth Dockyard, drew up plans for a smaller, three-masted ship carrying a single turret. In April 1865 the Admiralty appointed a committee to examine the

Below: Although the Admiralty were willing to mount turrets in ships, it was the general view at the time that ships could not manage without sails as an alternative form of propulsion to steam. A number of people considered that mounting turrets in ships carrying a full sailing rig was completely impractical as the rigging would severely impede the ability of the turrets to fire in any direction and would therefore nullify any advantage turrets might confer on a ship fitted with sails. (ACPL)

proposals. The Committee did not fully approve of Coles's proposals and, after detailed discussion, came out in favour of a rigged ship. Reed was ordered to prepare a design based on the Committee's proposals, and in compliance designed *Monarch*, the plans for which were forwarded to Coles in March 1866. Reed, however, had reservations about the advisability of mounting turrets in a fully-rigged ship, later stating, 'No satisfactorily designed turret ship with rigging has yet been built'. This statement was to be tragically confirmed in 1870.

As revised, the design showed a full-rigged vessel with pole masts and a fo'c'sle, which deprived her of end-on fire. This was considered essential to maintain seaworthiness in a vessel with such a shallow freeboard, but was to some extent compensated for by the siting of two 7in MLR guns in armoured positions on either side of the bow and a single 7in MLR aft.

Captain Coles was not at all pleased with the alterations made to his plans. He considered that at 17ft above the water the guns were mounted too high, and wished them to be lowered to a height of 15ft, where they would not make the ship too top-heavy. He also wanted the foc's'le removed to restore end-on fire, and the height of the turrets reduced.

Captain Coles complained bitterly about the alterations to *Monarch*, and in the end the First Lord, against the advice of the Controller, ordered another turret ship to be designed according to Coles's ideas. Coles selected the shipbuilding firm of Lairds at Birkenhead to design and build the new vessel, *Captain*, as it had the most experience in producing turret ships (such as *Scorpion* and *Wivern*). Basically, *Captain* turned out to be an enlarged *Monarch*. The major difference lay in the decks, *Captain* having only two, compared with the three of *Monarch*, which resulted in a very much lower freeboard than even *Monarch*, just 8.5ft compared with the *Monarch*'s 14ft. Another distinguishing feature was the masts, which were tripods in *Captain*, as opposed to the single pole in *Monarch*. At Coles's insistence the masts were the tallest and heaviest mounted in any ship in the Fleet. Protection for the fo'c'sle in *Captain* was dispensed with, and the whole structure was much enlarged to keep the ship dry when steaming against a head sea. When she was launched it was found that *Captain* floated with a freeboard two feet lower than that for which she had been designed. The turrets were mounted farther apart than in *Monarch*, but end-on fire was still obscured by superstructure fore and aft. To overcome this, *Captain* mounted a single 7in MLR on the foc's'le and another on the poop.

Reed was particularly sceptical about the design of *Captain*, and felt that the centre of gravity would be higher than that given by Laird. The Controller, too, strongly objected to the design, and especially to the low freeboard of only 8ft. However, both men's objections were overruled by the First Lord, who approved the design in July 1866.

Chapter 8

The Steel Navy

In 1870 the Royal Navy suffered a major disaster which shook the Service to its foundations. During the night of 6 September *Captain*, in company with the Channel Fleet comprising *Agincourt*, *Bellerophon*, *Bristol*, *Hercules*, *Inconstant*, *Lord Warden*, *Minotaur*, *Monarch* and *Northumberland*, forced her way through the teeth of a gale raging in the Bay of Biscay. Admiral Sir Archibald Berkeley Milne, Commander-in-Chief of the Mediterranean Fleet, who spent some time on board *Captain* during the day, remarked on what appeared to him to be a dangerous roll. *Captain* at the time was heeling between 12° to 14°. During the night the squadron became dispersed, and at daylight on 7 September, when it again came together, *Captain* was missing. Of her crew of 490, only 17 survived to reach land, Captain Hugh Burgoyne, VC, the commanding officer, and Captain Cowper Phipps Coles going down with the ship.

A court martial was at once convened to inquire into the cause of the loss. It was a particularly delicate inquiry to conduct, in view of the previous friction between Captain Coles and Reed, the Controller of the Navy, Sir Spencer Robinson, and the First Lord of the Admiralty, the Duke of Somerset. The controversy had grown to such an extent that on 9 July 1870 Reed had resigned over the argument concerning the danger of low-freeboard ships, while the Controller became even more implacably opposed to the concept.

After much discussion and heart searching, the court concluded that *Captain* did not possess 'the required amount of stability'. This resulted from her inadequate freeboard and heavy sails and masts, which gave the vessel a high centre of gravity. Furthermore, the design and construction had been left almost entirely to Laird and was largely unsupervised, Coles being ill for most of the period. Thus it was that, although Laird as naval architects had designed *Captain* according to Coles's requirements, modifications had been introduced which they felt were necessary, and insufficient quality control had been exercised in respect of the materials used. On the night of the accident the ship was rolling heavily, and a sudden extra-strong gust of wind striking the double-reefed topsails and fore-topmost staysail, coupled with a broadside wave hitting the ship along her keel line at the height of a roll, pushed the vessel past her point of no return. At the end of the report the members of the court martial concluded: 'the *Captain* was built in deference to public opinion expressed in Parliament and through other channels and in opposition to the views and opinions of the Controller of the Navy and his Department'.

In fact, Reed's assistant, Nathaniel Barnaby, together with F.K. Barnes, had conducted a number of experiments on stability in 1867. These had been ordered when it was proposed to cut down a number of two-deck ships, arm

Right: The '*Audacious*' class was ordered for overseas service to counter the growing threat of the French Navy. The design was prepared much more scientifically than previous designs, careful account being taken of stability and rolling in a seaway. They proved to be exceedingly steady gun platforms. The *Audacious* is seen here in 1890. (Imperial War Museum)

Left: The *Hotspur* was unique in that she mounted her guns in a fixed turret rather than one which could be trained on any bearing. (National Maritime Museum)

them with turrets and give them masts. Even then, Barnes had theoretically calculated that, if the edge of the deck on a low-sided ship should reach the level of the sea, she would be in a dangerous situation. He further calculated that, if the vessel continued to heel past this point, the position of minimum stability would soon be reached, and stability would then be dramatically reduced as the righting force of the vessel was diminished. This was only a theory, however, and it took the capsizing of *Captain* to prove the dangerous significance of a low-sided vessel equipped with a heavy weight of masts and turrets on an upper deck, giving rise to a high centre of gravity.

The loss of *Captain* had further repercussions in the Admiralty. The new First Lord, Hugh Childers, having lost his only son in *Captain*, felt that the Controller's Department was to some extent to blame for the loss of the vessel, and as Reed had resigned he transferred his adverse feelings to the Controller, Sir Spencer Robinson. With the passage of time the quarrel between the two men grew. The First Lord then produced a minute on the loss of *Captain* in which he placed the responsibility for the tragedy on the Controller and Reed, both of whom had opposed the design. Finally, in February 1871, Sir Spencer Robinson was forced to resign his post following an interview with the Prime Minister, W.E. Gladstone. A month later, after an illness, the First Lord, too, was forced to resign his post, being succeeded by Mr G.J. Goschen.

The loss of *Captain* created much apprehension about turret ships and was indeed tragic, but it was not calamitous and the defects in her design were clearly highlighted. However, steps had already been taken before the disaster to remedy one of the gravest errors. The Admiralty had realized that steam and sail did not mix, and that to install both systems in the new generation of warships would seriously impair a vessel's fighting efficiency, and was courting disaster. As a result of *Captain*'s loss, the turret ship *Monarch* was subjected to many exhaustive tests which proved the vessel to be entirely satisfactory.

In the meantime, with construction of *Monarch* under way and the authorization for *Captain* having been given, Reed was busy preparing other designs. To counter the growing fleet of French armoured cruisers on overseas stations, the Admiralty ordered a class of four, smaller, armoured ships, the 'Audacious' class. These ships were armed with a central battery of ten 9in MLR carried on two gun decks, the four guns on the upper deck being mounted in corner ports to improve end-on fire. The class was notable for the fact that, for the first time, the problems of stability and rolling in a seaway were addressed scientifically, using a new theory propounded by William Froude in 1861. Reed designed the class with a low metacentric height which would result in a long period for the roll. Inclination trials held in the autumn of 1870 showed that the metacentric height was too low for safety. This was corrected by adding ballast, after which the design proved safe and steady in a seaway. In service the ships proved to be the steadiest gun platforms in the fleet. They were, however, completed without any wing bulkheads, which in the case of *Vanguard* was to prove disastrous.

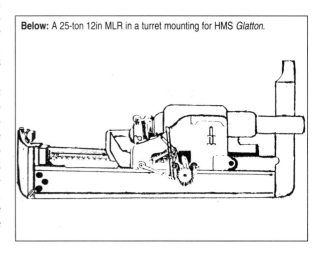

Below: A 25-ton 12in MLR in a turret mounting for HMS *Glatton*.

The last two vessels to be completed, *Swiftsure* and *Triumph* (which were single-screw vessels, as opposed to the rest of the class, which were twin-screw), were built for service in the Pacific, and were therefore experimentally fitted with copper sheathing as an anti-fouling device. The experiment was a success, only a slight loss in speed being recorded, although in the case of *Swiftsure* the tonnage was increased by almost 900 tons.

By the 1870s the ram bow had become a notable feature of many warships, and was so well supported by some members of the Admiralty, including the Chief Constructor, Reed, that in 1868 plans were drawn up for a ship specially designed for ramming. Although he supported the concept of the ram bow, Reed had very little faith in the new ship, *Hotspur*. She was the first and only ship in the navy to mount her armament in a fixed turret rather than a rotating one. The single 25-ton 12in MLR gun was carried on a trolley mounted on rails inside the fixed armoured citadel and manoeuvred into one of several ports in the structure. This arrangement was later replaced by a turret mounting two 25-ton MLR guns. The armoured belt, 11in thick amidships and tapering to 8in at the ends, was extended to reinforce the ram bow, which projected 10ft beyond the perpendicular line of the normal bow. Although *Hotspur* was designed for fleet duties, her short hull and low freeboard, combined with limited bunkerage, gave her poor seakeeping qualities which rendered her only suitable for coast defence duties.

Glatton, laid down in August 1868, enjoyed the dubious distinction of having the lowest freeboard of any ship in the navy, just 3ft. She carried two 12in 25-ton MLR in a single turret, and had an armour belt 12in thick. It was planned that her reserve coal bunkers would be flooded when joining action, reducing her freeboard even more, to a mere 2ft, and thus lowering her silhouette. *Glatton* was followed by the ram vessel *Rupert*. She was the last vessel of this type to be built, and was intended to be a sister to *Hotspur*. *Rupert*, however, was much larger, and reverted to the normal type of turret mounting two

18-ton MLR. Two 64-pounder MLR guns were carried aft in a fixed breastwork.

The war scare of 1870, and the fear that an enemy might attack unprotected ports and harbours with light armoured or unarmoured warships with shallow draught, led the Admiralty to order a class of four harbour defence ships (breastwork type monitors) known as the '*Cyclops*' class (*Cyclops*, *Gorgon*, *Hecate* and *Hydra*). Laid down in 1870, these ships entered service between March 1874 and May 1877. Armed with four 10in MLR carried in two rotating turrets and protected by 8in armour, they eventually came to be regarded as coast defence ships rather than just harbour defence vessels.

In January 1871, in the light of the disaster to *Captain*, the Admiralty set up a Special Committee on Designs under Lord Dufferin, its purpose being to draw up a report on all the designs then under construction and to make recommendations for future lines of development. The Committee made a close study of the current designs, which included *Monarch*, *Cyclops* and *Glatton*, and stated, 'As powerful armament, thick armour, speed and light draught cannot be combined in one ship, although all are needed for the defence of the country; there is no alternative but to give preponderance to each in its turn amongst different classes of ships which shall mutually supplement one another'. The report, on which there was much disagreement among the sixteen members of the Committee, made various other suggestions and recommendations. In general they favoured the *Devastation* design, which they saw as the model for the future development of capital ships in the navy. However, they also noted that larger guns would soon become available, and hence thicker armour protection of at least 24in would be required to provide adequate protection. Among the report's most important conclusions were: a need for improved fireproofing, a change in the way in which tonnage and power ratings were described (the Committee recommended a change to displacement tonnage and indicated horsepower, rather than nominal horsepower),

Left: The *Devastation* marked a radical departure in design and was the first major warship to be designed for the navy which carried no masts or sails, relying completely on steam engines for propulsion. For the first time the navy had a ship in service which could fire on almost any bearing with just two turrets. The *Devastation* marked the passing of the sailing ship era. (ACPL)

the fitting of instruments to measure trim at sea, the need to consider mounting a mix of both protected and unprotected guns, and – perhaps the most important recommendation of all, which would be of long-term benefit to the navy – the need to counter the ram by adopting a cellular method of construction. Many of these recommendations were eventually incorporated into the design of *Inflexible*.

As a result of the report, differing designs were produced which concentrated on the various aspects and led directly to the development of the scouting cruiser, battlecruiser and battleship concepts, for a completely defensible offensive fleet.

Devastation, to which the Committee on Designs had referred, had been conceived by Reed, modified by Barnaby, and laid down in November 1869. Completed in

Left: The *Inflexible* was notable for the fact that she carried the heaviest and largest guns ever mounted in a British warship – 16in MLR guns weighing 100 tons each. The *en-echelon* configuration of mounting the turrets did not prove entirely successful. She was completed with a full sailing rig, but this was removed in 1885, as shown here. (ACPL)

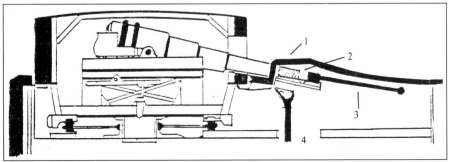

Left: Simplified turret on HMS *Inflexible* showing loading arrangement. 1, Glacis; 2, Shell being rammed home; 3, Hydraulic ram; 4, Ammunition hoist. (ACPL)

April 1873, she has been described as the most radical design to emerge in the 19th century. She was totally unlike any previous design, and was the first completely to do away with masts, sails and rigging. As a result her complement was almost halved compared with that of *Sultan* (358 to 633), and with no masts or rigging to interfere, her central battery now achieved far better arcs of fire, including full end-on fire from the turrets mounted on the centreline, each carrying two 12in MLR. The turrets were sited fore and aft high up in the breastwork amidships, which enabled them to fire over the foc's'le and quarterdeck without the blast affecting those areas. With *Devastation*'s entry into service, the era of the sailing warship passed into history, and steam became king.

Fury, designed as a successor to *Devastation*, was laid down in September 1870, and had been completed up to her armoured belt when the Committee on Designs began their deliberations. One of the designs investigated was that of *Fury*, and as it was of the same vintage as *Captain*, it was decided to suspend all work on the hull until the Committee's report was presented. Work ceased early in 1871, and she was subsequently redesigned by White to incorporate a number of the report's recommendations. Barnaby's secretary, W.H. White, redrew the plans, and the ship was renamed *Dreadnought* in 1872 and finally completed in 1879. She was the last true ironclad completed for the navy, and had a freeboard of uniform height throughout her length. In addition, she was completed without portholes in her sides, fresh air being provided by forced ventilation; she was the first ship to be so fitted.

There were one or two other notable features about *Dreadnought*. She was the first ship to be completed with a longitudinal bulkhead amidships, and was also among the first to be fitted with the new compound engines. Machinery had made many advances since it was first introduced into the navy. The compound vertical triple-expansion engines of *Dreadnought* developed 8,210hp on a displacement of 10,460 tons, to give her a speed of 14kts. Compared with this, the horizontal-trunk single-expansion engines of the first ironclad, *Warrior*, had developed 5,270hp, giving her a speed of 14kts on a displacement of 9,210 tons.

Another suggestion put forward by the Special Committee on Designs was that the armoured central citadel on warships should be considerably shortened, a practice followed in the Italian *Caio Duilio*. Having made suggestions concerning *Devastation*, the Committee next turned its attention to *Inflexible*, ordered under the 1873 Estimates, the plans for which had been completed in 1874. Previous adverse comment in the press and Parliament regarding vessels with low hatchway freeboards fore and aft, such as *Captain*, had very much influenced the design of the upperworks of *Inflexible*. As a result, she was planned with a high hatchway freeboard along her whole length, forcing the designers to place her two turrets in echelon. A new gun was being manufactured by Armstrong for the Italian battleship *Duilio*, and to ensure that the navy would not be outgunned in the Mediterranean, new guns were also adopted for *Inflexible*. These 16in MLR guns, although still of the muzzle-loading type, weighed 100 tons each and were the heaviest guns in the navy. Their barrels were much longer than the diameter of the turret which housed them, which meant that they had to be loaded from outside the turret, behind a specially constructed glacis. The turrets were protected by 16in compound armour which comprised a layer of thin hard steel welded on to soft wrought iron backing. However, the siting of the turrets in echelon did not prove very successful, the firing arcs being restricted, and cross-deck firing put too much strain on the deck. *Inflexible* was also equipped with two of the new torpedo tubes carried in submerged positions.

For its next ships the Admiralty opted for a smaller, cheaper version of *Inflexible*, the *Agamemnon* and *Ajax*, which were laid down in 1876 and launched in 1879-1880. They proved to be two of the most unsatisfactory battleships the navy had built. They were the last warships in the navy to carry muzzle-loading guns, and were the first battleships to carry a planned secondary armament.

In September 1873 another new type of ship, the Royal Navy's first armoured cruiser, was laid down. Completed four years later, *Shannon* was the first ship in the navy to be given an armoured deck. *Shannon*'s design went some way towards carrying out the proposals suggested by the Special Committee on Designs. Barnaby himself felt that the best means of defence was attack, and in carrying out this concept he concentrated more on the armament of ships than on the armour, as opposed to Reed, who had built vessels that were heavily armoured as well as being heavily gunned. In *Shannon*, Barnaby sacrificed protection in favour of heavier armament. Although it was fitted with an armoured belt, this was only 9in at its thickest part, and extended for only three-quarters of the waterline, ending some 60ft from the ram bow, where it was closed off by a 9in transverse armoured bulkhead. Extending forward from the bottom of the armoured belt to the ram bow was a 3in armoured deck. In addition, her hull was well subdivided, the forward subdivisions above the armoured deck, where there was no protective belt, being filled with the coal supply.

The new concept of armour protection, although at first regarded with some scepticism, was eventually adopted as the standard for all warships with armour protection, as it afforded much greater battle damage protection than an armoured belt alone. The armament of *Shannon* comprised two ahead-firing 10in MLR placed in embrasures, six broadside-firing 9in MLR and one stern-firing 9in MLR.

Although the basic concept of *Shannon* proved advantageous, the vessel herself proved a failure. Completed as a full-rigged ship, she was the last British armoured warship to be completed with sails, and was propelled by a single screw. The compound horizontal engines gave inferior results, and could only develop 3,370hp to give the vessel a speed of 12kts. The Admiralty were convinced that, although *Shannon* herself was a failure, further ships should be constructed with their plans based upon the same ideas. As a result *Nelson* and *Northampton* were built, but they unfortunately inherited the same faults as *Shannon*. Barnaby was also convinced of the practicability of the basic design, stating, '... they may be looked upon as armoured ships having to meet armoured ships — or, as protected cruisers...'. The Controller of the navy, Rear-Admiral Houstan Stewart, held different views to those of Barnaby as to the purpose for which ships of this

Vanguard the commander, Captain Richard Dawkins, had left the bridge to go below, having been on deck for some considerable time. The ship was left in charge of Lieutenant William Hathorn. The commander of *Iron Duke*, Captain Henry Hickley, had also gone below. In the absence of any signal from the Admiral, Captain Dawkins, who had returned to his bridge when the fog descended, discussed with Hathorn what course of action to take. He had just decided to make a steam whistle signal to reduce speed to 6kts and then 5kts when a sailing ship was spotted directly ahead.

Vanguard was now in an extremely difficult situation. If she continued at her present speed she would ram the ship ahead, if she slowed down she would herself be rammed by *Iron Duke* astern, who would not have time to

Left: Although rated a second class battleship, the *Shannon* is generally considered as being typically the first armoured cruiser to be built for the navy. In essence she was too weakly armed for a battleship and too slow for a cruiser. She is seen here at the Spithead Review in 1887. (National Maritime Museum)

type should be constructed. He felt that, 'their object was not to take part in a close engagement but to roam over the seas and drive away unarmoured fast cruisers from harrying our commerce'.

In September 1875 the Royal Navy suffered another major accident which gave rise to much thought concerning the design of its warships. The accident occurred at 1250 on 1 September, off Kingston in the Irish Channel, while the 1st Reserve Squadron of the Channel Fleet, under Vice-Admiral Sir Walter Tarleton in *Warrior*, was exercising. The four ships of the squadron were steaming in two divisions at 8kts, with *Warrior* (flagship) leading *Hector* in the starboard column, and *Vanguard* leading her sister ship, *Iron Duke*, in the port column. Suddenly a thick fog descended on the squadron, which in the absence of any signal from the Admiral continued at its speed of 8kts, twice the speed permitted in fog. On board

respond to her sound signal, and a turn to starboard would result in a collision with the starboard column. In the event Dawkins decided to make a slight turn to port, and stop to allow the ship ahead of him to pass safely. As he made his turn he could hear the Admiral to starboard making a sound signal, but nothing was heard from *Iron Duke* astern. As *Vanguard* slowed and swung to port, she was rammed amidships on her port side by *Iron Duke*, which had maintained her speed of 8kts. The ram pierced the bulkhead between the engine and boiler rooms, and both compartments were flooded, the ship sinking just over an hour later. Prompt rescue operations ensured that no lives were lost.

The subsequent court martial found that the main reasons for the accident arose from human error. These were: the high speed of the squadron in poor visibility; the captain of *Vanguard* leaving his bridge at the wrong time;

Right: On 1 September 1875, the *Iron Duke* rammed the *Vanguard* amidships in thick fog in the Irish Channel, the *Vanguard* sinking. (Imperial War Museum)

unnecessary reduction of speed by *Vanguard* without being ordered to do so, and without signalling such a move to *Iron Duke*; and the said ship improperly shearing out of line and not making fog signals. Apart from these human errors, the court also concluded that *Vanguard* foundered as a result of being holed in the most vital transverse bulkhead, between the engine and boiler rooms, and because of improperly closed watertight doors to the provision hold. Finally, the whole blame for the loss of the vessel was placed upon its captain, his second-in-command and the navigating officer, all of whom were severely reprimanded.

The accident immediately focused attention on the ram bow with which many warships were fitted, and the general design. A design feature of the ships of the time was the absence of any wing passages formed by the use of longitudinal bulkheads. As a result, if a ship's side was pierced below the waterline the large machinery compartments amidships would quickly be flooded, and this, combined with the fact that the main deck was only a

few feet above the waterline, would lead to flooding soon reaching the deck above, with a resultant loss of trim.

Between 1876 and 1879 yet another type of vessel designed by Barnaby was laid down for the Royal Navy. This was the 'Comus' class of eleven ships, rated as protected cruisers and designed for use on overseas stations. The design introduced an innovation in protection, in part based on the concept developed for *Shannon*. In the 'Comus' class an armoured deck 1.5in thick was sited over the machinery spaces and magazines. Above the armoured deck the space was subdivided by watertight compartments. This not only provided better protection, but ensured adequate buoyancy and improved stability in the event of flooding. Displacement was only 2,380 tons, and the ships carried two 6-ton MLR and twelve 64-pounder guns. Completed between 1878 and 1884, in service they attained speeds of up to 13kts.

One great advance made with the 'Comus' class was to have a profound effect on future warship construction. During the 1870s a number of experiments had been con-

Right: The 'Comus' class cruisers of the mid- to late 1870s were built of steel and marked the end of iron as a material for warship construction. Although designed for trade protection, the ships proved too slow to be of any use in this role. The *Calliope* is seen here in 1881. (ACPL)

ducted, both in England and abroad, with a view to improving the quality of the iron used in ships' boilers. These had, for some time, been giving trouble, and it was felt that the cracks that were appearing in the boiler tubes were probably caused by inferior quality iron used in their construction. As a result of the experiments a new process was evolved for purifying the iron, which led to the manufacture of steel. Steel was found to be much stronger and durable than iron. As a result the Admiralty specified that the 'Comus' class should be constructed entirely of the new material, and they were the first all-steel ships completed for the Royal Navy.

With construction of the 'Comus' class cruisers well under way, it was decided that a new class of protected cruiser, the 'Amphion' class, should be laid down. The first of these, Arethusa, was laid down in 1880, and three more followed. Although the displacement was only 4,300 tons the class was fitted with ten 6in guns and very soon gained a reputation for being overgunned. In addition, they proved to be inferior sea boats, but managed to maintain their speed well.

Throughout the 1880s France was still regarded by Britain as the potential enemy. With the French 'Formidable' class battleships mounting three 75-ton breech-loading guns newly commissioned, and Caiman, a super coast defence battleship, entering service, the Admiralty felt the need for a vessel to counter this impending threat. The First Sea Lord, Admiral Sir George Wellesly, ordered a design to be prepared for a vessel not larger than 10,000 tons. This limit on the displacement meant that the warship would be no better than a second class coast-defence vessel, and would certainly not be superior to the larger French and Italian vessels then under construction. The final design plans for the vessel were left in the hands of Barnaby's assistant, W.H. White.

The Controller of the navy, Vice-Admiral Sir William Houstan Stewart, recommended that a new mark of the 12in breechloader should be mounted in the vessel, which had been named Collingwood. In addition, Vice-Admiral Stewart proposed that the 12in guns should be mounted in a new barbette designed by George Rendel, instead of the more normal turret. The barbette concept, in which the gun was trained on a turntable inside an armoured breastwork, had certain advantages over the turret. The guns could be mounted much higher than in a turret because the mounting was far lighter, and elevation and depression were not restricted as in a turret. The echelon positioning used for the turrets in Colosus was dispensed with, and the barbettes of Collingwood were mounted fore and aft on the centreline. The compound armour protection was concentrated in a short, heavy waterline belt 8 to 18in thick amidships, protecting the engines, boilers and communication tubes of the barbettes. The ends of the armour belt were closed by bulkheads 16in thick, the whole being covered by a protective deck, flat over the armoured belt and slightly curved fore and aft. Collingwood proved to be an excellent design, the only fault being the low freeboard, which with the high speed of 16kts meant that mobility in a seaway was considerably impaired. Apart from mounting her guns in barbettes, Collingwood was also the first British battleship to have her secondary and light armament grouped in batteries, which enabled a much better concentration of fire to be achieved.

With Collingwood the navy at last crystallized its ideas on the development of the battleship, and all succeeding classes were really improvements and modifications of the Collingwood design. Future development differed in this respect from the previous two decades, where there were numerous separate designs, each emphasizing some particular aspect such as the ram bow, guns, turrets etc. The cause of the seemingly endless array of designs with widely differing capabilities which characterized the ships of the 1860s and '70s was a lack of any well defined strategy or naval policy. Warships were ordered and designed to meet each specific situation as it arose, incor-

Left: The Collingwood carried 12in BLR guns in open barbettes and exhibited a number of other novel features. Clearly seen along the hull are poles for carrying anti-torpedo nets. (ACPL)

Right: The Collingwood's guns were mounted in pear-shaped barbettes. With a reduced charge of 295lb (using a 400lb charge one of the original guns had burst on trials) the 12in shell could penetrate 20.5in of iron at a range of 1,000yds. (Imperial War Museum)

porating the latest technological developments. There was no study of strategy and tactics, so no designs could be developed to fulfil roles evolving from such studies. No formal naval requirement was promulgated, and no department had been formed or was charged with the task of studying tactics, or of gathering naval intelligence, or of determining the requirements for the defence of Britain's seaborne trade. Hence a diverse legion of designs appeared as the industrial revolution made its impact on the Victorian navy.

Gladstone's Administration of the 1880s was convinced of the economy of using sails whenever possible, instead of costly coal, and as a result a design was prepared which developed into the two armoured cruisers *Imperieuse* and *Warspite*, which were laid down in 1881 and were contemporaries of *Collingwood*. Designed principally to serve as flagships on colonial stations, these were the last major warships with a full rig to be built for the navy. The scheme of protection was basically that of *Collingwood* but lighter, except for the armoured deck fore and aft, which was thicker. For armament they carried four 9.2in BL guns of a new design, sited in single, shallow barbette mountings fore and aft and amidships to port and starboard (the gun disposition adopted in French warships). They were the only British vessels to so carry their armament. It was felt that such a placing of the guns would give the vessels a tremendous advantage in any cruiser action. Another unique feature of the ships was their tumblehome sides, again a design feature of French warships and hitherto unknown in the Royal Navy. Owing to poor inspection during construction and a considerable number of additions, the displacement was much greater than designed – so much so that the armoured belt was below the waterline.

Consequently they proved to be poor sea boats, a limitation which was not improved by the considerable top-weight resulting from the two masts and yards, a feature which was soon removed on the advice of the captain of

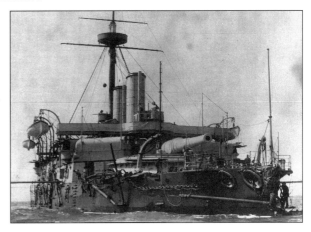

Above: The *Collingwood* was followed by the four ships of the 'Admiral' class, and the fifth ship, the *Benbow* is illustrated here. She differed from the other 'Admirals' in mounting a single 16.25in BLR gun in each barbette. Although problems had been experienced with the 13.5in gun, which lead to the *Benbow* mounting the 16.25in, even this gun was not as satisfactory as the 13.5in, proving too large and with too slow a rate of fire. (US Naval Historical Center)

Imperieuse. They were described in Parliament as, 'amongst the most complete failures of modern warships; badly designed; badly carried out; and absolutely dangerous'.

Following the large French programme of construction begun in 1880, the Board of Admiralty set about ordering more new vessels for the navy. They were undecided, however, as to what type of ship they should order. Finally, a class of four ships very similar to *Collingwood*, then still under construction, was ordered. Together with *Collingwood*, and later *Benbow*, this class — *Anson*, *Camperdown*, *Howe* and *Rodney* — came to be known as the 'Admirals'. By the time the four vessels were laid down (1882-83), the more powerful 13.5in BL gun had become available, and was fitted in the ships. Being slightly heavier than the 12in, the 13.5in put the second group of 'Admirals' on a par with recently completed French ships.

Delays in production of the 13.5in gun, and certain faults in the guns themselves which had to be eradicated before the ships could mount the weapon, meant that the second group of 'Admirals' did not finally enter service until the end of the decade. A repeat order for a fifth ship, *Benbow*, followed, in which it was decided to mount yet another new gun, the massive 16.25in Elswick BL gun. Unfortunately the considerable increase in weight of the 16.25in compared with the 13.5in (110 tons against 67 tons), and the extra space required to mount the gun, meant that only one weapon could be mounted in each barbette instead of two. Although the new gun enabled *Benbow* to be completed before any of her sister ships, the 16.25in was not as satisfactory as the 13.5in, being much slower in operation and having a much shorter life.

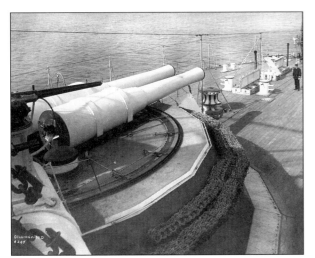

Chapter 9

The Victorian Navy at Peace

The latter part of the 19th century was one of consolidation and relaxation for the Royal Navy. The great changes wrought as a result of the Industrial Revolution were almost complete. The steam engine and its boilers were greatly improved, and slowly the engineers who operated them came to be accepted by their brother officers and men. Protection was also improved, new processes for the production of armour plate giving warships greater strength. This meant that improved guns had to be designed to penetrate armour. The race between gun and armour reached its height during this period, with new guns being produced almost yearly.

The British Empire was at its zenith at this time, and the small gunboats and cruisers of the Royal Navy were kept busy maintaining the peace. The only real actions were minor skirmishes in the Far East, where pirates and rebellions still caused trouble, and on the continent of Africa, where British interests came into conflict with other European powers.

The British governments of the day were unwilling to spend vast sums of money on the navy, as they were busily engaged in carrying out expensive programmes of social reform aimed at relieving the hardships of many at home. In the Spring Estimates of 1869 the First Lord, Hugh Childers, was forced, under the direction of Gladstone's Liberal Government, to reduce expenditure. In so doing he reduced the number of men serving on foreign stations from 17,000 to 11,000 in spite of the protests of the First Sea Lord. To accomplish this, the larger and more stable colonies such as Canada, Australia and New Zealand were requested to provide certain forces for their own defence.

The newly unified Germany under Chancellor Bismarck began building a navy, the nucleus of which had been formed after the Crimean War, when Britain had given Germany a frigate and a gunboat. The High Seas Fleet developed rapidly, and by 1872 two naval bases were in operation, at Kiel and Wilhelmshaven. In spite of these developments, and in the prevailing political climate, Great Britain still looked upon France as posing the greatest threat to peace. France had always been regarded as Britain's natural enemy, but the situation changed almost imperceptibly as the two countries found themselves more and more in accord over their views of the international situation, and especially with regard to German intentions.

Early in 1872 the Royal Navy fitted out an expedition under the command of Captain George Nares to carry out research in the Atlantic, Pacific and Antarctic oceans. Sailing in 1872 in the wooden steam corvette *Challenger*, the expedition remained away for three and a half years, covering a distance of almost 70,000 miles. On board *Challenger* was a team of three naturalists, a chemist, a geologist and a photographer, under the leadership of Professor Wyville Thompson. The purpose of the expedition was to take soundings and record sea temperatures, and to acquire samples of the ocean bed for animal life. In addition, the chemist was to analyze mineral content in the salt water. A certain amount of coastal surveying work was also undertaken and a number of magnetic observations made. *Challenger* finally returned to England in May 1876, when the results were processed and published in 15 volumes.

During a revolution in South America in May 1877, a British-built ironclad turret ship, *Huascar*, flagship of the Peruvian navy, was taken over by rebels. The *Huascar* stopped a number of British merchant ships, seizing their coal, and the British Government was forced to intervene. The unprotected *Shah*, flagship of the Pacific Station, accompanied by the smaller *Amethyst*, was ordered

Left: The 1870s and 1880s were the height of the period of the *Pax Britannica*, and ships of the navy could be seen in most major ports around the world, showing the flag. The navy's main base in the Mediterranean was Malta. The picture shows part of the Mediterranean Fleet, primarily comprising sailing vessels, in the early 1870s. From left to right: *Invincible, Pallas, Immortalité, Doris, Hibernia, Narcissus, Topaz* and *Rapid*. Partly in view at the far right is the *Endymion*. (ACPL)

Above: In 1877 the flagship of the Pacific Station, the *Shah*, was in action with the Peruvian ship *Huascar*, which had been taken over by rebels. The action was notable for the fact that it was the last time that a wooden ship of the navy was in action, and the first time that a British ship had fired a new weapon, the torpedo, in anger. (Imperial War Museum)

to intercept, and came upon the *Huascar* on 25 May. Admiral De Horsey on the *Shah* demanded that the rebels surrender the Peruvian ship, but this was refused. At 1500 *Shah* opened fire on *Huascar*, which was armed with two 10in MLR mounted in a Coles turret, and protected by a 4.5in armoured belt. *Shah* fired about 280 rounds at *Huascar*, of which about 30 struck, the upperworks suffering some damage. *Amethyst* scored a similar number of hits.

In return *Huascar*, with a totally untrained crew, was unable to score any hits on the British ships. The armour of the rebel ship proved impervious to the British shellfire, only one 9in shell piercing the upper belt, and causing little damage and only a few minor casualties. At 1714 *Shah* fired a 14in torpedo, but *Huascar* managed to outrun the 7-knot weapon, which finally sank when it ran out of compressed air. The fight reached an inconclusive end, and during the night *Huascar* sailed away and surrendered to the Peruvian forces. Had she stayed to fight the outcome might have been different, for after dark Admiral de Horsey launched a steam pinnace armed with two spar torpedoes, and a cutter armed with a 14in torpedo. The action was notable as being the last time that a wooden warship of the Royal Navy, armed with a broadside battery of muzzle-loading guns, was in action.

The *Huascar* incident proved to be just a passing scare. Of far more importance to the Admiralty were relations with Russia during 1877 and 1878. During the Russo-Turkish war these deteriorated to such an extent that the Admiralty fully expected that war would be declared, and that the navy would become involved. To prepare for such an eventuality the Reserve was mobilized in April 1878 and a motley collection of warships formed into the Particular Service Squadron under Admiral Sir Cooper Key. At the time three ironclads were under construction in Britain for Turkey, and another for Brazil. Under neutrality laws, warring states could not take over warships building in a neutral country, and they had to be kept in the country of build. In order that the British shipyards should not lose out, the Government purchased all four ships and gave them to the navy. This proved to be a false economy, for a considerable sum of money had then to be expended to bring the ships up to the standards of armament and equipment then current in the Royal Navy.

The Brazilian vessel was an improved *Monarch* designed by Reed, and on being commissioned into the navy was renamed *Neptune*. Her main claim to fame was that she was the first British warship to be completed with a bathroom. The Turkish vessels were never successful, one being an improved *Hercules* type of ship renamed *Superb*, and the other two being sister ships renamed *Belleisle* and *Orion*. All four vessels were obsolete when purchased, having long been superseded by newer designs already in service in the Royal Navy.

In 1880 Gladstone again took office as Prime Minister, with the First Earl of Northbrook, Thomas George Baring, as the First Lord and Admiral Sir Cooper Key, KCB, as First Sea Lord. Not for the first (or the last) time did an administration prove to be very unpopular after an extended term of service. Lord Northbrook had an obsession with economy, and did everything in his power to keep the Service estimates as low as possible. He was often unintentionally assisted by members of the Board of Admiralty, who could not decide on the type of warship that they should construct, and thus delayed construction, or designed vessels which caused much criticism within the Service. As a start to reducing expenditure, it was planned to pay off large numbers of ships, discharge many workmen from the dockyards and cease purchasing stores. The trend had been set by a previous First Lord, Hugh

Childers (see page 46), and Gladstone happily continued the process of whittling away the navy until it was not even strong enough to meet any possible opposition that the French Fleet might offer.

In September 1879, in the wake of the deficiencies in the navy's organisation and preparation for war revealed by the Russian scare of 1878, the Government set up the Carnarvon Committee to study the question of colonial defence. Included in the Committee's remit was a requirement to examine the ability of the navy to provide protection for commerce and defend overseas possessions. The Committee's report noted that the navy was inadequate in numbers to meet all of its commitments, and required an immediate increase in strength. This would require additional expenditure, which meant that the Government would be forced to raise the level of income tax to provide the necessary funds. Gladstone and his Cabinet could not countenance such a proposal, so the report was withheld and not revealed for ten years. Yet again the navy and the defence of the country fell foul of party politics, both political parties agreeing to withhold any increase in the Navy Estimates until 1884.

By the 1880s the problem of materiel had become a vital question in the navy, and in December 1881, in recognition of its importance, the Controller, Rear-Admiral Thomas Brandreth, was made a member of the Board of Admiralty. At the same time another important post, that of Civil Lord, was created. The Civil Lord was appointed to assist the Controller, and had not only to be an administrative assistant but also a qualified engineer. To fill this new post the Admiralty appointed George Rendel of Armstrongs. Apart from this, however, little was done to increase the navy's materiel strength during the early 1880s. The fleet was still a motley collection of hybrid vessels, very few of which could operate together as a homogeneous squadron. Submarines, then in the early stages of development, were thought to be an ungentlemanly weapon and rather impracticable. The voices of criticism were few and far between, and the general public knew very little of the real state of the navy and its weaknesses.

In July 1884 Lord Sidmouth drew attention to this poor state of affairs in the House of Lords, and asked that the Admiralty be given unlimited funds to build a new navy. Lord Northbrook replied for the Admiralty, making a most unfortunate statement:

> The great difficulty the Admiralty would have to contend with, if they were granted three or four millions tomorrow for the purpose referred to, would be to decide how they should spend the money ... Then there was another consideration, which made it doubtful whether it would be wise to spend a great sum of money now on such ships [ships with greater armour for protection against more powerful guns]. Some of the finest naval offi-

cers in Britain thought that, in the event of another war the torpedo would be the most powerful weapon of offence ... Then it would be most imprudent greatly to increase the number of these enormous machines.

This reply was completely misconstrued, as it gave the impression that Lord Northbrook regarded the navy as having adequate strength and that no more money was required. What Lord Northbrook meant, in fact, was that, with the apparent inability of large ships to defend themselves against attack by torpedo craft, the sudden expenditure of vast sums of money on these vessels would probably be wasted.

With the economies being forced on it by Gladstone's administration, the Board of Admiralty was finally forced to order some second class ships for overseas service, and to speed the rate of construction, which in the case of *Ajax* and *Collingwood* was being seriously delayed, the vessels finally taking seven years to complete.

Egypt had for many years seethed with discontent. A contributory cause was the bankruptcy in 1876 of the Khedive Ismail Pasha, ruler of Egypt. During the 1860s the French had completed the Suez Canal, which at once proved of inestimable value, the long sea journey round South Africa's Cape of Good Hope to reach the French Empire in the Far East no longer being necessary. It also proved of great value to the British, who were able to use the shorter route to get to India. With both Britain and France vying for influence in Egypt, the bankruptcy of the Khedive at last forced a *rapprochement* between the two countries.

Combining forces under the leadership of Lord Salisbury, who was determined not to allow the French to take advantage of the situation, the two countries at once set about the problem of recovering the money necessary to settle Egypt's debts, and an International Commission of the Public Debt was formed to collect the money. In effect, this meant that the Egyptians were placed under Anglo-French rule. Taxes were imposed which infuriated both the ruling classes and the peasants. Arising from the resulting discontent, many nationalist cells were formed in order to overthrow the foreign administration. Finally, in 1881, the Egyptian Army under Arabi Pasha took control of the Administration of the country.

By this time Gladstone had become Britain's Prime Minister, and, not wishing to release the British hold on the Suez Canal, he agreed to the sending of a joint British-French note to Arabi Pasha. The note, sent in January 1882, failed to have the necessary impact, and Arabi Pasha, inferring that armed intervention was hinted at in the note, began building up the fortifications of Alexandria. This act of provocation failed to stir the Allies, who waited until May before sending a combined squadron of warships. With such a powerful force outside Alexandria, the Khedive Tewfik Pasha, son of Ismail Pasha, was persuaded to dismiss Arabi Pasha, but so strong was the anti-British/French feeling throughout the country that five days later he was back in office.

The last straw was the massacre of 50 Europeans on 11 June. At this Gladstone instructed Admiral Sir Frederick Beauchamp Seymour to send an ultimatum to Arabi Pasha. Seymour, being rather over-zealous, demanded that Arabi Pasha disarm his forts or else be bombarded. The French declined to be associated with the Admiral's ultimatum and withdrew their warships from the squadron, leaving Seymour to act on his own. The squadron comprised a mixture of sail, steam, iron and wooden vessels, representative of all the major types of warship then in the Royal Navy, including eight battle-ships (the most modern being *Inflexible* with Captain J.A. Fisher in command), three gun vessels (including *Condor* under command of Commander Lord Charles Beresford) and two gunboats.

The squadron took up its prearranged bombarding position on the evening of 10 July. At 0700 the following morning the bombardment began, a number of the forts soon being heavily damaged. Tactically, the attack was an unfortunate error, as not only did it fail to subdue Arabi Pasha, but it brought the whole of Egypt into open revolt.

This forced Gladstone to send in the Army, who gradually restored the situation, until Egypt's rich protectorate, the Sudan, broke into revolt under the leadership of the Mahdi. The Egyptian Army sent to repress the rebellion was wiped out, and to cover British possessions on the Red Sea coast a squadron under Rear-Admiral Sir William Hewett was sent to the area.

As a result of the debacle in Egypt, British foreign policy underwent a change which was to have its effect on the navy, not least on the small gunboats which were often instrumental in carrying out that policy. The Empire began to wane, and almost imperceptibly Britain's isolated position was undermined as, at ever more frequent intervals, she was forced to enter into diplomatic negotiations with other European Powers.

With a general election in the offing, in the autumn of 1884 it was decided to print a series of articles entitled 'The Truth about the Navy', in the Liberal paper the *Pall Mall Gazette*. Although these were published anonymously, the author was W.T. Stead, the editor of the magazine, who had been persuaded to write them by H.W. Arnold Forster. The technical background for the articles was provided by Captain J.A. Fisher, commanding officer of the gunnery school *Excellent*. They completely damned

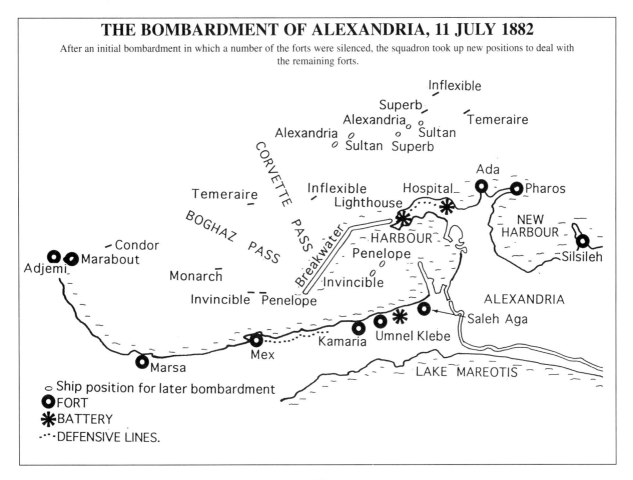

THE BOMBARDMENT OF ALEXANDRIA, 11 JULY 1882

After an initial bombardment in which a number of the forts were silenced, the squadron took up new positions to deal with the remaining forts.

the Board of Admiralty and the Government, showing the navy to be utterly deficient in men, organization, ships, stores and equipment.

As a result of the outcry that followed publication of the articles, Lord Northbrook was forced to institute a programme of reform and new construction. The resulting construction of armoured warships and cruisers was vital to the well-being of Britain, as by this time much of the food and materials for industry were being imported and the navy was responsible for the protection of this trade. The Estimates for 1884 voted an additional £3.1 million for a five-year plan of construction which included the *Sans Pareil* and *Victoria*, seven cruisers of the 'Orlando' class, six torpedo cruisers of the '*Archer*' class and fourteen torpedo boats. The Admiralty covered its previous failings by saying that, if a similar programme had been instituted before, there would have been such an outcry from the public that the Estimates would never have been passed. They also said that, as the feelings of the public had now been aroused in favour of the expenditure, it was in fact adequate.

In 1884, while the Admiralty was wrestling with its administrative problems, the country was yet again suddenly faced with the prospect of war with Russia. The scare materialized when Russia invaded Bulgaria and Afghanistan, and then gave an ultimatum that she also required India as a political necessity. The Government prepared for war and the Admiralty called out the Reserves, at the same time taking over the island of Port Hamilton, south of Korea, as an advanced base for warships.

In June 1885 a Special Service Squadron was assembled to constitute the Baltic Expeditionary Fleet under Admiral Sir Phipps Hornby. The squadron was a diverse collection of obsolete warships, none of which was suitable for such an operation. It consisted of twelve ironclads, *Polyphemus* and *Hecla*, six cruisers, thirteen gunboats,

eight armed merchant ships and sixteen torpedo boats. Many months passed before some of the vessels were ready for service, and some had not even finished fitting out when the scare eventually passed. As the situation eased it was decided to complete the mobilization of the squadron and then to keep it together as the Particular Service Squadron, employing it on exercises to test seagoing qualities and the value of the new torpedo boats, nets, mines etc.

In 1885 Gladstone resigned and Lord Salisbury again became Prime Minister (and also Foreign Secretary), with Lord George Hamilton as First Lord and Admiral Sir Arthur Hood as First Sea Lord. To appease public agitation over the state of the navy a Fourth Sea Lord was created, the post being filled by Lord Charles Beresford. This new Board of Admiralty was the last of its type to be formed, all future Boards being purely naval appointments made by the War Office (except that is, the post of First Lord, a civil post). The Chief Constructor, Sir Nathaniel Barnaby, resigned his post in 1885, as he had come into conflict with the Board in matters of design. The First Lord asked W.H. White to take over as Director of Naval Construction, and the post of assistant, previously held by George Rendel, was abolished.

Plans were drawn up to reform the navy, but before any material reconstruction was started a complete reorganization had to be undertaken which led to major changes in the administration of the Navy and the Dockyards, for which White was invited to take charge. In the reorganization the First Lord had all of Lord Northbrook's plans scrapped, except for the designs of *Nile* and *Trafalgar*. The previous years of financial stringency had wrought havoc with the state of the navy, and Lord Beresford prepared a memorandum on this aspect, putting forward proposals for the formation of a War Staff which were rejected by the Board of Admiralty as being unnecessary. At this Lord Beresford showed his plans to Lord

Left: Under the 1884 Estimates, the navy built the *Sans Pareil* and *Victoria* (illustrated here). The design was notable for the fact that the ships were the first to be fitted with the new triple expansion engines. (Imperial War Museum)

Right: The workhorses of the fleet on the more remote stations and rivers around the world were the small gunboats, epitomised by vessels such as the *Bramble*, seen here painted white for service in the tropics. (ACPL)

Salisbury, who at once set about forming a Naval Intelligence Department on the strength of his arguments.

During the 1890s Africa was to cause the Government many a headache, and already Britain and France were beginning to be at variance over their defined spheres of influence in the continent. Egypt and her difficulties were at the root of many of Britain's problems, and in the 1890s she was forced to make certain colonial concessions in Africa and the Pacific in order to obtain German approval for her policies in Egypt and South Africa. Trouble first became apparent in West Africa, where the French, no longer passive in that part of the continent, began to exploit trading possibilities on the lower Niger and Congo rivers. The lower Niger was looked upon as a British domain, and the French were offered Senegal and the upper Niger in return for their quiescence, but they refused. On the Congo, the British countered the French move by recognizing Portuguese claims to the area, hoping that the Portuguese would look after the area on their behalf. Again the French refused to be intimidated, and opened negotiations with the Germans. Without German support on the International Debt Commission (see page 48) British efforts to rule Egypt were doomed to failure, so the proposed British/Portuguese Treaty over the Congo proved to be abortive.

Following her retreat in West Africa, Britain was forced to concede certain parts of East Africa (opposite the island of Zanzibar) to Germany, a move which was to store up trouble for the country in the future. The Portuguese followed suit, making moves on the Zambesi River, which it hoped to use as a route to Central Africa. This was too much, and in 1889 the gunboat *Stork* was sent to the river to show the flag, surveying the mouth of the Zambesi at the same time. In 1890 Lord Salisbury at last asserted British rights. A small squadron composed of the gunboats *Herald*, *Mosquito*, *Pigeon* and *Redbreast* was assem-

Right: Life on the lower deck during the last decades of the 19th century was still hard, although improvements had been made with victualling; but food was poorly prepared and cooked. (ACPL)

bled with a view to intimidating the Portuguese. *Pigeon* and *Redbreast* crossed the bar at the mouth of the river and forced their way upstream, but *Pigeon* soon returned owing to the difficulties of navigation and the possible loss of the vessels. *Redbreast* continued upstream, finally breaking out into the open river, whereupon the Portuguese capitulated, recognizing British claims to the lakes. Thereafter *Herald* and *Mosquito*, being stern-wheel gunboats built especially for working on the Zambesi, patrolled the lakes.

The following year (1891) found the British and French in dispute over their boundaries in West Africa. The French fomented tribal unrest in the area of the Gambia River, and the gunboats *Alecto*, *Swallow* and *Widgeon* concentrated on the river and landed a number of sailors to restore peace. A further show of force was required at the end of 1891, and this time *Sparrow*, *Thrush* and *Widgeon* landed men. By the end of January 1892 nearly 500 men were engaged in the operation, which came to an end the following month when it was learned that the tribal chief responsible for the uprising had fled over the border to seek asylum in French territory.

The problems and difficulties which faced the Royal Navy during the 1890s were many and varied. On the question of welfare there was still much ground to be made. Training methods were also antiquated. The seamanship of both officers and men was still initially done on board sailing vessels, and life on the lower deck was still hard. The ordinary seaman was looked upon as a rather unintelligent creature with primitive habits. At mealtimes they ate their food with their fingers, as cutlery was regarded as an unnecessary expense. Improve-

ments had been made with the victualling, and rations were more varied, but they were poorly prepared and cooked. In spite of these hardships, morale in the navy was high.

In 1893 the navy suffered a disaster to one of its most modern battleships. On 22 June eleven ironclads of the Mediterranean Fleet were carrying out manoeuvres off the port of Tripoli. *Victoria*, flagship of the Fleet under the Commander-in-Chief, Admiral Sir George Tryon, and *Camperdown*, under Rear-Admiral Hastings Markham, were leading the two columns in line ahead six cables apart when Admiral Tryon gave the order for the two columns to turn inwards 16 points in succession. With the large turning circles of the vessels it was inevitable that under these conditions a collision would occur, and it did. *Camperdown* rammed *Victoria* on her starboard side just behind the anchor while the vessels were steaming at about 9kts. Sadly, there was insufficient time to shut many of the watertight doors, and the breach, occurring on a transverse bulkhead in the same place as *Vanguard* had been rammed (see page 42), let the sea flood through the large hole and gather along the starboard side, then pour in through open portholes, aided by the low freeboard. *Victoria* rapidly listed to starboard and suddenly capsized and sank, Admiral Tryon and 357 officers and men being drowned. The rest of the squadron managed to avoid similar collisions by dextrously jockeying with their screws.

The expansion of the German Empire in East Africa created grave misgivings in neighbouring African States, especially in the island of Zanzibar. Relations with Britain deteriorated as the mainland possessions of the Sultan were taken over by the Germans. In 1896 the Sultan died, and Prince Seyyid Khalid ben Barghash mounted a revolution with the full support of the army. He stormed the Royal Palace, broke out his personal flag, and proclaimed himself the new Sultan. The cruiser *Philomel* and the gunboat *Thrush* happened to be in the harbour at the time, and at once landed all available men. Later another gunboat arrived, and *Thrush* was then moved across the harbour where her guns could bear on the Palace.

The following day the cruiser *St George* (Rear-Admiral Sir Harry Rawson) and *Racoon* arrived and, together with the three other warships, moored in a line with all their guns trained on the Palace. At 0700 on 27 August 1896, the rebel Prince was given a final ultimatum to surrender. As the British vessels prepared for action all foreign vessels left the harbour, leaving *Glasgow*, the late Sultan's gunboat, now manned by the rebels. Two hours later, when the ultimatum expired, the British opened fire, the bombardment lasting just over half an hour. The Palace was destroyed, *Glasgow* was severely damaged and several dhows were sunk. At this Prince Seyyid Khalid ben Barghash surrendered, and a new Sultan was proclaimed.

At the beginning of 1897 the Royal Navy was again called into action on the west coast of Africa. The tribes of the Benin region posed a threat to the Niger Coast Protectorate, and a squadron of six cruisers and three gunboats under command of Rear-Admiral Sir Harry Rawson was sent to calm the area. On 9 February 1897 Admiral Rawson landed a force of 1,200 men, Hausa troops making up the numbers, and began a march on Benin through the fever-ridden bush. After fighting tribesmen most of the way the force finally reached the city of Benin on 18 February. Admiral Rawson garrisoned the abandoned city with Hausa troops and returned to the coast, leaving the politicians in Lagos to conclude a treaty with the Benin chiefs.

While Admiral Rawson was sorting out the problems in West Africa, the British Army had been advancing in the Sudan, at last forcing the Mahdi's Dervishes on the run. The Mahdi himself had died in 1886, but the Dervishes were still a force to be reckoned with under the leadership of the Khalifa. To supply the Army as it moved south into the wastes of the Sudan, a railway was constructed, closely following the course of the Nile, where river gunboats could protect the supply trains. In charge of the Army was Herbert Kitchener, and the navy seconded men to operate the gunboats under Kitchener's orders. In charge of the naval force was Commander Colville of the battleship *Nile*, assisted by Lieutenants

David Beatty, Walter Cowan and Horace Hood. The force consisted of four shallow-draught stern-wheel gunboats normally stationed on the Nile and armed with Maxim guns. In addition, three modern gunboats were shipped out to Egypt in sections and assembled on the Nile.

The gunboats followed hard upon the heels of the Army, negotiating the treacherous cataracts of the Nile with the help of bands of natives who acted as human tugs, towing the boats over the most difficult passages. After a number of brushes with the Dervishes, the Army and the gunboats finally reached Omdurman, where, after a close action, the Dervishes were completely routed, 10,883 of a total force of 80,000 being killed in precipitate charges against the Army, and by fire from the gunboats.

This, however, was not the end of the enterprise, for a few days later Kitchener received intelligence that a French force had arrived at Fashoda. Again use was made of the gunboats, which took Kitchener and a party of troops up the Nile to investigate. On arrival the British found that the French had laid claim to the Sudan as liberators of the territory. The French force was only a small one and, with the imposing strength of the river gunboats, Kitchener had no difficulty in persuading the French commander to recognize British sovereignty over the area.

June 1897 was the Diamond Jubilee of Queen Victoria. To mark the event the Royal Navy staged the largest and most impressive array of warships ever seen in the world. In all, 165 ships were assembled at Spithead, including 22 battleships, 40 cruisers and 20 torpedo boats, all drawn from home waters. This was a truly staggering comment on the strength of the Royal Navy, except that a number of the vessels in the review were unfortunately incapable of steaming and had to be towed to their positions. The Germans, however, were not to know this, and neither did they look upon the assembly as just a Jubilee Review. The Queen herself did not attend, not being very enamoured with the Royal Yacht *Victoria and Albert*, and she commanded the Prince of Wales to review the Fleet. To Admiral Tirpitz this was a frightening eye-opener, as every one of the vessels at Spithead came from bases around Britain. Not one vessel came from a foreign station. In response to such a display of strength Tirpitz at once set about goading the German nation into action, and the following year, 1898, the First German Navy Law was passed.

At long last it was realized that German intentions were not what they had at first seemed. The German Navy Laws could have only one purpose — to challenge the might of the Royal Navy. At first only a few farsighted men realized that these Laws posed a dire threat to the Royal Navy's supremacy at sea. Finally, after much argument, the Government was convinced of the German threat and new ships were designed and built. The arms race was on.

Chapter 10
New Weapons, Reorganization and Technological Advances

The art of gunnery lapsed dismally during the second half of the 19th century. In general the Victorian navy did not look favourably upon guns. Like the steam engines before them, they were viewed with some dismay, as firing them made an awful noise and the ships took hours to clean after a shoot. In many cases battle practices were a farce, the range being kept far too low and no real effort being made to improve efficiency. The intention was to get the exercise over as quickly as possible so that the ships could return to port, show the flag again, and allow their officers to continue the dashing social life. There were some, however, who did not enjoy indulging in all the social functions which were a feature of the Victorian navy. Very gradually, however, and under the guidance of a dedicated few who many regarded as cranks, the efficiency of the navy was improved.

In 1866 Robert Whitehead, manager of a factory at Fiume in the Austro-Hungarian Empire, built the first torpedo. In essence this was a long tube, the major part of which housed the propulsion unit driven by compressed air. Its offensive capability was in the form of an explosive charge placed in the nose of the weapon and fired by a pistol which was actuated on contact with a hard object. By 1868 Whitehead had developed 14in and 16in torpedoes which developed a speed of 7kts and had a range of about 700yd. The Admiralty was offered the exclusive rights to the weapon, but turned them down on the grounds that the torpedo would threaten Britain's naval supremacy. Limited rights on the weapon were then sold to Austria.

In October 1869, following receipt of a report from the Commander-in-Chief of the Mediterranean Fleet, the Admiralty asked Whitehead to demonstrate his new weapon, and in August 1870 14in and 16in weapons underwent trials against the old sloop *Oberon*. Following the trials, the Admiralty changed its views concerning the torpedo and bought the manufacturing rights in 1871, and 16in torpedoes began to be produced at the Royal Ordnance factory at Woolwich. Most major warships were soon fitted to launch torpedoes, and a number of the larger boats carried by the major warships were also fitted to launch them. In addition, a number of special Second Class Torpedo Boats were built to be carried by the large warships. The 14ft-long weapon carried 106lb of explosive at a speed of 9.5kts to a range of 200yd (800yd at 7kts). This was later improved to 300yd at 12.25kts or 1,200yd at 9kts. By 1877 the 16in weapon had been superseded by a 14in weapon with a much improved performance, viz 1,000yd at 22kts.

Realizing the weapon's potential, the commanding officer of the gunnery school HMS *Excellent*, Captain A.W. Hood, recommended that a new post be created at *Excellent* specifically to teach the mechanics of torpedo warfare. Reporting directly to the captain of the gunnery establishment, the new post was rated at the rank of commander, and appointments were to last for three years.

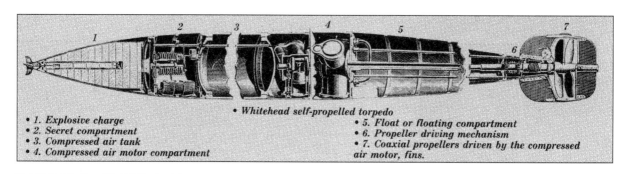

- *Whitehead self-propelled torpedo*
- 1. Explosive charge
- 2. Secret compartment
- 3. Compressed air tank
- 4. Compressed air motor compartment
- 5. Float or floating compartment
- 6. Propeller driving mechanism
- 7. Coaxial propellers driven by the compressed air motor, fins.

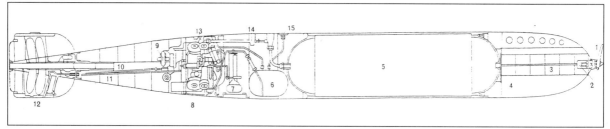

Right: In 1876 the navy took delivery of its first torpedo boat – TB No 1, the *Lightning*. Being small, the craft was confined to coastal waters and could only make high speed in a flat calm. Lacking seaworthiness, she did not prove to be very effective as a warship, but many lessons were learned from exercises carried out with her. Torpedoes were carried in frames, which were lowered over the side, the torpedo being fired when it was in the water. As these could not be used at higher speeds, they were replaced in 1879 by a bow-mounted torpedo tube. (National Maritime Museum)

On 16 July 1872 Commander J.A. Fisher was appointed to the post of Chief Torpedo Instructor at HMS *Excellent*, where he did all in his power to foster the new weapon. Meanwhile, the hulk of the old ship *Vernon* was being converted into a Torpedo Instruction Ship in Portsmouth Dockyard, but conversion progressed very slowly. Finally, in 1873, the new base was ready and Fisher moved into his new home. In 1876 *Vernon* was made an independent command, and when Fisher left for his next appointment he had achieved, as he put it: '...my utmost to develop it [the torpedo] from a conviction that the issue of the next naval war will chiefly depend on the use that is made of the torpedo, not only in ocean warfare, but for the pur-

poses of blockade'. The truth of this prophecy was not to be realized until 1917.

In 1876 the Thornycroft yard completed a prototype vessel for the navy specially built to carry and launch a torpedo. With a speed of 18.5kts she was commissioned as *Lightning* (*TB No 1*), the Royal Navy's first torpedo boat. With a displacement of 32 tons she carried a single 14in torpedo which was launched from a frame suspended from the side of the boat. *Lightning* was followed by a series of designs, most of them experimental.

In 1878 Phillip Watts, under the direction of Nathaniel Barnaby, designed the experimental vessel *Polyphemus* to test submerged broadside-mounted torpedo tubes. *Polyphemus* carried five of the new torpedo tubes, two on either beam and one in the bow at the base of the ram. The ship carried a total of eighteen torpedoes, and in addition was armed with six 6-pounder guns to repel any small boat armed with torpedoes. She was given a 3in-thick armoured deck and reached the high speed of 18kts. Launched in 1881, *Polyphemus* entered service in 1882.

The only defence against the torpedo at the time appeared to be the torpedo net, which was slung from long wooden booms strung high above the waterline.

Opposite page, top: General arrangement of a Whitehead torpedo. (ACPL)

Opposite page, bottom: The arrangement of a later compressed air and steam driven torpedo. 1, Pistol; 2, Primer; 3, Explosive charge; 4, Warhead; 5, Air bottle; 6, Fuel/water tank; 7, Depth governor; 8, Steam engine; 9, Gyro servomotor; 10, Propeller shafts; 11, After body; 12, Tail section; 13, Air regulator; 14, Air charging valve; 15, Fuel/water charging valve. (ACPL)

Below: General arrangement of TB No 1 - *Lightning*. (ACPL)

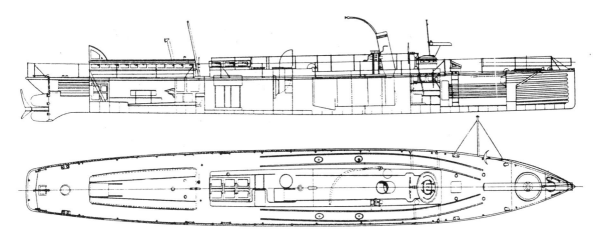

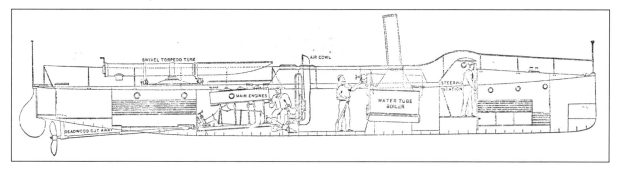

Above: General arrangement of a Second Class torpedo boat. (ACPL)

Left: Torpedo Boat No 2 seen here with a bow-mounted torpedo tube. Like TB No 1, No 2 was built by Thornycroft and incorporated some of the lessons learned from TB No 1. (Imperial War Museum)

Lower left: HMS *Ardent*, one of the 'A' class 27-knotters ordered under the 1893–4 Programme. Note the pronounced tumblehome on the forecastle, surmounted by a 12pdr gun. Two single 18in torpedo tubes are mounted abaft the funnels. (Imperial War Museum)

Experiments had proved that these nets could stop a 14in torpedo, but there was every possibility that the torpedo would explode and blow a large hole in the net, rendering it useless. Edward Reed then put forward an idea that he thought would provide an effective defence against torpedo attack. It consisted of giving a warship an armoured bottom with a thin outer shell, divided transversely and longitudinally, which ran under the magazines, boilers and machinery. This method of construction would raise the level of the machinery, exposing it to the destructive effect of shellfire which might penetrate the belt. Unfortunately the Admiralty calculated that if a torpedo should breach six compartments in the bottom, after both ends of the vessel had been flooded, there was a danger she might capsize. (Such a system of construction was used in the Japanese 'Yamato' class battleships of 1937, and *Musashi* took nineteen torpedo hits and seventeen bombs before sinking in 1944 in an identical situation to that envisaged by the Admiralty.)

In 1879 the Admiralty formed a Committee to investigate the possibilities of reintroducing the breech-loading gun into HM warships. The main fault of the earlier breech-loading guns was that the breech failed to close properly. Improvements to the muzzle velocities and penetration powers of guns had been dictated by the advancements in armour made during the previous decade. As a result of experiments it was found that increased muzzle velocity could be achieved with a slow-burning, large-grain powder. The new powder resulted in increased pressure in the gun barrel when ignited and gave the shell the extra speed required without increasing the weight and bore of the gun. However, the use of the new powder in the old muzzle-loading guns was unsatisfactory, the shell often leaving the muzzle before the charge was completely burnt. It was decided, therefore, to increase the length of the gun barrel to about 30 calibres. This meant loading the guns from outside the turrets, as in *Inflexible* (see page 41), a method which proved unsatisfactory.

Meanwhile, in 1878, Armstrongs had developed a new breech-loading gun in which the French idea of fitting automatic safety devices to the breech was adopted. This mechanism prevented the gun from being fired until the

Right: A large number of Second Class torpedo boats were built to be carried by the large battleships. TB 96 is seen here in her frame on board the battleship *Camperdown*. (National Maritime Museum)

interrupted-screw action had locked. The new weapon was offered to the Admiralty, but before it was finally accepted a number of experiments were conducted.

While the experiments with Armstrongs' new breech-loading gun were in progress, a group of naval officers were sent to Germany to witness trials of a new Krupp breech-loading gun. Following the report on the Krupp trials it was decided in August 1879 that the battleships *Colossus*, *Edinburgh* and *Conqueror* should be fitted with breech-loading guns instead of muzzle-loading weapons as originally intended. The War Office, up to that time responsible for all the ordnance and ammunition for the navy, at once ordered an experimental 12in breech-loading gun from Armstrongs, while Woolwich started a design of their own using Armstrongs' new breech mechanism. The Woolwich design was finally approved in February 1882. Details of the charge and shell, however, were not completed until March 1884.

This was not the only dangerous delay in the designing of the new guns, for the methods and materials used in their construction were also at fault. This was first realized in 1880, but very little was done about it until November 1886, when Captain J.A. Fisher was appointed Director of Naval Ordnance and rectified the faults. Following the appointment of Captain Fisher, a campaign was begun for the navy to assume responsibility for its own ordnance and ammunition, matters previously dealt with by the War Office.

While all the arguments were in progress over the new guns, a new class of battleships had been laid down. The new vessels, called *Colosus* and *Edinburgh*, were to all intents and purposes sister ships to *Agamemnon*. As soon as the design for the new 12in breech-loading gun was approved in 1882, they were fitted to the ships, their construction being seriously delayed in order to mount the new weapons. In addition, *Colosus*

Right: With the *Colossus* and *Edinburgh* (pictured here) the navy returned to the mounting of breech loading guns in battleships. Both ships mounted Armstrong's new 12in BLR gun in two twin turrets mounted amidships in an *en-echelon* configuration. The ships were also noteworthy for the fact that they were the first large warships in the Navy in which steel was used in the general construction. Another innovation was the use of compound armour instead of iron as used in all previous ships. (ACPL)

and *Edinburgh* were fitted with two 14in torpedo tubes. Steel was used in the general construction, and all the armour was of the compound type, instead of iron as hitherto. The new 12in guns had an unfortunate start to their lives when one being used in trials in *Collingwood* burst, in May 1886, owing to faulty materials. At the time *Colosus* was nearing completion, and to avoid any possible mishaps the commanding officer was ordered not to fire his new 12in guns until they had been removed and modified.

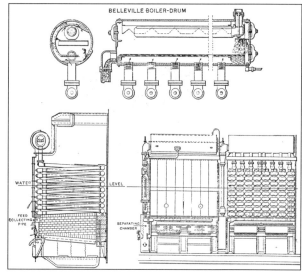

Two second class torpedo boats (designed for carriage aboard large warships) were ordered from John I. Thornycroft in 1884 and completed in 1885. Thornycroft had just perfected a new type of boiler, the watertube boiler. To test its capabilities torpedo boat *No 99* was fitted with the old type of locomotive boiler and tested against *No 100* with the watertube boiler. The main advantage of the watertube boiler was its greater heating surface compared with that of a locomotive boiler (606ft² as against 265.5ft²). The working pressure was increased from 130 to 145lb, and on trials torpedo boat *No 100* made 16.81kts, compared to the 16.13kts of *No 99*.

With an increasing number of torpedo boats being built for various navies, the Admiralty began to develop ideas to combat the menace. At the time the Yarrow shipyard was building a number of torpedo boats for foreign powers. Mr Yarrow was asked by the Controller, Admiral Fisher, if he could build a vessel that would be far superior to a new fast torpedo boat then under construction in a French yard. Yarrow went to France and saw the new vessels, and on his return put forward specifications for a vessel of 180ft by 18ft developing 4,000hp. The basic design was accepted, and two vessels were ordered, the *Havock* of 240 tons, armed with three 18in torpedo tubes, one 12-pounder and three 6-pounder guns and fitted with a locomotive boiler; and the *Hornet*, completed with a new watertube boiler designed by Mr Yarrow. *Havock* was launched in 1893, and on trials reached a speed of 26.7kts on 3,500hp, while in February 1894 *Hornet* became the fastest vessel in the world, reaching a speed of 28kts on trials. As a result of the successful trials, 36 vessels known as the 'A' class or 27-knotters, similar in design to *Havock*, were ordered under the 1893-1894 Programmes from firms specializing in torpedo boat construction. These early torpedo boat destroyers (TBDs), as they were known, were often prone to breakdowns, the high speed maintained when in operation often causing trouble to the hulls, where excessive vibration sprang plates and rivets.

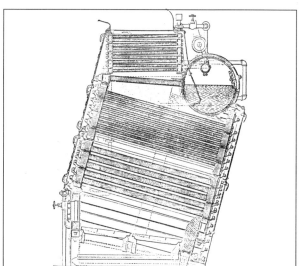

Problems soon began to manifest themselves with the new watertube boilers, however. Even after the proving trials in *Hornet* no vessels larger than the torpedo boat destroyer were fitted with the boiler, and all sorts of difficulties were foreseen should they be fitted to large warships. The French Belleville watertube boiler was the only one of its type sufficiently advanced to be fitted in large

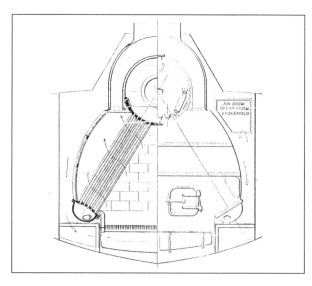

Top left: Cross section of a Belleville water tube boiler. (ACPL)

Centre left: Cross section of a Babcock & Wilcox water tube boiler. (ACPL)

Lower left: Cross section of a Yarrow water tube boiler. (ACPL)

warships. In spite of its many advantages, it did not prove fully satisfactory owing to its inexpert operation by officers untrained in handling the delicate machinery. Of course, as had happened before with other new inventions, there were many in the Admiralty and navy who were opposed to change, and they at once opened a vigorous campaign against the introduction of the new boiler. They were supported by a number of industrialists who had invested their money in the development of cylindrical boilers. The main problem, however, lay in the fact that the watertube boiler had been rushed into service in large warships before engineers could be trained in its operation, or firms became experienced enough in its construction.

Finally the outbursts against the watertube boiler became so vociferous that a Committee of Inquiry was appointed to investigate the claims for and against it. The Committee's first pronouncement was to recommend that no more Belleville boilers be fitted to HM ships until the invention had been thoroughly tested. In the meantime a ridiculous state of affairs existed, with vessels being completed with mixtures of cylindrical and watertube boilers. Instead of the Belleville, a number of other makes were tried in the navy, including the Niclausse, the Babcock and Wilcox and the Yarrow. After a number of tests the Niclausse was abandoned altogether, having none of the advantages of the Belleville and many of its alleged disadvantages. Instead, the Admiralty decided to fit the Babcock and Wilcox and the Yarrow large tube-type boilers. Fears about the watertube boilers gradually abated as the problems were ironed out, and the Admiralty proceeded to adopt the Belleville as its main watertube boiler for all new battleships.

Sans Pareil and *Victoria*, laid down under the 1884 Programme (see page 50), carried the development of the battleship one stage further by being fitted with the new triple-expansion engines. The horsepower developed was the same as in the *'Admiral'* class, but the number of boilers was reduced from twelve to eight and the working pressure raised from 90lb to 135lb. The general design, however, was misguided, being based on the earlier *Conqueror*, but with the proviso that they were to be seagoing vessels. They had a distinctive silhouette, with the funnel and bridge aft and a massive turret forward mounting two 16.25in guns, whose delivery was yet again delayed, holding up completion of the vessels.

In 1883–4 the four *'Mersey'* class protected cruisers, named after British rivers, were laid down. Built to an Admiralty design, Chief Constructor Barnaby being given the specification around which to plan the class, the *'Merseys'* laid the foundation for the Second Class Protected Cruiser category of warship. The basis of the concept was a ship carrying a much heavier protection (a curved armoured deck running the full length of the ship, 2in thick on the flat and 3in thick on the slope), and having higher speed on a lighter displacement.

In the early 1880s France promulgated her official naval policy for the future. Under the new policy the navy would avoid any major action between fleets. Instead, its new role would be to destroy the enemy's seaborne trade. Russia soon followed suit, and to this end both countries began building ships suitable for enforcing such a policy.

To counter this trend the Royal Navy had the *'Orlando'* class armoured cruisers designed, seven of which were laid down between 1885-6. These were basically an enlarged version of the *'Mersey'* class, but with a 10in armour belt amidships protecting the machinery area.

Right: The *'Mersey'* class cruisers laid the foundation for the Second Class Protected Cruiser category, of which a number were built up to the outbreak of war in 1914. The class were armed with two 8in and ten 6in guns. (National Maritime Museum)

However, during construction extra bunkerage, new machinery and additional equipment considerably increased the tonnage, to the extent that the protective armour belt was almost submerged and virtually useless. The ships were armed with two 9.2in and ten 6in guns, and achieved a maximum speed of 18kts.

As it appeared that armoured cruisers with a protective belt were ineffective, the Admiralty returned to a policy of building protected cruisers to counter the French and Russian plans. In 1888 two First Class Protected Cruisers, *Blake* and *Blenheim*, were laid down. Designed by White and completed in 1891-2, these ships established the basic design on which effective cruiser operations could be carried out. They were well armed (two 9.2in and ten 6in quick-firing (QF) guns), protected by a 4.5in armoured deck, had a good range (essential for cruiser operations in the open ocean), exhibited good seakeeping qualities, and with their maximum speed of 20kts were equally well suited to trade protection duties and operating with the main fleet.

Under the 1886 Estimates two battleships, *Nile* and *Trafalgar*, were ordered. Before the designs had been agreed, however, the Prime Minister, Gladstone, resigned. During construction of *Nile* and *Trafalgar* modifications were incorporated to such an extent that when completed the upper edge of the citadel was only 9.5ft above the waterline, instead of 11ft as designed. This brought to light a dangerous practice that had been carried out in dockyards for many years, that of adding extra equipment to vessels after the design had been passed. Many vessels had had their displacements so increased, often to a very dangerous degree. As a result the Board of Admiralty introduced the 4 per cent margin which allowed all future designs a leeway on the designed displacement, so that such additions or alterations could be made with safety.

One of the additions made to the '*Nile*' class was in the secondary armament, where, instead of the six 5in planned, a new Elswick 4.7in QF gun was fitted. The quick-firing gun now became the standard secondary armament for battleships, going a long way towards providing another antidote for the torpedo boat. The new 4.7in gun had great range and accuracy and also a high rate of fire (one round every eight seconds).

To keep pace with the advances in armament and protection, the old ironclad *Resistance* was fitted with special armour plates and commissioned as a target ship against which new weapons and armour could be tested, being subjected to shellfire from the new guns, explosives and torpedoes. Starting in 1886, these experiments continued for some years, the Admiralty gaining much from the results. One of the trials showed the power of a 14in torpedo to be far less than the Admiralty had been led to believe. To increase the charge the size was increased, first to 15in and later to 18in, speed and range remaining virtually the same as in the 14in.

In 1894 the Hon Charles Parsons made history when he ran the trials of a new vessel which he had designed. It was not so much the vessel herself that was unique, but her method of propulsion. Parsons had developed a principle that had been known for centuries. Turning theory into practice, he fitted the new ship with turbines, naming her *Turbinia*. With a compound radial-flow turbine driving a single shaft, the 44.5-ton vessel at once ran into trouble, the speed developed being only 19.75kts. Deciding that the slow speed was caused by cavities around the propeller blades, Parsons re-engined the vessel with three turbines, each driving a shaft. The new arrangement was successful, *Turbinia* reaching a speed of 29.6kts. It was then decided to change the propellers, and an even better result was obtained, the speed exceeding 32kts.

In February 1897 Admiral Fisher inspected *Turbinia*, and the following June she was present at the Jubilee Review, where she showed her capabilities by reaching a speed of 30kts in 40sec. With this success Parsons put forward a suggestion to the Admiralty that they should build a 30kt torpedo boat destroyer powered by turbines. The Admiralty accepted Parsons' tender in 1898, and in 1899 the torpedo boat destroyer (named destroyer for short) *Viper*, then under construction, was fitted with turbines. In 1890 the Admiralty purchased the turbine-powered *Cobra* from Elswick. Both vessels reached well over 30kts on their trials, a vindication of the faith Parsons had put in his turbines.

Below: In August 1886 the navy commenced a series of trials using the old hulk *Resistance*. The ship was fitted with special armour plates and coal bunker defences against which various calibres of gun were fired. The trials also involved testing new explosives and various types of torpedo. From the trials much data was gathered which was used to improve both design and methods of construction. The illustration shows torpedo trials being carried out against the hull in 1887. (ACPL)

Chapter 11

The Naval Defence Act

In 1885 the Conservatives had been elected to rule, partly as a result of public impatience over defence issues, and in particular because of the state of the Royal Navy. Speaking at the Jubilee Colonial Conference in 1887, the Prime Minister, Lord Salisbury, outlined the problem of colonial defence. He prophetically noted (and it is a truism which Britain has seemed to ignore regularly since the 19th century) that, 'The circumstances in which we live, and the tendencies of human nature as we know it, in all times of history, teach that where there is a liability to attack, and defencelessness, attack will come'. Lord Salisbury then went on to examine the problem facing Britain's rich overseas colonies and how they were enviously viewed by other European powers who were themselves expanding and building up their overseas colonies. In such a scramble for wealth and power it was inevitable that, in time, some of the European powers would fall into discord over such possessions. In the face of such potential for conflict it was only natural that Britain's colonies should look to the mother country for security which, perforce, would have to be provided mainly by the Royal Navy.

It was at the Jubilee Colonial Conference that extracts from the Carnarvon Commission's Report (see page 48) were finally published. The Royal Commission had been formed in 1879 to investigate and report on 'The Defence of British possessions and commerce abroad', and its report came like a thunderbolt. It revealed that the defences of overseas bases were practically nonexistent; Hong Kong and Singapore had none, while the remainder were so weak that they would never have stood up to a determined attack from the sea. Furthermore, the report noted that in its present state the navy would be incapable of defending the sea lanes or the bases. The vessels at present stationed overseas were largely slow and lightly armed gunboats, and were quite unequal to the task expected of them at that time. To complete the picture, the report summed up by saying that the navy was not even prepared for new tasks involving commerce protection. The 1886-1887 Estimates, for example, only provided for small weakly-armed cruisers which were incapable of fighting in heavy seas, a number of sloops, and the experimental torpedo boat *Sharpshooter*.

The following year, 1888, the Admiralty laid down that annual manoeuvres should henceforth be conducted. During the manoeuvres a partial mobilization of the Fleet would be carried out. Unfortunately the manoeuvres did not prove to be as worthwhile as had at first been hoped. Many of the exercises and movements were designed more for competition between ships than as a serious preparation for war. The gunnery exercises were looked on by many officers with distaste, as they made a fearful mess of the vessels, and cleanliness was the epitome of the late Victorian navy.

To study all the aspects of the manoeuvres a Committee was appointed, with the special instruction to look at the feasibility of blockading an enemy squadron in its home port. Special importance was placed on the ratios of capital ships and cruisers in the blockading and blockaded fleets, the possibility of keeping watch on the blockaded fleet by fast cruisers while the main battle fleet remained at home, or the possibility of keeping the battle squadron off an enemy port, supported by an inshore squadron. Apart from these important considerations, the Committee was also asked to note, 'the value of torpedo gunboats and first class torpedo boats both with the blockading and blockaded fleets, and the most efficient manner of utilising them'. In addition, the qualities of various new vessels in the Royal Navy were also to be studied.

The Committee's report on the 1888 manoeuvres presented to Parliament early in 1889 was the final straw. It noted that to maintain an effective blockade a superiority of at least 5:3, and preferably greater, was necessary. If, however, an anchorage near to the blockaded port was suitable, the superiority need only be 4:3, but in this case the blockading fleet would need to be very well supported. Torpedo boats as an adjunct to a blockading force were dismissed as being of little value, although it was thought that they might be of some use to the blockaded fleet. Torpedo gunboats, such as *Rattlesnake*, were thought to be ideal for blockading purposes. Finally the report severely criticised the performance of various vessels and concluded that the navy was '... altogether inadequate to take of offensive in a war with *only one Great Power* [author's italics]'.

Consequent upon this report and the outcome of the Jubilee Colonial Conference, the Government formulated the future principle of British sea power, which was to maintain the absolute necessity for adhering to a 'Two Power Standard'. This laid down that the strength of the Royal Navy must be equal to the combined strength of any other two navies, generally the largest at any time, and at that time the two most powerful navies were those of France and Russia. On the basis of this the Admiralty began reforms which were to affect the whole state of the navy.

On 7 March 1889 the First Lord, Lord George Hamilton, introduced the Naval Defence Act, which covered

Left: The eighteen torpedo gunboats of the *Sharpshooter* class, ordered under the Naval Defence Act, introduced the Armstrong 4.7in QF gun. The *Assay* is illustrated. (Imperial War Museum)

the four years from 1889 to 1892 and which provided for the construction of 70 new warships. The programme, which was estimated to cost £21.5 million, provided for the building of seven 'Royal Sovereign' class and the *Hood* first class battleships, two 'Centurion' class second class battleships, nine first class 'Edgar' class cruisers, twenty-one 'Apollo' class and eight 'Astrea' class second class cruisers, four 'Pallas' class third class cruisers and eighteen 'Sharpshooter' type torpedo gunboats. In addition, it included a list of 72 vessels that White proposed to scrap as obsolete. The Admiralty, however, could not bring themselves to authorize the scrapping of so many vessels, and the only ships deleted from the lists between 1889 and 1894 were *Defence, Hector, Valiant,* and *Warrior,* eight wooden cruisers, eight wooden sloops and ten gun vessels. The remaining 'obsolete' vessels were reboiled and modernized.

The genesis of the Naval Defence Act formed part of a continuous programme of construction that was to ensure Britain's naval supremacy in the future. Very soon the results of White's reorganization of the Controller's Department and the Dockyards (see page 50) became apparent. The lead ship of the 'Royal Sovereign' class, *Royal Sovereign,* was completed in 32 months and *Majestic* in 22 months by Portsmouth, while Chatham completed *Magnificent* in 24 months. At that time this was the shortest time in which a battleship had been completed anywhere in the world.

Following the plans laid down for the new Defence Act, White was ordered to draw up a design for a new battleship. The Admiralty had already asked him (in 1888) to draw up outline plans for a follow-on design to *Trafalgar.* For this he had prepared both turret and barbette outline designs, the latter being preferred as it offered a higher freeboard, a feature which had been shown to be necessary from previous experience with vessels such as *Captain.* White therefore developed the barbette proposal into the *Royal Sovereign* design, which was basically an enlarged 'Admiral'.

Displacement was increased to 14,000 tons, the guns were mounted 23ft above the waterline, and protection, while similar to that of the 'Admirals', was deeper and

longer. The armour, manufactured by Jessops of Sheffield, was an alloy of nickel steel and proved extremely hard and durable compared to other types of armour. The greater tensile strength of the new armour meant that, to achieve the same protection as in earlier vessels, the 20in compound armour of *Trafalgar* could be reduced to 18in of nickel steel. In addition, the 'Royal Sovereigns' had an upper belt of 4in closed at the end by a screen bulkhead, while the barbette armour was extended down to the level of the armoured deck. The ships mounted four 13.5in guns, as in the 'Admirals', while the secondary battery was increased to ten of Armstrongs' new 6in QF guns. The four 6in on the main deck were mounted in casemates instead of in the open as hitherto, and the remainder were given plain shields. In addition, sixteen 6-pounder QF were carried, together with twelve 3-pounder QF.

Seven 'Royal Sovereign' class vessels were ordered to the new design. The main feature was the extra deck, resulting in a high freeboard which greatly improved seakeeping qualities and enabled high speeds to be maintained in heavy seas. To help counter any tendency to instability arising from the extra deck, the sides of the hull had a distinctive tumblehome. With their excellent seakeeping qualities, heavy armament and high speed (for a battleship) of 17kts, they came to be regarded as the finest ships in the world, and completely outclassed any other ships then afloat. They set the pattern in battleship design for the next 15 years.

An eighth ship of the class was ordered, but she differed in a number of ways from the earlier vessels. The First Sea Lord, Admiral Hood, was strongly opposed to the barbette, preferring the heavily protected turret ship with low freeboard. As a gesture in recognition of Admiral Hood's feelings, White planned that the last ship of the class, named *Hood* after the First Sea Lord, should be completed to a modified turret design. The extra deck was omitted, which left the guns only 17ft above the waterline. As a result, *Hood* lacked the good seakeeping qualities of the earlier vessels and her stability was poor. It was so poor, in fact, that the designers were forced to dispense with the casemates for the 6in guns, as they would have brought the centre of gravity to a dangerous level. Although in herself not successful, *Hood* more than vindicated White's views on barbette ships with high freeboard.

In March 1889 the Controller requested plans for two second class battleships (the *Barfleur* and *Centurion*) with a draught not exceeding 26ft, for use on the China and Pacific Stations — a reflection of the concern expressed at the 1887 Jubilee Colonial Conference regarding the defence of overseas colonies. The specified radius of action was 6,000 miles (the same as that of the *Imperieuse*), for which an estimated bunkerage of not more than 750 tons was to be provided. For reasons of economy the price was kept as low as possible, forcing the displacement to be reduced by 4,000 tons. As a result the vessels could only mount 10in and 4.7in QF for their armament, and protection had to be greatly reduced.

The *Barfleur* and *Centurion* were notable for the fact that the barbettes for their 10in guns were fitted with an armoured hood, and the guns could be loaded with the barbettes trained in any direction. In an effort to reduce weight the barbettes were circular, as opposed to earlier mountings, which had all been pear-shaped. Training was achieved either by steam or hand, steam proving unsatisfactory in service as it failed to stop the turret quickly enough. Although only designed to carry 750 tons of coal under Service conditions, the vessels actually carried a maximum of 1,125 tons, giving them a radius of action of 9,750 miles. A speed of 18.5kts was made on a forced draught of 13,000hp, 1.5kts more than the '*Royal Sovereigns*'. Although they were only rated as second class battleships, they were quite powerful vessels and could be considered the forerunners of the battlecruiser, where a ship carried fewer guns of slightly smaller calibre than a battleship at a higher speed and with rather less protection.

TABLE III: Comparison of *Royal Sovereign* & *Centurion*

Class	Royal Sovereign	Centurion
Displacement	14,100 tons	10,500 tons
Horsepower	13,000	13,000
Speed	17kts	18.5kts
Radius	7,900 miles	9,750 miles
Protection (belt)	18in	12in
Armament	4 x 13.5in,	4 x 10in,
	10 x 6in	10 x 4.7in

While the '*Royal Sovereigns*' and '*Centurions*' were under construction, the new cruisers of the Naval Defence Act were being developed. Following the poor results obtained from the '*Orlando*' class armoured cruisers, this category fell into disfavour. Under the Naval Defence Act, White concentrated on developing first, second and third class cruiser designs primarily for use on trade protection duties and on the overseas stations, and also as scouts for the main battle fleet. The '*Edgar*' class first class cruisers were simply smaller versions of the earlier '*Blenheim*' class of 1888, mounting the same armament but with reduced horsepower and lighter protection. Six of this class were launched between 1891 and 1892, armed with two single 9.2in guns. They proved to be extremely good sea boats, and all exceeded their designed speed on trials, the machinery being very reliable.

The second class cruiser category proved most popular, however, and 21 of the 3,400-ton '*Apollo*' class were ordered, armed with two 6in and six 4.7in. However, in service they proved to be undergunned and poor sea

Right: With the '*Royal Sovereign*' class, White set the pattern for battleship design for the Royal Navy for the next fifteen years. Among the notable features of the design was the all-steel armour protection and the siting of the secondary armament in casemates. The *Repulse* is seen here in 1897. (National Maritime Museum)

Left: Similar in general appearance, but smaller than the 'Royal Sovereign' class were the two Second Class battleships *Barfleur* and *Centurion.* Contrary to the views held by White concerning Second Class ships of any category, these 10,500 ton vessels were built specifically for duty in the Far East. Armament consisted of four 10in and ten 4.7in QF. The illustration shows the *Centurion* in 1894. (National Maritime Museum)

boats. They were followed by the eight vessels of the 'Astrea' class, which sought to overcome some of the faults of the 'Apollos'. In this class displacement was increased to 4,300 tons, which enabled a slightly higher freeboard, increased speed and greater endurance, vital qualities for trade protection duties. However, in spite of these improvements, they were still regarded as ineffective, still being considered to be undergunned with only two 6in and eight 4.7in. A number of third class cruisers were also ordered, together with thirteen gunboats built to an improved 'Sharpshooter' design which were completed at the turn of the decade.

During the early 1890s a new type of 12in gun was under development which was to be mounted in a new vessel specially designed for it. Failing to get the gun into production in time, the Admiralty was forced to redesign the vessel, *Renown,* as a modified *Centurion* armed with 10in guns. Laid down in February 1893, *Renown* was completed in January 1897. With *Renown* the importance of secondary armament for use against torpedo boat attack went a stage further, with the placing of the upper deck guns in armoured casemates. The major feature of *Renown,* however, was her protection. For the first time a British warship was given all-steel armour. In addition, the armoured deck sloped down to the lower level of the armour belt, which resulted in a protected space immediately behind the belt. Hence, any shell penetrating the main belt would also have to penetrate the sloping armoured deck before reaching the magazines or machinery spaces. It also gave additional protection in the event of flooding.

Left: A category of warships that came to be built in large numbers was the Second Class cruiser, of which 21 examples of the 'Apollo' class were built under the Naval Defence Act. The cruiser illustrated is the *Rainbow,* which became the second ship to serve in the Canadian Navy, arriving in Canada on 7 November 1910. (ACPL)

All-steel Harvey armour plate was much stronger than nickel steel, being fashioned without any welds, and with a certain amount of carbon on its face so that, as it cooled, an extremely hard face was produced on the plate. This enabled the belt on *Renown* to be reduced to 8in on the lower belt and 6in on the upper belt. The only problem was that Harvey armour could not be used on curved surfaces.

During 1893 concern began to be expressed over the future state of the navy, as there appeared to be no follow-on to the Naval Defence Act, which was due to expire the following year. In presenting the Naval Defence Act, the First Lord, Lord Hamilton, had expressly noted that the Act should form the start of a policy which should see a steady build-up of naval strength year-by-year, corresponding to national requirements as they were deemed necessary.

Three battleships had been planned for the 1892 Estimates and two for 1893, but due to the delays with the 12in gun only *Renown* was laid down under the 1892 Programme. In an address to the London Chamber of Commerce, Lord Charles Beresford remarked upon Britain's apparent naval weakness and asked for Estimates totalling £25 million to be spread over a period of three and a half years to provide for trade protection. He called especially for more cruisers. At once support appeared in the form of letters to the press from many naval officers.

In 1893 Gladstone's Liberal Administration had been returned to power, and regarded a reduction in defence expenditure as a moral obligation. Gladstone would require considerable persuasion before he would countenance any increase in the naval Estimates. Early in November 1893 Lord Spencer asked White to prepare a statement showing the estimated expenditure on new construction over the next five years, together with dates for the laying-down and completion of ships it was proposed should be built to match the French programmes.

It was at once seen that the critical years were 1896-97. In 1894-95 the Royal Navy would have available nineteen first class battleships, against ten French and three Russian, a number of those available to the navy when the Naval Defence Act of 1889 was promulgated having been relegated to second-line duty in the interim. At their present rate of construction it was noted that the combined French and Russian fleets would have nearly reached parity with the Royal Navy by 1896, and almost nullified the effect of the Two Power Standard. The Director of Naval Construction, White, regarded it as imperative that at least six first class battleships should be laid down and completed by 1898, this being the absolute minimum which would guarantee the maintenance of the Two Power Standard against France and Russia. Even when presented with the facts the Government vacillated, Gladstone assuring the House in 1893 that '... the country need entertain under the existing circumstances, the smallest apprehension as to the distinct supremacy of

Great Britain', carefully omitting any reference to the critical period of 1896-97.

At this the Board of Admiralty threatened to resign in a body. Faced with a mass resignation, Gladstone's Administration had no alternative but to accept the proposals. Gladstone resigned over the question of the increased expenditure and was succeeded by Lord Rosebery, and on 8 December 1893 what became known as the 'Spencer Programme' was passed. As envisaged by Lord Spencer, the five-year programme allowed for an expenditure of £31 million (slightly less than that asked for by Lord Beresford) for the construction of 159 ships. This included seven *'Majestic'* class first class battleships, two *'Powerful'* class cruisers, six *'Diadem'* first class cruisers, twelve *'Eclipse'* second class cruisers, four *'Pelorus'* third class cruisers, six ram cruisers, seven torpedo gunboats, two sloops, eighty-two torpedo boat destroyers (30kt *'B'*, *'C'* and *'D'* classes), thirty torpedo boats and one torpedo depot ship. In spite of Lord Beresford's plea for more cruisers for trade protection, the number planned in the programme was actually reduced, the *'Diadems'* not being ordered until much later and only nine of the *'Eclipses'* laid down. On the other hand, the number of first class battleships was increased to nine.

The *'Majestic'* class of first class battleships, laid down between 1893-95, was the largest class of battleships built up to that time. With them, White reached the zenith of his career as a designer, and from then until he left the Admiralty all of his designs were based upon this class. Often regarded as the true pre-Dreadnoughts, the *'Majestics'* combined the basic features of the *'Royal Sovereign'* with the improvements in protection incorporated in *Renown*.

The new 12in 35-calibre gun was at last ready for service, and was fitted in all of the ships. It was a vast improvement on the 13.5in, its great advantage being its lighter weight compared with the 13.5in gun. The weight thus saved was put to use in mounting two extra secondary weapons, a total of twelve 6in and sixteen 12-pounders being carried. A change was also made to the charge of the 12in shells. Instead of the gunpowder previously used, the new slow-burning cordite was introduced. Cordite gave a far greater pressure in the gun barrel when ignited, and as a result it was possible to make reductions in the size of charges needed (a 12in charge needed 167.5lb of cordite, compared with 295lb of powder). The reduction in the size of the charges meant a large saving in space and weight in the magazines, which was used for an extra 100 rounds of ammunition for the secondary guns. The new 12in gun remained the standard main armament for the navy's battleships for the next 16 years.

In all, nine vessels were built to the *'Majestic'* design, and when completed *Mars* became the first ship in the Royal Navy to use oil fuel for firing her boilers. Gradually, as they became due for refit, the rest of the class were also

Left: The *Majestic* class battleships (the *Prince George* is illustrated) were considered to have been the finest battleships of their time. They marked a return to the 12in gun and were the largest class of battleship ever built. (National Maritime Museum)

fitted for oil firing, except for *Jupiter* and *Illustrious*. The last two vessels in the class, *Caesar* and *Illustrious*, differed from the rest in having their turrets fitted in round barbettes as opposed to the pear-shaped ones of the earlier vessels. This design emanated from *Renown*, and was made possible by the all-round loading system. By using hydraulic power instead of steam for training the guns, the faults of *Renown* were overcome. Furthermore, the all-round loading position of the guns gave them a much increased rate of fire, in addition to improving the safety of the turret by introducing a break in the ammunition hoist.

As the construction of the 'Majestic' class proceeded, the cruisers ordered under the Spencer Programme began to be laid down. The two 'Powerful' class vessels laid down in 1894, although rated as cruisers, were almost as large as the 'Majestics' (14,200 tons against 14,900 tons). They were designed as answers to the Russian *Rurik* and *Rossiya*. They featured a very strong protective deck 6in thick amidships on the slope, but had no armoured belt. For armament they carried a new gun, the 9.2in, which was electrically operated and mounted in a barbette protected by 6in Harvey armour. Two of these were carried in single mountings fore and aft, while the secondary battery of twelve 6in guns was disposed in two superimposed casemates on either beam forward, the remainder being in single casemates protected by 6in armour. This set the pattern for the armament of first class cruisers until White retired in 1902.

The cruisers were fitted with 48 of the the new Belleville watertube boilers (see page 59). The new boiler was far superior to the old cylindrical type and, with the powerful new engines, materially assisted the 'Powerfuls' in maintaining their maximum speed of 22kts throughout their career. The Belleville boilers were very much lighter than cylindrical ones and,

mechanically, were easier to maintain and repair. They were also very economical in their use of fuel, and steam could quickly be raised if the occasion demanded. However, they proved troublesome throughout the whole of the cruisers' lives.

Following the 'Majestic' class the Admiralty ordered the six vessels of the 'Canopus' class, primarily for duty in the Far East, where they would counter the Japanese naval build-up. The design was to embody all the best features of *Renown*, *Centurion* and *Majestic*. The main armament was the new 12in gun, while the secondary armament, fuel capacity and speed were to be the same as those of *Renown*. Finally, watertube boilers were to be fitted, and these were the first British battleships to have the new boiler. The Belleville boilers did, however, give rise to certain problems of stability owing to their light weight.

The sketch designs for *Canopus* were submitted in May 1895, but before any decision could be reached Lord Rosebery was defeated in a general election and the Conservatives returned to power with Lord Salisbury as Prime Minister and Mr Goschen as First Lord. Finally, in December 1895, the plans were passed, the first five vessels being laid down under the 1896 Estimates and *Vengeance* under the 1897 Estimates. In the autumn of 1896 it was proposed that the vessels should carry twelve 6in guns in casemates instead of the ten planned, those on the main deck being sponsoned to increase end-on fire. The number of 12-pounders was increased from eight to ten, and the number of 3-pounders reduced to six, as the fighting tops in the masts were to be dispensed with. In addition, the 'Canopus' class were the first British warships to carry Krupp cemented armour. This had largely superseded the Harvey steel, its main advantage being that it could be applied to curved surfaces, so affording better protection to gun turrets.

Right: Also laid down under the 1893 Spencer Programme were two large cruisers, the *Powerful* and *Terrible*, the largest Protected cruisers ever built. They were armed with two 9.2in and twelve 6in. (ACPL)

Right: Six '*Diadem*' First Class cruisers were ordered under the Spencer Programme. They were armed with sixteen 6in guns. (ACPL)

Right: The Spencer Programme also provided for twelve '*Eclipse*' Second Class cruisers. Here a broadside-mounted 12 pounder gun is manned by its crew aboard HMS *Talbot*. (Imperial War Museum)

Chapter 12

The Pre-Dreadnought Navy

In the 1897 Programme a larger and more powerful British battleship was designed to match the French and Japanese battleships *Jena* and *Shikishima*. This resulted in an order for the three vessels of the *'Formidable'* class. A newer and heavier mark of 12in gun that developed a far higher muzzle velocity and energy than earlier marks was fitted in a new mounting which allowed rapid loading in any position of elevation or training. However, the new gun needed a much heavier turntable and mounting and a much larger barbette, and these took up most of the weight saved by fitting lighter boilers and thinner Krupp armour. White intended to keep to the displacement of the earlier *Majestic* design, while at the same time introducing all the improvements which had emerged since that ship was completed. He also hoped to increase the secondary armament to fourteen guns. The Admiralty, however, only requested twelve 6in guns, but asked that the protection on the citadel be increased to 9in. In spite of all the modifications and ensuing extra weight, the final displacement of the *'Formidable'* class exceeded that of the *'Majestic'* by only 100 tons. They were far superior vessels, being easier to handle and answering well to the helm.

In addition to the *'Formidable'* class, six armoured cruisers of the *'Cressy'* class were ordered in the 1897-1898 Esti-mates, and completed between 1898 and 1902. These were very similar to the *'Powerful'* class but slightly smaller, and with an identical armament of 9.2in and 6in, as opposed to just the 6in of their eight predecessors, the 11,000-ton *'Diadem'* class, completed between 1895 and 1903, and an armoured belt 6in thick. The *'Cressys'* were followed by the four *'Drake'* class armoured cruisers, in which the design faults of earlier vessels were eradicated. Displacement was increased by 2,000 tons, back to the 14,000 tons of the *'Powerful'* class, which allowed the ships to mount four extra 6in casemate guns. The calibre of the main armament was also increased from the 40 of the *'Cressy'* class to 45. In addition, speed was increased by 2kts to 23kts. All in all, the *'Drake'* class cruisers proved far superior to the *'Cressy'* class.

At long last Lord Beresford's pleas for more fast cruisers to protect trade routes had been heeded by the Admiralty, and many cruisers of all categories were now under construction.

The *'Drakes'* were followed by ten cruisers of the *'Kent'* class which were much smaller than the *'Drakes'*. In place of the 9.2in guns they carried 6in guns in electrically controlled twin turrets fore and aft. It had originally been intended that these cruisers would mount 7.5in, but this proposal was discarded in favour of twin 6in which, how-

683

Right: The six cruisers of the '*Cressy*' and four '*Drake*' cruisers were almost identical, the '*Drake*' class mounting four extra 6in guns and incorporating design improvements over the '*Cressy*' class. The *Drake* is shown here shortly after completion. (ACPL)

ever, proved somewhat of a failure, the turret's working space being exceedingly cramped, greatly reducing the efficiency of the weapon. The guns were not nearly powerful enough, and for their size the ships were considered to be undergunned. The 7.5in originally planned for the vessels would have been ideal, but even then the ships were far too lightly protected and no more than rather better versions of the earlier '*Eclipses*'. Had they been rated as first or second class protected cruisers and used accordingly, they would have been ideal.

Under the 1898-1900 Programmes eleven more battleships were ordered. Five of these belonged to the '*London*' class, which were virtually repeats of the '*Formidables*'.

The other six vessels, the '*Duncan*' class, were a new design. The Admiralty laid down the specifications for the class after obtaining details of the Russian *Osliabia* and *Peresviet*. The '*Duncans*' were slightly smaller than the '*Formidables*' and lacked ventilators, a feature which distinguished them from previous battleships. When completed they were far superior to the Russian vessels, but in order to obtain a higher speed they had sacrificed some of their protection. By reducing the amidships belt from 9in to 7in, a saving of 1,000 tons was made on the displacement, while the horsepower was increased by 3,000. In spite of all this, the speed of the vessels was only raised by 1kt over that of the '*London*' class.

Left: Gun crews at practice on the two 6in guns mounted on the quarterdeck of HMS *Andromeda*. (Imperial War Museum)

Right: The design displacement of the six battleships of the '*Duncan*' class was restricted to 14,000 tons, which resulted in a compromise on the scale of protection incorporated. The *Duncan* is illustrated. (ACPL)

By 1900 the submarine had become a weapon in its own right, adopted by the American, French, Russian and Turkish navies. During the summer of 1900 Isaac Rice of the American Electric Boat Company, who owned the patents of Holland's submarine designs, came to Britain on a sales visit, hoping to gain orders from European navies for submarines. Lord Rothschild introduced Rice to various members of the Admiralty, and before the end of the year it had been agreed that the firm of Vickers Son and Maxim Ltd at Barrow-in-Furness would be asked to build submarines for the Royal Navy. This was a major change in policy, for previously the Admiralty had been implacably opposed to the submarine, and the current Controller, Sir Arthur Wilson, remained opposed to the idea of the navy acquiring submarines. Even so, an order for five *Holland*-type boats was placed with Vickers in December 1900. In the 1901-02 Navy Programme the change in policy was explained by the statement that the boats were being acquired so that destroyer captains could be trained in anti-submarine operations.

Captain Reginald Bacon was sent to Vickers to oversee the construction of the submarines, and the first, *Holland I*, was launched on 2 October 1901 and started sea trials in January 1902. The hull was cigar shaped, and propulsion on the surface was provided by a single petrol engine, with electric motors for submerged power. Regarded as experimental boats, the *Hollands* were used for evaluation, training and instructional purposes. Having placed the order for the *Hollands*, the Admiralty now appeared to abrogate all interest in the boats, Bacon being left to develop the concept on his own. Before the last of the *Hollands* had been completed, Bacon and Vickers had designed the first serviceable submarine for the navy, the 'A' class. The Admiralty was persuaded to order four of these boats in the 1902 Programme and nine in 1903.

Basically enlarged Hollands, the 64ft long 'A' class were single-hulled boats, in which the ballast tanks were sited inside the hull. There was no internal subdivision, and no accommodation, most of the space being taken up by the batteries and electric motor, which gave the boat a submerged range of 25nm at 7kts. Apart from the ballast tanks, control was exercised through a single rudder, and a single aft-mounted hydroplane which was used to control the boat's attitude while submerged. The design featured a small conning tower which was used while navigating on the surface. A novel item proposed by Bacon was a periscope, which was stowed horizontally along the side of the hull when not in use. The boats carried a single 18in torpedo tube mounted in the bows.

From then on, development of the submarine proceeded rapidly under the guidance of James McKechnie. Working with him on submarine development was T.G. Owens Thurston, who carried out many experiments in the Vickers experimental tank at St Albans. Short periscopes and high conning towers were characteristic features of these early submarines. *A 13* was experimentally fitted with a heavy diesel oil engine, which was a vast improvement on the petrol engine and was subsequently fitted to all new submarines. The fuel oil of the diesel engine had a much higher flash point than petrol, and much reduced the danger of the fuel supply igniting from any stray sparks.

The 'A' class were followed by eleven vessels of the 'B' class, *B 1* actually being *A 14* renumbered. Following the tragic loss of *A 1* in March 1904 (she was accidentally rammed by the liner *Berwick Castle*) all of the 'B' class were fitted with two periscopes, one for navigation and the other for search purposes.

The year 1900 found the Royal Navy yet again on active service, this time in the Far East. European incursions into Chinese affairs and trading interests had aroused the displeasure of a large section of the Chinese community. The Dowager Empress, Tzu Hsi, was also contemptuous of the foreigners in her land, and incited a

Left: The first submarines to enter service in the Royal Navy were five boats of the *Holland* type. The picture shows Nos 2 and 5 alongside the depot ship *Thames*. (ACPL)

Right: The first indigenous submarines were the 'A' class, whose design was very similar to the *Holland*s. (ACPL)

Right: The first major class of submarine to be built for the Royal Navy was the 'B', class which was followed by the large 'C' class, of which *C21* is illustrated. (ACPL)

band of fanatical Chinese known as the Society of Righteous Fists, popularly referred to as Boxers, who proceeded to harass Christian communities and foreign sympathizers.

The incidents spread until, in June 1900, a Relief Expedition of 2,000 marines and seamen under Admiral E.H. Seymour was sent to protect the settlement. The force was repulsed, and returned to the ships on 26 June. On 4 August a second Allied Expeditionary Force, eventually comprising some 18,700 men, began an overland march up the river to relieve Peking, which was finally captured on 14 August. Among the outstanding naval officers taking part in the action was Commander Beatty of the *Barfleur*, who was promoted to Captain for his part in the fighting around Tientsin.

By 1900 the Royal Navy had, either in service or under construction, 36 modern first class battleships, compared with 11 French and 13 Russian; a ratio of 3:2. With superiority achieved there followed a marked slowing down in battleship construction, and only two 'London' class were begun in 1901.

As soon as details of the latest American and Italian battleships became known, the Controller, Sir Arthur Wilson, ordered a series of new designs to be prepared which would allow for a heavier secondary armament. As the Admiralty did not lay down any specifications for the new vessels, it was left to the Director of Naval Construction to make suggestions and draw up plans. White was ill at the time, and the task fell to the Chief Constructor, Mr Deadman, and his assistant J.H. Narbeth. The Admiralty did not accept the design prepared by Mr Deadman, whereupon Mr Narbeth designed a vessel based upon the *Duncan*, but having an intermediate armament of either 9.2in or 7.5in. The Admiralty approved a design which mounted eight 7.5in guns on the upper deck in pairs, and a secondary battery of 6in

sited on the main deck. However, White returned before the design was completed, and the Board of Admiralty asked him to prepare a report on it. White asked Narbeth if there were any improvements he would like to make to his design, and an alternative plan with a single 9.2in gun in place of the paired 7.5in was proposed. White, who concurred with his assistant's proposals, then requested the Admiralty to accept the new plans. The change from 7.5in to 9.2in had so little effect on the general design and displacement that the plans were redrawn and completed in a very short time.

Finally, the ill health that had dogged White for so long forced him to leave the Admiralty, and in 1902 he was succeeded by Philip Watts from Elswick. Watts also approved of the new design and signed the plans for the new battleship, *King Edward VII*, the last of the pre-dreadnoughts. Eight vessels of the new class were ordered under the 1901-02-03 Estimates. When they entered service there was some criticism of the mixed main armament of four 12in and four 9.2in (the latter mounted in single turrets on either beam abreast the masts), which created many problems with fire control. At the time the 9.2in was an excellent weapon, being as easy to handle as the 6in and almost as quick to fire.

The secondary 6in battery, sited in a box battery on the main deck instead of in casemates as in previous ships, was also criticised. The main criticism was that it was only 12.75ft above the waterline, and in a heavy sea would be continuously swept by the sea and almost impossible to operate. Much more serious, however, was the fact that if the vessels rolled to 14° the barrels of the guns would dip into the water. Consequently a number of the vessels later had these guns removed. Protection was similar to that of the 'London' class, but was rendered obsolete during their construction by the introduction of the capped shell, which had a much higher velocity and

Left: The 'King Edward VII' class battleships (the name ship is shown here) featured a mixed armament of four 12in, four 9.2in and ten 6in. The intermediate 9.2in battery was sited at the four corners of the superstructure. The diverse armament was severely criticised within the navy, as it gave rise to major problems in spotting the fall of shot, it being difficult to distinguish between the 12in and 9.2in shells. (ACPL)

increased powers of penetration. With the Belleville boiler abandoned, the ships were fitted with a mix of watertube and cylindrical boilers, the mix not proving entirely satisfactory.

The loss in 1901 of the torpedo boat destroyer *Cobra* during a gale led to an examination of the methods of destroyer construction. In the 1902 Programme a new class of destroyer, the *'Rivers'*, was ordered, with a high forecastle deck instead of the turtle-back construction of the earlier vessels. It was also realised that the speed of 30kts at light load requested for the earlier vessels was unrealistic, especially in heavy seas, and this was reduced to 25kts in the new class, this speed to be attained under service conditions and normal load. In addition the class were to be fitted with reciprocating machinery, in spite of the problems encountered in the preceding classes, and only *Eden* was fitted with a Parsons turbine.

With a major plan of expansion envisaged under the 1900 German Navy Law, the Royal Navy was severely compromised. Having been brought to a Two Power Standard (see page 61), with France and Russia being regarded as the two most likely opponents, the Royal Navy could not hope, in the state it was in at the time, to compete with the German navy as well. Britain, no longer able to isolate herself from continental involvement, was forced to look for an alliance, and in 1901 a treaty was signed with Japan. Attempts at reconciliation with France and Russia were also begun. These finally bore fruit when the Entente Cordiale came into being in 1904. At the same time Germany, in spite of her increasingly antagonistic outlook towards Great Britain, was invited to join the alliance with Japan.

In June 1902 Admiral Fisher was appointed Second Sea Lord with responsibility for the manning and training of the Fleet in preparation for war, a post he held until the following August, when he was made Commander-in-Chief Portsmouth. For Fisher this was an extremely important post, and during this period of command he

crystallized his ideas on battleship design, which finally led to the ordering of the *Dreadnought* and high speed battlecruiser. Apart from theoretical matters, Admiral Fisher also busied himself with practical plans. For many years the higher education of officers in the Royal Navy had been a disgrace. The methods and subjects taught were old fashioned, and independent thought or action was discouraged. Admiral Fisher was well aware of this sad state of affairs, and one of his first tasks was to improve the educational standard of the navy. As a start he put forward proposals for the establishment of two naval colleges, at Osborne on the Isle of Wight and at Dartmouth in Devon.

For some years Captain Percy Scott had complained about the state of the navy's gunnery, and on being appointed to the command of the gunnery school HMS *Excellent*, at Whale Island, in 1903, he at once set about putting into practice his ideas. The old methods of instruction using a book were discarded, and future gunnery efficiency was achieved by practical methods. The long-range gunnery Battle Practices held by the Fleet were deemed to be useless, as vessels were not provided with the necessary instruments or instructions. The problem was how to register hits.

To test his theories, Scott asked the Admiralty if he could use the armoured cruiser *Drake*, commanded by Captain J.R. Jellicoe, as a target. To spot the fall of shot accurately Scott believed that broadside firing was essential, and for this purpose he intended to have *Drake* straddled with broadsides. The Admiralty, not unnaturally, refused to allow Scott to use *Drake* for such a purpose. Instead, the Admiralty instructed Rear-Admiral Sir Reginald Custance and Rear-Admiral Sir Hedworth Lambton of *Venerable* and *Victorious* to test the theories using long-range firing, for which purpose no restrictions were placed on the amount of ammunition to be used.

Scott had also frequently complained to the Admiralty about the poor sights used on the guns. This also took some years to improve, and not until 1905, when director fire was first instituted, did gunnery really begin to show an improvement.

Under the new Director of Naval Construction, Philip Watts, the concept of the armoured cruiser underwent a major change. Watts believed that armoured cruisers should be faster and more heavily armed and protected, so that they could scout for enemy battleships ahead of the main Battle Fleet. Watts's ideal was a vessel mounting a large number of heavy guns, preferably the 9.2in. With such views the 'Duke of Edinburgh' class of armoured cruisers was designed, armed with a single 9.2in fore and aft, and two on either beam fore and aft. They were designed to make 23kts under service conditions, but this meant that they would not be able to have the protection of a battleship, or carry such a heavy broadside. A broadside of 6in guns was, however, felt to be perfectly adequate.

Although on paper the concept of the 'Duke of Edinburgh' class appeared sound, in practice they proved to be a failure. To reduce the silhouette, the 6in battery had been mounted low down and was found to be unworkable in anything except a very calm sea. In the mock battle manoeuvres of 1906 Black Prince, continually washed by heavy seas, was soon put out of action by Leviathan. In addition, the anti-destroyer armament was found to be totally inadequate. The twenty 3-pounders were well sited, but were far too small to be of any use against a destroyer.

The 'Duke of Edinburgh' class was followed by four similar vessels of the 'Warrior' class, laid down in 1904. They were to have been of the same type as the 'Duke of Edinburgh', but, with the 6in secondary armament proving inadequate, they were redesigned to mount 7.5in guns on the upper deck in turrets. With gunnery becoming more scientific and complex, fire control platforms were fitted on the masts, from which the guns were directed. The cruisers proved to be formidable opponents and were excellent sea boats, the guns being workable in practically any kind of weather.

The 'Minotaur' class followed, being laid down in 1905. They carried only four 9.2in guns in twin turrets, but an extra six 7.5in. It was at last realized that the 3-pounder gun was too small to be any good as a weapon, and so the 'Minotaur' class carried sixteen 12-pounders. Difficulties over the watertube boiler had at last been resolved, and the class carried a full set of the new boilers.

Only two new battleships were ordered in the 1904 Estimates, instead of the three originally planned, as two ships under construction for Chile had been purchased in 1903. Watts put forward plans for a vessel mounting four 12in in twin turrets fore and aft, and twelve 9.2in in twin turrets amidships. Although the plans were passed by the Controller, Sir William May, the Board of Admiralty failed to approve them. The main problem was the beam required to carry the 9.2in turrets, which would have been so great that the docks at Chatham or Devonport

would not have been able to accommodate the vessels. Consequently, the plans were recast for the 'Lord Nelson' class, carrying ten 9.2in in four twin and two single turrets amidships in place of the 6in secondary armament. The navy thus became the first to have first class battleships mounting an intermediate battery. Armour protection was also much improved over that of earlier ships. Although considered to have been the most successful of the pre-dreadnought designs, the ships were obsolete when completed, having been superseded by the Dreadnought design.

In October 1904 Admiral Fisher was appointed First Sea Lord, a post which gave him the opportunity to initiate many of the reforms and much of the reorganization which had held his attention for so many years. Upon taking office he at once set about defining the duties of the Board of Admiralty (see Appendix 2). For many years the Board had carried on its affairs in what almost amounted to confusion, the different problems and day-to-day matters being dealt with by whoever happened to be at hand. Having set the Board of Admiralty on a clear course, Admiral Fisher began his great programme of reform and organization, some details of which he had already set in motion during his period as Commander of Portsmouth (see page 72).

Admiral Fisher's first main concern was to get an efficient fighting fleet. As a step towards this he set up a great economy drive, cutting out much wastage and duplication. During the first four years of the decade the Navy Estimates had nearly trebled, and Fisher set up the Estimates Committee to scrutinize the Estimates and find ways of reducing the rising expenditure. One example of wastage caused by duplication concerned glass water tumblers. It was found that the medical department ordered one set while the supply department ordered another.

The next area where Fisher felt economies could be made was the Fleet itself. The Admiralty had always been loth to scrap old vessels, and many antiquated ships, better suited as museum pieces, were kept on the lists, entailing the expenditure of vast sums of money on maintenance and repairs. Admiral Fisher scrapped them all, including many of the protected cruisers, which under modern conditions had been made obsolete by the advent of armoured cruisers. In all, 154 vessels were removed from the Fleet, and even then this was not as many as Fisher had requested be scrapped. The dockyards were also reorganized and 6,000 men sacked, while the overseas dockyards were greatly reduced in size.

The new Selborne education scheme, begun while Fisher was in command at Portsmouth, was also expanded. The two new colleges at Osborne and Dartmouth opened the way for a common entry for men in all classes of society to have equal chances of becoming officers, with part of their fees paid by the State. In addition, the initial training of all officer branches in the

Royal Navy was amalgamated into the two colleges, instead of each branch being trained separately as previously. On reaching the rank of lieutenant, at about 22 years of age, officers at last began to specialize in the gunnery, torpedo, navigation, engineer or general branch. At the start the Royal Marines had also been combined in the scheme, but this was soon found to be impracticable, and Marine officers continued to have a separate training.

Simultaneously with the improvements in education, Fisher also modernized the promotion boards and conditions of service. There had been an age limit at which officers could reach flag rank, and this led to many older Admirals being given commands which they could not really manage. The First Sea Lord believed that, with a modern navy, younger officers with new ideas were needed. To recruit these men the age limit was lowered by approximately four years. At the same time it was decided to pension off officers two or three years earlier if there were no suitable posts for them. With these changes in force, the average age of officers was considerably lowered, Captains gaining their rank at about 36 years old, Rear-Admirals at 41 and Vice-Admirals at 52 years of age.

Conditions on the lower deck were still poor, which greatly concerned Admiral Fisher. He realized that unless the men were happy and contented the fighting efficiency of the Fleet would not be at its best. For example, the quantity of food allocated to each man every day was increased, and to give the men the opportunity of having fresh bread each day, bakeries were fitted in all the larger warships. Cutlery was also provided for the seamen's messdecks. Living quarters were also improved, with better ventilation and heating, and the sanitation was modernized.

To ensure that all the valuable training given to a man was not lost, the First Sea Lord formed the Royal Fleet Reserve. On leaving the navy, ratings were encouraged to join the Royal Fleet Reserve, which to some extent reduced the importance of the Royal Naval Volunteer Reserve, which was composed of merchant seamen. The training of the Royal Naval Reserve was improved, the men being sent to sea in commissioned ships, the old sailing vessels previously used as training hulks being scrapped. The Royal Naval Volunteer Reserve had been formed in 1903, created from volunteers drawn from yachtsmen and fishermen who were prepared to give up their own jobs in time of war and serve in the navy.

Admiral Fisher had also initiated the War Course in 1900, and he now had this extended in scope and purpose. This was a compulsory course lasting eight months for officers of Commander and Captain rank. Its aims were to study the methods of conducting war and investigate different tactical problems. After a few courses had been held it was found that eight months was too long a period over which to conduct the lectures. In 1903 the prospectus was altered slightly and two four-month courses were held every year. The syllabus ranged over a wide area of naval affairs, including naval history, strategy, tactics and international law.

In 1890 and 1900 German Navy Laws posed a serious threat to the Royal Navy's mastery of the seas. To counter this threat Admiral Fisher began to reorganize the composition of the fleets. The problem was most serious in home waters, where for the larger part of the year the Channel Fleet (renamed from the Channel Squadron in 1903) was on exercise in Irish and Spanish waters. While it was away there were no organized squadrons available to deal with any difficult situations. The only vessels available were antiquated battleships of the Reserve Squadron, renamed the Home Fleet in 1903. This force was practically useless, the vessels being deployed in harbours all round the coasts of Britain, and manned by only two-thirds of their complement. Even if fully manned, the squadron was incapable of meeting an organized force, as it only exercised for about a fortnight every year, the ships being left at anchor for the rest of the time.

In an even worse state were the ships of the Fleet Reserve and Dockyard Reserve. These vessels were almost completely closed down, with only care and maintenance parties on board the Fleet Reserve vessels and watchmen on those of the Dockyard Reserve.

As a start to building up the strength in Home waters, Fisher introduced the nucleus crew system, whereby those vessels in the Fleet Reserve, later renamed Reserve Fleet, were crewed with all the officers and specialists necessary for the fighting efficiency of the vessel, giving them two-fifths of their normal complement. These vessels were then concentrated in the dockyards of Devonport, Portsmouth and Sheerness. In addition to this the ships were regularly taken to sea for fortnightly training cruises, and their complements brought up to full strength for the annual manoeuvres in which the vessels participated. The extra men needed to man these vessels were taken from the ships which Fisher had scrapped.

Apart from improving the state of the Reserve Fleet, Admiral Fisher also completely reorganized the Active Fleets. In view of the international situation (the Alliance with Japan, friendlier relations with France and the forming of the Entente Cordiale, and rising German naval power), the major part of the navy was held in home waters. The number of active squadrons was reduced from nine to five, based on Alexandria, Dover, Gibraltar, Singapore and Simons Town. From 1904 two Fleets were kept in home waters, these being the Home Fleet, based at Dover, and the Atlantic Fleet, based at Gibraltar. To increase the strengths of these fleets a number of battleships were brought home from the Far East and the Mediterranean. Being based at Gibraltar, the Atlantic Fleet was in an ideal position to reinforce either the Mediterranean or Home Fleets. In addition to this strengthening of the navy, the new armoured cruisers, as they were completed, were formed into squadrons and attached to the Home and Atlantic Fleets.

Chapter 13

The Dreadnought Era

In the 1903 edition of Fred T. Jane's annual *Fighting Ships*, Constructor General Cuniberti of the Italian Navy set forth ideas he had been formulating since the early 1900s concerning future battleships. Cuniberti pointed out that there were two ways of dealing with an enemy — either by a knockout blow or a slow process of attrition, which would require two totally different types of action. The destruction of an enemy by attrition was the method practised by the Royal Navy in 1905, and was necessitated because most of the world's warships were of comparative fighting power. The other method, the knockout blow, would require a type of vessel which the Royal Navy did not at that time possess. Its armour would have to be impervious to all known weapons, and its armament heavy enough to penetrate an enemy's armour at his most vulnerable point, the waterline belt. In addition, the speed would have to be higher than that of any other known vessel. With six such vessels, General Cuniberti felt that the Royal Navy could easily retain the mastery of the seas. The specifications for such a vessel were a displacement of 17,000 tons, dimensions of 521ft x 82ft x 27ft with a 12in armour belt along the waterline and round the battery, twelve 12in guns with ample ammunition and anti-torpedo weapons, and a speed of 24kts.

At first these plans were ridiculed in Britain as being technically impractical and unrealistic, as they would render the present fleet of capital ships obsolete. Following the Russo-Japanese War in 1904-5, the Japanese laid down the *Aki* and *Satsuma*, whose conception followed the lines of General Cuniberti's idea. The Americans also took note of the ideas and ordered the two battleships *Michigan* and *South Carolina*.

At about the same time as Cuniberti was developing his ideas, Fisher, at that time C-in-C of the Mediterranean Fleet, began to formulate ideas for a new super battleship in association with W.H. Gard, the Chief Constructor at Malta dockyard. Gard followed Fisher to Portsmouth, and together the two men worked out a series of sketches for two principle types of warship; a battleship which Fisher called the *Untakable*, and an armoured cruiser which he called *Unapproachable*. By 1902 Fisher had embodied a 10in gun into the designs, but following arguments put forward by Captains Madden, Jackson and Bacon, Gard redrew the designs for Fisher based on a uniform main armament of 12in guns.

Various alternative designs for both battleship and armoured cruiser were placed before a special Committee on Designs appointed by Fisher on 22 December 1904. The designs and proposals were studied, and a sketch plan was approved on 13 January 1905. The approved sketch design formed the basis on which detailed plans for the new battleship, to be named *Dreadnought*, were drawn up. With the new design being draughted it was recommended that all battleships currently building for the Royal Navy should be completed, but that no new

Right: The *Dreadnought*, seen here dressed overall in 1907, heralded in a new era in battleship design, introducing the concept of the all-big-gun armament. The other novel feature of the *Dreadnought* was her turbine machinery, which gave her a speed of 21kts. (ACPL)

TABLE IV: *DREADNOUGHT* PROPOSALS				
	Displacement	Speed	Armament	Protection (Belt)
Cuniberti design	17,000 tons	24kts	12 x 12in 18 x 12pdr	12in
Dreadnought	17,800 tons	21kts	10 x 12in 27 x 12pdr	11in
Invincible	17,250 tons	25kts	8 x 12in 16 x 4in	6in

Right: Coincident with the *Dreadnought* concept, Fisher developed his battlecruiser idea, based on the concept of the *Dreadnought*, but with protection sacrificed for speed. One of the early battlecruisers, the *Indomitable*, is seen here in 1918. (ACPL)

battleship should be ordered until trials of the new ship were completed.

The design for the *Dreadnought* showed a vessel carrying ten 12in guns in five turrets, three on the centreline (two aft) and a turret on each beam between the second and third funnels. This siting was chosen so that eight guns could bear on each broadside and six ahead or astern. The grouping of eight guns on a broadside was chosen because it was found to be the most efficient unit for fire control when firing salvoes for ranging. Eight guns was also the maximum number that could probably be fired simultaneously with full charges without seriously straining the vessel. The designed speed was 21kts, 3kts less than the speed suggested by General Cuniberti. The design for the new battleship was finalized in March 1905, it was laid down the following October, and it was ready for trials in October 1906, an incredibly short time for so large and complex a vessel.

At one fell stroke *Dreadnought* made all the world's existing battleships obsolete. She was extremely well protected, the hull generally being immensely strong and the scantlings very heavy. The armour itself was disposed as in *Lord Nelson*, with additional armour applied internally below the waterline for protection against the possibility of the detonation of two torpedoes in any position. *Dreadnought* also had solid bulkheads. Apart from armament (she also carried 27 12-pounders in addition to her main guns), she was also unique in being powered by turbines. Previously these had only been fitted to destroyers and small cruisers. The plans to equip *Dreadnought* with turbines gave rise to much apprehension, especially when the three other vessels ordered under the 1906 Programme were also given turbines. It was the fitting of these engines which gave *Dreadnought* her high speed of 21kts, 3kts more than *Lord Nelson*.

Fisher's concept for the armoured cruiser, which became known as the battlecruiser, was a high speed version of the battleship. The outline sketch for the new armoured cruiser was approved by the Committee on Designs in March 1905. It was planned that the ships, with their superior firepower and speed, would be able to operate either alone in a scouting role or as part of the main battle fleet, ready to engage enemy armoured cruisers. Their high speed would also enable them to avoid action with slower, more heavily armed ships. In the battlecruiser, protection was sacrificed to gain a speed of 25kts (the armour belt was thinned from 11in to 6in), to bring it more in line with General Cuniberti's ideal.

Unlike the beam turret disposition in *Dreadnought*, the midships turrets in the battlecruisers were sited *en echelon*. By such siting it was planned that the they would obtain the same broadside as *Dreadnought* with only four turrets. In practice, however, it was found that only six guns could bear on either beam instead of the eight planned. By this time the Admiralty had realized that some sort of secondary armament was essential to a large warship, so it was decided to arm them with sixteen of the new 4in QF that had just been designed. Three 'Invincible' class ships were ordered, *Invincible*, *Indomitable*, and *Inflexible*, *Invincible* going to sea in March 1908.

In some respects *Dreadnought* did not quite come up to the specifications suggested by General Cuniberti, and neither did the battlecruiser.

Just before the end of its term of office at the end of 1905, the Conservative Government laid down the shipbuilding policy to be followed for the navy by the next Government, irrespective of who was returned to power. Known as the Cawdor Programme, after the Conservative's First Lord of the Admiralty, it specified that four armoured ships of the dreadnought and battlecruiser type be ordered each year, thus ensuring that at any time eight such vessels would be under construction. The programme planned that by 1908 the Royal Navy should have in commission five dreadnoughts and three battlecruisers, as opposed to Germany's two dreadnoughts. The Liberal Party under Sir Henry Campbell Bannerman was returned to power at the general election, and although not in favour of heavy expenditure on armaments, accepted the principles set out in the Cawdor Programme.

The 1906-07 Estimates provided for the construction of one dreadnought and three battlecruisers. At first the Liberal Party accepted these figures, but after having passed the Estimates the Government had a change of mind, and, in an effort to reduce arms expenditure so that it could carry out its programme of social reform, the Estimates were reduced to three improved Dreadnought-type vessels. The three vessels finally ordered were *Bellerophon*, *Superb* and *Temeraire*. They were almost identical to *Dreadnought* but of slightly greater displacement.

In October 1906 Admiral Fisher set about reorganizing the Fleets. This at once led to controversy, and Lord Beres-

ford was highly critical of Admiral Fisher's decisions. With the nucleus crew system (see page 74) now well established, Admiral Fisher felt able to carry out far-reaching reforms among the warships stationed around Great Britain. Until 1906 there had been three independent battleship divisions stationed around British coasts, but in that year these divisions, the Nore, Portsmouth and Devonport, were combined into one fleet – the reformed Home Fleet. This fleet, under the command of one Commander-in-Chief, became the main force when the Channel Fleet was away on exercises. To bring the reformed Home Fleet up to a strength capable of meeting any threat, two battleships were withdrawn from each of the Channel, Atlantic and Mediterranean Fleets, the remaining seven vessels of the Home Fleet being drawn from the former Fleet Reserve. Gradually the Home Fleet was built up until, finally, the Nore Division on its own was powerful enough to meet any threat posed by the German navy.

In spite of the growing strength of the German navy and Admiral Fisher's continued efforts to build up the Royal Navy, the Liberal Government was still bent on making economies with the Service Estimates. In the 1907-08 Estimates yet another dreadnought was dropped from the programme planned by Lord Cawdor. Before the Estimates were presented, however, the Prime Minister had asked the First Lord, Lord Tweedmouth, if he would be prepared to accept a 50 per cent reduction in the dreadnought programme. Very grudgingly the Board of Admiralty agreed to the proposal, which led to a furious outcry in the press. On presenting the Estimates, however, Lord Tweedmouth said that if no satisfactory agreement could be reached at the Hague on the question of disarmament, three dreadnoughts would be built instead of the two proposed. The talks came to nothing, so the Government gave the Admiralty permission to construct the extra dreadnought. The three vessels of the 1907-08 Programme were *Collingwood*, *St Vincent* and *Vanguard*, all sister ships and practically repeats of the 'Bellerophon'

class, themselves merely a slightly larger *Dreadnought* with improved underwater protection.

The 1908-09 Estimates saw yet another reduction in the dreadnought programme, when only *Neptune* and the battlecruiser *Indefatigable* were ordered. *Indefatigable* was just an improved *Invincible* with a better siting arrangement for the guns which improved the arc of fire. *Neptune* also had her main armament arranged differently from earlier dreadnoughts. The midships turrets were sited in echelon so that all the main armament could bear on either broadside in a very wide arc, while the first of the two after turrets was superimposed, the first time a turret was so sited on a British battleship. Moreover, the Admiralty had become aware of the possible part that airships could play in a future war, and in recognition of this the *Neptune* had her upper deck built to withstand the explosion of small bombs dropped from a height.

In February 1908 Germany passed a new Navy Law which increased the rate of construction of dreadnought-type warships to four per year, an increase of one over the previous Law. In addition, the eight large cruisers of the 1900 Law were reordered as battlecruisers. This would give Germany a total of 58 dreadnought-type battleships and battlecruisers, as opposed to 38 dreadnought-type warships and 20 armoured cruisers. The publication of these figures led to a vigorous press campaign throughout Great Britain, with the Conservative press demanding that six dreadnoughts be ordered in the 1909 Estimates. Admiral Fisher, when presented with the figures for Germany's dreadnought construction, at once requested eight dreadnoughts, but the First Lord, Reginald McKenna (who had replaced Lord Tweedmouth when Sir Henry Campbell Bannerman died in 1908 and was succeeded by Herbert Asquith as Prime Minister), only pressed for six.

With the Admiralty undecided as to how many dreadnoughts should be ordered, the Chancellor of the Exchequer, Winston S. Churchill, at once asked to inspect the Admiralty's figures of the estimated rate of expansion of

TABLE V: CAPITAL SHIP CONSTRUCTION

Year laid down	Dreadnoughts		Battlecruisers	
	Germany	Britain	Germany	Britain
1905 –	1	–	–	
1906	–	1	–	3
1907	4	3	–	–
1908	3	2	1	–
1909	2	4	2	2
1910 3	3	–	3	
Laid Down by 1912	12	14	3	8
Completed by 1912	10	14	3	8

TABLE VI. COMPARISONS OF MAIN ARMAMENT, 1905

Calibre	Length	Weight	Weight of shell	Muzzle velocity	Range
13.5in/Mk V	45cal	76 tons	1,400lb	2,450ft/s	23,200yd
12in/Mk XII	50cal	67 tons	850lb	2,825ft/s	20,900yd

Right: The *Colossus* and *Hercules* (illustrated here) formed part of the famous 'We want Eight' programme. Note the 'flying bridge' on which were carried the ship's boats. These were later removed. (ACPL)

the German navy. These had been reckoned at 17 and possibly 21 dreadnoughts in commission by 1912. After close scrutiny it was felt that the Admiralty had overestimated the rate at which Germany could build dreadnoughts, and the Liberal Government, feeling there was no need for a rushed programme of construction, would only agree to the construction of four dreadnoughts under the 1909 Estimates. They did, however, insert a clause to the effect that, if it was felt necessary for the national security, a further four dreadnoughts could be constructed under the 1909 Estimates.

This led to further outbursts of angry comment, especially among those who agitated for a large navy, among them a number of influential Conservatives. It was at this time that the famous phrase 'We want eight and we won't wait' was first coined. However, the Government was not to be shaken in its resolve, and the 1909 Estimates remained at four dreadnoughts, with a further four conditional vessels. The controversy over the dreadnought programme gave rise to a number of fortuitous side-effects, among which was an offer by the Australian and New Zealand Governments to provide funds for the construction of two extra dreadnoughts for the Royal Navy. The offers were accepted, and led to the construction of *Australia* and *New Zealand*, sister ships to *Indefatigable*. Another side-effect which was to prove helpful in the future was that the publicity concerning the German Navy Laws, along with the publication of a number of novels in which future wars were described, indoctrinated the general public to the fact that war with Germany sometime in the future was certainly a possibility.

The first four vessels of the 'We want eight' programme were the 22,200-ton *Colossus*, *Hercules*, *Lion* and *Orion*. They were laid down almost immediately in the summer of 1909, about three months before work would

normally have begun on them. In the spring of the following year it was decided to lay down the four conditional vessels — *Conqueror*, *Monarch*, *Princess Royal* and *Thunderer*. *Colossus* and *Hercules* were practically repeats of *Neptune*, except that the after tripod was suppressed, it being seriously affected by the smoke from the funnels. This structure was also found to be unnecessary for supporting the wireless aerials, just a short mast aft proving satisfactory for the purpose. *Lion* and *Orion* of the first group were classed as super dreadnoughts, being armed with a new 13.5in gun instead of the 12in of the earlier dreadnought-type vessels.

The new 13.5in gun was a vast improvement on the model fitted in the earlier 'Royal Sovereign' class, the great advantage being its greatly increased penetration capabilities (22in against 9in on Krupp cemented armour at a range of 5,000yd). *Orion*, the first vessel to carry the new 13.5in, had all her main armament sited along the keel line, instead of in echelon as in the previous dreadnoughts. To a certain extent this was a necessary improvement forced upon the Admiralty to prevent serious strains being set up when the guns fired across the deck. The siting also allowed far greater firepower to be developed, and the new arrangement was soon adopted for other vessels in the Royal Navy.

Orion, together with the three vessels of the conditional order, *Conqueror*, *Monarch* and *Thunderer*, formed another new class of super dreadnought, while *Lion*, *Princess Royal* (the remaining vessel of the conditional order) and *Queen Mary* (ordered under the 1910 Programme) were battlecruisers mounting eight of the new 13.5in guns. A number of minor problems were encountered with *Lion*, including some necessary repairs to the turbines which somewhat delayed her completion. Another problem was the heat generated

Right: The 'Colossus' class was followed by the four 'Orion' class, which reverted to the 13.5in gun for main armament, in reply to the German decision to mount 12in guns in their new dreadnoughts. Previous dreadnought-type battleships in the Royal navy had all mounted 12in guns. (ACPL)

Right: The battlecruiser counterparts to the 'Orion' class were the three ships of the 'Lion' class. The *Lion* is seen here in 1918 with various modifications – all three funnels the same height, and foremast sited in front of the first funnel. (ACPL)

in the fore funnel, which was so great that the fire control position on the tripod mast sited just behind it became untenable, and navigating instruments were damaged. Before she was finally accepted into service, *Lion* had the forward tripod removed and replaced by a light mast, the bridge much enlarged and placed behind the conning tower, the fore funnel sited further aft and the height of all funnels increased.

By 1908 the Fisher-Beresford feud had become so subversive that it was endangering the morale of the whole Service, and the press was continually calling for someone to take a hand in the affair and bring it to a close, one way or another. The opposite occurred, and the row became more intense, those unfortunate enough to take sides sometimes falling foul of the contestants and having their careers hindered. One of these was Admiral Scott, who disagreed with Lord Beresford over a signal made during manoeuvres in 1908. Had he carried out the order from Lord Beresford a collision would have resulted, so Admiral Scott refused to obey the order. A first-class quarrel ensued, and in the end Admiral Scott was moved to another command. Lord Beresford himself was also highly insubordinate, continually questioning orders from the Admiralty, criticizing Admiralty policy and orders, and generally being completely tactless. He was absolutely opposed to the First Sea Lord and his reforms, and the incidents between the two became so bitter that discipline within the navy was seriously threatened.

Admiral Fisher's reorganization of the Home Fleet was the final blow. Lord Beresford held command of the Channel Fleet, but in 1909, when it was joined with the Home Fleet in a unified command, Lord Beresford was finally told to haul down his flag (see Appendix 3). Now a free man and no longer hidebound by Service discipline, Lord Beresford freely spoke his mind to all and sundry, condemning Admiral Fisher and Admiralty policy over the inadequate state of the navy, poor strategy, bad composition and disposition of the fleets, lack of war plans, insufficient cruisers and destroyers, and many other, minor points.

These disclosures, at first made privately by Beresford to the Prime Minister, Herbert Asquith, forced the Government, with the First Lord's agreement, to form a subcommittee of the Committee of Imperial Defence to investigate Lord Beresford's accusations in private. The formation of the committee infuriated Admiral Fisher, who thereupon threatened to resign, but he was persuaded to remain, finally saying, 'I am not going till I am kicked out'.

At the same time as the inquiry began, some of Beresford's supporters published a series of letters from Captain Bacon in the Mediterranean to Admiral Fisher, which complained of the handling of the Mediterranean Fleet. As a result of the publication of these letters, and the outcry from the papers and the general public, Admiral Fisher was finally forced to resign from the Admiralty. In the five years he had been in office as First Sea Lord, Admiral Fisher had completely revitalized the Royal Navy, set in train many reforms and thoroughly prepared the Service for the great struggles that lay ahead. He was succeeded by his staunch supporter, Admiral Sir Arthur K. Wilson. The report of the inquiry, published in August 1909, showed that Admiralty policy had not at any time placed the country's safety in jeopardy.

To counter the German construction of second class cruisers, a type of vessel which had been completely omitted from the Estimates in recent years, five protected cruisers of the 'Bristol' class, were ordered in the 1908-09 Estimates. Their armament consisted of two 6in and ten 4in, and although the specifications only asked for a speed of 25kts, all of the vessels exceeded 26kts on trials. In the Estimates for the following year (1909-10) four similar vessels of the slightly larger 'Weymouth' class were ordered, mounting eight 6in. These were followed by six 'Chatham' class (eight 6in) and four 'Birmingham' class (nine 6in).

Left: The five cruisers of the 'Bristol' class were ordered under the 1908–9 Estimates in reply to the light cruisers of the 'Kolberg' class under construction for the German Navy. (ACPL)

Right: HMS *Rifleman* of the 'Acorn' or 'H' class built under the 1909–10 Programme. A total of twenty destroyers were built to this design, which introduced the new 21in torpedo to the fleet. Two tubes were mounted. (Tom Molland)

Right: Submarine *D2*. The 'D' class submarines featured saddle tanks instead of internal ballast tanks and incorporated wireless telegraphy (W/T). The boats carried three 18in torpedo tubes (one stern, two bow) and also carried a 12pdr gun, which was withdrawn into the base of the conning tower when not in use. (ACPL)

In 1906 the first of a new standard design of destroyers, known as the 'Tribal' class, was laid down. Between 1906 and 1910 thirteen of these vessels were built, all reaching a speed of 33kts on fuel oil only. The first five vessels carried an armament of five 12-pounder guns and two 18in torpedo tubes, and the remainder of the class had two 4in in place of the 12-pounders.

Seeking to avoid the duplication of torpedo boats and torpedo boat destroyers for similar tasks, the Admiralty proposed an intermediate type of vessel that could perform the duties of both types. This led to the design of the 'Beagle' class destroyers ordered under the 1908-09 Programme. Displacing about 900 tons and armed with one 4in and two 12-pounder guns and two 21in torpedo tubes, the vessels reached a speed of 27kts. It was decided to revert to coal for firing the boilers instead of the more costly oil. This decision resulted from reports on comparable new coal-fired German vessels, which showed that they were capable of steaming at speeds very much the same as Britain's oil-fired vessels. Added to this, Britain had an abundant supply of very good coal from Wales, which was far cheaper than transporting oil from the Middle East.

The 'Beagles' were followed by the twenty 'Acorn' class vessels ordered under the 1909-10 Programmes. These were slightly smaller than the 'Beagles' and were fitted with fully oil-fired boilers. The contract speed of 27kts remained the same, but the radius of action was increased

by 200 miles. Armament consisted of two 4in, two 12-pounders and two 21in torpedo tubes. These were followed by the 20 'Acheron' class of 1910-11, 12 'Acasta' class of 1911-12 (armament standardized at three 4in), and 22 'Laforey' class of 1912-13 (with the torpedo armament doubled to four 21in). These were the last destroyers to be completed before the outbreak of war.

In 1906 the first of the eight 'D' class submarines began to be laid down, being a development of the earlier 'C' class, 38 of which had been built, with more under construction. The 'D' class were almost double the size of the 'C' class, displacing about 600 tons submerged. Surface speed was increased to 16kts and three torpedo tubes were fitted — two superimposed in the bow and one in the stern. The new bow arrangement resulted in a much better hydrodynamic hull form. The 'D' class differed radically from previous classes in that the main ballast tanks were mounted in saddle tanks outside the pressure hull. Power was provided by vertical four-cycle diesel engines (first experimentally fitted in *A 13*) driving two propellers, as opposed to the single screw of previous boats. *D 1* was experimentally fitted with wireless telegraphy. The remaining seven vessels of the class proved more successful than *D 1*, displacement being increased slightly and horsepower increased from 1,200 to 1,750. It had been intended to build nineteen vessels of the 'D' class, but while they were under construction an improved design was prepared which superseded them.

Chapter 14

The Road to War

In January 1911 the Japanese ordered the battlecruiser *Kongo* from Vickers. Under the 1911 Programme, the Admiralty had planned a fourth battlecruiser of the 'Lion' class, but with the details of the *Kongo* before them they began to have doubts about the wisdom of ordering another 'Lion'. *Kongo* had much better protection than *Lion*, and was the first foreign battlecruiser to mount a gun heavier than 12in. The siting of the four turrets, the secondary armament, and the design generally gave the Admiralty much food for thought concerning their own designs. With such a superior vessel under construction, the British battlecruiser was redesigned. The original plans called for 85,000hp, but this was now raised to 108,000hp, increasing the speed by about 2kts to 28kts. The initial design was approved in August 1911, and the final drawings in December of that year.

The new battlecruiser, *Tiger*, was finally laid down at John Brown's shipyard in June 1912. When war broke out in August 1914 the shipyard worked round the clock to speed her completion. She was the largest and fastest warship afloat, and the only battlecruiser to mount 6in guns as secondary armament. Not only was she an extremely well built vessel, but she was also the last to be built to satisfy the sailor's ideal of what a ship should look like. Under the influence of the *Kongo* design, the midships turret was resited behind the after funnel instead of in front of it, as in *Lion*. This had the effect of increasing the turret's arc of fire to 60° before the beam and 90° after it on either side.

In 1911 Anglo-German relations took a turn for the worse. Tension arose when, in the spring of the year, the French were forced to send troops to Fez in Morocco to put down a revolt against the Sultan. This was the first of a series of French moves aimed at annexing Moroccan territory. In retaliation, and without any real motives, except to create a rift in the Entente Cordiale and cause a war, the Germans laid claim to the port of Agadir, on the Atlantic coast of Morocco. Unable to discern the German intentions, the Liberal Government split over the issue. No one knew, if it came to the test, whether the Government would be united in its condemnation of German policy. Both the Home Secretary, Winston Churchill, and Chancellor of the Exchequer Lloyd George were pacifist in their outlook. However, after a period of uncertainty, Lloyd George, with the consent of the Prime Minister, Mr Asquith, and the Foreign Secretary, Mr Grey, took the initiative at an after-dinner speech at the Bankers' Association on 21 July 1911, stating:

> If the situation were forced upon us in which peace could only be preserved by the surrender of the great and beneficent position Britain has won by centuries of heroism and achievement by allowing Britain to be treated, where her interests were vitally affected, as if she were of no account in the Cabinet of Nations, then I say emphatically that Peace at that price would be a humiliation intolerable for a great country like ours to endure.

The speech caused an uproar in Germany, and the First Lord, told of the German reaction to the speech, warned the Royal Navy of the possibility of war. It was indeed fortunate that war was not declared, and that the Germans did not make a surprise attack on the navy, for the First Sea Lord, in spite of the continual warnings from the Foreign Secretary, remained totally unconvinced of the possibility of war. The Atlantic Fleet remained in the north of Scotland, while the First Division of the Home Fleet was at its base in Ireland. The Second Division was at Portland with its crews on four days' leave and boilers shut down, and not even the torpedo nets were put out as a precaution. The Third and Fourth Divisions were at their various

Left: The design of the last battle-cruiser, the *Tiger*, built before the outbreak of war, was strongly influenced by the Japanese *Kongo* built by Vickers. (Tom Molland)

Right: The first all-big-gun battleships to return to a full-sized secondary armament of 6in guns was the third series of super-dreadnoughts, the four ships of the '*Iron Duke*' class. The return to a 6in secondary armament was dictated by the increasing size and power of destroyers. The picture shows the *Emperor of India* in 1916. (ACPL)

bases around the coasts with only their nucleus crews on board. In addition, there was a strike in South Wales, and no coal was available for the Fleet.

Gradually the situation eased, and the German navy continued its build up, much to the anxiety of the Admiralty. The Entente Cordiale remained intact, and in November an agreement was finally signed with Germany, recognizing French claims in Morocco, in return for which a large part of the French Congo was handed over to Germany.

As a result of the Agadir crisis the Prime Minister convened a special meeting of the Committee of Imperial Defence on 23 August 1911, to discuss war plans in the event of war with Germany. At the morning seminar the Army put forward the probable moves of the German army and the British counter moves, while in the afternoon the First Sea Lord, Sir Arthur Wilson, outlined the navy's proposed operations. At once it became obvious that opinions differed, the Admiralty feeling that a close blockade of German ports would suffice to force the Germans to surrender. The Admiralty looked on the plans of the Army's General Staff for sending an expeditionary force to France as unnecessary, preferring to have such a force ready for a surprise landing on the German coast. The Army, however, was absolutely opposed to such a plan.

With the two services at variance, the Secretary of State for War, Mr Haldane, threatened to resign from the War Office unless the Board of Admiralty formed a Naval War Staff to co-ordinate plans with the General Staff. Admiral Wilson, like his predecessor Admiral Fisher, and also the First Lord, McKenna, found the proposals for the formation of a Naval Staff completely unacceptable.

However, there were others who also doubted the wisdom of the Admiralty's policies of close blockade. Among these was Winston Churchill, who also favoured the formation of a War Staff. With the Agadir crisis abating, and the Admiralty's apparent lack of plans and poor relations

with the General Staff, the Prime Minister decided that it was time for changes at the Admiralty. He therefore asked Winston Churchill if he would like to become the new First Lord. Churchill accepted, and he and McKenna (who privately did not readily accept the arrangement) exchanged offices in October 1911.

On taking office, Churchill, like Admiral Fisher, at once put in hand sweeping reforms. His first task was to set up the Naval War Staff, which so many of his colleagues in the Cabinet had urged on the previous First Lord. The new staff was made up of three sections — operations, intelligence and mobilization. It was found, however, that there were not enough officers with specialized knowledge to man the War Staff, so in 1912 the Staff College was set up at Portsmouth to train officers for the positions.

Next on the list for reform were the Admiralty war plans, which, it seemed, had always been kept in Admiral Wilson's head. In particular, the plans for close blockade of Germany were closely scrutinized. It was found that destroyer flotillas three or four times the size of the German flotillas would be needed to enforce a close blockade of the Heligoland Bight, and Britain simply did not have that number of destroyers. To find sufficient numbers of vessels for the task, it had been necessary to reduce the patrol strength of existing flotillas by two-thirds. This enabled a flotilla to maintain one third of its strength on patrol, the other two parts returning from and going out to the patrol area. This was a most unsatisfactory arrangement, and Churchill insisted that the navy institute a system of distant blockade with the Home Fleet, based upon the new base of Scapa Flow and with destroyer patrols deployed across the straits of Dover, supported by older battleships and minefields.

At the same time the Fleets were reorganized so that the number of vessels immediately ready for action was increased. Measures were also taken to guard against surprise attacks. To carry out the reforms as directed,

Left: In 1912 a wooden platform was fitted over the forward turret of the battleship *Africa*. On 10 January, Commander Samson took off from the platform using a modified Short S28 pusher biplane. (Imperial War Museum)

Below: A Short biplane on the flying platform mounted over the forward gun turret of the *Hibernia*. The 'plane was flown off from the ship as she steamed along in Weymouth Bay during a Review of the Fleet. (ACPL)

Churchill appointed a new Board of Admiralty with Sir Francis Bridgeman (late Commander-in-Chief of the Home Fleet) as First Sea Lord, and Prince Louis of Battenberg as Second Sea Lord. Sir George Callaghan was appointed Commander-in-Chief of the Home Fleet, with John Jellicoe as his Second-in-Command.

With the Agadir crisis over, Lloyd George adopted a more conciliatory attitude towards Germany. Talks between the two countries were opened with a view to ending the naval rivalry between them. Basically the terms offered to the Kaiser were: the acceptance of British supremacy at sea; no increase in the size of the German navy programmes, and if at all possible a reduction; British recognition of German colonial aims; and proposals for mutual declarations that the two countries would not formulate treaties or plans that could be considered aggressive to each other. The Kaiser's response to these proposals was to send the Prime Minister the plans of the new 1912 Navy Law. Churchill, after studying the proposed Navy Law, was greatly perturbed. The planned programmes of British dreadnought construction had allowed for a total of 21 vessels over the six years, compared with 12 German. The new German Navy Law, however, increased their number to 15, which meant that if Britain was to maintain a superiority of 60 per cent in dreadnoughts, as planned, the Admiralty's rate of construction would have to be increased to 27 ships over the next six years.

Nor was this all, for the new German Navy Law also planned for the formation of a third dreadnought squadron in full commission. This posed a very serious threat to the Royal Navy's supremacy on its present state. The First Lord suggested that if the Germans were to arrange to complete their proposed programme in twelve years instead of six, it would be possible to resume more cordial relations. It might also then be possible for Britain to reduce her planned rate of dreadnought construction. The First Lord was convinced that an attempt at mutual agreement on these terms should be made, and that if it was successful it might, as a result, achieve twelve years of peace.

The Secretary of State for War left London with the proposals on 6 February 1912, returning two days later with a promise from Admiral Tirpitz that Germany would cancel the construction of one of her dreadnoughts. The British Government, in a reciprocal gesture, sacrificed two planned dreadnoughts, leaving its declared programme at 25 ships. The figure for the first year was, however, increased to five again when the Federated States of Malaya made a gift to the British Government for the construction of a 'Queen Elizabeth' class battleship.

The formation of the third German dreadnought squadron forced the Admiralty to accelerate reorganization of the Fleets. Previously both the Home and Atlantic Fleets had been available for Home defence. These were now reorganized into three Fleets with a total of eight battle squadrons, each of eight battleships, supported by cruisers and destroyers. The First Fleet had the Fleet Flagship and four battle squadrons, each fully in commission. To achieve this strength the former Atlantic Fleet was based on home ports instead of at Gibraltar as hitherto, and the Mediterranean Fleet moved from Malta to Gibraltar. To compensate the Mediterranean Fleet for the loss of its 'King Edward' battleships, it was allocated the Second Battlecruiser Squadron and the First Armoured Cruiser Squadron. In addition, to counter the threat posed by the growing Austrian navy, a dreadnought squadron was earmarked to join the Mediterranean Fleet by 1915.

The two battle squadrons of the Second Fleet, although fully commissioned, had only 60 per cent of their complements on board, the remainder being under training or on courses ashore. The Third Fleet, also of two battle squadrons and five cruiser squadrons, was formed from the older classes of warship and manned by care and maintenance parties. This Fleet could not be fully commissioned until after mobilization of the reserves had been carried out. To speed up mobilization of the Third Fleet a special reserve, the Immediate Reserve, was formed of men who were given periodic training and higher pay. They were liable to be called up before a general mobilization was ordered. This reorganization brought the strength of fully commissioned battleships to 49, as opposed to the German increase from 17 to 25. After mobilization Britain could put 65 battleships to sea, while Germany had only 38.

During the early 1900s the aeroplane began to prove itself. Under Captain Murray F. Seuter and Commander C.R. Samson, adventurous elements in the navy took a keen interest in the new-fangled machines. On 1 March 1911 four officers were sent on a course to be trained as pilots, and in December that year a Naval Flying School was established at Eastchurch, the aircraft being formed into a Naval Air Wing. Meanwhile, Commander Samson had developed a flying-off platform for aircraft which could be fitted to large warships. An experimental wooden platform was fitted on the foredeck of the battleship Africa at Sheerness, and on 10 January 1912 Samson flew Short S.38 pusher biplane No T2 from the platform. On 2 May 1912 Samson repeated the experiment off Portland. This time the aircraft took off from a slightly longer platform fitted on Hibernia, which was steaming at 5kts. The platform was subsequently transferred to the London, and another flight took place on 4 July, with the ship steaming at 12kts.

In May 1912 the Naval Air Arm joined with the army's air arm to form the Royal Flying Corps (RFC), the navy retaining full control of its Naval Wing. Commander Samson was placed in charge of naval personnel in the air arm, while the air bases came under control of HMS Vernon, the torpedo school. Then, on 25 November 1912, the Admiralty formed a new branch, the Air Department, under Captain Seuter, which was to have a major impact on the future of naval operations. After this successful beginning the new arm fell into decline, and it was not until 1 July 1914 that enthusiasm for the new form of warfare was again aroused, when the Naval Wing of the RFC was renamed the Royal Naval Air Service (RNAS).

In the meantime a number of experiments had been conducted with the old cruiser Hermes. In 1913 she was fitted with a short flight deck and seaplanes were launched from wheeled trolleys which fell into the sea when the aircraft became airborne. Progress was painfully slow, however, and by the start of the war only experiments for launching aircraft had been conducted. To return, aircraft alighted on the sea alongside their parent ship, supported on floats or by flotation bags, and were then hoisted back on board by cranes; a slow and clumsy operation.

Under the 1912 Programme, the basis of which had already been agreed when Churchill took over as First Lord, the Admiralty were to construct three battleships, one battlecruiser, three cruisers and twenty destroyers. The designs for the battleships had all been prepared and only awaited a final signature before being presented to Parliament. However, uncertainty hung over the three battleships of the 'Queen Elizabeth' class. Already Japan and America had battleships mounting 14in guns under construction. The Royal Navy had increased the calibre of its main armament once from 12in to 13.5in, and there were those who felt it was time that the calibre was raised again. But there were formidable problems to be overcome if the size of the guns was to be increased. To carry a 15in gun, which was the next satisfactory calibre, the 'Queen Elizabeth' class battleships would have to be increased in size, and they would thus cost more. Also, there could be no delay in having the guns and mountings ready, or completion of the ships would be delayed. The First Lord decided that the risks must be taken, and the requisite number of 15in guns were ordered for the new battleships, without first constructing a model and having it thoroughly tested. The ordnance factory did, however, manage to hurry the construction of one gun, and completed it four months ahead of the remainder. A number of basic tests were carried out on this gun to enable range tables, etc, to be compiled. The tests showed the gun to be satisfactory in every way, with a much longer life than the 13.5in.

TABLE VII. COMPARISON OF 13.5in AND 15in GUNS

Calibre	Length	Weight	Weight of shell	Muzzle velocity	Range
15in	42cal	97 tons	1,920lb	2,450ft/sec	23,600yd
13.5in	45cal	76 tons	1,400lb	2,450ft/sec	23,200yd

The initial plans for the 'Queen Elizabeth' class allowed for a vessel mounting ten of the new guns, but it was seen that if the vessel mounted only eight the broadside would still be heavier than that provided by the ten 13.5in guns of the four preceding 'King George V' class of the 1910 Programme and the four 'Iron Duke' class of the 1911 Programme. If, therefore, the midships turret was dispensed with, the space thus saved could be used for extra boiler rooms which would enable the vessel to achieve a higher speed. With an extra 4/5kts these battleships would be able to turn the van of the German Fleet and destroy the head of the line, enabling the slower British vessels systematically to destroy the enemy's rear line. The First Sea Lord felt that vessels built to this design were of far greater value than the battlecruisers, and said:

> If it is worth while to spend far more than the price of your best battleship upon a fast heavily gunned vessel, it is better at the same time to give it the heaviest armour as well [the 'Queen Elizabeth' class battleships had armour belts of 13in, the heaviest of any ship then afloat]. You then have a ship which may indeed cost half as much again as a battleship, but which at any rate can do everything ... The battlecruiser in other words should be superseded by the fast battleship.

The War College felt that for the Royal Navy to maintain an advantage over the High Seas Fleet of 1914 a speed of 25kts would be necessary. It was impossible to achieve speeds of this nature using coal-fired boilers, and the only other alternative which would give this speed was oil. Until then, only destroyers had been fitted with fully oil-fired boilers, larger vessels still being coal-fired

Below: The British Fleet being reviewed by the King on 20 July 1914. (Imperial War Museum)

but using oil sprayed on the coal to assist combustion. To go completely over to oil-fired boilers for the new battleships would create many problems, not least of which would be supply and transport of the fuel and the high cost of the initial outlay of the storage facilities and purchase, etc. Nonetheless, the plunge was taken, and the 'Queen Elizabeth' class completed with fully oil-fired boilers. At the same time an agreement with the Anglo-Persian Oil Company was concluded at a cost of £2 million (later increased to £5 million), and a controlling share in oil properties obtained which later led to a considerable reduction in the price the Admiralty had to pay for oil. The success of this operation was mainly due to the Commission on Oil which the First Lord set up under the leadership of Admiral Fisher.

With their high speed, excellent armour and powerful broadsides, the 'Queen Elizabeth' class were more than capable of operating with, and providing a formidable backup to, the battlecruiser force. As they combined all the advantages of battleships with the high speed of battlecruisers, it was decided that no more of the latter need be ordered for the time being. Not until the success of the battlecruisers at the Battle of the Falklands in 1914, when Fisher had returned to the Admiralty, was the battlecruiser concept revived, Fisher persuading the Cabinet to allow two battleships to be completed as the battlecruisers Renown and Repulse, which were then followed by others.

The 'Queen Elizabeth' class was followed by the five vessels of the 'Revenge' class ordered under the 1913 and 1914 Programmes. Again these vessels mounted the 15in gun, but otherwise were merely enlarged editions of Iron Duke. Protection was to a certain degree improved, and Ramillies was additionally fitted with shallow external bulges, the first British battleship so fitted. Although the decision had been taken to give the 'Queen Elizabeths' oil fuel, there were doubts as to the reliability of the supply should there be a war. In consequence it was decided that the 'Revenge' class should revert to the use of coal, but this retrograde step was averted when Admiral Fisher returned to the Admiralty in October 1914 and rescinded the order.

The programme of increased dreadnought construction gave rise to a number of problems, one being a serious manpower shortage, especially in the officer branches. This had been accentuated by the growth of the submarine arm and the rise of the dominion navies, to which large numbers of officers were seconded for training purposes. To overcome the manpower problems a supplementary scheme of entry was begun in March 1913, by which it was hoped that boys between the ages of 17½ and 18½ from Public Schools could be encouraged to enlist in the officer category. On joining they would undergo an intensive training course lasting 18 months, during which they would receive a thorough grounding in seamanship, both in the naval colleges ashore and on seagoing warships in commission.

Vast sums of money had already been expended on the navy, and in the autumn of 1913 the First Lord requested that the annual manoeuvres planned for 1914 should be cancelled on the grounds of economy. Instead, the First Sea Lord was asked whether all the reserve ships and men of the Third Fleet (the Reserve Fleet) could be mobilized as for a war. It was then planned that, towards the end of 1914, all the Royal Naval Volunteer Reserve men would be mobilized and embarked for a week's training cruise on the vessels of the First Fleet.

Meanwhile the political situation in Europe had been rapidly deteriorating. At the end of June 1914 two squadrons of the Royal Navy were on official visits to Kronstadt and Kiel. While the Kaiser was inspecting the units at Kiel, news was received of the assassination of the heir to the Austro-Hungarian throne, the Archduke Franz Ferdinand, at Sarajevo, the capital of Bosnia-Herzegovina, by a Bosnian student. In an air of impending doom the regatta at Kiel was quickly brought to a close and the units returned to England.

While Europe tottered on the brink of war and statesmen hurried to and fro between the different embassies in an effort to avert a catastrophe, the Third Fleet began its mobilization on 15 July. The Fleet coaled and raised steam, leaving soon after for a grand review at Spithead where the ships were to be inspected by the King. The morning after the review, 19 July, the Third Fleet put to sea for exercises, preparatory to dispersing to its home ports to pay off on 23 July. That same day Austria-Hungary gave Serbia a 48hr ultimatum, which was rejected on 26 July. Fortunately only the smaller vessels of the Third Fleet had begun to pay off, and with the situation critical the First Sea Lord, Prince Louis of Battenberg, cancelled the demobilization order. By 28 July, when Austria declared war on Serbia, the Royal Navy had been put on a war footing. The following day, 29 July, the First Fleet sailed from Portland for its new war base in Scapa Flow, passing the Straits of Dover during the night with all ships blacked out. By 31 July it was at its battle stations, and the Second Fleet was busy assembling at Portland.

By evening on Saturday, 1 August, all the major powers were busy mobilizing. The next day the Germans seized a number of British merchant ships at Kiel, and with war now almost certain it was decided to replace the Commander-in-Chief of the First Fleet, George Callaghan, by Admiral Jellicoe. This was done because the First Lord felt that Admiral Callaghan's health would not stand up to the strains of a war. By 3 August the mobilization of the Royal Navy was complete, and the next day the Fleet was informed that the telegram ordering the start of hostilities against the Central Powers would be issued at midnight. Everything had been done, there was no surprise attack, and the Royal Navy was ready for its first major war since 1815.

Chapter 15

The Outbreak of War

On 3 August 1914, the Royal Navy completed mobilization for its first major war since 1815. All was prepared and the ships were on station ready for the commencement of hostilities at midnight. The German Navy could be met on a more than equal footing, or so it was thought. The Grand Fleet was full of confidence, and its morale had never been better; but these factors alone do not win wars or battles, as was soon to be seen. Events were to prove that in some respects the Navy was not as ready for war as some believed, and before it emerged victorious the Navy was to suffer serious setbacks and grievous losses in men and *matériel*.

Within a few weeks of the commencement of hostilities the Admiralty realized it was facing an enemy fully prepared and ready to use every means at its disposal for the prosecution of war. The German mine offensive made itself felt in no uncertain terms and found the Navy woefully short of minesweepers and lacking an efficient sweep. Other factors soon began to manifest themselves and created unease at home, where questions were asked as to whether the Navy was capable of defending the nation: certain sections of the press carried out a vigorous campaign of criticism over the conduct of naval operations. Sadly there were grounds for criticism. Amongst the charges levelled at the Admiralty were those of poor allocation and disposition of forces. These were made patently obvious when three obsolete cruisers were sunk in the North Sea, the South Atlantic Squadron was destroyed at Coronel, and when German battlecruisers raided the east coast ports with apparent impunity. Sub-

sequent actions were to highlight poor signalling arrangements and poor and inaccurate reporting of enemy forces, which led to lost opportunities. Early actions showed up the poor state of gunnery within the Grand Fleet, while tragic losses at Jutland pointed to other failings in the design of British battlecruisers.

On 4 August 1914, Great Britain declared war on Germany. Just three hours after the declaration, the navy grasped the initiative when two submarines, E6 and E8, carried out a reconnaissance of the Heligoland Bight and brought home a great deal of information concerning German warship movements in that area. As a result of this operation, the Harwich Force (First and Third Destroyer Flotillas under Commodore Reginald Tyrwhitt in the light cruiser *Amethyst*) left port on 5 August to carry out a sweep of the area. Soon after leaving Harwich a trawler informed Tyrwhitt that a suspicious vessel was in the area throwing unidentified objects overboard. The vessel, the minelayer *Königin Luise*, which had laid about 180 mines, was soon sighted by the destroyers *Lance* and *Landrail*, and was sunk in the brief ensuing action. The following morning, as the Harwich Force was returning from its sweep, the light cruiser *Amphion* struck two of the mines and sank within a few minutes.

As well as being the navy's first loss in the war, the *Amphion* was also the first to be sunk by mine. Although warship losses due to minelaying did not assume disastrous proportions, it was at once apparent that this form of warfare could put the navy at a serious disadvantage and might seriously disrupt the free flow of trade in

Left: The *Amphion*, a Scouting cruiser of the '*Active*' class, formed part of the Harwich Force and was the first warship to be lost by the Royal Navy during the First World War, and the first to be sunk by mine. (Tom Molland)

Above: Following a reconnaissance of the Heligoland Bight, the Harwich Force carrier out a sweep of the area which led to the first action between British and German forces at sea. (Tom Molland)

Right: The onset of the German minelaying campaign in 1914 found the navy without an effective mine countermeasures capability. Although warship losses from mines did not assume major proportions, the mining campaign did place a severe strain on the navy's resources as it attempted to ensure that the movement of merchant ships was not completely disrupted by the campaign. (Imperial War Museum)

merchant ships. To begin with, there was no permanently organized force of minesweepers (apart from ten converted torpedo gunboats and thirteen trawlers), although the navy had under charter 82 trawlers manned by fishing crews with merchant seamen officers of the RNR trained in minesweeping. Furthermore, very few arrangements had been made to combat mine warfare, in spite of the fact that a German minelaying campaign was one of the Admiralty's greatest fears; neither had much thought been given to countermining measures. All the Navy had at its disposal was seven old cruisers converted to carry 100 mines each; no modern vessels designed specifically for minelaying existed in the Royal Navy. This was hardly surprising for the navy did not possess an efficient mine, and total stocks in 1914 amounted to no more than 4,000, a completely inadequate number to lay defensive mine barriers around ports and anchorages, let alone involvement in offensive mine warfare. The mines available were of an old design which posed a greater danger to Britain than to the enemy. They were troublesome to lay (a number of minelayers losing their sterns through premature ignition); easily broke adrift whereupon their fail-safe devices often refused to become operative; and finally, when they were struck, they often failed to explode, those that did so failing to inflict serious damage.

With the onset of the German minelaying campaign in the autumn of 1914, the British Cabinet, supported by the Commander-in-Chief of the Grand Fleet, Admiral Jellicoe, and many naval officers, put forward plans for a British countermining offensive. These plans were opposed by the First Lord – Winston Churchill – and the Chief of the Admiralty War Staff, Henry Jackson, who were only prepared to sanction defensive anti-submarine mining off certain harbours and in certain defined areas around the British coast (the Dover Barrage being one such field laid to prevent submarines using the English Channel; it was, however, not as successful as had been hoped). There were many who felt that a large mining offensive would impede the navy's ability to conduct fleet and submarine operations. The Foreign Office was also against a mining offensive and considered that large-scale mining operations off

THE BATTLE OF HELIGOLAND BIGHT, 28 AUGUST 1914

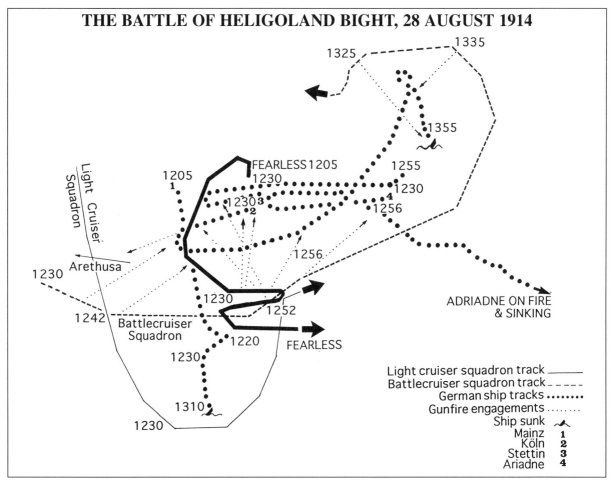

the European coast and in the North Sea would antagonize neutrals. These views held until 1917, by which time only three offensive minefields had been laid in the area of the Heligoland Bight.

At first the Admiralty was not greatly perturbed over the question of mine warfare. Their fears of a massive German minelaying campaign appeared to be unfounded, in spite of the fact that in its first action the Navy had sunk a minelayer and that the loss of the battleship *Audacious* in October 1914 was directly attributable to mine damage.

On 28 August came the first major action between the opposing navies. Early in the morning, just as it was getting light, the cruisers *Arethusa*, *Fearless* and twenty destroyers of the Harwich Force, carrying out a sweep off the coast of Heligoland, sighted dim shadows. These were identified as German destroyers, and soon after the *Arethusa* opened fire on a German cruiser. The action developed into a general mêlée, the British forces becoming rather scattered. The German fire was fairly accurate and the *Arethusa*, completed only three days previously, was soon hit and forced to haul out of line when only her forward 6in guns remained operational. The German

force also suffered casualties, a number of their destroyers being hit and a cruiser severely damaged. By this time the Admiralty had been informed of the action and the Battlecruiser Squadron was at once ordered to the assistance of the Harwich Force. At 1230 the *Lion* sighted the *Arethusa* and soon after opened fire on a German cruiser, which caught fire and disappeared sinking into the mist. As the remainder of the Battlecruiser Squadron came up, the Germans retired from the scene, leaving the cruiser *Mainz* in a sinking condition, a heap of wreckage where the *Köln* had already sunk, and the little *Ariadne* ablaze from stem to stern.

With only a month gone by, the Royal Navy had shown, in spite of some harsh queries from the British press as to what the Fleet was doing, that it was fulfilling its duty, protecting the sea lanes so that the merchant ships could bring vital imports to the country without interference from the High Seas Fleet.

The moral ascendancy gained by the navy on 28 August was rudely shattered the following month in very tragic circumstances. The failure in certain quarters of the Admiralty to appreciate the potential of the submarine to carry out offensive warfare, and the almost total lack of

Right: The first serious loss suffered by the Navy was the battleship *Audacious*, sunk on 27 October 1914. (Imperial War Museum)

means to counter a submarine attack effectively, was brought sharply into focus on 22 September, when in a very short space of time the old submarine *U9* sank the obsolete cruisers *Aboukir*, *Cressy* and *Hogue*.

These cruisers of the 'Bacchante' class formed part of the Seventh Cruiser Squadron, which was deployed to support the Harwich Force in keeping the area around the Dogger Bank and the Broad Fourteens to the south of it clear of German warships. On 21 September the destroyer patrols had been withdrawn, owing to bad weather, and the cruisers were called in to cover the potentially dangerous area of the Broad Fourteens on their own. In a mistaken effort to conserve coal, the officer commanding the squadron had decided to steer a steady course at about 10kts, and in this inviting situation (the high seas of the previous day having abated), *U9* found and sank the vessels early on 22 September. The first to be sunk was the *Aboukir*, and she was quickly followed to the bottom

when the other two vessels, in an error of judgement, stopped to lower boats and rescue survivors.

Towards the end of October the Navy was beginning to feel the strain of continuous concentrated operations against Germany. Admiralty policy laid down in 1889 (see page 61 had stated that the battleship strength of the Royal Navy was to be twice that of any possible opponent. The opponent now was Germany, whose Fleet at this time had a strength of fifteen dreadnoughts and five battlecruisers. The strength of the Royal Navy, on the other hand, was nowhere near what the Admiralty had hoped it would be under the Two Power Standard. The strain of war operations had begun to take its toll, and although Britain had lost only one battleship (*Audacious*), three others for various reasons, mainly connected with machinery problems, were in dire need of dockyard attention; while two more just commissioned (the *Benbow* and *Emperor of India*) were not yet ready for active service. In addition, one of the bat-

Right: The dangers from submarine attack began to strike home in a very dramatic way towards the latter part of 1914. The picture shows the cruiser *Hermes* sinking after being torpedoed in the English Channel on 31 October by the submarine *U 27*. (ACPL)

tlecruisers was in dry dock undergoing refit. This left the Grand Fleet with a total of seventeen dreadnoughts and five battlecruisers to meet any possible threat from the High Seas Fleet — a margin of superiority which, under favourable circumstances for a German attack, could have led to disaster. The strength of the Grand Fleet was soon to be further weakened when the *Inflexible* and *Invincible* were detached to track down Von Spee in the South Atlantic (see page 96). The Grand Fleet was, however, due to be reinforced by two new dreadnoughts (*Queen Elizabeth* and *Warspite*) and a battlecruiser (*Tiger*), but these could not be counted as fully operational until they had completed working up.

On top of these problems, the submarine menace suddenly affected the ability of the Grand Fleet to carry out operations. The main base was at Scapa Flow in the Orkneys, where the fleet conducted gunnery and torpedo exercises. It was in an ideal position for war against Germany. However, owing to lack of foresight and ignorance of the possibilities of submarine warfare and, as Churchill had claimed, to the potential problem of heavy expenditure in peacetime, nothing had been done to provide the base with any anti-submarine defences. Nor had any other port on the east coast of England or Scotland been prepared as a naval base. At Scapa there was a complete lack of nets, booms, minefields, coastal fortifications or searchlights, except for a few blockships and guns sited by Jellicoe, and which were completely inadequate for the task in hand. With the very real dangers from submarine attack now becoming apparent (the loss of the *Aboukir*, *Cressy* and *Hogue*, the cruiser *Hawke* sunk on 15 October and the abortive attack of *U15* on the First Light Cruiser Squadron when she was rammed and sunk by the *Birmingham*), Jellicoe became very apprehensive regarding the safety of the Grand Fleet. His anxiety was further heightened on 16 October, the day he received news of the loss of the *Hawke*, when a report was received of the sighting of a submarine periscope inside the anchorage at Scapa. At the time only four battleships were in the base,

and they put to sea at once. But the fear of a submarine attack inside the unprotected base took hold, and numerous sightings of periscopes were claimed, although in actual fact only one submarine — *U18* -managed to penetrate Hoxa Sound on 23 November 1914. The numerous false scares and lack of adequate anti-submarine defences finally forced Jellicoe to move the Grand Fleet to the safer anchorage of Lough Swilly in Northern Ireland.

The mine menace also assumed threatening proportions, and it was soon apparent that the 82 chartered minesweeping trawlers were completely inadequate in number to cope with the indiscriminate mining carried out by the Germans. Consequently vast numbers of trawlers and drifters were requisitioned for minesweeping duties, and by the end of September 1914 nearly every major port was provided with a flotilla of these vessels. They were not, however, capable of providing protection for the fleet at sea. Fortunately there was an invention available that could be fitted to warships which could provide a measure of protection against the mine while steaming at sea. This device, the paravane, consisted of a wire with a cutter at the end. This was trailed from the bows of a warship, and the forward motion of the vessel forced the mine aside, where it was caught by the wire of the paravane and pulled to the cutter at the end, which severed the mine from its mooring wire. The mine then floated to the surface to be destroyed by rifle fire. By May 1915 the paravane was ready for trials and proved so successful that in time all capital ships and cruisers were fitted with it.

By October 1914 the Admiralty's conduct of the war at sea was increasingly coming under fire, both in the press and in parliament — and even within the Fleet itself. The actions of the First Lord, Churchill, came in for a great deal of criticism. His own attitude engendered mistrust

Below: At the start of the war submarines were ordered in large numbers. The 'E' class boats particularly distinguished themselves under daring commanders. (ACPL)

Above: The standard sweep of the First World War was the A type. This consisted of a 2.5in wire whose depth was regulated by a 'kite' towed in the water between two vessels about 500 yards apart. The speed of the sweep was deemed sufficient to cut a mooring wire, but it was found that trawlers had insufficient speed to accomplish this. Generally a trawler would circle a mine with its sweep and either drag the mine out to sea or else beach it where it would be destroyed by gunfire. In 1916 a serrated sweep wire was introduced which enabled even slow sweepers to cut a mine free. In time, as many as seven or eight sweepers working abreast were used to clear a path through a minefield. The picture shows the A sweep gear at the stern of the 'Acacia' class fleet sweeping sloop *Primrose* in 1917. (ACPL)

amongst his cabinet colleagues and hatred from the opposition, and his position at the Admiralty became very unstable. The series of reverses suffered by the Navy, and in particular the losses of warships and men, led the public to believe, contrary to the real facts, that the Navy was in severe trouble. The actual *matériel* value of the vessels lost up to that time was small, for nearly all were obsolete; but the shocking losses of men were such that they could not be quickly or easily replaced.

The press were the first to do battle with the Admiralty, certain sections making much of the fact that the First Sea Lord, Prince Louis of Battenburg, was a German by birth. He was in a most vulnerable position, but this failed to deter him from his duty and devotion to the Navy; the cause of the reverses suffered could in no way have been laid upon him. The King greatly valued the loyalty of Prince Louis to his adopted country, Britain, but to the ordinary man in the street he was a German, and that was sufficient. Eventually, the public outcry became so great that to save further embarrassment Prince Louis resigned his post. There now followed a great

discussion as to who should be his successor. The First Lord suggested that Fisher be recalled as First Sea Lord, and he was backed in his proposal by the Prime Minister, Herbert Asquith. The King, however, was not in favour of Fisher and put forward a number of other suggestions, all of which were rejected by Churchill and Asquith. Finally the King agreed to accept Fisher, but made known his feelings concerning the admiral and the fact that he felt the navy did not take kindly to Fisher or his methods. (See Fisher's resignation from the Admiralty, page 80). The country, however, was overjoyed to find that a man with the energy and drive of Fisher was back at the Admiralty. Public confidence in the navy returned, and the furore against Churchill died down as it was felt that Fisher would be able to check some of the First Lord's more hair-brained schemes. True to his old form, Fisher made a number of changes to the Admiralty War Staff, most of which were fortunately for the better.

Apart from shaking up the Admiralty, Fisher also breathed new life into the shipyards, and a vast programme of warship construction was embarked upon. Fearing the war would last some time, large numbers of new destroyers were laid down (22 'M' class in November 1914, 18 'M' class in February 1915 and a further 22 in May 1915). In addition Fisher put forward plans for greater use of that 'ungentlemanly weapon' the submarine, development of which had sadly been allowed to fall behind under Commodore Keyes' direction, or so Fisher thought. Submarines were ordered in large numbers — 37 'E', and eight 'G' in November 1914. That as yet still barely appreciated weapon of war, the aeroplane, was also given a boost. A soon as he took office Fisher undertook the study of the possibilities of air warfare vis-a-vis the naval aspect, and in June 1915 a number of non-rigid airships, or blimps were ordered.

This foresightedness on Fisher's part was to pay dividends later in the war, especially in 1917 at the height of the U-boat campaign, when airships were used to scout for submarines. These first blimps were just a bag filled with gas under which was slung under the fuselage of a BE2C aircraft powered by a Renault engine. They had an endurance of eight hours at 45mph, and 29 were operational by the end of 1915. Also in November, Fisher purchased the old Cunard liner *Campania*, then at the shipbreakers, and plans were drawn up and conversion begun to fit the vessel out as a seaplane carrier, with a

flight deck over the forecastle from which the aircraft could be launched. This would give the aircraft of the RNAS the flexibility they lacked at that time, for although the Admiralty had three seaplane carriers already operational (*Empress*, *Engadine* and *Riviera*) they had no flight deck, and launching had always to be carried out from the sea with resultant restrictions according to the prevailing sea state. Owing to the fragile construction of the seaplanes, flying operations could only be conducted when there was a dead flat calm, a situation which severely hampered the development of air operations. It was intended that the *Campania* should operate with the Grand Fleet, her seaplanes carrying out reconnaissance missions and attacking Zeppelins scouting over the Fleet.

Above: For defence against aircraft attack, warships were equipped with kite balloons. The picture shows the '*Arabis*' class sloop *Pentstemon* with a balloon in 1917. (ACPL)

Left: The light cruiser *Pegasus* beached and abandoned at Zanzibar after being shelled by the German light cruiser *Königsberg* on 20 September 1914. (ACPL)

Chapter 16

Coronel and the Falklands

While Fisher was involved in introducing new technology into the fleet at home, events were building up to a climax in the Atlantic. From the numbers of merchant vessels reported overdue, the Admiralty knew that raiders were at large, but by far the greatest threat came from Admiral Von Spee's Far East Squadron, which was heading across the Pacific for Cape Horn, to enter the Atlantic in an attempt to reach Germany. The Admiral on the South Atlantic Station, Admiral Craddock, had under his command the obsolete and newly commissioned armoured cruisers *Good Hope* and *Monmouth*, crewed mainly by eager reservists and no match for the fast modern vessels of Von Spee's Squadron; the obsolete battleship *Canopus*, which it had been intended to scrap in 1915 and which could steam no faster (so her Engineer Commander reported) than 12kts (she could and did in fact manage 16.5kts); the cruiser *Glasgow* and the armed merchant cruiser *Otranto*. Craddock's orders were to watch the west coast of South America for Von Spee while Admiral Stoddart kept an eye on the east coast.

Just after midday on 1 November 1914, while the British squadron (less *Canopus*, 300 miles astern coaling and convoying colliers) was cruising off the port of Coronel, *Glasgow* sighted smoke. Craddock had found Von Spee, but concentrated in strength contrary to his expectations. The outcome of the action, which Craddock could have avoided had he wished to do so, and which the newly appointed Board of Admiralty led by Fisher had sought desperately to avoid, was a foregone conclusion. The undergunned *Good Hope* and *Monmouth*, having had no chance to carry out gunnery drills, were no match for *Scharnhorst* and *Gneisenau*, the most proficient gunnery ships in the Kaiser's navy. The Germans avoided the British moves to join action until after sunset, when Craddock's Squadron was clearly silhouetted in the twilight. It was not long before *Good Hope* was seriously damaged, but even so she managed to return the enemy's fire before she finally blew up and sank. *Monmouth*, also seriously damaged, drifted away from the action only to be found and sunk later by the *Nürnberg*. *Otranto*, realizing her limitations in such an action, kept well out of range, while *Glasgow* miraculously escaped serious damage and managed to elude the German squadron to inform *Canopus*, heading to the scene of the action, and the Admiralty, of the disaster.

With this event coming so soon upon the earlier losses, British naval pride suffered a very serious blow from which it did not recover for some time. Not even the sinking in the Far East of the outstandingly successful raider *Emden* by *Sydney*, nor the final destruction of the cruiser *Königsberg* in the Rufiji river, after a long siege involving the use of monitors and seaplanes, helped to restore neutral and home opinion on the might of the Royal Navy. The fact that Craddock's Squadron was not nearly so powerful as had been thought, or that the loss of two obsolete vessels made little difference to the materiel strength of the navy, failed to influence public opinion at home regarding the conduct of naval affairs.

With Craddock's Squadron destroyed, Von Spee was free to attack merchant shipping along both the east and west coasts of South America, to go to the assistance of German land forces in South Africa, or to speed north, pass through the Panama Canal and escape home to Germany. To guard against the last, the battlecruiser *Princess Royal* was detached from the Grand Fleet to guard the exit routes from the canal, while cruiser reinforcements were sent to the South Atlantic to cover the African coastline. The gravest and most immediate problem, however, concerned the rich shipping lanes off the South American coast. To cover this area Fisher secretly ordered Jellicoe to

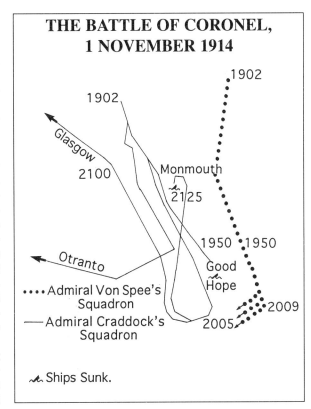

THE BATTLE OF CORONEL, 1 NOVEMBER 1914

1902
1902
Glasgow 2100
Monmouth 2125
Otranto
1950 1950
Good Hope
2005 2009

•••• Admiral Von Spee's Squadron

— Admiral Craddock's Squadron

⚓ Ships Sunk.

release the battlecruisers *Invincible* and *Inflexible* from the Grand Fleet. They were placed under the command of Vice-Admiral Sturdee, who was given *carte blanche* in the Atlantic and South Pacific to seek out Von Spee and destroy him. Sturdee was made senior officer of the whole area, with authority to give orders to any other British officer who came within his sphere of action, a move unprecedented in Admiralty procedure.

Sturdee worked his way down the east coast of South America towards the Falkland Islands, and arrived at Port Stanley on the morning of 7 December. The following morning the Squadron (*Invincible, Inflexible, Bristol, Carnarvon, Glasgow, Kent, Cornwall* and *Macedonia*) began coaling in relays. While this was in progress the wireless station set up on the island by the crew of *Canopus*, which on Fisher's orders had been grounded in the inner harbour of Port Stanley to act as a fort, reported two unidentified warships approaching the island from the south.

Sturdee was in a dangerous situation. His vessels were very low on coal, and only *Carnarvon* and *Glasgow* had completed coaling. *Bristol* had drawn her fires and *Cornwall* was carrying out engine repairs and would be unable to sail for six hours, while *Invincible* was in the midst of coaling. It was in this compromising situation that Von Spee found the British Squadron. But surprise was not all on the British side, for Von Spee had expected to find only *Canopus* and *Glasgow*. He was horrified when lookouts reported sighting two sets of tripod masts, for this could mean only one thing – British battlecruisers – and

Von Spee knew that in spite of his superb gunnery he would be no match for such vessels. Not only was he faced by a force at least the equal of his own, but, owing to the heavy expenditure of ammunition during the Battle of Coronel, he was in no state to engage in another major action, for *Scharnhorst* had only 350 8in shells in her magazine, and *Gneisenau* 528.

Canopus was first to open fire, her second salvo straddling *Gneisenau*, which turned and headed out to sea to meet the rest of Von Spee's squadron coming up from the south. Two hours later all of the British Squadron, except *Bristol*, had raised steam and were engaged in a general chase of Von Spee, who was heading southeast at top speed. The action gradually settled down to a stern chase, with the light cruisers lagging behind *Invincible* and *Inflexible*. Slowly the two battlecruisers overhauled Von Spee, opening fire on the rearmost cruiser, *Leipzig*, just after midday. At this Von Spee ordered his light cruisers to scatter and escape to South America where they could become raiders, while he headed out into the ocean at top speed in an effort to draw off Sturdee.

The ruse failed, for in accordance with instructions the British light cruisers gave chase to the German cruisers, while the battlecruisers continued to pursue Von Spee. The action continued intermittently, but after about two hours the fire from *Scharnhorst* suddenly slackened and she rapidly lost speed. The ship was soon reduced to

Below: The *Invincible* seen working up to full speed during the chase at the Battle of the Falklands, 8 December 1914. (ACPL)

wreckage, and about 2½hr after the opening of the action she capsized and sank, taking her entire crew with her. *Gneisenau* continued to return an ineffectual fire on the British force, but her fate was already sealed and, about 1½hr after *Scharnhorst* sank, *Gneisenau* followed her to the bottom.

In the meantime the British light cruisers had continued to overhaul the German cruisers, *Nürnberg* being sunk by *Kent*, while *Leipzig* was pounded into a wreck which finally sank about an hour later, at 2035.

At the end of the battle only *Dresden* remained afloat to harass merchant shipping. The disaster at Coronel had been avenged, but the lesson learnt, namely that modern efficient warships of the Royal Navy should always be concentrated in sufficient strength in areas of action, was not always put into practice. Tactically, the action was not the success it should have been, and Fisher was furious with Sturdee for allowing *Dresden* to escape. The lack of an effective system of fire control and the need for more intensive gunnery practice was not, unfortunately,

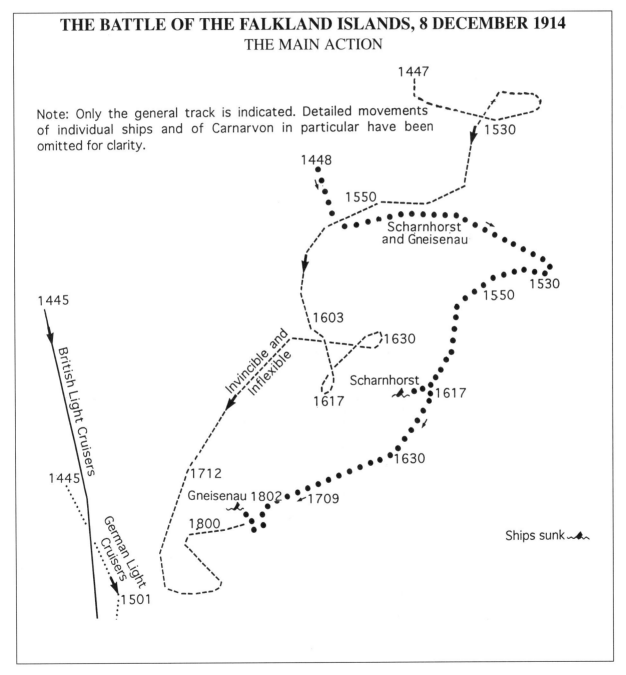

THE BATTLE OF THE FALKLAND ISLANDS, 8 DECEMBER 1914
THE MAIN ACTION

Note: Only the general track is indicated. Detailed movements of individual ships and of Carnarvon in particular have been omitted for clarity.

1447

1530

1448

1550

Scharnhorst and Gneisenau

1530

1550

1445

British Light Cruisers

1603

1630

Invincible and Inflexible

Scharnhorst

1617

1617

1630

1712

Gneisenau 1802

1709

1800

German Light Cruisers

1445

1501

Ships sunk

Above: The *Invincible* and *Inflexible* seen from the *Kent* at about 1100 on 8 December at the Battle of the Falklands. (Imperial War Museum)

made abundantly clear at the time. Strategically, however, the action was a brilliant success, and there were now no German forces of any significance left at sea to attack merchant shipping.

Following the successful conclusion of the Falkland Islands battle, Fisher was more than ever convinced that the potential of the battlecruiser just could not be ignored, and he obtained Cabinet approval for the construction of two more. At this time Fisher had devised a pet scheme known as the Baltic Project. In essence, the plan was to land an army on the Baltic coast and attack Germany from the rear. To support such a force he required large numbers of vessels of all types, including heavy ships of shallowish draught with high speed and powerful gun armament. The battlecruiser concept was ideal, and it was perhaps with this project in mind that Fisher ordered the two vessels of the 'Renown' class. As previously, protection was to be sacrificed completely to speed and armament (32kts and six 15in guns). Work on the design began in December 1914, and the two ships were laid down on 25 January 1915 for delivery, as Fisher requested, in only fifteen months. In fact *Repulse* was completed in nineteen months and *Renown* in twenty. Unfortunately the ships were so lacking in armour and general strengthening that the first time they fired their guns they severely strained their hulls.

Two months after the 'Renown' class had been laid down, Fisher laid down a further three vessels, designed specifically for the Baltic Project. To obtain Cabinet approval, as no more money was to be made available for large armoured ships, Fisher described the new vessels as large light cruisers. The First Sea Lord specified that the three vessels (two 'Courageous' class and *Furious*) should carry only a few guns of the largest calibre practicable, and have only light cruiser protection, a speed of no less than 32kts, and a maximum draught of 22ft to enable them to operate in the shallow confines of the Baltic Sea where the High Seas Fleet could not follow them. The vessels were so thinly armoured to meet these specifications that they were vulnerable to a dangerous degree to any shell of 6in or larger. Owing to the Baltic Project never being implemented these ships, together with the 'Renown' class, were put to uses for which they were never intended, although many of the other 612 special vessels Fisher had built for his Baltic Project proved invaluable in the Dardanelles campaign.

When completed, in January 1917, the 'Courageous' class mounted four 15in guns in twin turrets and eighteen 4in in triple mounts, and were the first large vessels to be completed with all-geared turbines. *Furious* was completed in July 1917, and mounted one 18in gun and eleven 5.5in guns. (She was designed to carry two 18in guns, but in the meantime the Baltic Project had faded into obscurity and, as there was a crying need for fast aircraft carriers, *Furious* was redesigned and completed with a flight deck forward in place of the single 18in gun.)

Chapter 17

The East Coast Raids

On 3 November 1914 there occurred the first of a number of hit-and-run raids on the East Coast of England by powerful squadrons of the High Seas Fleet. These raids spotlighted many deficiencies in the navy, not the least being the poor disposition of forces covering the East Coast and the North Sea. Other failings were also highlighted, namely poor signalling arrangements between units of the Grand Fleet and, had they been recognized at the time, certain grave faults in the design of our battlecruisers. The first raid on the port of Yarmouth was in fact a cover for a minelaying operation which the Admiralty felt was the prelude to a much larger operation, possibly even an invasion of the East Coast.

The Germans planned a far more ambitious raid for the middle of December. With the knowledge that two battlecruisers had been detached from the Grand Fleet to track down Von Spee off South America (see page 96), and knowing the narrow margin of superiority the Grand Fleet held over the High Seas Fleet, especially in the battlecruiser category, it was decided to stage a bombardment of Scarborough and Hartlepool with the five battlecruisers of Admiral Hipper's Scouting Group, while at the same time carrying out yet another mining operation. The raid was to be covered by the High Seas Fleet, which would be in position in the North Sea. The purpose of the raid was to lure a section of the Grand Fleet away from Scapa to the East Coast, where it would run into a minefield to be laid by the *Kolberg*. Should the British force escape and follow Hipper's squadron, it would run into the High Seas Fleet and be annihilated.

Fortunately, owing to the capture of the German naval codes early in the war by the Russians, who passed them on to the British, the Admiralty were aware that an operation was planned, but were not able to divine its purpose. Nor were they aware of the fact that the High Seas Fleet would be coming out in support. The Admiralty laid its plans, and Jellicoe ordered Admiral Beatty and the Battlecruiser Squadron to catch the German vessels on their way home after the raid. In addition, the most powerful battle squadron of the Grand Fleet (the Second, with six dreadnoughts under the command of Vice-Admiral Warrender, who was also in overall command of the British forces) and two cruiser and one destroyer flotillas were sent to the area in support. As well as this powerful force, eight submarines were to be in position off Terschelling, while Commodore Tyrwhitt and the Harwich Force were sent to the area off Yarmouth to await orders. Jellicoe wished to send the whole of the Grand Fleet to catch the German squadron, but was overruled in this by the Admiralty.

Just before dawn on 15 December the destroyer flotilla, which had become separated from the Second Battle Squadron, met up with an outlying destroyer screening the High Seas Fleet. Instead of trapping the German battlecruiser squadron as they had hoped, the British forces were in grave danger of becoming trapped by the whole of the High Seas Fleet. For a while the two fleets steamed on parallel courses about 10 miles apart, but owing to poor shadowing reports the Second Battle Squadron was unaware of the proximity of the High Seas Fleet. Fearing a torpedo attack, the German commander, whose advanced units continued sparring with the British destroyers, turned for home and was promptly chased by Beatty, who was under the impression that he was only overhauling the German battlecruisers. At this point Beatty received reports that battlecruisers were bombarding Scarborough, and he at once reversed course for the port, to be closely followed by Warrender.

The bombardment of Scarborough, Whitby and Hartlepool had accomplished little apart from the destruction of a number of houses and the killing and wounding of a few civilians. But it had succeeded in its main purpose, that of drawing a part of the Grand Fleet away from its base and into an area where the High Seas Fleet was waiting for it. However, the fear of torpedo attack from the British destroyers had forced the High Seas Fleet to run for home before it had even begun the task for which it had sailed. Although the Germans had failed to inflict any material damage on the British squadron, they had dealt another severe blow to British morale, especially to the people along the East Coast.

The German battlecruisers, their part in the action successfully accomplished, set course for Germany, unaware that the High Seas Fleet had fled. Nor was Hipper aware that Beatty and Warrender were heading for what they thought was Hipper's only exit through the minefields off Whitby. In case Hipper decided to retire north between the minefield and the East Coast, Jellicoe ordered the Third Battle Squadron to cover the area. The tables had now been turned on the German forces, and it was they who were caught in a trap. Unfortunately, the relative positions of Beatty and Warrender forced them to pass north and south respectively of the shallow part of the Dogger Bank, and at this point they lost sight of each other.

Soon after this, rain reduced overall visibility to 4,000yd, then Goodenough in *Southampton* sighted part of Hipper's advance screen. Goodenough ordered his squadron to close, and with *Birmingham* began to engage

THE BATTLE OF THE DOGGER BANK, 24 JANUARY 1915

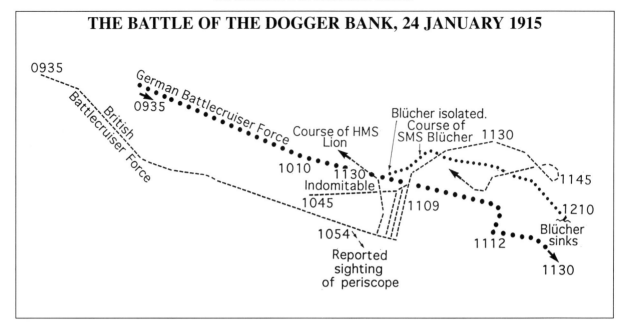

the Germans, but the order was countermanded by Beatty, who wished to retain part of the squadron for his screen. Owing to a signalling error, Goodenough took Beatty's order to mean that the whole of his squadron was to disengage and resume scouting ahead of Beatty. Hipper, unaware of the British forces in the vicinity, altered course to support his screen. But for Goodenough's reluctant action in breaking contact, Beatty would have been able to engage Hipper. Contact was regained by the Second Battle Squadron, but Hipper managed to escape northward in the rain squalls which now sped across the area.

The first year of the war ended with a raid carried out on Christmas Day by seaplanes of the Royal Naval Air Service. The aircraft, Short seaplanes carried aboard *Empress*, *Engadine*, and *Riviera* bombed the Zeppelin sheds at Cuxhaven and flew over the High Seas Fleet anchored in Schillig Roads, their sudden appearance causing the fleet to put hurriedly to sea.

The year 1915 opened full of promise for the Royal Navy's efforts to contain the High Seas Fleet. The navy had lost a number of warships, but they were nearly all obsolete and of little fighting value and the materiel losses were inconsequential. The resulting manpower losses, however, were grievous, but they too were made good, and the strength of the Fleet was maintained at a level more or less sufficient to meet the High Seas Fleet on an equal footing should it ever venture into the North Sea.

The German Commander-in-Chief, Admiral von Ingenohl, was hamstrung by the Kaiser's wish that the High Seas Fleet should maintain its strength, and that risks were not taken which might entail the loss of a warship. This greatly restricted Ingenohl's movements, but

he did manage to wring a concession from the Kaiser, allowing sorties to be made into the North Sea with the aim of attracting part of the Grand Fleet into a trap where it could be annihilated. This had already been tried in December 1914 and had almost succeeded (see above).

Following the sighting of Beatty's forces in the North Sea on 19 January 1915, Ingenohl ordered the Scouting Force under Hipper to ascertain the extent of British operations in the area of the Dogger Bank, and to destroy any forces sighted. Beatty, forewarned by the Admiralty, who had read the German coded signals that they would sail on 23 January, left Rosyth towards evening with the First and Second Battlecruiser Squadrons and the First Light Cruiser Squadron, while the Harwich Force sailed to rendezvous with him the following morning. The Third Battle Squadron and the Third Cruiser Squadron also left Rosyth to cover the East Coast and provide distant support for Beatty. Late in the evening of 23 January, the Admiralty further ordered the Grand Fleet to leave Scapa to carry out a sweep of the southern North Sea and to cover the East Coast. Thus it was that the Admiralty left Beatty and the Harwich Force to intercept the Germans, while the remaining forces covered the East Coast.

Early on the morning of 24 January, Beatty's forces reached the area where interception with the German force had been anticipated, and the Harwich Force arrived soon after. The first to sight the enemy was the cruiser *Aurora*, which reported its presence to Beatty in *Lion*. Beatty altered course towards the Germans while his cruisers and destroyers started shadowing, reporting the composition and course of the German force.

The action soon settled down to a long stern chase as the Germans turned and headed for home. Gradually the rearmost German cruiser, *Blücher*, was overhauled, and at 0852 *Lion* fired the first shot of the action at a range of about 20,000yd (up to that time an unheard-of range, 16,000yd on an experimental shoot in the spring of 1914 being the greatest range achieved up to that time). Twenty minutes later *Lion* hit *Blücher* for the first time. As the British squadron came abeam the Germans, Beatty ordered his squadron to concentrate fire on their opposite numbers.

Lion became the principle target of the German squadron and received a number of hits, one piercing her armour belt and allowing salt water to contaminate the port fuel tank, causing the port engine to be stopped. As *Lion* hauled out of line, Beatty signalled the other ships to close the German squadron. When Beatty had fallen some two miles astern of the rest of his squadron a seaman reported sighting a submarine to starboard.

Believing that his squadron was heading into a submarine trap, and remembering Jellicoe's Battle Orders, which stressed the dangers of allowing British forces to be drawn into an area possibly infested with mines and submarines, Beatty ordered a turn to port. Compliance with this order unfortunately forced the British ships to break off the action. There then occurred a most unfortunate situation. *Lion* had already suffered numerous hits and was left with only two sets of signal halyards; the dynamos had all ceased functioning, and there was no power for the searchlights or wireless. With the British squadron astern of the Germans, Beatty ordered his ships to attack the rear of the enemy. However, this signal was mistakenly hauled down together with the previous signal ordering a turn to port. The British squadron, unaware of Beatty's preoccupation with a possible submarine attack, read the two signals as one and bore away to the northeast (to port) after the rear of the only German vessel in that quarter, *Blücher*, by then well on fire and sinking.

Owing to the smoke emitted by *Lion*, Beatty's final signal, 'Keep nearer the enemy', was obscured and the squadron continued to pound the luckless *Blücher* for target practice while the remainder of Hipper's force was able to escape unmolested. By the time Beatty had managed to transfer his flag to *Princess Royal* and resume tactical command it was too late to catch up with Hipper, and he was forced to turn back for Rosyth.

Following this rather abortive action, a number of technical and administrative improvements were made to warships of the Royal Navy. At long last the Admiralty came to appreciate the potential value of an integrated fire control system controlled from a central director tower. Such a system had first been devised by Admiral Percy Scott, but it was not until the action of the Dogger Bank in January 1915, and the atrocious gunnery of the newly commissioned *Tiger*, that the question of the advisability of fitting a fire control system was precipitated. (It so happened that *Tiger* was provided with a rudimentary fire control system, being the only British vessel in the action so equipped.) Further to the poor gunnery of *Tiger* (she mistook *Lion*'s fall of shot on Hipper's flagship, *Seydlitz*, for her own, which were 3,000yd over, and instead of concentrating on her opposite number, *Moltke*, she concentrated on *Seydlitz*, which was also the target of *Lion*), Admiral Jellicoe's Battle Orders regarding the concentration of fire were reworded so that no confusion could arise in the future as to which target a ship should engage, and all vessels of the Grand Fleet henceforth paid greater attention to gunnery practice. The unfortunate misinterpretation of Beatty's signals resulted in the fitting of an extra wireless set and improvements to the signalling arrangements.

Right: On Christmas Day 1914, three seaplanes carriers, the *Empress*, *Engadine* (shown here) and the *Riviera* launched seaplanes which carried out a raid on the Zeppelin sheds at Cuxhaven. (ACPL)

Chapter 18

The Submarine Campaign Begins

February 1915 saw the start of the German submarine campaign, which in 1917 was to reach such proportions and cause such heavy losses to the world's merchant fleet, much of which was used to bring vital supplies to Britain, that at one time it was thought that Britain might be forced to sue for peace. Unfortunately, owing to lack of foresight in certain quarters at the Admiralty, the navy totally lacked any means with which to combat the submarine. There was no suitable equipment for detecting submarines or destroying them. Finally the Admiralty was forced to revert to sailing ships in convoy, when an immediate drop in losses became apparent. The Admiralty's stubborn refusal to accept the concept of the convoy as a suitable means by which some measure of protection could be afforded to merchant shipping had led to the grievous losses.

On 2 February Germany at last made known her intentions regarding the opening of a submarine campaign, and announced that from 18 February 1915 any enemy merchant ship found in waters surrounding Great Britain and Ireland, or in the English Channel, would be sunk. Germany pointed out that although the vessels of neutral nations would not be included in this directive, it would not always be possible for a submarine to distinguish between a neutral and one sailing under the British flag. This was total warfare, in which the submarine would not necessarily surface to warn her intended victim of the fate about to befall her, but would in all probability torpedo

any such vessel found within the prescribed area from a submerged position. This edict was made in a desperate effort to break the Royal Navy's blockade of Germany, which was having severe economic repercussions within the country.

The Admiralty was ill prepared to meet a large-scale attack on merchant shipping. An Admiralty committee had been studying anti-submarine warfare before the war, but was disbanded when war broke out. It was, however, reconvened on 1 December 1914. The navy was totally without means of detecting submarines, except by look-outs, a most inefficient method which resulted in numerous unfounded scares or missed sightings which led to tragic losses. A weapon to attack the submarine, the depth charge, had been invented early in the war, but development and production was slow. Apart from a number of ludicrous suggestions and inventions put forward to combat the submarine menace, the only really practical idea used extensively during the first year of war was the explosive sweep. By late 1915 no means of detecting submarines had been invented, and until a suitable system was devised, all ideas for destroying submarines were virtually useless.

Forewarned by the German declaration, the best the Admiralty could do was to suggest that merchant ships timed their arrival and departure from ports to coincide with the hours of darkness. The convoy system, used with success in previous wars through the centuries when the

Left: At the start of her submarine campaign in 1915, Germany only had four submarines ready for sea. One of these, *U 8*, sank five steamers in the English Channel during the first few weeks, but was herself sunk on 4 March 1915 by the destroyers *Gurkha* and *Maori*. Boats are seen picking up the survivors of the U-boat. (Imperial War Museum)

merchant fleet was facing destruction, was totally ignored, and indeed was discounted as probably being ineffective. Furthermore, shipowners were loath to sail their vessels in convoy as it would entail loss of revenue when vessels were forced to wait for a convoy to assemble, and when the convoy had to proceed at speeds often well below the best economic speeds of individual ships. From the Admiralty's point of view convoys were regarded as impractical as there were insufficient escorts available to protect them, and those destroyers that were available could not be spared from their duties protecting the Grand Fleet. It was felt, therefore, that unprotected convoys, in which a large number of vessels were assembled in a relatively small area, would provide excellent targets for submarines.

Fortunately for Britain, Germany started her submarine campaign with just twenty submarines, of which only four were immediately ready for sea. But these were sufficient, for during the first few weeks of the campaign *U8* sank five steamers in the Channel, and *U20* and *U27* between them sank another six ships. Up to the end of April a total of 57 submerged attacks were made on merchantmen in which 38 vessels were sunk, and a further 50 vessels were sunk by gunfire out of a total of 93 vessels attacked, and all this for the loss of just five submarines. Even more ominous was the fact that 25 submarines entered service during this period. If such a situation were to continue, sheer numbers of submarines could overwhelm the merchant fleet, and the rate of sinkings might well outstrip the ability of the shipyards to replace losses.

Then, on 7 May 1915, came the sinking of the Cunard liner *Lusitania*, with the loss of 1,198 lives, off the southern coast of Ireland. The Germans claimed that the ship had been armed and was carrying arms, and that as such she was a legitimate target. The *Lusitania* was carrying a large number of Americans, and the sinking caused a serious deterioration in German/American relations, so much so that German submarines were henceforth ordered to exercise greater restraint when carrying out attacks against liners of any nationality, and to be much more careful where ships flying the American flag were concerned. At this time America was still neutral, and Germany had no wish to bring her into the war. Gradually the submarine campaign gathered momentum. Between June and July German submarines sank between 40 and 50 ships in the war zone, of which 41 were British.

On 19 June *U24* sank the White Star liner *Arabic* with the loss of 42 passengers, including three Americans. This led to a further deterioration in relations, and for a time the resulting diplomatic moves saved Britain from further serious losses, for German submarine commanders were thenceforth ordered not to sink any passenger vessels without first warning the ship and then ensuring that passengers and crew were all safe before sinking the vessel. This procedure meant that the submarines had to surface, exposing themselves to attack by surface vessels. As a result the campaign slackened to such an extent that by the end of 1915 there were only about six submarines at sea. During the year 748,000 tons of British merchant shipping had been sunk for the loss of only twenty U-boats. A temporary respite had been gained by the expedient of requisitioning a number of rusty old tramps and arming them with guns disguised as hatch covers, coamings, etc, so that they could be used as anti-submarine vessels. These decoy, or 'Q' ships as they were known, achieved a number of successes, but after one or two submarines had escaped from the traps to disclose their secret the success of the 'Q' ships was reduced.

Right: On 7 May 1915 the Cunard liner *Lusitania*, carrying 1,951 passengers and crew, was sunk by *U 20*. Only 761 people were saved. (Tom Molland)

Chapter 19

The Dardanelles

During 1915 a terrible tragedy began to unfold in the Mediterranean, leading to events which were to have repercussions on the whole of the British war effort. The struggle for the command of the Dardanelles was to prove a dismal failure of British arms, and showed grave failings on the part of the Admiralty, a lack of initiative amongst the leaders of the future expedition, and above all divided support from the Government at home.

On the same day that the Germans bombarded Scarborough (15 December 1914), a combined British and French squadron began a bombardment in the Mediterranean that was to signal the start of a long and unsuccessful struggle by the Allies for the command of the Dardanelles and the entrance to the Black Sea. The bombardment was carried out in retaliation for a raid against Russian Black Sea ports by *Goeben* and *Breslau*. These two ships were now operating from Turkish ports, whence they had sailed after units of the British Mediterranean Fleet had unsuccessfully tried to prevent their passage to Turkey in August, thus swaying the Turks into joining the war on the side of the Central Powers.

Following the bombardment, the Government had been persuaded that the Royal Navy would be able to force the Narrows, enter the Sea of Marmara and proceed to Constantinople, seat of the Turkish Empire, and so force the Turks to seek an armistice. With Turkey out of the war, a vital sea route to Russia would be opened. Furthermore, it might ease the grave crisis faced by the Russians on the Eastern Front, where their army was in difficulty against the Turks.

Had the initial bombardment been carried through with vigour it might well have succeeded, as at the time the forts along the Dardanelles were undermanned and not ready for action, while other defences were practically non-existent. It might well have shortened the war by nearly two years, as some have speculated.

All of these arguments, recriminations and tragic defeats were, however, in the future. At the time the purpose of the bombardment begun on 3 November 1914 was to discover the extent of the damage that could be inflicted on the forts from the sea, and to estimate the range of the Turkish guns.

The action led some to believe that the forts could be overcome by bombardment (in fact only one fort was damaged), but many, however, remained sceptical as to the ultimate results that could be achieved by such methods. Unfortunately the November bombardment had alerted the Turks and their German advisers to the possibility of a determined attack on the Narrows. As a result

the defences had been greatly improved, new minefields, anti-submarine nets and torpedo tubes being sited along the shoreline. The forts were placed on a permanent war footing, and new ones constructed, and, finally, a number of mobile artillery batteries were brought into the area. These new defences, together with the very strong tides encountered in the Narrows, were to prove formidable obstacles to future Allied efforts to attack the position.

When the First Sea Lord was consulted regarding the Dardanelles situation, he favoured a large-scale attack by both the Army and the Royal Navy, the navy forcing the Narrows with old battleships of the '*Majestic*' and '*Canopus*' classes, which were all due to be scrapped. Kitchener refused to move men from France for such an operation, but the First Lord took up the naval part of Fisher's plan, feeling that the navy alone could accomplish the task. Churchill then requested the Admiral commanding the Aegean, Admiral Carden, to give his views on the matter, and to state what forces would be required for such an operation. On 11 January 1915 the First Lord received

Carden's suggestions, which envisaged the operation being carried out in three phases:

1 The bombardment of the forts
2 The clearing of the minefields in the Narrows
3 The journey up Straits into the Sea of Marmara and thence to Constantinople.

To carry out the operation, Carden estimated that he would need twelve battleships, three battlecruisers, sixteen destroyers, six submarines, four seaplanes to carry out reconnaissance duties, twelve minesweepers and a number of miscellaneous craft. In addition, as expenditure of ammunition was expected to be very heavy, there had to be an ample supply available to replenish the ships. If these conditions were met, Carden was confident that the navy could force the Narrows, but it was an operation which would take time and could not be rushed. The First Lord and the Admiralty Staff approved the plan, and in addition offered the new battleship *Queen Elizabeth*, the most powerful warship afloat. It so happened that *Queen Elizabeth* was due to go to the Mediterranean to calibrate her guns, and it was decided that the calibration shoot might as well be carried out against the forts in the Dardanelles as against the more normal towed target used in such tests.

Kitchener approved the plan, as it would not entail the use of any units from the Army, but the War Office and the Admiralty pressed for certain preparations to be made in case military intervention should be required. While these discussions were in progress, Carden precipitated the situation by starting a bombardment of the forts on 19 February. The bombardment achieved a measure of success, considerably damaging the forts at Kum Kale and Sedd-el-Bakr. At 1445 the squadron, consisting of *Vengeance*, *Cornwallis*, *Triumph*, *Suffren*, *Gaulois* and *Bouvet*, moved in closer, to a range where their secondary armament could engage the forts, and by evening it appeared that all the Turkish guns, bar one on the Asiatic side of the Narrows, had been silenced.

On the following morning seaplanes from *Ark Royal* carried out a reconnaissance of the area to discover the extent of the damage.

At this point the weather unfortunately deteriorated, preventing the navy from exploiting the apparent success of the bombardment. Not until 25 February was it reopened, at long range, by *Queen Elizabeth*, *Agamemnon*, *Irresistible*, *Triumph*, *Suffren*, *Charlemagne*, *Vengeance*, *Cornwallis*, *Gaulois* and *Albion*. The guns at Cape Helles were soon put out of action, and by 1715 all of the forts had been silenced. The next task was to sweep the Narrows for mines. This was scheduled for nightfall, when a force of trawlers from the North Sea were to enter the Straits.

By daylight a passage four miles into the Straits had been cleared, and *Albion* and *Majestic*, supported by *Vengeance*, steamed up to the limit of the swept area to bombard the forts at Dardanos and the new batteries concealed on the Asiatic side. The final destruction of these guns was accomplished by naval landing parties sent ashore from the three battleships. Operations continued as often as the doubtful weather would allow, until the preliminary task of destroying the outer forts had been completed and a mine-free path cleared.

The next phase of the attack, on the heart of the defences, began on 5 March. The forts now under attack mounted far heavier guns than those at the entrance, and the bombarding squadron frequently suffered hits, which fortunately did not inflict severe damage. Two days later it was decided to suspend the indirect bombardment as results were not up to expectations; radio communications between the ships and the seaplanes spotting the fall of shot often broke down at a crucial moment.

The minesweeping operations were not proceeding successfully either. The raw recruits in the trawlers were becoming completely demoralized by the fire from the dozen or so mobile shore batteries which opened up every time the sweepers entered the Narrows. In exasperation, Commodore Keyes, Carden's Chief of Staff, called

Left: The major focus of attention for the navy in 1915 was the Mediterranean and support of the Dardanelles campaign. A large number of ships were assembled in an effort to force a passage through to the Black Sea. The picture shows the *Agamemnon* bombarding Turkish positions. Note the camouflage. (ACPL)

Right: The 9.2in guns of HMS *Agamemnon* bombarding Turkish batteries in the Dardanelles. (ACPL)

for volunteers, and on the night of 13 March made a determined attempt to clear a way through the minefield, but again without success. Once more the Turkish batteries and searchlights forced the minesweepers to retreat.

It was now becoming clear that warships alone would not be able to force the Dardanelles. Before any significant progress could be made the minefields had to be swept, but this was impossible to accomplish until the batteries had been silenced. It had now been proved that,

though the bombardment might succeed in silencing the static forts for short periods of time, it could not hope to silence the mobile batteries. The only way they could be silenced was for the Army to mount an expedition to land troops in sufficient strength to overcome the Turkish defenders.

On 15 March Carden resigned owing to ill health and was succeeded as Commander-in-Chief of the Dardanelles operation by Admiral De Robeck. On 18 March a

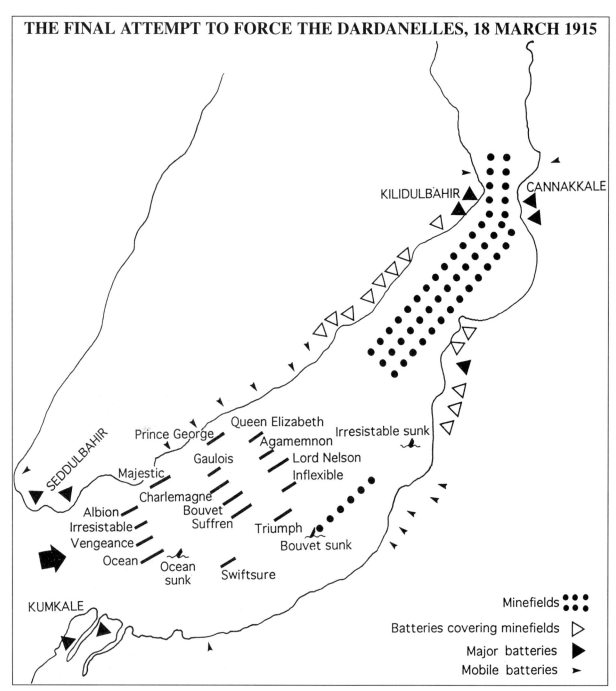

THE FINAL ATTEMPT TO FORCE THE DARDANELLES, 18 MARCH 1915

KILIDULBAHIR

CANNAKKALE

Queen Elizabeth

Prince George

Irresistable sunk

Agamemnon

Gaulois

Lord Nelson

Majestic

Inflexible

SEDDULBAHIR

Charlemagne

Albion

Bouvet

Irresistable

Suffren

Vengeance

Triumph

Ocean

Bouvet sunk

Ocean
sunk

Swiftsure

KUMKALE

Minefields

Batteries covering minefields ▷

Major batteries ▶

Mobile batteries ➤

final attempt was made to break through the minefield in daylight, rather than under the darkness of night as previously. The powerful squadron entered the Straits and opened a long-range bombardment of the forts in the Narrows. At midday the shore forts ceased firing, and the opportunity was taken during the brief lull to relieve certain vessels in the squadron. During the exchange of units the French battleship *Bouvet* hit a drifting mine and sank within three minutes. The disaster failed to deter the Allied squadron, which quickly resumed firing when it became clear that the shore batteries had not been completely silenced. The Turks, however, were elated with their success and released more drifting mines into the strong current that swept down the Dardanelles.

At 1605 they scored another success when *Irresistible* was struck, sinking three-quarters of an hour later. Then, at 1805, another mine struck *Ocean*, which quickly sank in deep water. *Gaulois* was severely damaged by the shore batteries. *Inflexible* was also damaged by the shore batteries and soon after struck a mine. The battlecruiser only just managed to reach Tenedos safely. With the onset of darkness on that fateful day the bombardment died away and the Allied squadron withdrew. So ended in failure the naval attempt to force the Dardanelles. The net result of the attempt was the destruction of two 14in guns and two or three smaller ones in the forts, and a number of

others temporarily disabled. On 21 March the Admiralty issued a statement on the bombardment, which concluded, '... the power of the Fleet to dominate the fortresses by superiority of fire seems to be established'. So it might have been, but only for short periods of time, for the navy had failed to destroy completely the forts and their guns, let alone force its way through the minefields in the Straits to support the Russians.

De Robeck was still of the opinion that the navy could succeed in its enterprise, and as the minefields were the main obstacle to success he decided to reorganize the sweeping force completely. More ships were sent to the Dardanelles to replace losses, but the Army remained sceptical as to the outcome of any future naval operations. At a meeting at Mudros on 22 March, De Robeck presented a complete *volte face*, stating that he felt the navy would not be able to force the Narrows without assistance from the Army.

Although the failure of the attempt to force the Narrows on the 18th did not signal the end of the navy's participation in the Dardanelles campaign, it had, nevertheless, suffered a severe reverse at the hands of Turkish minefields and shore batteries. As a result it was eventually forced to play a secondary role when plans were drawn up for a major operation involving the Army, which would be landed to secure the peninsula.

Right: For the first time in the history of war, aircraft actively cooperated with warships, Short 184 seaplanes from the seaplane carrier *Engadine* are seen here carrying out reconnaissance and spotting missions for the bombarding force in the Dardanelles. The *Engadine* is seen at Mudros with a Short 184 seaplane on her stern. (ACPL)

Right: The bombardment having failed to achieve its objective, it was decided to carry out amphibious landings at several points around Cape Helles at the tip of the Gallipoli peninsula. The steamer *River Clyde* was assigned to land troops at V beach, but the troops were bloodily repulsed. (ACPL)

Left: On 27 May 1915 the battleship *Majestic* was sunk off Cape Helles by the submarine *U 21*. (ACPL)

The landings started on 25 April, and although all went well on some beaches, at others the troops were bloodily repulsed with heavy losses and only a few yards of sand gained. The whole operation was a fiasco, and by November it was obvious that the Army could not hope to capture the heights that dominated the Straits, so the Allied force was withdrawn at the end of the year.

Overall, the Dardanelles campaign was a dismal failure of British arms. Not, it must be emphasized, as a result of any failing on the part of the ordinary sailors and soldiers, but more as a result of political machinations at home and lack of resolve amongst some of the commanders on the spot. The failure of the operation had results far outreaching the purely military defeat suffered by the Allies.

As First Lord, and one of the prime instigators and supporters of the ill-fated Dardanelles and Gallipoli operations, Churchill took a major part of the blame for the failure. He already had much to answer for in the eyes of many, who felt that politicians should not meddle in military operations about which they knew little and for which they had had no training. Churchill had already come in for some severe criticism over some of his previous schemes and plans. For some time, relations between the First Lord and First Sea Lord had slowly been deteriorating. The Dardanelles operation finally put an end to what had been a brilliant partnership, one which, both before the war and up to 1915, had doubtless saved England from what must, without the energy, drive and determination of these two individuals, have ended in a resounding naval defeat, leading in all probability to the surrender of the nation.

Fisher began to lose heart in the Dardanelles operation when the ever-increasing demands for more ships led to a gradual erosion of the strength of the Grand Fleet, which he realized should be concentrated in strength ready for a conclusive encounter with the High Seas Fleet. Churchill was all for the Dardanelles operation, as he believed it might lead to the opening of a Second Front, thus breaking the stalemate of the trench warfare on the Western Front, which entailed gigantic losses in men and material for the gaining of just a few yards of desolated no-man's land. This clash of ideas and personalities finally forced Fisher regretfully to hand in his resignation on 14 May, and he was replaced as First Sea Lord by Admiral Sir Henry Jackson.

The fiasco of the Dardanelles operation leading to Fisher's resignation, coupled with newspaper disclosures spotlighting the desperate shortage of high-explosive shells, forced the Prime Minister, Asquith, to form a Coalition Government with the Conservatives. Churchill, under the terms the Conservatives set for the formation of a Coalition, was replaced as First Lord by Arthur James Balfour. The Liberal/Conservative coalition under Asquith took office on 25 May.

Left: British submarines played a major part in the Dardanelles campaign, the *E.11* penetrating the Narrows and entering the Sea of Marmara, where she severely disrupted Turkish shipping. The picture shows the submarine *E.2* at Mudros during the campaign. *E.2* also penetrated the Narrows and entered the sea of Marmara, where she sank a steamer and destroyed nineteen sailing vessels in a patrol lasting 24 days. (ACPL)

Chapter 20

Jutland – Defeat or Victory?

At the beginning of 1916 Admiral Scheer became the German Commander-in-Chief when Admiral Von Pohl was forced to resign his post through ill health. Scheer's dynamic leadership had a profound effect on German operations, and eventually led to the situation which both sides had been trying to achieve since the start of the war — a fleet action under conditions favourable to whichever side initiated the first moves.

Scheer had conceived just such a plan. He was convinced that if the High Seas Fleet could be concentrated in sufficient strength and deployed at exactly the right moment to bring all units into action simultaneously, he would gain superiority over the Grand Fleet and achieve victory. Similar ideas put into practice by Von Ingenohl had always ended in dismal failure, with results totally incommensurate with the effort and losses suffered. Scheer's plan was to involve the whole of the High Seas Fleet, the submarine arm, which had already proved its capabilities during 1915, and the naval Zeppelins. By skilful use of all three forces he hoped to trap a portion of the Grand Fleet near the German coast and destroy it. The plan was for the submarines to make a concerted attack on British merchant shipping, forcing the Royal Navy to divert a large number of destroyers from the Grand Fleet to protect the merchant fleet. The Zeppelins, meanwhile, would be carrying out a continuous reconnaissance of the Grand Fleet to ascertain the moment when it was at its weakest, with the destroyers deployed elsewhere. Part of the Grand Fleet would then be lured into German waters, where the High Seas Fleet would be waiting for it.

Across the North Sea, Jellicoe had been wrestling with the parallel problem of how to bring the High Seas Fleet to action. Previous operations, which in the main consisted of sending a decoy of light forces into German waters to lure the High Seas Fleet to sea, where the Grand Fleet could destroy it, had always been frustrated when the Germans refused to leave port in pursuit. With the public outcry following the raids on the East Coast, and the disastrous portents of the submarine campaign of 1915, pressure was being exerted on Jellicoe to make a determined effort to bring the High Seas Fleet to action and destroy it. Basically, Jellicoe's plan was for two squadrons of light cruisers, supported by a single battle squadron, to penetrate far into the Kattegat to act as a decoy and lure Scheer to sea in pursuit. The Grand Fleet would be out of sight to seaward, waiting to pounce on Scheer as he left port.

Surprisingly, Scheer was unaware of the Admiralty's ability to intercept and decode German radio messages.

His order to sail was duly intercepted by the Admiralty who, although they were unable to divine the full purpose of the message, were aware from the method of its transmission and the fact that it was addressed to all vessels of the High Seas Fleet, that major moves were afoot. To cover all possible contingencies, it had always been policy on the receipt of such messages to send the whole of the Grand Fleet to sea, so by 2230 on 30 May 1916 the Grand Fleet, including Beatty's Battlecruiser Force, was at sea awaiting developments. Unfortunately the Admiralty overlooked the vital fact that it was normal practice in the German navy to transfer a flagship's callsign to the shore base when the Fleet sailed, so Jellicoe was under the impression that the High Seas Fleet was still in harbour.

On 31 May, a fine summer day with a glassy calm sea and good visibility, Jellicoe, unaware that the High Seas Fleet was at sea, continued his eastward advance at a steady speed of 15kts in an effort to conserve his destroyers' fuel. At 1415 Beatty's force, also heading eastwards, turned to the north to effect a rendezvous with the rest of the Grand Fleet. At this moment *Galatea*, in the First Light Cruiser Squadron, sighted smoke and the masts of a small Danish steamer to the east. *Galatea* and *Phaeton* turned to investigate, followed by the rest of the squadron. Meanwhile Hipper, Beatty's opposite number, in command of the German Scouting Force of battlecruisers, had also been sailing on a northerly course. Part of his cruiser screen had also sighted the Danish steamer, and on Hipper's orders they, too, turned to investigate the ship. Thus it was that the small Danish steamer *H.J. Fjord* brought the opposing fleets into contact. At 1428 *Galatea* fired the first shots in the opening moves of the Battle of Jutland.

But the trap had been sprung too soon. The Germans were unaware that the whole of the Grand Fleet was at sea 65 miles to the north, and Beatty was unaware that his own light cruisers were in action with the screen of Hipper's Scouting Force, and that the whole of the High Seas Fleet was following up astern of Hipper. At this point confused signalling on both sides led to a muddled action. On the British side the scouting cruisers, instead of shadowing and reporting the German forces, turned towards the north, hoping to draw Hipper further away from his base towards the Grand Fleet and so enable Beatty to interpose his battlecruisers between the Germans and their base. In the German squadron the vessels of Goodenough's First Light Cruiser Squadron were reported as battlecruisers, and a further report was later misread to give a total of 26 battleships.

Left: The battlecruiser *Indefatigable* of the 2nd Battlecruiser Squadron entering action at the Battle of Jutland 31 May 1916. (Imperial War Museum)

Hipper, following the plan laid down by Scheer, turned towards the British force, hoping to present a target tempting enough for the British to attack, at which point he would turn and lure them on to the rest of the High Seas Fleet. Hipper and Beatty thus found themselves on converging courses at a combined speed of more than 45kts. At this point Beatty ordered the seaplane carrier *Engadine* to send up an aircraft to scout ahead. The seaplane radioed three reports back to *Engadine*, which attempted to pass them by searchlight to both *Lion* and *Barham*, but unfortunately they never reached Beatty. Beatty, therefore, was still unaware that German battlecruisers were in the vicinity, the First Light Cruiser Squadron only having sighted German light cruisers.

Further signalling difficulties now bedevilled the British forces, leading Beatty into a grave situation which could have led to the complete destruction of the Battlecruiser Force. Beatty gave the order to turn towards the German forces, but the Fifth Battle Squadron ('Queen Elizabeth' class) was unable to see the signal, and for eight minutes the two squadrons steamed on diverging courses. Finally, the Fifth Battle Squadron turned to follow Beatty, but it was some time before the ships could work up speed to match the 24kts of the battlecruisers. By then Beatty was some 10 miles ahead, and although the gap was to some extent reduced, it was still great enough to have an almost disastrous effect on the battlecruiser action that was about to start.

At 1532 the tripod masts of Beatty's battlecruisers were visible to Hipper, and a sighting report was sent to Scheer. Sixteen minutes later the two forces opened fire, and after a few salvoes the Germans found the range. Three minutes after the action began, Beatty's flagship, *Lion*, and *Princess Royal* and *Tiger* received hits. A turret on *Princess Royal* was put out of action, and two turrets on *Tiger* were temporarily disabled and the ship almost lost her ability to direct the fire of the others. The British took some time finding the range of Hipper's vessels, but at 1555 they at last scored a hit, the *Queen Mary* landing two shells on *Seydlitz*, putting one of her turrets out of action.

In spite of comments made following the Battle of the Dogger Bank (see page 101), there was still confusion as to which enemy vessel a ship should engage. As at the Dogger Bank, a German battlecruiser was left unengaged, in this case *Derfflinger*. This was soon realized, and the Fleet champion gunnery ship, *Queen Mary*, quickly found the range and scored a number of hits. The remainder of the British squadron, however, continued having great difficulty in finding the range. At about 1600 *Lion* received a hit on her midships turret, and but for the brave action of Royal Marine Major F.J.W. Harvey, who ordered the flood valves opened to prevent a cordite fire from reaching the magazine, the ship would surely have been destroyed. A further six salvoes hit *Lion*, which was severely damaged, and *Princess Royal* received another hit which put her after turret out of action.

Left: The battlecruiser *Lion* is struck on Q turret amidships during the battlecruiser action. (Imperial War Museum)

THE BATTLE OF JUTLAND, 31 MAY 1916
THE BATTLE CRUISER ACTION, 1600 TO 1640

Tracks have been simplified for clarity.

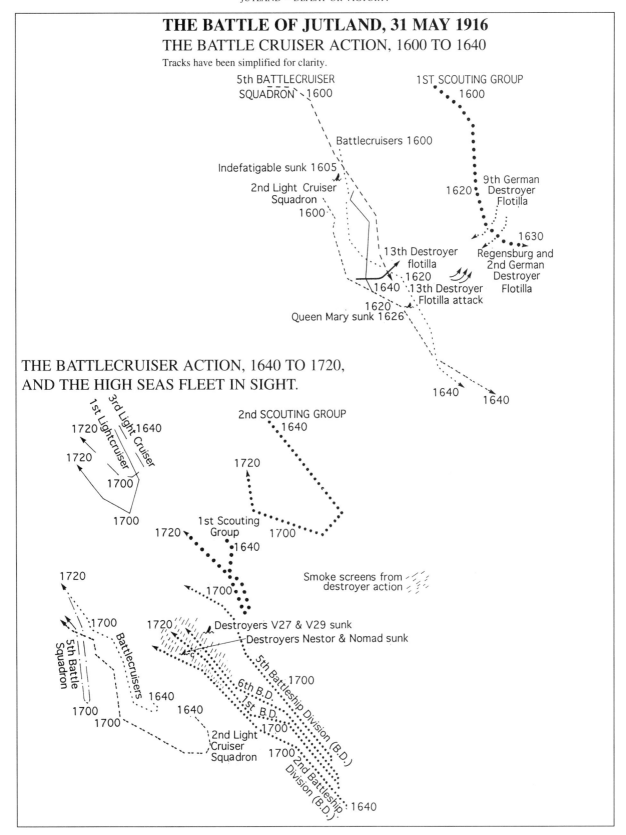

5th BATTLECRUISER SQUADRON ~1600

1ST SCOUTING GROUP 1600

Battlecruisers 1600

Indefatigable sunk 1605

2nd Light Cruiser Squadron 1600

9th German Destroyer Flotilla

1620

1630

Regensburg and 2nd German Destroyer Flotilla

13th Destroyer flotilla 1620

1640

13th Destroyer Flotilla attack

1620

Queen Mary sunk 1626

1640

1640

THE BATTLECRUISER ACTION, 1640 TO 1720, AND THE HIGH SEAS FLEET IN SIGHT.

3rd Light Cruiser

1st Lightcruiser

1720 1640

1720

1720

1700

1700

2nd SCOUTING GROUP 1640

1720

1700

1st Scouting Group

1720

1700

1640

1640

1700

Smoke screens from destroyer action

1720

1700

Destroyers V27 & V29 sunk

Destroyers Nestor & Nomad sunk

1720

5th Battleship Division (B.D.)

1700

5th Battle Squadron

1700

Battlecruisers

1640

6th B.D.

1st B.D.

1700

1700

1700

2nd Light Cruiser Squadron

1700

2nd Battleship Division (B.D.)

1640

111

At the rear of the British line *Indefatigable* disappeared in a cloud of smoke and debris as a salvo from *Von Der Tann* penetrated her armour and ignited a magazine. At this point Beatty ordered the First Destroyer Flotilla to attack and ease the pressure on the battlecruisers. At last, at 1605, the Fifth Battle Squadron arrived and quickly entered the action, finding the range almost at once. *Von Der Tann* was hit by a number of 15in shells which caused severe flooding, and *Moltke* was hit soon after. Unfortunately the British armour-piercing shells broke up on impact instead of piercing the armour and exploding behind it, so a number of hits which should have wreaked havoc on board the German ships had little or no effect on their fighting ability.

An even worse defect now became patently apparent on the British ships. At 1626 *Queen Mary*, then bearing the brunt of the fire from Hipper's squadron, who no longer found *Lion*, wreathed in smoke from her fires, a worthwhile target, reeled under a number of hits. Horrified observers watched a great sheet of flame shoot out from the stricken vessel, and this was followed by a thunderous explosion as her magazine exploded. Further explosions completed the destruction of *Queen Mary*, and she sank with 1,266 of her crew. This was the second

Below: The *Queen Mary* is struck by a salvo from the German battlecruisers and disintegrates in a huge cloud of smoke during the battlecruiser action as a German shell penetrates her turret, and the resulting flash shoots down the trunk to the magazine below. (Imperial War Museum).

British battlecruiser to be lost that afternoon when the flash from a cordite fire penetrated a magazine.

In spite of his success, however, Hipper was now in great difficulty, as the Fifth Battle Squadron with its powerful 15in guns began to score heavily. At this point the German destroyers went into the attack, and met the oncoming British destroyers bent on the same duty of relieving pressure on their own battlecruisers. In the ensuing melée two German destroyers were sunk and the remainder were forced to fire their torpedoes at an ineffective range. The German destroyers, however, achieved their object, for the Fifth Battle Squadron temporarily turned away from the torpedo attack, relieving the pressure on Hipper's sorely pressed battlecruisers. The British destroyers pressed home their attack, and, having been scattered during their action with the German destroyers, in which *Nomad* was disabled, came under heavy fire. Beatty then reversed course and recalled his destroyers, for Commodore Goodenough in *Southampton* had sighted the main body of the High Seas Fleet.

From the signals he received from Hipper, Scheer was under the impression that the only British force in the vicinity was Beatty's. Believing his plan had succeeded, Scheer altered course to the north to support Hipper. Beatty, meanwhile, having confirmed with his own eyes the *Southampton*'s report of the presence of the High Seas Fleet, reversed course to the northwest towards Jellicoe and the main body of the Grand Fleet. By the time the last ship in the Fifth Battle Squadron had turned, the van of the German Battle Fleet was within range and had opened fire, scoring hits on *Barham* and *Malaya*. While *Warspite* and *Malaya* engaged the leading ships of the High Seas Fleet (*Grosser Kurfürst* and *Markgraf*), the remainder of the Fifth Battle Squadron continued to engage Hipper's battlecruisers, scoring hits on *Lützow*, *Derfflinger* and *Seydlitz*. Only the *Moltke* of Hipper's force remained comparatively undamaged. As they raced northward towards Jellicoe, the superior speed of the British ships began to tell and the range gradually opened. Still unaware that the Grand Fleet lay ahead, Scheer gave the order 'General Chase', but the range had opened to such an extent that neither Hipper nor the leading battleships could reach Beatty's force.

Visibility gradually decreased during the day, and a haze from the gunfire spread over the action. The Grand Fleet remained in its compact cruising order, with the heavy cruisers of the First and Second Cruiser Squadrons forming a scouting screen 8 miles ahead, and the Third Battlecruiser Squadron (Rear-Admiral the Hon. H. Hood) 20 miles ahead of the main battle fleet. On receipt of information that the enemy was steering a northerly course, Hood altered to a more easterly course in an effort to cut the enemy off from any possible escape route through the Skaggerack.

With the skies overcast and the constant zigzagging at high speed, accurate plotting of positions became almost impossible, with the result that Jellicoe was farther south than he thought and Beatty was farther north. With the battlecruisers in action on a southerly course, it seemed as though the Grand Fleet might miss its chance to engage the enemy, and Hood was ordered to press ahead at full speed, leaving the slower battleships of the main body behind. With *Lion* severely damaged, Jellicoe received little information during the day as to the outcome of the battlecruiser action, and was unaware of the grievous losses suffered by Beatty. It was not until he received *Southampton*'s sighting report of the High Seas Fleet that Jellicoe had any detailed knowledge of the forces opposing him. From then onwards, Goodenough's reports formed the basis on which Jellicoe arrived at all his decisions regarding the forthcoming battleship action.

At 1740 the two battlecruiser forces again joined action. This time the situation was reversed, with Hipper's Squadron in full view of Beatty's vessels, which, apart from gun flashes, remained almost invisible to Hipper. *Derfflinger* suffered further severe damage and began to sink by the head, *Seydlitz* was again hit and set on fire and Hipper, unable to reply effectively to the British fire, turned away to open the range. This enabled Jellicoe and the Grand Fleet heading down from the north to approach the High Seas Fleet unreported.

If Scheer was unaware of the approach of the Grand Fleet, Jellicoe was in nearly as bad a position, for poor and erroneous reports left him with a very inaccurate picture as to the state of the action and the correct position and composition of the various forces involved. Deprived of accurate information, and with darkness soon to fall, Jellicoe was placed in an almost impossible position for making the final decision as to when and how to deploy his fleet. Not until 1750 was the necessary information received from which an assessment of the situation could

be made. Then *Marlborough*, leading the starboard wing column of the Grand Fleet, sighted Beatty and reported his relative position. From this information and further knowledge gleaned from *Southampton*'s reports regarding the relative positions of Hipper and Scheer to Beatty, Jellicoe realized that he would sight the High Seas Fleet at least 20min sooner than anticipated. With this vital information, Jellicoe was at last able to decide how he should deploy the Grand Fleet.

It was not a moment too soon, for, as the last of Jellicoe's battleships completed the deployment, Scheer's High Seas Fleet appeared out of the smoke in view of the First Battle Squadron. The Third Battlecruiser Squadron, meanwhile, had had a brief encounter with a number of German light cruisers, during which the light cruiser *Chester* was severely damaged, *Wiesbaden* was gunned into a floating wreck, *Pillau* was severely damaged in her boiler room and the destroyer *Shark* was sunk. Hipper had suffered further heavy damage from Beatty's battlecruisers, *Seydlitz* being severely flooded and *Lützow* almost battered into a wreck and rapidly losing speed. The news of Hood's action with the light cruisers, and a misleading report from the German commander, led Hipper to believe that he was facing the whole of the Grand Fleet. In this seemingly uncompromising position he fell back on Scheer, who assumed that Hood's Squadron was the van of the Grand Fleet. At this stage Jellicoe had almost completed his deployment, and the Grand Fleet opened fire on the High Seas Fleet.

Scheer was well and truly caught in a trap and ringed by fire. Fortunately the excellent design of the German ships and their sturdy construction saved Scheer from annihilation as hit after hit crashed home on the battlecruisers and leading battleships. Even so, the German vessels were severely damaged, but not to the extent that they were unable to return fire, for as they turned away from the solid line of the Grand Fleet the leading ships concentrated their fire on the nearest British ships. These

Below: The Grand Fleet (*Bellerophon* on the left) steaming into action at Jutland. (ACPL)

THE BATTLE OF JUTLAND, 31 MAY 1916
THE GRAND FLEET DEPLOYS, THE BATTLESHIP ACTION AND THE FIRST TURN AWAY BY THE HIGH SEAS FLEET

Tracks have been simplified for clarity.

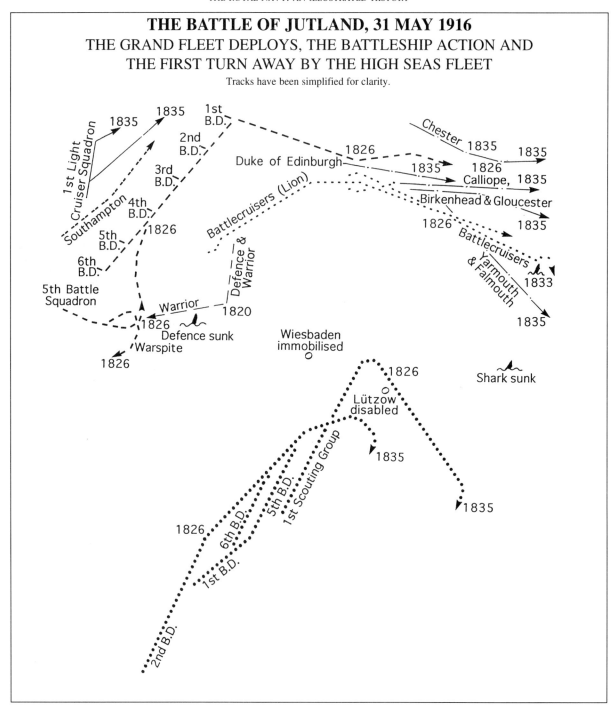

were the unfortunate vessels of the Third Battlecruiser Squadron. Almost at once *Invincible*, Hood's flagship, was hit on her midships turret and, as with *Lion*, *Indefatigable* and *Queen Mary* earlier in the day, the resulting cordite flash penetrated the magazine, which blew up, breaking the ship in half.

Scheer now displayed that genius which marks a great commander, executing a move which the High Seas Fleet had practised time and time again in preparation for an identical situation to that in which Scheer found himself. Even so, the move — the Battle Turn Away — was a most complicated and difficult manoeuvre to accomplish, for the German line was under heavy fire from the Grand Fleet. At 1836 Scheer began his Turn Away, torpedo boats covering the move by making smoke across the rear of the turning ships, and in the failing light and smoke skil-

Above: The *Revenge* (left), followed by *Hercules*, with guns trained to starboard at Jutland. (Imperial War Museum)

fully accomplished his object. As the gunfire died away Scheer was under no illusion that he was facing the whole of the Grand Fleet, which might well be in chase after his battered fleet behind the smoke.

Jellicoe was unaware that Scheer had turned away, and did not become cognizant of the fact until 1855. Yet again, scouting reports, or the lack of them, had let Jellicoe down, and once again it was left to Goodenough in

Below: The *Superb* (left) opening fire at Jutland. *Canada* is astern of *Superb*. (Imperial War Museum)

Southampton to inform him of Scheer's movements. On receipt of these facts, Jellicoe at once altered course and manoeuvred the Grand Fleet into a position where he could again cross Scheer's 'T'. This was achieved when Scheer reversed course to the east, in an attempt to throw Jellicoe off balance and gain sufficient time and space in which to extricate the High Seas Fleet by breaking through astern of the Grand Fleet and heading for home in the twilight.

Scheer, however, was as poorly served by his scouting cruisers as Jellicoe. As he reversed course he was unaware that the whole of the Grand Fleet still lay across his path. Just after 1900 the head of the High Seas Fleet again came into sight, and the Grand Fleet opened a murderous fire on the German ships, *Derfflinger*, *König* and

Grosser Kurfürst being repeatedly hit. The High Seas Fleet was in a desperate plight, being silhouetted against the setting sun and only briefly able to sight the British ships through the smoke and haze. In desperation Scheer ordered Hipper to charge and ram the Grand Fleet. This was a desperate signal indeed, for the four battlecruisers had much of their armament out of action and were all carrying thousands of tons of sea water in flooded compartments. They were to be supported in their death ride by every available destroyer. The desperate gamble succeeded, for Jellicoe, mortally afraid of a massed torpedo attack, at once ordered a turn away. As he turned, Jellicoe lost his last chance of trapping the High Seas Fleet, for in the failing light, and under cover of the attack by the battlecruisers and destroyers, Scheer yet again brilliantly executed another turn away.

Apart from a few minor skirmishes which occurred during the night, the main battle was over. Jellicoe, fearful of a major night action in which his large and unwieldy fleet might well suffer at the hands of the smaller and more manoeuvrable High Seas Fleet, assumed a night cruising disposition. In this compact formation, totally unsuitable for action, Jellicoe hoped to remain astride Scheer's line of retreat without actually encountering the High Seas Fleet. Scheer, on the other hand, reformed his battered fleet and headed on a southerly course in an effort to get to eastward of the Grand Fleet before daylight, when he would have a clear run home.

As the High Seas Fleet slowly passed astern of the Grand Fleet a number of actions between small units took place in which the light cruisers of both sides suffered hits. Later, a number of destroyers of the Fourth Flotilla collided with the head of Scheer's battle fleet. The leading German battleships sheered away to avoid British torpedoes and opened fire, the cruiser *Rostock* being torpedoed and sunk in the ensuing confused melée for the loss of three British destroyers sunk and a number of others seriously damaged. To the rear of the German line the cruiser *Black Prince*, having become detached from the rest of the British force, was disabled by *Thuringen*, thereafter providing night target practice for the remainder of the High Seas Fleet as they passed the drifting, burning wreck. It was just after midnight on 1 June that the Ninth, Tenth, Twelfth and Thirteenth British destroyer Flotillas crossed the 'T' of the retreating Germans. The leading German ships opened fire on the rearmost British destroyers, sinking *Turbulent* and seriously damaging *Petard*. Meanwhile, the Twelfth Flotilla, having become detached from the other flotillas, soon found itself in an excellent position to attack, steaming on a parallel but opposite course to the Germans. A number of torpedoes were fired just as it was getting light, and the pre-dreadnought *Pommern* was struck and blew up.

With this final skirmish the Battle of Jutland ended, and by daylight Scheer had passed behind the Grand Fleet and was safely heading for home. On board Jellicoe's flagship, *Iron Duke*, daylight showed a sea empty of the High Seas Fleet and the Grand Fleet widely scattered, the Battlecruiser Force being nowhere in sight. The destroyer flotillas, as a result of their night actions, were scattered over a wide area of the ocean, and the Grand Fleet was in enemy waters without an effective anti-submarine screen. At 0239 Jellicoe, realizing that the High Seas Fleet had escaped and that he was in enemy waters in an uncompromising situation, reluctantly turned north in Battle Order, finally ending any hopes he might have entertained of bringing the High Seas Fleet to a conclusive action.

In Britain, a bitter and acrimonious controversy raged over the outcome of the Battle of Jutland, the protagonists firing verbal broadsides at each other long after the two leading figures on the British side, Jellicoe and Beatty, were dead. In view of his past dashing performances with the Battlecruiser Force, Beatty was already a national hero. Jellicoe, on the other hand, was a rather retiring Admiral who certainly had no wish for brash publicity. Because of his rather unfortunate manner, the press gained the impression that Jellicoe was reluctant to engage the High Seas Fleet, and he was made a scapegoat for what the press and public regarded as a lost opportunity to annihilate the High Seas Fleet.

This was unfair. Under the conditions prevailing, Jellicoe had done remarkably well, in spite of the fact that for a large part of the action he had no detailed information from which to make assessments of the situation as it developed and accordingly formulate plans and orders. Beatty was not entirely blameless in this respect, for his forces were very lax in reporting the development of the action.

To compound the agony, the Admiralty was slow to release a statement to the press on the outcome of the action. However, here again it is true to say that this was not entirely their fault, for they did not receive detailed reports from the various commanders until well after the Germans, who, being much closer to their base port, were able to issue a communique claiming a victory and giving figures of losses well before Jellicoe returned to Rosyth. Jellicoe himself was unaware of the full extent of British losses until he returned home, but by then it was too late to rectify the German statement; the damage had been done. When the losses were studied it certainly seemed that the Germans had achieved a victory, but it was only a statistical victory. The true victory lay with the British, who were left in command of the battle area, Scheer having retired from the scene of the action.

The Grand Fleet retained command of the sea, and the High Seas Fleet only once more reluctantly ventured into the North Sea, towards the end of the war. Nevertheless, the fact that the High Seas Fleet remained a fleet in being forced the Admiralty to keep the Grand Fleet concentrated in Scapa, tying up thousands of men and vessels, particularly destroyers, which would have been invaluable during the submarine campaign of 1917.

Chapter 21

The Submarine Campaign

As long ago as 1901, in a lecture to the Institute of Mechanical Engineers, Commander Sir Trevor Dawson noted that 'Submarine boats have sufficient speed and radius of action to place themselves in the trade routes before the darkness gives place to day, and they would be capable of doing almost incalculable destruction against unsuspecting and defenceless victims'. The accuracy of this prophecy was now to become tragically apparent. Although 1917 was to see little action between large warships, the Grand Fleet was continually at sea, exercising and carrying out sweeps of the North Sea, proving beyond doubt that it retained the initiative and ensuring that the High Seas Fleet remained in its base. The major effort at sea during 1917, however, was to be devoted to combating the new submarine campaign, which gathered great momentum until at one time it was feared that Britain might be forced to sue for peace.

However, means were at hand by which the navy could at long last fight back. The campaign in 1915 had failed to convince the Admiralty of the necessity of carrying out a complete reappraisal of anti-submarine measures, but some improvements had been made. Additions were made to the strength of the anti-submarine forces in the shape of the new patrol boats of the 'Kil' and 'P' classes, and new equipment began to enter service. A device for detecting sounds emanating from a submerged submarine had finally been devised – the hydrophone – but it was primitive in operation and not particularly effective. Successful results required a calm sea and a number of hydrophone sets in widely dispersed vessels, from which accurate cross-bearings could be obtained. In addition, so that extraneous noises should not confuse the hydrophone operator, all machinery nearby had to cease functioning, including engines, which thus rendered the escort extremely vulnerable to submarine attack.

A new weapon, the depth charge, had also been developed. Two designs were available, one for use on large, fast submarine chasers, with a 300lb explosive charge, and another for use on small craft, containing 120lb of high explosive. Detonation was achieved by a hydrostatic pistol set to actuate at either 40ft or 80ft. To be sure of a kill, the charge had to explode within 14ft of the target, a singularly difficult feat to accomplish without accurate detection and plotting of a submarine's exact position. A continuous depth charge attack in the near vicinity of a submarine did, however, have an extremely demoralizing effect on the crew, and the resulting shock waves from the explosion could seriously damage the vessel.

During 1916 the anti-submarine forces were gradually equipped with hydrophones and depth charges, but to achieve any measure of success a far more accurate submarine detector, less susceptible to weather conditions and surrounding ambivalent noise, was required. The only real achievement during 1916 was the equipping of merchant ships with guns which, although of small calibre, were quite capable of piercing the vulnerable pressure hull of a submarine, rendering it incapable of diving and in some cases even sinking the vessel. By April 1916 1,100 merchant vessels had been defensively armed, and of the 310 so equipped that were attacked (nearly always, it must be admitted, by gunfire from a surfaced submarine — an ideal situation for the defence of an armed merchant ship, and a tactic resorted to by many submarine commanders in an effort to conserve precious torpedoes), 236 were able to escape. Compared with this, only 67 of 301 unarmed ships which were attacked managed to escape.

However, losses continued to rise alarmingly during 1916, in part due to the Admiralty's misconception of the way in which anti-submarine operations should be conducted. The methods employed consisted mainly of patrolling the trade routes used by merchant ships, or carrying out searches of areas where a submarine was thought to be operating. These efforts failed completely, firstly because the searching vessels were either inadequately equipped with anti-submarine equipment or had none at all, and relied on their mere presence to keep a submarine out of an area, and secondly because the submarines submerged and shut down all machinery until the patrol had passed, when they resurfaced, free to resume their mission. Although the trade routes were altered from time to time, submarine commanders soon discovered the new routes and sinkings continued to increase.

Faced with increasing losses, the Admiralty's only antidote was to increase the number and quality of anti-submarine vessels. The most effective vessel for patrol and search duties had proved to be the destroyer, but the majority of these were required for attendance on the Grand Fleet, and few could be released from screening duties. Jellicoe realized the potential of the destroyer as a positive counter to submarine attack, and in October 1916 wrote to the First Lord, Balfour, pointing out that, 'the destroyer is very efficient defensively as a screen to individual ships or to a large number of ships'. Unfortunately Jellicoe did not point out that this large number of ships could be a merchant convoy, rather than units of the Grand Fleet. Nor did he mention that such a convoy would provide far too tempting a target for a submarine commander to ignore, and that instead of sending patrol boats on fruitless searches for submarines, they might be far better employed escorting a convoy and waiting for submarines to attack, when they could retaliate with a far better chance of a kill. Instead of sending out patrol boats to hunt for submarines, let the submarines come to the hunters.

The Admiralty had already gone part of the way to meeting Jellicoe's note by ordering large numbers of destroyers under the Emergency War Programme. Many were in fact already under construction, but they were destined for duties with the Grand Fleet.

Table VIII. Destroyer Orders Placed During the War*

Programme	Ordered	Number	Type
Emergency War	9/14	20	M class
"	11/14	32	,,
,,	2/15	18	,,
,,	11/14	3	Leaders
,,	2/15	2	,,
,,	5/15	20	M class
,,	7/15	3	Leaders
,,	7/15	26	R class
,,	12/15	1	Leader
,,	12/15	10	R class
,,	3/16	21	R & Mod R class
,,	4/16	5	,,
,,	4/16	5	V class
1916-17	4/16	6	Leaders
,,	6/16	25	V & W class
,,	12/16	9	Leaders
,,	12/16	23	V & W class
1917-18	4/17	33	S class
,,	6/17	36	,,
1918-19	1/18	16	Mod V & W class
,,	4/18	38	,,

*A number of destroyers ordered under the 1917–19 Programmes were cancelled after the end of the war. See Chapter 21.

During April 1916 37 ships were lost to submarines, and another six were sunk by mines — a total of 140,000 tons. However, another U-boat attack which took American lives relieved pressure on Britain's hard-pressed merchant fleet. At the end of March 1916 the French cross-channel steamer *Sussex* was sunk with the loss of many lives, some of them American. This produced a strong American reaction and, fearing a further deterioration in her already strained relations with America as a result of such incidents, Germany perceptibly slackened off her submarine campaign.

Following the Battle of Jutland, Scheer was forced to admit that the High Seas Fleet would never again be able to meet the Grand Fleet on equal terms, so in October 1916 he ordered that the U-boat campaign be intensified. During the first six months of 1916 500,000 tons of British merchant shipping were sunk (2.5 times the output of the shipyards). During October, however, a staggering total of 176,000 tons of British shipping was sunk, 30,000 tons more than the worst month (August) of 1915, and the total tonnage sunk in all areas during the month was 337,000 tons.

In the light of these increasing losses, Jellicoe realized that the major threat facing Britain came not from the High Seas Fleet but from the U-boat campaign. From June to December 1916 only fifteen submarines were sunk, compared with a total of 74 commissioned, and at the end of the year Germany had a total of 140 submarines in service. The greater range of the latest submarines entering service, and the increase in the number in commission, enabled Scheer to extend the areas of the U-boat campaign to the East Coast of America, as well as covering the North Sea, the Arctic, the Mediterranean, and even down into the South Atlantic. By November the British Government had become completely dissatisfied with the lack of drive in the Admiralty over the handling of the submarine campaign, and Jellicoe was given the specific task of defeating the submarine.

The press, also dissatisfied with the conduct of naval operations, was agitating for changes in the Admiralty. This reaction so annoyed the First Lord, Balfour, that on 22 November 1916 he appointed Jellicoe First Sea Lord in place of Jackson, whom many regarded as being responsible for the debacle. Beatty took over as Commander-in-Chief of the Grand Fleet. Balfour, however, was not to last much longer in office either, for by this time the country as a whole had become dissatisfied with the conduct of the war, and after the staggering losses in the Battle of the Somme, the seeming fiasco of Jutland, and the row over the supply of munitions, Asquith, the leader of the coalition, was forced to resign and a new coalition was formed under Lloyd George, with Sir Edward Carson as First Lord.

When Jellicoe took over as First Sea Lord, the anti-submarine measures in force were completely inadequate for the task. The only means of detection remained the hydrophone, and efforts to make the instrument directional had failed. In June 1917 a new device, ASDIC, which picked up the reflection of a sound beam bounced off a solid object, was tested. Unfortunately the tests and trials took such a long time to complete that the war was over before the equipment entered service. In addition, depth charge production had been so slow that on average destroyers were only allocated four during July 1917. However, production gradually improved, and by the end of the year factories were producing a total of 2,000 a month.

In his efforts to combat the submarine, Jellicoe instituted a number of new measures, and on 15 December

Above: The major effort in 1917 was devoted to combatting the submarine. The first of the new anti-submarine vessels, the 'P' class (*P 24* is seen here at Dover in 1917), armed with a single 4in gun and two 14in torpedo tubes, began to enter service. Forty four of these vessels with a low silhouette and specially strengthened bows for ramming submarines were built. The torpedo tubes were later replaced by depth charges. (ACPL)

Right: New equipment was also developed to detect submarines. Here officers and crew of the drifter *Thrive* are seen using the hydrophone while on patrol in the Otranto barrage in the Mediterranean. An officer wears headphones ready to pick up the sound of a submarine, while a rating (right) prepares to lower the hydrophone into the water. (Imperial War Museum)

Right: In April 1917 the convoy system was instituted, which led to an immediate drop in sinkings. Further protection for convoys was afforded by aerial patrols carried out by airships of the Royal Naval Air Service. The picture shows a non-rigid coastal airship No C23A over a convoy. (Imperial War Museum)

1916 he formed the Anti-Submarine Division of the Naval Staff under Rear-Admiral Alexander Duff. By this time, moves were afoot in Germany for the opening of unrestricted submarine warfare, which would enable U-boats to attack merchant vessels of any nationality in any area, without warning. There were fierce debates for and against such a campaign. Those against argued that such a move would force America into the war on the side of the Allies and eventually lead to the defeat of Germany, if for no other reason than the fact that American industrial capacity was far greater than that of Germany, and even of any of the Allies. Others felt that the actual American military contribution would be negligible, and that if an unrestricted submarine campaign were begun, Britain would be defeated in six months, before America could give significant assistance. In the end the protagonists of an unrestricted submarine campaign won. The campaign began on 1 February 1917, and two months later America declared war on Germany.

The opening of the new campaign heralded disaster for Britain. In February alone a total of 520,000 tons of merchant shipping was sunk, of which 256,394 tons were British. Losses in April were cataclysmic, with a total of 860,000 tons sunk for the loss of two U-boats. Of this staggering total, 516,394 tons were British. These figures surpassed even German expectations, and if such losses continued, the prediction that 39 per cent of the merchant tonnage available to Britain would be sunk within six months would soon come true. Germany fully expected Britain to sue for peace, but owing to the introduction of rationing, and careful control of stocks, Britain still had sufficient reserves with which to continue the war, and the Government made no overtures to open negotiations for peace.

Sinkings continued at an astronomical rate, but the antidote was there for all to see, though many could not, or did not, wish to see it. The answer was the convoy, a method which had been used with great success by the troop transports sent to France since the start of the war,

and by the coal transports which had been sent in convoy to France since January 1917. Both types of convoy had sailed with practically complete immunity from submarine attack.

To Jellicoe, the main problem with the introduction of a convoy system was ensuring an adequate supply of escorts, something he had always refused to provide for when he was Commander-in-Chief of the Grand Fleet. It was felt, wrongly as it happened, that the ratio of escorts to merchantmen in a convoy should be two to one. However, the staggering losses of April 1917 finally forced a decision on the convoy issue. For some time Commander Reginald Henderson in the Anti-Submarine Division, unbeknown to the First Sea Lord, had been supplying figures to Lloyd George which showed that the Admiralty was perfectly capable of providing escorts for convoys. Lloyd George was already dissatisfied with the results that Jellicoe was achieving, and on 25 April asked the War Cabinet if he could attend the Admiralty's discussions. This, together with the terrible losses of April, forced Jellicoe's hand. When Lloyd George appeared at the Admiralty on 30 April he that found Jellicoe had already decided to institute convoys on the West Coast and Scandinavian routes, and intended to try an ocean convoy for practicability. The system at once proved successful, and no losses were sustained in the first convoys, nor were any submarines sighted.

By this time public criticism and press agitation, as well as his own observations, had already convinced Lloyd George of the need to replace Jellicoe and Carson as soon as practicably possible. As a start, in May 1917, he appointed Sir Eric Geddes Controller of the Navy, the first time a civilian had held the post. Geddes was given the honorary rank of Vice-Admiral, and on 20 July he replaced Carson as First Lord, Carson being given a position in the War Cabinet.

Below: To bolster the anti-submarine forces, large numbers of destroyers were ordered. The *Restless*, one of the 'R' class is illustrated. (ACPL)

Chapter 22

Changes in the High Command

In July 1917 a committee was set up to study the state of development in air warfare and to make recommendations for the future development and strategy of the air services, which Lloyd George felt could well make the major contribution to winning the war. A previous body, the Air Board, set up in July 1916, had been formed to investigate and advise on ways and means of reducing wasteful expenditure by the air services (RNAS and RFC) and to co-ordinate their war efforts to avoid duplication, but the unco-operative attitude of the Admiralty had made working conditions for the Board intolerable.

The Committee formed in July 1917 recommended the formation of an Air Ministry which would exercise control over the military air services, which would be merged into one body. This would avoid waste and duplication of effort, with the Air Ministry being responsible for procurement, control and administration of all military aircraft.

At the time the Board of Admiralty was preoccupied with other problems, notably the submarine campaign, and few voices were raised in opposition to the proposed merger of the RNAS and RFC into a unified Air Force, those that did so being ineffective in their arguments. The Board of Admiralty finally acquiesced to the forma-

Below: By 1917 development of the navy's air capability was proceeding apace. The first ship designed from the outset as an aircraft carrier with a full length flush flight deck was the *Argus* (originally laid down as a liner, but whose construction had been suspended), seen here in her First World War camouflage. She was originally designed with an island bridge, but this was removed before completion, following the unsatisfactory trials with the initial conversion of the *Furious*. (ACPL)

tion of a unified Air Ministry as long as they could have some say in the type of aircraft ordered for naval use, and control over operations carried out for the navy. Thus it was that on 1 April 1918 all personnel and aircraft in the RNAS (5,500 men and 2,500 aircraft) were transferred to control of the newly formed Royal Air Force (RAF).

In August 1917 Vice-Admiral Wemyss replaced Jellicoe's close personal friend, Sir Cecil Burney, as Second Sea Lord. Wemyss was also given the newly created post of Deputy First Sea Lord, a sure indication that Jellicoe was on the way out. Then, in September, Admiral Heath replaced Wemyss as Second Sea Lord, allowing Wemyss to devote his entire energies to the duties of Deputy First Sea Lord. Jellicoe, meanwhile, had become more and more immersed in paperwork and trivialities which he could not bear to delegate to subordinates. Finally a series of disasters, for which the First Sea Lord was held to be responsible, completely destroyed any confidence the Prime Minister had in Jellicoe as head of the navy.

On 17 October a German force of two light cruisers attacked a Scandinavian convoy, destroying the two escorting destroyers and nine of the twelve merchant ships. On 12 December four German destroyers attacked another Scandinavian convoy, sinking the destroyer *Partridge*, disabling a second destroyer and sinking the entire convoy of six ships. On each occasion the Germans escaped without damage, even though there were British cruisers in the vicinity at the time of the second attack, acting as distant escort to the convoy.

On 17 November a British force consisting of four battlecruisers, eight light cruisers, the new cruisers *Courageous* and *Glorious* and nineteen destroyers carried out a

Above: While work was progressing on the first true carriers, a number of ships were converted to operate aircraft, some being fitted with a small deck for landing on and flying off aircraft. One such conversion was the *Furious*, seen here as first converted with a flying off deck in place of the forward gun. (Imperial War Museum)

sweep in the North Sea in an attempt to catch a German force engaged in sweeping British minefields. The German force covering the minesweepers consisted of four light cruisers and eight destroyers, with two battleships in support near Heligoland. The two forces made contact early in the morning in good visibility, but German smokescreens frustrated the British attack, and because those on board the British ships had an incomplete knowledge of the extent of the British minefield, they were obliged to abandon the chase and allow the German ships to escape.

The final straw which led directly to Jellicoe's dismissal concerned the fiasco of the Dover Barrage. This mine and net barrage, laid under the direction of Admiral Bacon, a close friend of Jellicoe's, had proved to be singularly ineffective in preventing U-boats from entering the Channel. Geddes, as First Lord, set up an enquiry under the chairmanship of Keyes to investigate ways of improving the efficiency of the barrage. Bacon, who had always regarded the Barrage as successful, considered the enquiry a waste of time. As a result he adopted an unco-operative attitude towards the committee. The committee finally put forward a suggestion for illuminating the Barrage at night. This, it was hoped, would force submarines to submerge and become trapped in the minefield.

The system went into operation on the night of 19 December, and was an immediate success. The submarine *UB 56*, forced to submerge, became caught in the minefield and was sunk. Bacon's judgement had proved to be flawed, and on 28 December he was replaced by Keyes, who was promoted to Vice-Admiral. Jellicoe refused to endorse Bacon's dismissal, and stubbornly fought against the order. As a result the First Lord, Geddes, also lost confidence in Jellicoe, and following vociferous condemnation of the First Sea Lord's handling of the raids on the Scandinavian convoy, the debacle of 17 November, and finally the Dover Barrage enquiry, Geddes sent Jellicoe a curt note on 24 December, informing him that he was dismissed from his post. On 27 December Wemyss took over as First Sea Lord.

By the end of 1917, when the ocean convoy system was in operation in all theatres, it seemed that the U-boat campaign had at last been brought under control, even though the submarines themselves had not been resoundingly defeated. During December 1917, 76 British merchant ships, totalling 227,195 tons, were sunk by submarine, but during the first five months of 1918 the total number of British vessels sunk fell to about 66 per month, with a total average tonnage of about 200,000 tons. Shipping losses fell steadily during 1918 as the convoy system was extended throughout the oceans, and in June new shipbuilding at last exceeded the rate of sinkings. The situation was further eased as the average number of U-boats available for operations at sea each month steadily declined from 70 to 60. By the end of the war the losses exceeded new construction by three, an insignificant number, it is true, but the trend was plain to see. When the figures were analyzed at the end of the war, it was found that only 0.6 per cent of the ships sailing in ocean convoy were lost, while in home waters the percentage was slightly lower at 0.24 per cent.

A further attempt to combat the submarine menace was made on 22 April 1918, when the navy carried out raids on the ports of Ostend and Zeebrugge, exit routes for 30 U-boats and 35 destroyers stationed at the inland base of Bruges, in Belgium. At the heavily defended port of Zeebrugge a powerful force of assault ships with storming parties and block ships partially succeeded in blocking the canal from Bruges, while the submarine *C3* managed to destroy the viaduct carrying the vital railway from Zeebrugge to the mole on which was sited a number of batteries, sheds, submarine pens and a seaplane base. The operation at Ostend, on the other hand, was a failure. Unbeknown to the British, the Germans had moved two buoys near the harbour entrance which the navy planned to use for navigation. Their resiting by the Ger-

Right: Shortly after the *Furious* commissioned in July 1917, the first successful landing was carried out on 2 August 1917 by Squadron Commander E.H. Dunning in a Sopwith Pup (illustrated). In a third attempt on 7 August the engine stalled, and the flight deck crew, who had to manually hold on to the aircraft to stop it, were unable to prevent it from rolling over the side out of control, and Dunning was killed. (Imperial War Museum).

Centre right: Plans were also drawn up to convert the two large light cruisers built as part of Admiral Fisher's pre-war Baltic project. These were the *Courageous* (seen here as Vice-Admiral Charles Napier's flagship) and *Glorious*, which had proved unsatisfactory as designed. (ACPL)

Lower right: On 22 April 1918 the Navy carried out raids on the Belgian ports of Zeebrugge and Ostend. The raids were designed to block the U-boats and destroyers of Germany's Flanders Flotilla in their base at Bruges. The illustration shows the gap in the viaduct made by the submarine *C 3*. (ACPL)

Below: The last major loss suffered by the Royal Navy during the First World War was the battleship *Britannia*, seen here on fire and sinking off Cape Trafalgar after being torpedoed by submarine *UB 50* on 9 November 1918. (ACPL)

mans led to the blockships for Ostend being sunk in the wrong place. A second attempt to block the port was made on 9 May, but this, too, ended in failure.

Thus ended the last major First World War action involving the Royal Navy. The chief problem facing the navy following the Armistice was how to revert to a peacetime role. Large numbers of men would have to be demobilized, and only a relatively small number of ships would be required to carry out peacetime duties. Means would have to be found of phasing vessels out of service. This problem was not quite so acute, for many of the vessels were obsolete, while others were worn out after their arduous wartime duties, when maintenance and repairs had been kept to a minimum to keep as many vessels as possible in commission.

Chapter 23

Peace, and the Run-down of the Royal Navy

On 11 November 1918 the war finally ended. Unfortunately the end of the First World War did not signify a complete cessation of hostilities as far as the Royal Navy was concerned, for a number of units became involved in what was known as the 'War of Intervention', more generally referred to as the Russian Revolution. Royal Navy vessels based at various ports in Russia remained after the outbreak of the Revolution in 1917 to protect British interests and to protect supplies and bolster forces still fighting the Germans on the Eastern Front. With the formation of an Allied Force, the Royal Navy became actively involved in assisting the White Russian forces supporting the deposed Czar.

The years 1919-39 tell a sorry tale as far as the navy is concerned. The sheer destruction and losses suffered during the First World War convinced many that Britain should never again be involved in such a conflict, and through their beliefs and strenuous efforts, combined with an ever declining economic outlook and the disastrous slump of the 1920s, naval strength suffered more at the hands of its own Government than it had when fighting the Germans. Succeeding Estimates were continually slashed, both by passively minded Labour Governments bent on reducing Britain's armaments expenditure to the barest minimum, and by Conservative Governments anxious to defeat inflation and improve the economy by reducing expenditure in all areas.

Not until Hitler began asserting his authority was it at last realized that peace would not be achieved by disarmament. A few farsighted people realized that Britain might well become involved in another war with Germany, and that if such were the case, the navy was woefully inadequate to meet a threat from Germany's new navy, which was rising like a phoenix from the ashes of the High Seas Fleet. Urgent programmes of construction were instituted and crash programmes of recruiting begun, but even so, many of the new vessels laid down in the middle of the 1930s had not been completed when war broke out on 3 September 1939. As in 1914, the navy immediately seized the initiative when war broke out, but, as before, beneath the surface of the highly efficient and well organized Senior Service lay deficiencies which, in the strenuous operations carried out under exacting war conditions, would soon make themselves felt only too well.

In November 1918 the Cabinet ordered a number of cruisers and destroyers under the command of Rear-Admiral E.S. Alexander Sinclair to the Baltic, to protect the states of Estonia, Latvia and Lithuania and ensure that Bolshevik forces did not try to take over these small countries. Sinclair was relieved by Rear-Admiral Sir W. Cowan, who had under his command three or four light cruisers, approximately twelve destroyers, five submarines, two depot ships and a number of minesweepers. In May 1919 a number of clashes took place between Cowan's force and Bolshevik-crewed Russian warships. The following month, coastal motor boat *CMB 4* scored a singular success when she sank the cruiser *Oleg*, which was engaged in bombarding the forts at Kronshtadt. Subsequently, Cowan received a number of reinforcements, including eight coastal motor boats, a further minesweeping flotilla and the carrier *Vindictive*. With these additional vessels at his disposal Cowan immediately put into effect a plan using the carrier. On 18 August aeroplanes from *Vindictive* carried out a diversionary raid on Kronshtadt while coastal motor boats penetrated the harbour and sank the battleships *Andrei Pervosvanni* and *Petropavlovsk* and the submarine depot ship *Pamiat Ozova*.

In October 1919 trouble broke out on board a number of the British ships. Some of the minesweeping crews

Left: HMS *Queen Elizabeth*, the flagship of Admiral Beatty, Commander-in-Chief of the Grand Fleet, with the destroyer *Oak*, escorting units of the High Seas Fleet on their way to internment in Scapa Flow. (ACPL)

Right: One of the more unsatisfactory campaigns conducted by the navy was operations in support of the White Russians against the Bolsheviks in 1919. The picture shows the wreck of the minesweeper *Sword Dance* on the River Dvina in September 1918. She had been mined on 24 June. (ACPL)

Right: With the ending of the First World War orders for many ships were cancelled. The most modern battleships in the Navy were the four units of the '*Revenge*' class. The *Revenge* is seen here on trials in 1916. (ACPL)

Right: The most modern battlecruisers were the *Repulse* (seen here as completed in 1916) and *Renown*, built following the success of the Navy's battlecruisers at the Battle of the Falkland Islands, and before the disasters at the Battle of Jutland. (ACPL)

refused duty, a small mutiny occurred on *Vindictive*, and there was even trouble on board Cowan's flagship, the cruiser *Delhi*. The main cause of the trouble was pay, a grievance which also affected the rest of the navy, as well as indifferent food and a poor system of leave allocation. Partly as a result of these disturbances, and partly because of Government policy, the Baltic Fleet was run down during the spring of 1920, later being finally withdrawn when it became obvious that White Russian forces, in spite of local successes, had little real chance of ousting the Bolsheviks from power. Under difficult conditions, and with little support and guidance from the government at home, the Baltic Fleet under Cowan had succeeded in sinking a number of Bolshevik ships, including a cruiser and two battleships, for the loss of the destroyers *Vittoria* and *Verulam*, the submarine *L 55*, two minesweeping sloops, seven coastal motor boats and a store carrier, plus 127 men killed or missing.

The major problem facing the navy at the end of the First World War was how to comply with the Government's order to proceed with demobilization and reduce the size of the peacetime fleet. The Admiralty had already taken steps towards preparing for the run-down of the fleet when, towards the end of 1918, they cancelled the *Anson*, *Howe* and *Rodney*, three sister ships of the battle-cruiser *Hood*. *Hood* had been designed in 1915 in reply to the 15in-gunned '*Mackensen*' class battlecruisers that Germany was building. Orders had been placed for the '*Hood*' class in 1916, but after the Battle of Jutland, in which British battlecruisers suffered heavily through lack of adequate protection, it was decided to redraught the requirement for the class.

The battlecruiser concept laid down by Fisher (see page 76) with its 'speed is the best protection' dictum, was obviously no longer true. Instead a new concept, the high speed battleship, came into being, and the design of the '*Hoods*', with second class armour, was redrawn. Some of the lessons learnt from the Battle of Jutland were incorporated in the new design, including an antiflash arrangement between the shell hoists and the magazine,

Below: The last battlecruiser to be built for the navy was the *Hood*, laid down in September 1916 and completed in March 1920. She is generally regarded as aesthetically the most beautiful ship ever built for the navy. However, in warships beauty often belies capability, and the *Hood* lacked adequate protection in the face of modern naval firepower. Continuous inter-war parsimony over defence resulted in little being done to modernise the *Hood* to enable her to face modern warships. Finally, in 1939, modernization plans were approved, but it was too late. Before any of the plans could be implemented, the Second World War broke out and she was fully occupied on war service. The *Hood* is seen here shortly after commissioning. (ACPL)

Right: In the cruiser category the latest types were the 'C' and 'D' classes. The picture shows the *Calypso* of the 'C' class. (ACPL)

Right: The 'D' class were very similar to the 'C' class, the picture showing the *Durban*. Armament usually consisted of six (five in the 'C' class) 6in and two 3in guns, and twelve 21in torpedo tubes (the 'C' class carried fewer torpedo tubes). (ACPL)

the lack of which had caused the disastrous losses at Jutland. Extra armour was also to be fitted at the expense of speed and an increase in draught. These improvements increased the tonnage from 36,300 to 41,200. Further delays occurred while the Commander-in-Chief approved the final details, and the leadship, *Hood*, was not finally completed until 1920.

The future strength of the Fleet was further curtailed when, following the cancellation of the '*Hoods*', the Admiralty cancelled eighteen destroyers of the 'V' and 'W' classes and 198 submarines of the '*L*' class. In the cruiser category four vessels of the 'D' class, ordered in March 1918, were cancelled in the following November (eight had already been built or were under construction, the first two of the class being ordered in September 1916), while the *Euphrates* of the '*Emerald*' class was also

cancelled in the same month. The design of the 'D' class resembled that of the earlier 'C' class, but they mounted extra 6in guns and were equipped with triple instead of twin torpedo tubes, giving them the heaviest torpedo armament mounted in a cruiser at that time.

The three 'E' class cruisers (*Emerald*, *Enterprise* and *Euphrates*) had been designed and ordered on the supposition (later proved to be unfounded) that the Germans were planning to build high speed light cruisers as a counter to the 'C' and 'D' classes. The Admiralty stipulated that everything in the 'E' class should be subordinated to the overriding need that they must be capable of reaching a speed of 32kts at maximum displacement. The resulting design gave the vessels an armament almost identical to that of the preceding 'D' class on a hull whose length had been increased by 100ft to accommodate the powerful machinery required to reach 32kts, and whose displacement was 2,700 tons greater than that of the 'D' class (7,550 tons, compared with 4,850 tons).

The question of whether or not to continue with development of the submarine placed the Board of

Left: After the war orders for eighteen destroyers of the 'V' and 'W' classes were cancelled. The picture shows the *Warwick* of the 'W' class. Note the triple torpedo tube mounts and the 3in high-angle gun abaft no 2 funnel. (ACPL)

Admiralty in a dilemma. The sheer destruction accomplished by the German submarine campaign had led many to feel that the submarine was a weapon which certainly ought to be banned, and moves were made at the Peace Conference to obtain unilateral agreement on the total abolition of the submarine as a weapon of war. During the First World War, submarine development in the Royal Navy had progressed at a steady pace. In August 1914 the main strength of the submarine fleet was vested in the 72 boats of the 'B', 'C', 'D' and 'E' classes. The 'E' class was followed by the fifteen almost identical boats of the 'G' class. These, in turn, were followed by the much improved 'L' class with increased battery power giving an increase of 3kts submerged speed, and armed with the much more powerful 21in torpedo in place of the 18in weapon mounted in earlier boats. Smaller coastal submarines, the 'H' class, were also built during the war, together with the ten boats of the 'R' class, which carried six 18in torpedo tubes. This class had been specially designed to hunt U-boats, and their powerful batteries gave them a submerged speed of 15kts.

In addition to these standard designs, a number of experimental boats had been built, none of which proved successful. The most notorious of these were the eighteen ill-fated boats of the 'K' class. This class had been designed to operate with the Grand Fleet, and to give them sufficient surface speed for this role they were fitted with steam turbines instead of diesels (the earlier 'J' class, with conventional propulsion, could reach only 19kts maximum, insufficient for fleet duties). These engines gave rise to many problems and, together with poor longitudinal stability and the large number of tragic accidents which befell 'K' class submarines, led to them being deemed a failure. The surviving vessels were soon sold out of service.

The last four vessels of the 'K' class were completed with diesels, and underwent some interesting modifications when they were fitted with a single 12in gun. Dubbed submarine monitors, the 'M' class, these also proved unsuccessful as the gun could only be loaded when the boat was surfaced, although it could be fired from periscope depth. Of these four vessels, M4 was cancelled, M3 was converted into a minelayer, and M2 into a seaplane carrier. However, she was tragically lost on 26 January 1932 when she failed to resurface after submerging. It is believed that a mishap with the hangar door led to the submarine being flooded.

Left: Submarine development reached its peak with the 'L' class design. A total of 40 of this type were built between 1917 and 1920. A large number already ordered were cancelled at the end of the war. This class formed the mainstay of the submarine fleet during the early post-war years. Armament comprised a single 4in gun (two in later units) and six 21in torpedo tubes. (Wright & Logan)

Lower left: The Admiralty regarded the submarine as an integral part of the fleet and to this end designed the 'K' class, powered by steam turbines, which gave the boats the incredible surface speed of 24kts, allowing them to keep up with major fleet units. Standard electric motors were provided for submerged propulsion. The design proved a failure, the complexities of operating steam turbines in a submarine never being successfully overcome. The boats also suffered from a tendency to bury their bows in a seaway which necessitated redesigning the bow section. The class was dogged with ill luck and a number of boats were involved in disastrous accidents. Armament generally comprised two 4in and one 3in guns, and ten 18in torpedo tubes. (ACPL)

Anticipating that the Peace Conference would agree to the abolition of the submarine, the Admiralty reduced expenditure on the development programme to a minimum. However, as the submarine was an ideal weapon for smaller nations, providing them with great offensive potential for a modest outlay and being cheap and easy to produce with low manpower requirements, certain other nations at the Peace Conference refused to sanction its abolition, and placed on record their determination to proceed with its development. The prospect that Britain might soon fall behind in submarine development forced the Admiralty to review its policy, and a decision was made to continue with development of the weapon. This decision led to the ordering of the *X.1*, a cruiser submarine developed after close study of the German cruiser submarines and launched in June 1923. At the time she was the largest submarine in the world, with a surface displacement of 2,780 tons and an armament of four 5.2in guns carried in two twin turrets. Six 21in torpedo tubes were fitted in her bow. Although she suffered a certain amount of engine trouble, it was planned to build more of this type, but restrictions set by the Washington Treaty prevented the Admiralty from pursuing the idea and she was scrapped in 1937 to enable the navy to build three

smaller submarines (the *'U'* class) under the terms of the Treaty.

A further run-down in the fleet followed the end of the war when, with far fewer ships in commission and the consequent reduction in manpower needed to meet peacetime requirements, the Admiralty decided to reorganize the navy in home waters into three main fleets. These were the Atlantic Fleet (the main fleet, with all ships in full commission – 11 battleships, 5 battlecruisers, 6 light cruisers and 54 destroyers in three flotillas, about 30 submarines in five flotillas, and the entire air strength including carriers and seaplane carriers), the Home Fleet and the Reserve Fleet. Overseas forces would consist of the Mediterranean Fleet, China Fleet, and cruiser squadrons in the East Indies, Cape of Good Hope, South America and Western Atlantic. To man these fleets the manpower strength of the navy was set at 134,000. This reorganization was carried out early in 1919, and gave the navy a total of 33 battleships, 8 battlecruisers, 60 light cruisers and 352 destroyers to provide for the naval defence of Britain. The Admiralty further proposed to the Cabinet that the navy should complete a proportion of the vessels already under construction as a way of alleviating labour problems being caused by demobilization.

Right: A number of experimental boats were also built. Four *'M'* class boats were built using the hulls of discarded *'K'* class boats. Armed with a single 12in gun removed from obsolete battleships, they were classed as submarine monitors. The gun could only be loaded when the boat was surfaced, which made the boats extremely vulnerable to attack. The picture shows *M.1* firing her 12in gun. (ACPL)

Right: Further experimental submarine designs resulted in the *X.1*, a cruiser submarine armed with four 5.2in guns in twin turrets. (ACPL)

Above: The standard fighter serving with the navy during the 1920s and 1930s was the Fairey Flycatcher. The small aircraft served on all the navy's carriers, as well as being flown from the short take-off platforms fitted over the gun turrets of capital ships. (ACPL).

Below: *M.2* subsequently had her 12in gun removed and the housing altered to serve as a hangar for a tiny Parnall Peto seaplane. The submarine was lost with all hands off Portland in 1932 when the hangar flooded on surfacing.

Chapter 24

Pay, Conditions of Service and the Ten-year Rule

In addition to providing for the peacetime strength of the Royal Navy, the Admiralty also had to face the problem of improving the conditions of service. These had remained practically unaltered throughout the war, and there was a certain amount of discontent within the Service over welfare. The main bone of contention was pay, and at the beginning of 1918 the First Lord, Geddes, set up a Committee to investigate the question and to recommend increases. These were duly forwarded to the Treasury, where they lay unattended for nine months. This led to further unrest and there was even talk of strike action, but fortunately it came to nothing, except in the Baltic, where the navy was engaged with the Bolsheviks (see 126).

In April 1919 further proposals were fowarded to the Treasury. The majority of the revised figures were approved by the Cabinet, and led to substantial increases in pay being awarded. Unfortunately no provision had been made in the recommendations to allow for any rise in the cost of living index, which after the war and the economic slump in the 1920s rocketed sky-high, leaving the men poorer than before. This was to have tragic results in 1931, when the Admiralty proposed a cut in naval pay. Owing to poor communications between their Lordships and the Lower Deck, the reasons were not properly explained, and in September 1931 the crews of the ships at Invergordon refused to take their ships to sea, seeing strike action as the only means by which they could impress upon their Lordships the fact that they would be unable to live on the reduced pay. This incident came to be known as the notorious Invergordon Mutiny.

In August 1919 the Board of Admiralty took another step towards improving conditions in the navy when it set up the terms of reference of the Welfare Committee. Unhappily this Committee was composed entirely of officers. Representatives from the Lower Deck were drafted to act as advisors only, and would be attached as required. The Committee had been convened in this way in an

Below: The carrier *Eagle* was converted from a battleship under construction for the Chilean navy but purchased in 1917. She was completed with an unobstructed flight deck with an island bridge, and was noted as being the only carrier to have two funnels in her bridge superstructure. The *Eagle* carried about 25 large aircraft or 30 small, depending on mix of types. Under the terms of the 1921 Washington Treaty it was proposed to build four small 17,000-ton carriers between 1926and 1935, in which case it was planned that the *Eagle* would be scrapped in 1939. But the carriers were not built and the *Eagle* served on until sunk in the Mediterranean by *U 73* on 11 August 1942. (ACPL)

effort to forestall any attempt by the Lower Deck to set up a trade union. The Committee first met in February 1920, but owing to the exclusion of members from the Lower Deck it was not a success. Such important details as Naval Policy, discipline and individual claims and grievances were excluded from the terms of reference, and these were the main bones of contention among the Lower Deck. With these matters barred from discussion, the Lower Deck felt it was hardly worth their while putting forward recommendations, as those that were proposed were being ignored by the Admiralty. In the end this led to a virtual boycott of the Committee by the Lower Deck. As a result, the Board of Admiralty decided to suspend the Committee and await a more favourable opportunity for its reinstatement.

Tied up with the conditions of service was the vexed question of promotion, which mainly affected the more junior officers and ranks. A plan was put forward which would enable promising men from the Lower Deck to join the Special Entry Cadets, which had been formed in 1913 to cater for entries from the Public Schools. The majority of the Board of Admiralty were not in favour of the proposal, and the Second Sea Lord, Vice-Admiral H.L. Heath, even stated, 'To be a good officer it is necessary to be a gentleman'. There was much vacillation over the Committee's proposals, but in the end nothing was done and more than ten years elapsed before a Labour Government altered the situation.

Apart from the difficulties of promotion from the ranks, there was also a grudge in the engineer branch over their prospects, and particularly their exclusion from Flag Rank. This controversy raged until well after the Second World War and the introduction of the General List, which at long last made it possible for engineers to attain Flag Rank. Finally, there was the problem associated with the operation of electrical equipment. The number of electrically controlled pieces of apparatus had grown tremendously, and a committee which investigated the question in 1920 proposed that a new branch be formed to maintain and operate this equipment. However, after due deliberation the Board of Admiralty still could not make up its mind. Not until 1929 was a final decision reached which gave the engineer branch responsibility for high powered electrical equipment, while the torpedo branch was made responsible for the maintenance of low powered equipment. Thus the formation of a separate electrical branch was held in abeyance for many years by a most unsatisfactory interim solution.

In August 1919 the Cabinet asked the Admiralty to make an exhaustive study of the whole field of naval expenditure with a view to greatly reducing the Naval Estimates. At this point the Admiralty asked the Government what its policy would be concerning the strength of the navy vis-à-vis any possible combination of foreign naval powers. The Government view was that the British Empire would not become engaged in any major war for

at least ten years, and they put forward the notorious 'Ten-year Rule' which gave the Treasury unlimited statutes of power. Every time the Estimates were presented the Treasury, by quoting the 'Ten-year Rule', could veto any part of the Estimates and thus effectively prevent the navy from engaging in any increased construction or expenditure. This rule was extended several times during the 1920s, and in 1929 was made self-perpetuating, to the great detriment of the navy's strength and its capability of meeting any maritime threat. The Rule stifled British naval development and policy, and was not finally abrogated until the end of 1932. Under the 'Ten-year Rule' the Cabinet directed the Admiralty to limit expenditure in the 1920-21 Estimates to £60 million. This forced the Board of Admiralty to cancel or scrap all warships under construction which could not be completed within a few months.

TABLE IX. STATE OF WARSHIP CONSTRUCTION AT 1920-1 ESTIMATES

Type	Ordered/under construction	Subsequently cancelled
Battlecruisers	4	3
Light cruisers	21	4
Flotilla Leader Destroyers	} 108	44
Submarines	73	33
Carriers	2	—

These vast reductions would leave the navy with a peacetime strength of about 126,000 men and 20 capital ships in full commission, as opposed to the 29 originally planned. When the figures were placed before Parliament the Admiralty pointed out in no uncertain terms that, as far as the navy was concerned, Britain would henceforth be regarded as a European power, and emphasized that 'Great Britain will no longer be supreme at sea'.

The major problem confronting the Admiralty in the Estimates of this period was the question of battleship construction, about which an urgent decision was required. In the Defence White Paper presented in March 1920 the First Lord set forth his views on the battleship, stating, 'The unit in which sea power is built up is the battleship'. No provision had been made in the 1920-21 Estimates for designing or ordering a new class of battleships, and those completing or in commission at the time of the Estimates had all been designed during the war and would soon become obsolete. There was, therefore, an overriding need to start work on designs to replace these vessels, incorporating lessons learnt from the war.

In July 1920 the Admiralty made a study of the relative future strengths of the United States Navy and the Royal Navy, and in view of a recent statement in Parliament by the First Lord (Long) to the effect that the navy should not be inferior in strength to any other single navy (The One Power Standard), it was seen as impera-

Above: The first purpose-designed carrier built for the navy was the *Hermes*. The aircraft complement comprised twelve aircraft in the hangar with a further ten small aircraft stowed in a hold forward of the hangar. *Hermes* spent much of her career in the Far East where she was sunk by Japanese carrier aircraft on 9 April 1942. (Tom Molland)

tive that new battleships should be laid down as soon as possible. It was therefore proposed that four such vessels be laid down in 1921, another four in 1922, and that they should all be completed between 1924 and 1927. To keep within the Government's ruling concerning expenditure, it was agreed that, as long as the destroyers and cruisers then under construction were completed, there would be no need to construct any of these types of warship under the 1921-22-23 Estimates, and money which would have been spent on them could go towards covering the cost of the new capital ships. This proposed plan was not, however, to interfere with the completion of the conversion of the carrier *Eagle*, nor with the completion of the first purpose-designed aircraft carrier in the navy, *Hermes*.

The end of the First World War had done nothing to end the struggle for supremacy at sea. Already a new naval arms race was in progress, and Cabinet insistence on a reduction in the Defence Estimates, backed up by public opinion and a vigorous press campaign for disarmament, plus the deteriorating state of the national economy, left the navy with the unpalatable prospect that by 1925 the only post-Jutland ship which it could match against the six 'South Dakota' class battleships and six 'Lexington' class battlecruisers of the USA, and the four 'Kagas' and four 'Akagis' of Japan, would be *Hood*. Moreover, each of the foreign ships on its own would be more powerful than *Hood*, mounting 16in guns as opposed to *Hood*'s 15in weapons.

Churchill, First Lord Long and First Sea Lord Beatty voiced the opinion that if the One Power Standard was to be maintained, more capital ships ought to be laid down immediately, but, in spite of an inquiry to investigate the Admiralty's claims, nothing was done, nor were any plans for a new battleship drawn up. After a certain amount of wrangling the Admiralty managed to persuade the Cabinet to allow them increased expenditure, but with certain provisos.

The final figure agreed allowed the Admiralty to proceed with a design for four battlecruisers of an advanced *Hood*-type design, orders for which were placed in October 1921. An entirely new layout for the armament was drawn up. It was decided that the main armament of nine 16in guns in triple mounts should be concentrated forward of the machinery spaces, which would be sited aft. Half of the secondary armament battery of sixteen 6in guns would be sited around the superstructure aft of B gun and immediately in front of Y gun, while the remaining eight twin turrets were to be sited aft, near the stern. The secondary armament thus commanded a very wide arc of fire and would form a formidable defence, especially as the guns were to be mounted in turrets instead of open batteries, as hitherto. The bridge, chart rooms, control positions, rangefinders and all other associated equipment were to be concentrated in a tower structure sited immediately aft of B gun, rather similar to the pagoda-style structure later adopted in Japanese battleships.

The final Estimates as approved for 1921-22 gave the navy a strength of sixteen capital ships in full commission (reduced from the twenty of the previous Estimates), while the remaining fourteen capital ships available were to be placed in reserve. Manpower was further reduced from 126,000 to 121,700, and other economies were achieved in the dockyards and in the number of civilians employed therein. Overseas squadrons were reduced in size, and the South America Squadron was temporarily disbanded. Rampant inflation and the generally poor state of the economy pointed to the possibility of even greater cuts in future Defence Estimates, and it was not difficult to foresee that the navy would have severe difficulty obtaining approval for replacements and new construction. The Admiralty was placed in an exceedingly difficult position, for if the Estimates were reduced any further the navy might be unable to fulfil its commit-

Left: The Blackburn Ripon, which replaced the Dart in 1929, became the navy's standard two-seat torpedo aircraft, remaining in service until replaced by the Baffin in 1934. The Ripon was fitted for catapult operations and, with armament removed and extra fuel tanks added, could be used for long-range reconnaissance. (ACPL)

ments, and would certainly be unable to keep up with naval developments abroad.

In a further effort to reduce expenditure, in 1921 the Cabinet set up a committee under the chairmanship of Sir Eric Geddes to investigate the expenditure of the nation as a whole. The report dealt a decisive blow to the strength of the navy, and became known as the 'Geddes Axe'. It noted that the lack of co-ordination between the three armed services often led to a duplication of effort and entailed wasteful expenditure. To improve co-ordination and reduce duplication the Committee recommended that a body responsible for all military development and operations be formed, such as a Ministry of Defence, but the proposal was turned down in 1923 and the Ministry was not finally created until 1946. It was argued that the Committee of Imperial Defence (CID), formed in 1902, already provided some of the answers to the problem, and to improve the situation further a Chiefs-of-Staff subcommittee of the CID was created in 1924.

In addition, the Geddes report recommended individual cuts in the services, which in the navy led in part to the voluntary retirement of 200 lieutenants, with another 350 'selected' to retire. These retirements went part of the way to meeting the problem of surplus officers in the Service left over from the First World War, but in view of the run-down in the material strength of the navy even this was insufficient, and incentives were offered to officers surplus to requirements in an effort to induce them to retire early. Despite this, the problem of too many officers seeking too few seagoing appointments existed until well into the 1930s.

The Ten-year Rule had already imposed severe restrictions on military development, the newly formed RAF suffering the severest cuts. With responsibility for naval air operations resting with the Air Ministry, it was obvious that this area should suffer first in whatever cutbacks had to be made in the RAF. Consequently the maritime side of RAF operations was practically non-existent, the

maximum strength being just three squadrons, with a few extra Flights embarked in capital ships and cruisers in home waters. Although Air Vice-Marshal Vyvyan had voiced the opinion that shipborne aircraft were a vital and integral part of Fleet operations, carrying out reconnaissance, spotting and fighter duties and executing bombing and torpedo attacks against enemy aircraft and vessels, the RAF had done little to develop aircraft to meet the navy's needs.

It had already been decided that, to meet the navy's air requirements, a fleet of five modern carriers was required, and that when in commission three would serve in the Atlantic Fleet and two in the Mediterranean. Proposals that the carrier fleet should come under the control of the RAF were always vigorously opposed by the Board of Admiralty. The possibility of aircraft co-operating in convoy defence was unfortunately dismissed from these considerations, in spite of the apparent success obtained when airships were used for convoy defence in 1917. The main objection was that convoy protection was regarded as a defensive strategy, and both the RAF and the Admiralty considered that aircraft were primarily for use in an offensive strategy. This view prevailed right up to 1941.

In December 1919 the Admiralty had laid down guidelines along which it expected the Air Ministry to develop the naval air service. These listed as a main priority the development of a three-seat gunnery spotter aircraft. The Admiralty also requested development of a torpedo bomber and a number of large and small flying boats and seaplanes for reconnaissance work, the latter for use on capital ships and cruisers. In addition, all naval aircraft up to a certain size were to be designed for carrier operations (see Appendix 4). The Admiralty also asked for an armour-piercing bomb to be developed for use against enemy warships, but the bombing trials held in 1921 against the radio-controlled target ship *Agamemnon* proved a failure, the aircraft being forced to descend to 400ft to obtain 50 per cent hits.

Chapter 25
Disarmament Conferences and Naval Reductions

In July 1921 America called the world's principal naval powers together for a conference to discuss ways and means of limiting naval arms races, particularly the Anglo-American race then in progress, and to limit the increasing strength of Japan's navy, which was threatening to upset the balance of power. The British proposals had been drawn up to set limits which would permit a reasonable defence of the vital interests of the Empire, and the delegation was to press for the largest possible reduction in armament expenditure within these limits and for a reduction in the number of capital ships rather than the tonnage. The delegation was also to press most strongly for the abolition of the submarine.

The first session of the conference took place in Washington, DC, in November 1921, and the Treaty was finally signed on 6 February 1922. Under the terms of the Treaty, Britain was forced to accept parity with America over the quotas of capital ships and carriers allowed. Naval opinion in Britain, however, condemned the terms of the Treaty, which forced the Admiralty to scrap 20 capital ships of 408,500 tons, leaving the navy with 22 capital ships of 580,450 tons. As a result the Admiralty was forced to cancel the order for the four super 'Hoods', work on which had been suspended in November 1921 pending the outcome of the Treaty. Britain was, however, allowed to build two new battleships of 35,000 tons under the Terms of the Treaty as a counter to the battleships *Mutsu* and *Nagato*, which the Japanese declared they would retain in commission. The sketch design for the two battleships (*Nelson* and *Rodney*) was passed on 6 February 1922. The design was practically identical to that of the 1921 battlecruisers, but much reduced in size, and when completed they were the first capital ships to have their main armament

in a triple turret and the only British ships to mount 16in guns.

At the Washington Conference the British delegation refused to entertain any limitations on the number of cruisers a nation might retain in commission, for with long sea routes linking the Empire, the Admiralty rightly demanded that as many cruisers as possible be kept in commission, as they were vital for the protection of the trade routes. The Conference did, on the other hand, accept the British recommendation that the tonnage of cruisers should not exceed 10,000 tons, and that they should not mount guns larger than 8in. As soon as the Japanese made known their plans to construct 8in gunned cruisers, the Admiralty prepared plans for the 'County' class of 10,000-ton, 8in gunned cruisers for the Royal Navy, the first of which were ordered in the 1924 Estimates. Plans were also drawn up to convert the battlecruisers *Glorious* and *Courageous* into aircraft carriers, for under the terms of the Washington conference they would have had to be scrapped.

Under the 1922-23 Estimates, the first since the Washington Treaty, orders were placed for the two 'Nelson' class battleships and the cruiser-minelayer *Adventure*, and although no new construction was planned for in the Estimates for the following year, work began on converting *Courageous* and *Glorious* into aircraft carriers. Plans were also drawn up for the complete modernization and reconstruction of the 'Queen Elizabeth' class battleships. The modernization (allowed under the Washington Treaty) included the provision of extra deck armour to provide improved protection against bombs and plunging shells, and the addition of bulges to guard against damage from torpedo attack. The extra deck protection was, however, felt to be subordinate to the overriding

Right: Built under the terms of the Washington Treaty, the two battleships of the 'Nelson' class - *Nelson* and *Rodney* (illustrated) - exhibited a number of novel features unique to ships of the Navy. They were the first to carry triple turrets and mount 16in guns, all sited forward of a tower mast. Main deck batteries were replaced by turret mountings, which were all carried aft, mounting three twin 6in on either beam. (ACPL)

Left: The 'County' class heavy cruisers were all ordered and built strictly to the limits laid down in the Washington Treaty. They were divided into three sub-groups: the *Kent* (seven ships), *London* (four ships) and *Dorsetshire* (two ships). In attempting to achieve the best possible speed and armament within the displacement restrictions, they sacrificed protection. The design featured a long hull and high freeboard, and armament consisted of four twin 8in turrets and a secondary battery of eight 4in grouped in single mountings (later replaced by twin mountings) abaft the funnels. The illustration shows the *Norfolk* in the mid-1930s with a Fairey III floatplane forward of the after superstructure. (ACPL)

Left: The conversion of the *Courageous* and *Glorious* from large cruisers to aircraft carriers was completed in 1928/30. The *Courageous* (illustrated), was the first carrier in the Navy to be fitted with a transverse arrestor wire system. Aircraft complement totalled 42. (ACPL)

Left: During the latter part of the 1920s and early 1930s, the 'Queen Elizabeth' class battleships were extensively modernised, the major noticeable difference being the trunking together of the uptakes into a single funnel. The *Queen Elizabeth* is shown at the 1937 Coronation Review. (ACPL)

need for bulges, and as it was doubted whether funds would be forthcoming to meet both requirements in the prevailing financial situation, the question of increased deck protection was neglected. In the end sufficient armour was provided to give protection against 550lb bombs, the heaviest that could at that time be dropped by carrier aircraft. Unfortunately the Admiralty neglected to take into consideration the load that could be carried by shore-based aircraft, and this was to have dangerous repercussions in the future.

Sea trials of ASDIC were carried out in July 1923, and their successful conclusion and the introduction of the new equipment into the navy led to the formation of a new branch, the Anti-Submarine Specialist branch. ASDIC enabled escorts to determine the range and bearing of a submarine, but not its depth. Numerous exercises to test its effectiveness in screening a battle fleet were carried out, but curiously, especially in view of the disastrous losses suffered during the 1917 submarine campaign, no trials involving the use of ASDIC in convoy defence were carried out. Yet again Britain had ignored the potential of the submarine to dominate mercantile warfare.

The Admiralty were not completely lacking in foresight, however, for the new class of submarines then under design, the 'O's, equipped for greater endurance as it was realized that war with Japan might be a possibility, were fitted with ASDIC. The 'O' class boats unfortunately suffered from oil leaks from their fuel tanks, which were sited outside the pressure hull. The subsequent 'P' and 'R' classes suffered from the same trouble, and all three classes experienced trouble with their machinery.

In June 1923 the Admiralty put forward proposals for a ten-year programme of construction to replace the larger part of the fleet, which was rapidly becoming obsolete, especially the cruisers and destroyers. The plan provided for eight 10,000-ton 'County' class cruisers to be laid down in 1924, and, starting in 1927, two flotillas of nine destroyers ('A', 'B', 'C' and 'D' classes of eight units each, plus one leader) to be built every year, for by that time 87 of the total of 207 destroyers available would have reached their age limit. In addition it was proposed that, from 1924 onwards, seven overseas patrol submarines should be built annually, and in addition a submarine depot ship and two destroyer depot ships were urgently needed. In November 1923 the Board of Admiralty approved an immediate plan for the construction of eight 10,000-ton cruisers, three patrol submarines, a submarine and destroyer depot ship, a minelayer, two destroyers and new carrier.

Treasury approval was sought for the new programme, but in January 1924, before a decision could be reached, the Government fell when the Prime Minister, Baldwin, resigned. Ramsay Macdonald led into office a Labour Government fully committed to carrying out a programme of disarmament. The new First Lord, Lord Chelmsford, had to begin all over again with the new ten-year programme of construction. This resulted in a new set of figures being presented in which the major difference lay in submarine construction, which was reassessed at 60 overseas patrol, 12 cruiser and eight fleet types, all to be built during the succeeding decade. In addition, four new 30kt carriers totalling 68,000 tons were to built, while *Eagle*, *Hermes* and *Argus* were to be scrapped. In addition, two new minelayers were required as well as four submarine and five destroyer depot ships. A new class of minesweeper was also to be developed and, if the design proved successful, a total of 40 were to be in service by 1939. The immediate design of an experimental anti-submarine vessel was also proposed, and in conclusion the Board of Admiralty stated that they required a number of auxiliaries capable of supplying the fleet's needs at sea – the first move towards providing a Fleet Train of replenishment ships.

Right: The nine 'O' class submarines were the first to be fitted with ASDIC. The 4in gun was carried in a revolving mount in front of the conning tower. Eight torpedo tubes were fitted. (ACPL)

The total cost of this Ten-year Programme was put at £262.5 million. With the Labour Government in office, however, it was not easy to gain Treasury approval for the implementation of such a large programme. The Government finally agreed to the Estimates for 1924 providing for five 'County' class cruisers instead of the eight originally planned, and two experimental destroyers (*Amazon* and *Ambuscade*). Construction of the five cruisers was permitted solely as an economic measure, to relieve the desperate unemployment situation.

In 1927 a further conference on disarmament took place under the auspices of the League of Nations at Geneva. Like the previous Washington Conference, this was another attempt by the major powers of the world to come to mutual agreement concerning disarmament. It was felt that this would be a way of ensuring a lasting peace, and would prevent arms races which could lead to another great war. The conference finally disbanded without having achieved any results, mainly because Britain and America, with differing strategic requirements, were unable to agree on limitations concerning cruiser construction. Britain was again adamant that she could not, under any circumstances, consider reducing her cruiser strength, or placing an upper limit on it.

Above: The *Boadicea* (illustrated here) was one of the 'B' class destroyers which, together with the 'A', 'C' and 'D' classes, formed the mainstay of the Navy's destroyer flotillas throughout the 1930s. In general, armament consisted of four 4.7in guns and eight 21in torpedo tubes in two quadruple mounts. (ACPL)

Left: In the mid-1930s the Blackburn Baffin began to replace the Blackburn Ripon as the standard torpedo-bomber in naval service. Baffins of 810 NAS had the honour of leading the formation of Fleet Air Arm aircraft taking part in the Jubilee Naval Review in 1935. (ACPL)

Chapter 26

The Naval Air Battle

Towards the end of 1928 the Government at last announced that work was to start in 1930 on the carrier planned in the 1925 White Paper. Admiral Pound, at the time Assistant Chief of the Naval Staff, drew up a memorandum detailing his proposals for the expansion of the naval air service, and estimated that by 1937 the navy would require an effective strength of 251 front line aircraft (in 1929 the total strength was 150 carrier-borne aircraft). Pound felt that, with the three converted carriers having entered service, as well as *Eagle*, *Argus* and *Hermes*, the strength of the carrier fleet was adequate, and construction of the new carrier could therefore be deferred until 1932-33. The Board of Admiralty concurred, and agreed to review the position regarding the new carrier in 1930. This was done and the vessel, *Ark Royal*, was finally ordered in the 1934 Estimates.

Some improvement in naval tactics was seen during the 1920s and certain advancements were made, notably in anti-submarine techniques. A number of exercises to investigate the possibilities of carrier operations were also conducted, and some of the problems thrashed out. Unfortunately these experiments had to be conducted with the obsolete aircraft of the naval air service. The general performance of the aircraft then in service was below standard, mainly because of the greater all-up weight of

Below: The *Ark Royal*, completed in December 1938, differed from previous carriers in having side plating extended right up to the flight deck. She was fitted with a double storey hangar, two catapults and a crash barrier and eight arrestor wires. Her 60 aircraft (she was designed for 72) could operate in practically any weather. (ACPL)

the aircraft compared with their RAF counterparts. This was due to all the extra equipment, such as arrester gear, wing-folding apparatus, etc, with which naval aircraft were fitted. In addition, the restricted space in the hangars on the carriers forced aircraft to be designed to fulfil a number of roles, instead of concentrating on one function, which led to consequent loss of performance in each role.

Experiments were conducted with the carrier *Courageous* in an attempt to overcome the problems of landing aircraft on a moving deck. At the end of the First World War aircraft were arrested by claws on the aeroplane's undercarriage, which caught longitudinal wires raised by transverse flaps sited along the deck. This clumsy arrangement naturally led to a number of accidents and damage to aircraft. As a result the system was abandoned in 1926, and thenceforth aircraft landed on deck without any means of arresting their forward movement save a crash barrier used in emergencies. In 1931 the deck of *Courageous* was fitted with a number of transverse wires, and the arrester equipment was finally perfected in 1933, when tests were carried out using a Fairey IIIF. The new hydraulic equipment then became standard for all existing and future carriers.

All carriers, capital ships and large cruisers were already fitted with catapults for launching aircraft, following successful trials carried out on the carrier *Vindictive* using a Fairey IIID in October 1925. Night landings were also standard procedure by 1931, the first successful landing by night being carried out on *Furious* in May 1926 by a Blackburn Dart.

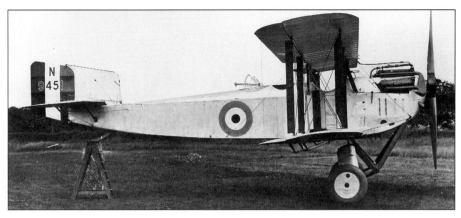

Left: For most of the 1920s the Fairey IIID was one of the mainstays of the Fleet Air Arm. It was the first of the III series to enter service in large numbers, the aircraft illustrated being the second of its type. These units were powered by Eagle engines. In 1925 a Fairey IIID became the first standard seaplane of the Fleet Air Arm to be catapulted from a ship at sea. (ACPL)

Left: The heavy cruiser *Exeter* (illustrated) with streamlined bridge. *York* differed in having a tiered bridge structure. Built under the terms of the Washington Treaty, the two cruisers were armed with three twin 8in turrets and mounted a catapult and aircraft abaft the funnels. (ACPL)

In spite of all the trials and successful exercises carried out involving naval aircraft, the concept of a major fleet action between capital ships was still adhered to. Exercises conducted in 1931 and 1932 showed conclusively that large fleets of capital ships were extremely vulnerable to a concerted air attack. During these exercises, torpedo bombers scored nine hits on the battleships, and out of a total of 32 torpedoes fired at the warships the aircraft scored a total of 21 hits. A notable omission in Fleet exercises at that time was the total lack of training involving the assembling and protection of slow moving merchant convoys, which was especially surprising in view of the disastrous losses suffered during the First World War and the undoubted success of the convoy system.

The Admiralty was also busy carrying out other trials and tests during the early 1930s, a number of which involved amphibious warfare techniques. Three experimental assault craft underwent evaluation, but the design and development of landing craft progressed slowly, and it was not until April 1939, with war imminent, that substantial contracts were placed for the construction of a number of different types of landing craft designed during the previous years.

A third naval conference was called by Britain and America in January 1930, and the British delegation most surprisingly stated that the Labour Government felt that, in view of its tremendous size and cost, the battleship was considered of doubtful fighting value, and that the British Government would welcome an agreement whereby the battleship would in time become obsolete and disappear completely from the fleet lists. The delegation also proposed that the question of the replacement of existing battleships be left until the next conference, due to be held in 1935, and that in future the maximum displacement of battleships should be limited to not more than 25,000 tons and that guns no larger than 12in should be mounted, a retrograde step indeed when one considers the designs that Germany, Italy, Japan and America then had under consideration.

Under the final terms of the agreement, Britain agreed not to lay down any new battleships until 1936, and to scrap four 'Iron Dukes' and *Tiger*. This left the navy with twelve capital ships. In the cruiser category Britain was at last forced to accede to America's request to limit her cruiser construction. By the terms of the Treaty Britain was compelled to reduce her cruiser strength from 70 to 50, and to construct a total cruiser tonnage of no more than 91,000 tons by December 1936. This limit was to have serious repercussions when war broke out in 1939, as it left the navy with only 62 cruisers to carry out trade protection and perform fleet duties. In addition, many of the cruisers were becoming obsolete (the 'C' and 'D' classes) and replacements were urgently needed, but in view of the Treaty limitations and the grave economic sit-

Right: In January 1930 the Admiralty approved the final design for the '*Leander*' class cruisers, a total of eight eventually being ordered. The vessels were armed with four twin 6in turrets of a new design and two sets of quadruple 21in torpedo tubes. A Fairey IIIF aircraft was carried on a catapult abaft the funnel. (ACPL)

Right: The four units of the '*Arethusa*' class light cruisers were armed with only three twin 6in turrets, X turret being omitted. The general lack of space topside led to the secondary battery being very cramped for space, while there was only room for triple torpedo tubes instead of the quadruple mounts of the '*Leander*' class. (ACPL)

uation facing the country the navy was forced to accept a severe cutback in the cruiser construction programme, to three per year.

These limitations led to the design of the smaller 7,000 ton '*Leander*' class cruiser, armed with 6in guns, and the slightly smaller '*Arethusa*' class, also armed with 6in guns. By the time the 1933 Estimates were presented, both America and Japan had resorted to constructing 10,000-ton 6in gunned cruisers, and in an effort to keep pace the navy dropped the orders for a '*Leander*' and two '*Arethusas*' so that two 6in-gun cruisers of an enlarged design could be constructed. The original design of the new class was based on the '*Leander*' class, but had four triple 6in turrets and improved protection. Known as the '*Southampton*' class (later referred to as the 'Town' class), these vessels bore little resemblance to the '*Leanders*'. The design was considerably enlarged to allow for the extra turrets and improved protection. In addition, the ships were equipped with a hangar amidships to enable the spotter aircraft to be maintained in a serviceable condition.

A Second London Conference was convened in December 1935, before the expiry date of the Washington Treaty of 1921 and the First London Treaty of 1930. The Conference opened on 9 December 1935, amid a worsening world situation. Germany had repudiated the Versailles Treaty and was busy rearming, and had come to a separate agreement with Britain to limit her fleet to 35

per cent of the total British tonnage. No longer bound by the London Treaty of 1930, German naval rearmament forced Britain to make a further separate agreement in 1937 to limit German construction in the various naval categories. Japan had already announced her intention of withdrawing from the Washington Treaty, and indeed had little real intention of signing any other Treaty as she was busy formulating plans for expansion in the Far East. Italy had invaded Abyssinia and allied world opinion against her, and she finally refused to sign the 1935 Agreement as a result of the hostility over her African ambitions.

Consequently there was little the Second London Conference could achieve. Restrictions on various categories of warships were abandoned, and instead agreement was reached on 25 March 1936 that each of the main signatories (Great Britain, France and America) would exchange advance information on new designs. In addition, no more heavy cruisers of 10,000 tons would be built after the end of 1942, when the Treaty expired, while light cruisers were limited to a maximum of 8,000 tons. The deteriorating world situation and growing likelihood of war caused the inclusion of a clause enabling signatories who found themselves in an impossible situation to relinquish their obligations to the Treaty, provided they first informed the other parties of their intention to withdraw.

Chapter 27

Rearming for War

The British Government was at last forced to realize that the armed services were woefully inadequate to meet any major threat from a rearmed Germany equipped with the most modern weapons available. Reluctantly the Government decided to approve a vast increase in the Defence Estimates to enable the armed forces to replace their obsolete equipment with more modern weapons, and to increase their strength.

In the Navy Estimates for 1936, orders were placed for two new battleships of the 'King George V' class, to be completed in 1940. At first there was some indecision as to the calibre of the guns to be mounted, but time was pressing and the deteriorating international situation forced the Admiralty to agree to a 14in gun. A 16in gun was preferred, but this would have meant a year's delay in the completion of the vessels. The 14in mounting permitted a better design to be adopted for the battleships, and at first they were to have three quadruple turrets mounting the 14in, but after finding that extra armour protection was required round the magazine, B turret was reduced to a twin mounting. The need for a heavy anti-aircraft defences, while at the same time having to provide for anti-destroyer armament, led to the adoption of a dual-purpose secondary armament of sixteen 5.25in high-angle/low-angle guns grouped amidships. In addition to the orders for the 'King George V' class, orders were also placed for the first of the 'Illustrious' class aircraft carriers, the first of the 'Southampton' class cruisers, and new classes of destroyers. Unfortunately the Government had left matters too late, and the majority of these vessels were still uncompleted when war broke out in 1939.

The 'Illustrious' class carriers were to be ordered at the rate of two per year from 1937 onwards. The first two, *Illustrious* and *Victorious*, were followed by *Formidable* and *Indomitable*, ordered in 1938. The carriers were to be larger than *Ark Royal* (23,000 tons), but the aircraft complement was to be reduced by 40 per cent to allow the ships to be fitted with an armoured flight deck, a decision which was to prove wise in the forthcoming war. Greater attention was also paid to the aerodynamic qualities of the design, to improve aircraft handling by reducing deck turbulence.

In 1936 the Spanish Civil War broke out, and Germany, Italy and Russia all supplied men and munitions to both sides in the conflict in an endeavour to train their armed forces for war and to test new weapons and equipment under war conditions. Although the Royal Navy was not an active participant in the bloody conflict, it carried out neutrality patrols. On numerous occasions destroyers from the Home Fleet on patrol around the Spanish Coast were called to assist British merchant ships caught up in the war, rescue stranded British civilians, and evacuate people all along the coast.

Below: To counter the latest Japanese cruisers, the navy developed the 'Town' class cruisers, ordering two under the 1933 Programme, three under the 1934 Programme, three more under the 1935 Programme and two modified units under the 1936 Programme. The ships were armed with four triple 6in turrets and eight twin 4in mounts sited on either beam just abaft the after funnel. To maintain aircraft in a serviceable condition it was realised that some form of hangar was essential. This was a sizeable structure which housed two Walrus amphibians sited on either side of the fore funnel, immediately forward of the athwartships catapult. The picture of the *Southampton* shows the enormous hangar under the fore funnel. (ACPL)

Right: During the mid-1930s a number of coastal patrol escorts, designed for anti-submarine tasks, were completed. Typical of these vessels was the *Kingfisher*, seen here at the 1935 Jubilee Review. (ACPL)

Right: For ocean-going anti-submarine/AA escort duties the larger 'Bridgewater', 'Hastings', 'Shoreham' and 'Falmouth' classes (fourteen ships) were built. The *Bridgewater* is seen here at Portland just prior to the outbreak of war. (ACPL)

Right: This picture of the 1935 Jubilee Review shows the Royal Yacht *Albert and Victoria* about to pass between the *Revenge* and *Devonshire*. (ACPL)

In 1937 Parliament at last announced that a decision had been reached concerning the future of naval air co-operation. Following a long and often bitter controversy, responsibility for the naval air element was at last to be handed back to the Admiralty in 1939. The Admiralty would then be able to have its own shore stations, and all personnel in the Fleet Air Arm (FAA, renamed as such in April 1924) would be naval. Moves in this direction had already been made as early as 1921, when the Air Ministry began to train naval officers as Naval Observers, and again in 1923, when a Committee recommended that 70 per cent of the pilots manning naval aircraft should be naval, but given a dual RAF rank to enable them to meet the Air Ministry's requirements. This same Committee had, however, refused the First Lord's request that control of naval aviation be returned to the navy. At this the Sea Lords had threatened to resign in a body, but had been persuaded not to do so.

The years after 1936 saw more orders placed for warships of all categories as Hitler gradually widened his sphere of influence in Europe. Austria was annexed in March 1938, and in August of that year Germany began mobilization. In April 1938 the Sudeten Germans in Czechoslovakia demanded autonomy, fully backed by Hitler. France and Britain resisted Hitler's demands for the adjustment, and in September 1938 the British Prime Minister met Hitler in an attempt to dissuade him from carrying out his threat to destroy Czechoslovakia. On 23 September the Czech Army was mobilized, and as war seemed imminent the Royal Navy was mobilized on the 27th, but demobilized when the crisis receded. On 30 September 1938 Chamberlain acceded to Hitler's wish that the Sudetenland be transferred to Germany, and returned from Munich with a piece of paper, proclaiming 'It is peace in our time'.

In November Hungary annexed southern Slovakia and the dismemberment of Czechoslovakia was almost complete, without any nation lifting a finger in its defence. On 15 March 1939 German troops entered the remaining territories of Czechoslovakia, and Hitler announced that the country had ceased to exist. On 31 March Chamberlain said that Britain and France had agreed to guarantee the status of Poland, should Hitler turn his attention to that country. In April 1939 Hitler denounced the Anglo-German naval pact and repudiated the German-Polish non-aggression pact. The way was now open for the domination of Europe by Hitler, and in a secret pact with Russia the two countries agreed on their partition of Poland.

On 23 August the Admiralty sent orders that all warships in home waters were to proceed to their war stations, and on 29 August the Fleet was ordered to mobilize for war.

Although Chamberlain had seriously misjudged Hitler's aims concerning Europe in the past, he was in no doubt when German troops invaded Poland in the early hours of 1 September 1939. The following day he sent an ultimatum to Hitler, demanding the withdrawal of German troops from Polish territory. Hitler ignored this, and on 3 September 1939 Britain, France, Australia and New Zealand declared war on Germany.

At 1100 the Admiralty sent off the war telegram to all ships, 'Commence Hostilities at once against Germany', and once again the navy found itself at war with Germany. It had two new leaders; Churchill, who returned as First Lord, and Admiral Pound, who was appointed First Sea Lord in July 1939, on the death of Admiral Sir Roger Backhouse.

Left: By the late 1930s the 'H' and 'L' class submarines were becoming obsolete and two new designs for their replacement were prepared. The 'S' class, designed to replace the 'H' class, proved so successful that production was re-started on the outbreak of war and continued until the end of hostilities. The *Snapper* is illustrated. (ACPL)

Left: The 'T' class boats were designed to replace the obsolete 'L' class and superseded the 'O', 'P' and 'R' classes. The class was notable for mounting a torpedo tube on either beam amidships. The two external bow tubes in the first group were enclosed in a bulbous nose which created a large bow wave at periscope depth. Later vessels had a streamlined bow. Shown is *Triton* of the first group. (ACPL)

Chapter 28

The Second World War: Opening Moves

For the second time within a century, and only 21 years after the ending of The Great War, the Royal Navy found itself involved in a war with Germany spanning the seven oceans of the world. It was a war which would eventually bring all the major nations of the world into conflict on one side or the other. Unlike 1914, the margin of superiority between the Royal Navy and the new *Reichsmarine* of resurgent Germany was greatly in favour of the former. In his 'wisdom', Hitler, who had no experience in naval matters, had ignored the advice of his Admirals that the navy was not yet fully up to its planned strength for a major war, and pressed ahead with the invasion of Poland.

Within hours of the outbreak of war, maritime operations had begun, with the German submarine *U 30* sinking the liner *Athenia*, which it had mistaken for an auxiliary cruiser, south of Rockall. The survivors were soon rescued by warships of the Royal Navy and nearby merchant ships, but even so 112 passengers and crew lost their lives. With the memory of the submarine campaign of the First World War still relatively fresh in their minds, the Admiralty assumed that Germany had begun an unrestricted submarine campaign. This was not the case, however, and in view of the controversy aroused by the sinking, the German naval commander-in-chief, Admiral Raeder, issued more detailed instructions to the U-boat arm, designed to prevent such incidents recurring.

Below: The first of the new 'armoured' carriers, HMS *Illustrious* entered service in May 1940. She is shown here as first completed, and still carrying workmen's huts on her flight deck abaft the superstructure. The effect of the streamlined bow configuration can be clearly seen. (ACPL)

The outbreak of war immediately put the Royal Navy at the forefront of the fighting, for it was clearly recognized that, whatever happened in the coming months, the whole future of Britain and her Empire depended entirely on the safe arrival and departure of merchant ships from every corner of the world. Oil was the vital lifeline to Britain's war effort, and every effort had to be made to ensure the safe arrival of oil tankers with their precious cargo.

At this stage, Germany had relatively few U-boats with which to wage a mercantile campaign. However, the surface fleet had been built up with just such operations in mind, and within a week two pocket battleships, *Admiral Graf Spee* and *Deutschland*, had broken out into the Atlantic with a view to carrying out raids against merchant ships bound for Britain. They were soon to be followed by others, including a number of disguised and heavily armed merchant ships, well provisioned and designed to remain at sea for extended periods of time, supported by a network of supply ships which also sailed from Germany.

At first it was the surface raiders which demanded the full attention of the Royal Navy, and a number of hunting groups were formed in an effort to track down these independent marauders and put a stop to their attacks. But it was the U-boats that were the first to score success, primarily against units of the Royal Navy. On the outbreak of war, carriers from the Home Fleet, supported by screening destroyers, had been formed into small groups to hunt for U-boats. Although the concept seemed sound, the value of air patrols to reduce the effectiveness of U-boat operations during 1917 having been proven, the

capability of the aircraft to attack the U-boats was severely limited, and the destroyers were not that well equipped to hunt modern submarines. Furthermore, the carriers themselves were high-value units which the Royal Navy could ill afford to deploy on duties which turned out to be rather fruitless.

This was soon proved when, on 17 September, the carrier *Courageous* was sunk by *U 17* off Ireland. The ability of the U-boat to strike anywhere at any time, virtually without warning, was again highlighted the following month when, in a daring raid, *U 47* penetrated the fleet base at Scapa Flow and sank the old battleship *Royal Oak*. The loss of life was tragic, but the loss of the old battleship was not of great significance. What was significant, however, was that a submarine had been able to penetrate what was considered to be a safe anchorage. Fortunately the main bulk of the fleet was not in the base at the time of *U 47*'s attack, or the story might have been very different.

In October the first indications that units of the *Reichsmarine* were roaming the oceans in mercantile raiding operations became apparent. A number of merchant ships were reported overdue, and very little news as to their fate had reached the Admiralty. With the knowledge that a number of warships and armed merchant cruisers had sailed to carry out raiding operations, the British and French formed eight hunting groups to search for and track down the pocket battleship *Admiral Graf Spee*. Between 5 and 12 October *Graf Spee* sank four ships of 22,368 tons. Further sinkings by *Graf Spee* led to the formation of more hunting groups in the Indian Ocean, but it was like looking for a needle in a haystack. While the British raced to the lone raider's last reported position, *Graf Spee* slipped back into the Atlantic. All the groups could do was sail to the last reported position of merchant ships sending out the RRR distress message — Raider, Raider, Raider.

Meanwhile, in the middle of October, U-boats attempted to carry out their first co-ordinated operation using a tactical commander, Commander W. Hartmann on *U 37*. The operation was not entirely successful, *U 40* being mined in the English Channel and *U 42* and *U 45* being sunk by the escorts to convoys OB.17 and KJF.3, which were attacked. The remaining three U-boats then went on to attack the unescorted convoy HG.3, which lost three ships. The entire operation resulted in sixteen merchant ships of 98,800 tons being sunk for the loss of three U-boats.

In an attempt to clear British patrols in the North Atlantic and entice the groups hunting for *Graf Spee* away from their task, and also to enable the German raiders to operate with greater impunity, the battleships *Scharnhorst* and *Gneisenau* sortied into the Faroes-Iceland passage. There, on the evening of 23 November, *Scharnhorst* came upon the armed merchant cruiser *Rawalpindi*, which was sunk after a brief gun duel. At once the Admiralty ordered

all available warships to the area in an effort to catch the Germans, and all convoys due to sail for the North Atlantic were recalled. However, the onset of bad weather, in which many ships suffered considerable damage, enabled the Germans to return safely to their home base.

Nearer to home, and in the area of the main shipping channels around the home ports, German submarines, destroyers and aircraft were busily laying mines, many of them of a new magnetic type. Aware that a new mine was being deployed, the Admiralty made strenuous efforts to capture one of the weapons intact. Their efforts were finally rewarded on 23 November, when Lieutenant Commander Ouvery succeeded in defusing a magnetic mine which had been dropped in the mud flats off Shoeburyness and had been uncovered at low tide. German minelaying operations continued to claim victims, but with the secrets of the magnetic mines revealed, the navy was able to set about designing a means of sweeping and destroying them.

The depredations of the *Graf Spee* continued. Finally, on 2 December *Graf Spee* seized the British SS *Doric Star*, which was able to transmit an RRR message. This was picked up, and immediately indicated the general area of operations of the raider, off the northern region of Brazil. The C-in-C South Atlantic, Admiral Sir G. H. d'Oyly Lyon, organized a search northwards, while Force G, comprising the 8in-gunned cruiser *Exeter* and the smaller 6in-gunned cruisers *Ajax* and *Achilles*, under the command of Commodore Henry Harwood, deduced that *Graf Spee* would make for the rich shipping lanes to the south of Brazil, off the mouth of the River Plate, between Uruguay and Argentina. Force G assembled in the general area off the River Plate on 12 December, and not long after daybreak on the following day *Ajax* sighted smoke to the north. *Exeter* was ordered to investigate, and at 0615 she signalled 'Think it is a pocket battleship'. The rest of the squadron joined the chase, *Exeter* shadowing and firing on *Graf Spee* from the south while the two light cruisers shadowed from the east.

The British force was heavily outgunned (*Exeter* mounted three twin 8in turrets and the two smaller cruisers four twin 6in turrets, while *Graf Spee* was armed with two triple 11in turrets), but by splitting his force Commodore Harwood hoped to force *Graf Spee* to divide her own fire, rather than concentrate on one ship. These tactics would also provide accurate fall of shot observations for the British force, maximizing the effectiveness of its gunnery. Fire was opened at the maximum range of the British guns, and at once *Graf Spee* responded as Commodore Harwood hoped, dividing her fire against both groups of British ships. Soon after, *Graf Spee* directed all her fire on *Exeter*, which was identified as being the more dangerous threat with her 8in guns. *Exeter* suffered a number of serious hits, losing the use of one of her three 8in turrets and her main steering. At this, *Exeter*'s captain, Captain F.S. Bell, decided to move in on *Graf Spee* and

THE BATTLE OF THE RIVER PLATE, 13 DECEMBER 1939

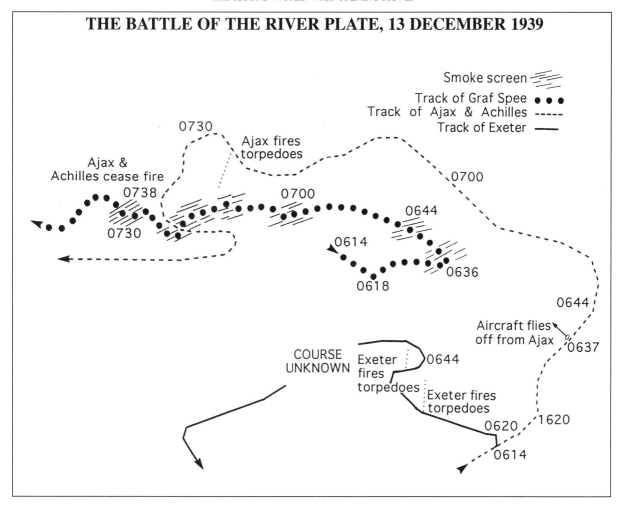

Smoke screen
Track of Graf Spee ● ● ●
Track of Ajax & Achilles - - - - -
Track of Exeter ——

0730

Ajax fires torpedoes

Ajax & Achilles cease fire

0738

0730

0700

0700

0644

0614

0636

0618

0644

Aircraft flies off from Ajax

0637

COURSE UNKNOWN

Exeter fires torpedoes

0644

Exeter fires torpedoes

0620

1620

0614

attract all her attention, to allow the two lighter cruisers to close and attack unseen from a different angle. Reaching her maximum speed of 32kts, *Exeter* raced towards *Graf Spee*, hoping to carry out a torpedo attack. The cruiser suffered terrible punishment until only one turret was left working. At this point, with a bad list to starboard, *Exeter* was forced to withdraw from the action.

In the meantime, the two lighter cruisers had been exchanging fire with *Graf Spee*'s secondary 5.9in guns. *Ajax* suffered some serious damage, while *Achilles* suffered light damage. At this the Commodore put up a smoke screen and withdrew out of range of *Graf Spee*'s main armament. *Graf Spee* turned towards the River Plate, the British cruisers continuing to shadow out of range of her 11in guns and occasional salvoes being exchanged as the ships came within range. *Exeter*, meanwhile, had turned south to limp towards the Falkland Islands for temporary repairs. The fourth cruiser of Force G, *Cumberland*, had left the Falklands immediately on hearing of the action, and raced northwards to join the remaining two cruisers.

Graf Spee had suffered relatively minor physical damage, but the crew's morale was at a low ebb and she had been

away from home and out of sight of land for a long time, so she put into the neutral Uruguayan port of Montivideo. Under neutrality laws, the captain of the *Graf Spee*, Captain Hans Langsdorff, was allowed just 24 hours' stay in the port to make emergency repairs. At the end of that time he would be forced to leave and face the British forces.

As soon as the action had begun, the Admiralty had directed all available forces to the scene, but it would be some time before reinforcements could arrive to support *Ajax* and *Achilles*. Both sides sought to extend the 24-hour stay, and eventually the German Embassy in Montivideo gained permission for the *Graf Spee* to remain in port for 72hr. This was further helped by the British sending merchant ships to sea from the port. Under neutrality laws, the Germans had to allow each ship 24 hours' grace before they themselves could leave. The British continued to build up pressure on the Germans, making public radio announcements as to the strength of the forces assembling off the River Plate (long before any such forces could hope to reach the area). On 16 December Langsdorff cabled from the German Embassy to Admiral Raeder in Germany, seeking instructions.

The only escape, as Langsdorff could see it, was to fight his way out of Montivideo and across the estuary to Buenos Aires, Argentina, where there was strong sympathy for the German cause. Any attempt to break out to sea was, as far as he could see, foredoomed to failure. The only alternatives were internment in Argentina or, as a last resort, scuttling his ship. Raeder consulted Hitler over the problem, which by now had hit the world's headlines. Hitler refused to endorse internment, and grudgingly agreed to scuttling if fighting a way out became impossible. On 18 December, 24hr after receiving the reply from Germany, Captain Langsdorff sailed from Montivideo, watched with bated breath by many hundreds of people ashore, and with considerable trepidation by the two British light cruisers and the recently arrived *Cumberland*, the only force available to bar the way out into the Atlantic.

This, of course, was unknown to Langsdorff, who, together with the Germans in Uruguay and Argentina, had been fooled by the British propaganda concerning the strength of forces awaiting him in international waters off the River Plate. *Graf Spee* moved out to the edge of the three-mile limit, where she transferred members of her crew to a waiting German steamer which had followed her. Shortly after, the night sky was lit by enormous explosions on *Graf Spee* as her magazines exploded from scuttling charges. The crew and captain were taken to Argentina for internment, and there, on 20 December, Captain Langsdorff shot himself. Captain Langsdorff and his ship had sunk a total of nine merchant ships of 50,089grt during her brief career, and not a merchant seaman's life had been lost.

There was a sequel to the scuttling of *Graf Spee*. This concerned one of her attendant supply tankers, the *Altmark*, which carried 299 of the merchant seamen captured by *Graf Spee*. On hearing of the loss of *Graf Spee*, *Altmark* sailed south until the furore died down, and then headed for Germany. She managed to evade waiting British forces, and holed up in a fjord in Norway. There, on 16 February 1940, in a daring operation after persuading Norwegian naval forces to withdraw, the destroyer *Cossack* rescued the merchant seamen held in *Altmark*'s stinking holds.

During April 1940 the focus of maritime operations switched to Norway. Concerned over the amount of trade, and in particular Swedish iron ore, reaching Germany from Norwegian ports in German merchant ships, the navy carried out a mining operation, Operation Wilfred, in Norwegian waters on 5-8 April, which was to be backed up by landings at Narvik, Trondheim, Bergen and Stavanger. A mining operation had already been proposed by Winston Churchill on 19 September, in a note to the Cabinet. The Foreign Office, however, was opposed to any such operation, which would violate Norway's neutrality. The debate spread beyond Parliament and reached the press. It was not long, therefore,

before the news concerning the possibility of British moves against Norway reached Hitler. The following month Admiral Raeder told Hitler what the strategic disadvantages of such an occupation of Norway by Britain would mean to Germany. Raeder also noted that German possession of bases in Norway would be of advantage to U-boat operations. Hitler, however, was not convinced of the advantages, preferring Norway to remain neutral.

Further hints concerning possible Allied moves against neutrals, and against Norway in particular, were given in speeches in Britain during January. On 27 January Hitler ordered comprehensive plans to be prepared for an invasion of Norway, should this prove necessary. Finally, the *Altmark* incident convinced Hitler of the necessity of invading Norway to pre-empt any British attempt at intervention in that region. On 1 April Hitler ordered German forces to begin Operation Weserübung, the invasion of Denmark and Norway, on 9 April.

When the news of Operation Wilfred reached Hitler, German naval forces were already at sea bound for Norway. Part of the covering force for Operation Wilfred included the battlecruiser *Renown* (flying the flag of Vice-Admiral Whitworth) and the destroyers *Hyperion*, *Hero*, *Greyhound* and *Glowworm*. During a heavy storm on 8 April *Glowworm* became separated from the rest of the force when she stayed behind to rescue a seaman who had fallen overboard. At this point she encountered the German cruiser *Admiral Hipper*, which formed part of a naval force convoying German troops to Trondheim. In a desperate attempt to fight back, *Glowworm* rammed *Hipper*, but was herself then sunk.

Unbeknown to the British, *Hipper* formed part of the much larger Operation Weserübung, which involved a series of landings along the Norwegian coast by strong

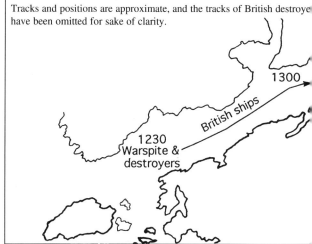

THE SECOND BATTLE OF NARVIK IN OFOTFJORD, 13 APRIL 1940

Tracks and positions are approximate, and the tracks of British destroyer have been omitted for sake of clarity.

1300

British ships

1230
Warspite & destroyers

German forces. By the end of 9 April the Germans had taken possession of the capital, Oslo, and all the main ports, including Narvik in the far north. The British government, under the premiership of Mr Chamberlain, was slow to realize the gravity of the situation, considering that the German operation was probably only aimed at southern Norway, and that the invasion could easily be contained and dealt with by British forces. Problems between the French and British Allies led to a delay in the start of Operation Wilfred, allowing the Germans to have a head start.

The news of the loss of *Glowworm* alerted the Admiralty and the Government to the German moves, some details of which had already become known. But the government and the Admiralty were slow to react, which allowed the German forces time to consolidate their position ashore. Although they had viewed the potential of air power with scepticism before the war, the Admiralty now became intensely concerned over the air threat, and not without reason, as events were soon to show. In an effort to counter the German invasion, Operation Wilfred was upgraded and stronger Allied forces belatedly embarked to invade northern Norway and sweep south to evict the Germans from the country. The operation was a fiasco, the entire British force having to be re-embarked from most places within a fortnight. Only those at Narvik remained for a month, then they, too, were re-embarked as the Germans began their invasion of France.

On the evening of 7 April, upon receiving news of the German invasion, the C-in-C Home Fleet, Admiral Sir Charles Forbes, sailed from Scapa Flow with the battleships *Rodney* and *Valiant*, the battlecruiser *Repulse*, the cruisers *Penelope* and *Sheffield* and a number of destroyers. They were later followed by a number of French warships. Other British naval forces also converged on Norway

from a wide area, while one convoy, ON.25, was actually recalled and her escort ordered to join the Home Fleet forces. Vice-Admiral Sir Max Horton, Flag Officer Submarines, also ordered all available submarines to positions off the Norwegian coast to intercept German naval forces and their support convoys. On 8 April the Polish submarine *Orzel* sank the troop transport *Rio de Janeiro*, and the submarine *Trident* sank the tanker *Posidonia*. The submarines were then given permission to attack transports without warning, and finally, on 11 April, to attack without warning all ships sailing within 10nm of the Norwegian coast. A number of ships were sunk, including the German cruiser *Karlsruhe*, initially torpedoed by the submarine *Truant* and later sunk by her own forces. The submarine *Thistle* was sunk by *U 4* on 10 April, *Tarpon* by the minesweeper *M 6* on 14 April, and *Sterlet* by German submarine chasers on 18 April.

Meanwhile, further out to sea, the German battleships *Gneisenau* and *Scharnhorst*, providing distant cover against British forces, fell in with the battlecruiser *Renown*. An inconclusive action followed, *Renown* and *Gneisenau* each taking hits. A number of units were detached from the British force under Vice-Admiral Layton to carry out an attack on Bergen. The ships were forced to turn away when they came under air attack, *Gurkha* being sunk and the cruisers *Glasgow* and *Southampton* being damaged by near misses.

At daylight on 10 April, in poor visibility, the 2nd Destroyer Flotilla (Captain Warburton-Lee) with *Hardy*, *Hunter*, *Hotspur*, *Havock* and *Hostile* entered Ofotfjord to attack German shipping around the port of Narvik. In the ensuing action a number of merchant ships were sunk, three German destroyers were damaged and *Hardy* and *Hunter* were sunk. On 13 April the battleship *Warspite*, accompanied by the destroyers *Bedouin*, *Cossack*, *Eskimo*,

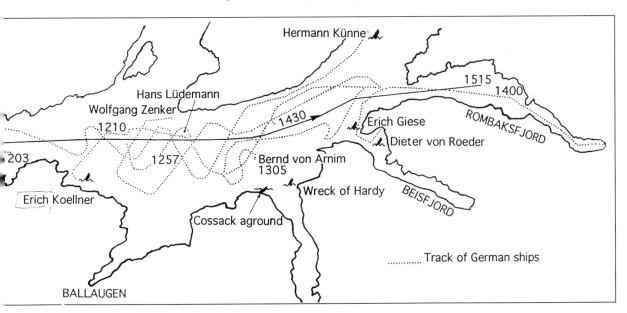

.... Track of German ships

Forester, *Foxhound*, *Hero*, *Icarus*, *Kimberley*, and *Punjabi*, entered the fjord to deal with the remaining German destroyers. All eight destroyers were either sunk or scuttled, and the submarine *U 64* was sunk by a Swordfish floatplane from *Warspite*. Three of the British destroyers suffered varying degrees of damage. Later in the day Skua dive bombers of Naval Air Squadrons 800 and 803 sank the cruiser *Königsberg* in Bergen harbour.

With the German forces temporarily neutralized and the Royal Navy in command of the northern waters off Norway, the belated Allied landings were able to take place. However, the Germans were ashore in such strength, and with such total command of the air, that the Allied forces were able to accomplish little of significance. German air attacks carried out from bases in Norway continued to dominate the operation. The forces at Andalsnes had to be evacuated on 29 April, and those at Namsos on 2-3 May, in the face of severe air attacks. At Namsos the sloop *Bittern* was sunk, and the destroyers *Afridi* and *Bison* (French) were sunk when returning from Norway with the rearguard after covering the evacuation from Namsos.

On 24 May the decision was finally taken by the Allied Supreme Command to evacuate all Allied forces from Norway. Once again, operations had to be undertaken in the face of severe air attack. On 26 May the anti-aircraft cruiser *Curlew* was sunk. The final evacuation of Narvik began on 4 June, and in five successive nights 24,500 men were evacuated. Aware that the Allies were evacuating, the Germans mounted a major naval operation against the convoys with the battleships *Gneisenau* and *Scharnhorst*, the cruiser *Hipper* and a number of destroyers. This resulted in the sinking of the empty troop transport *Orama*, the tanker *Oil Pioneer* and a trawler on 8 June.

The German battleships then detached from the rest of the force and came upon the carrier *Glorious* and the destroyers *Acasta* and *Ardent*. *Glorious* had embarked all of the RAF's Hurricane and Gladiator aircraft from Norway, and with her decks crowded with aircraft was unable to fly off air reconnaissance which might have warned of the presence of the two German battleships. In the action which followed, all three ships were sunk, but the main troop evacuation convoys managed to reach England safely. The loss of the carrier was serious, but even more calamitous was the loss of so many pilots, both naval and RAF, for they were soon to be sorely needed in the Battle of Britain.

Even before events in Norway had reached their disastrous conclusion, another disaster had loomed much closer to home across the English Channel. There, the Allies had been forced back from the Franco/German border in a lightning *blitzkrieg* operation by the German Army. By the middle of May the BEF had been forced back to the Channel ports. During 23-24 May 4,368 troops were evacuated from Boulogne in the face of heavy German artillery fire. By the end of May the main bulk of the BEF was holed up in Dunkirk and the surrounding area. On 28 May Belgium capitulated and the main evacuation from France began.

Between then and 4 June, when Operation Dynamo, as the evacuation was codenamed, ended, 338,226 troops were evacuated from Dunkirk, including 123,000 French. Over three-quarters of the BEF had been saved, but the Army had had to leave all of its equipment behind. The whole operation was carried out under the most intense air attack, as well as shelling from the land. In spite of valiant efforts by the RAF to cover the evacuation (they flew 4,822hr and lost 106 aircraft), losses were heavy, a total of nine destroyers being sunk, together with many

Left: Three Blackburn Skuas of 803 NAS. The Skua was the navy's first operational monoplane and the first specifically designed for the dive-bombing role. 803 Squadron served on board the carrier *Ark Royal*, and a Skua from this squadron is credited with the first enemy aircraft claimed by the Fleet Air Arm in the Second World War, a Dornier Do 18 shot down off Norway. Skuas from 803 NAS were also involved in sinking the German cruiser *Königsberg* in Bergen Fjord. The Skua was replaced in 1941 by the Fulmar. (ACPL)

Right: The *King George V* shortly after completion in her dazzle camouflage. She was the lead ship of the new class of four battleships ordered under the 1936 Programme. The design reverted to the 14in gun for main armament, four of which were mounted for the first time in a quadruple turret. They were also the first ships to carry the new 5.25in high-angle/low-angle AA gun in eight twin turrets. (ACPL)

small craft which had been hastily volunteered into service by amateur yachtsmen and RNVR officers. Pleasure craft, cross-Channel ferries, and in fact almost anything that would float was pressed into service for the greatest evacuation in history. It was indeed a miracle, and no-one who was involved in the operation could have believed that it would succeed to the extent that it did.

This, however, was not the end, for other troops still remained in France, and had to be evacuated from other ports stretching right down the coast along the Bay of Biscay. One of the most tragic losses was sustained at St Nazaire, where the liner *Lancastria* was bombed and about 3,000 of the 5,800 troops embarked were killed. Finally, on 22 June, France capitulated and signed an armistice with Germany, leaving the whole of the English Channel coast and the Atlantic coast in German hands. Large parts of the French Fleet were disarmed but not taken over, and this was to result in further distressing operations against former allies in the future.

On 27 June Britain announced that she would enforce a total blockade of Europe from the North Cape to Spain. At this point Germany turned her attention to the English Channel, and heavy air attacks, together with attacks by small surface units and minelaying operations, were launched against British shipping using the Channel. In France the Germans began developing the newly captured French naval bases from which they would be able to conduct U-boat operations in the Atlantic against Allied convoys. Bases in western France cut many hundreds of miles from the U-boats' transit journeys to the Atlantic convoy routes, enabling them to spend much longer on patrol and to deploy much further out into the Atlantic, beyond the furthest point at which the convoys were escorted.

With the collapse of France and the evacuation from Dunkirk, Britain found herself alone against Germany. The maritime scene of operations now switched to the Mediterranean and the Atlantic.

Right: The end of May 1940 saw the evacuation of the BEF from France, in which the navy played a major part. Here a destroyer returns, loaded with hundreds of soldiers lifted from the beaches at Dunkirk. (Imperial War Museum)

Chapter 29

The Battle for the Mediterranean

On 10 May 1940 Italy entered the war. Mussolini, not to be outdone by Hitler's successes in France and Norway, and continuing to seek to improve his position with Hitler, decided to take advantage of the desperate situation of Britain in an effort to consolidate his empire in North and East Africa, and to gain as much as he could before the war ended with Hitler in overall control. But the Italians were slow to embark on military operations, and it was to their discomfiture that, when they did, they were severely ousted by a greatly inferior British army in North Africa, and also suffered severe losses in East Africa.

In the meantime, and before naval operations grew in intensity in the Mediterranean, Britain was forced to ensure that the French Fleet in North Africa did not fall into German hands. As Britain failed to gain satisfactory assurances after France's surrender that this would not happen, Force H, under the command of Vice-Admiral Somerville, attacked French naval units in the port of Mers-el-Kebir near Oran. A British ultimatum was rejected by Admiral Gensoul, at which Force H, which included the battlecruiser *Hood*, the battleships *Resolution* and *Valiant*, the carrier *Ark Royal*, the cruisers *Arethusa* and *Enterprise* and a number of destroyers, opened fire on the French ships. In the resulting bombardment, codenamed Operation Catapult, the battleship *Bretagne* and the destroyer *Mogador* were destroyed and the battleships *Dunkerque* and *Provence* badly damaged, but the battleship *Strasbourg* and five large destroyers managed to escape to Toulon.

In Britain, other units of the French Navy which had escaped to England were seized by British forces. Some eventually served under the Free French Forces in Britain, while the remainder were interned. Further attacks on French warships in North African ports resulted in more losses to French ships. The actions against the French ships left the Royal Navy feeling very uneasy, but the government and the Admiralty considered them necessary to prevent French warships being seized by the Germans, for it was felt that the French would be unable to resist German demands for their hand-over.

In the central Mediterranean the land battle in North Africa was at last beginning to have an effect on naval operations. For the Italians, control of the Mediterranean was essential to enable them to supply their land forces. Consequently, numerous small convoys were run from Italy to the North African coast, escorted by small units and with occasional distant support provided by major units of the Italian fleet.

One such convoy sailed from Naples on the evening of 6 July 1940, bound for Benghazi. On board were over 2,000 troops and large quantities of armoured vehicles and transport. The Italians, aware that a British cruiser force had arrived in Malta, decided to provide the convoy with a powerful escort comprising two battleships and a number of heavy cruisers and destroyers. At the same time, the British Mediterranean Fleet was also at sea to

Below: Operation 'Coat'. The carrier Ark Royal (Force H) under air attack in the Sicilian Narrows on 9 November 1940. Force H from Gibraltar was escorting reinforcements for the Mediterranean Fleet, including the battleships *Barham* and cruisers *Berwick* and *Glasgow* and four destroyers. The photograph was taken from HMS *Sheffield*. (Imperial War Museum)

support two convoys sailing between Malta and Alexandria. On 8 July Force H from Gibraltar also put to sea. The Italian convoy reached its destination without loss, whereupon the Italian Fleet rendezvoused to carry out an attack on the Mediterranean Fleet. The plan was for the Italian air force to carry out heavy raids on the British forces and weaken them before the Italian Fleet joined action. The Italian air force failed to locate the British forces, but British air reconnaissance detected the Italians. Air raids were mounted from the carrier *Eagle*, but were evaded by the Italians. The two opposing forces clashed in the late afternoon, in what became known as the Battle of Calabria, but the action was inconclusive. The Italian battleship *Giulio Cesare* was hit by *Warspite*, and the cruiser *Bolzano* was slightly damaged. The Italian destroyers attacked the British forces and laid a smoke screen, at which contact was lost, the British forces turning away. Belatedly, the Italian air force carried out a number of air raids in which a number of Royal Navy warships suffered near misses (including *Hood*, *Ark Royal* and *Resolution*), but received only slight damage.

British and Italian forces again clashed on 19 July, in what became known as the Battle of Cape Spada. British air reconnaissance had detected Italian ship movements between North Africa and Europe, and, during the action, which involved the Australian light cruiser *Sydney* and five destroyers, the Italian light cruiser *Bartolomeo Colleoni* was sunk.

Units of the Royal Navy continued to carry out aggressive patrols in the Mediterranean, while the Italians carried out a series of minelaying operations which claimed a number of British warships. In another minor operation a major success was achieved when three Swordfish of NAS 824 from the carrier *Eagle* attacked the Italian submarine *Iride* and a depot ship near Tobruk. The submarine, which was in the middle of preparing for the first operation to deploy human torpedoes against units of the Mediterranean Fleet in Alexandria, was sunk and the operation was abandoned.

The Mediterranean remained relatively calm until November 1940, when the Royal Navy laid on a major night air raid against Taranto, designed to cripple the Italian Fleet in its main base. On 10 November aerial reconnaissance of Taranto by RAF aircraft based at Malta showed that the bulk of the Italian Fleet was at anchor in the base. Accordingly, Admiral Cunningham decided to

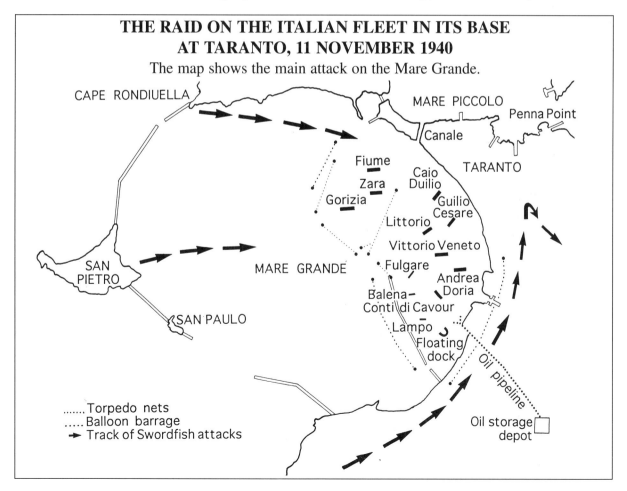

THE RAID ON THE ITALIAN FLEET IN ITS BASE AT TARANTO, 11 NOVEMBER 1940

The map shows the main attack on the Mare Grande.

Above: Operation 'Collar'. The battle off Cape Spartivento, Sardinia, on the morning of 27 November 1940. The destroyer *Defender* and two cruisers are seen taking up positions ready to meet the Italian Fleet. (Imperial War Museum)

mount the raid during the night of 11 November. During the day the carrier *Illustrious*, escorted by a powerful force from the Mediterranean Fleet, flew off 21 Swordfish from a position some 150 miles from the base.

The first strike of twelve aircraft (six armed with torpedoes and six with bombs) left the carrier's decks at 2040, followed by a second strike of nine aircraft (six armed with torpedoes) at 2110. As the aircraft flew in over the base, the target was illuminated by flares. The new battleship *Littorio* and the modernized battleships *Caio Duilio* and *Conte di Cavour* were all torpedoed, three torpedoes striking the *Littorio*, and one torpedo hitting each of the other ships. Two Swordfish were lost, but the remainder returned safely to *Illustrious*. As the carrier and her aircraft returned from their successful operation, other Royal Navy forces attacked an Italian convoy in the Straits of Otranto, sinking three of the Italian convoy's four ships.

At one stroke the Royal Navy had showed that it could retain mastery of the closed Mediterranean sea through the use of naval air power. The successful raid had far-reaching consequences. Not only did it sweep away any remaining prejudices as to the efficacy of carrier-borne aircraft compared with land-based power, but it also convinced any remaining skeptics within the Royal Navy that carrier air power could win battles and dominate maritime operations. Furthermore, it also confirmed to the Japanese that their ideas concerning the use of organic naval air power against the American Fleet at Pearl Harbor would be valid, and, ironically, paved the way for the defeat of Japan herself in the immense carrier battles that were later to be fought in the Pacific. Taranto confirmed that, for the forseeable future, the new naval capital ship would be the carrier.

However, while the raid showed that organic naval air power could pose a formidable threat to naval forces, it did not solve the problem of how to secure the sea lines of communication between Alexandria, Gibraltar and Malta in the face of a massive land-based air threat operating from air bases very close to those sea lines of communication. During December the German *Fliegerkorps X*, highly skilled in antishipping attacks, arrived in Sicily.

With such short lines of communication available to them the scale of the air threat from Italy and Sicily could be rapidly built up by the Luftwaffe and the Italian air force. As a consequence they were soon able to dominate the Mediterranean skies completely in the face of the much weaker British organic naval air arm, supported by the RAF as and when fighter aircraft could be convoyed into Malta.

The Germans realized that the key to the control of the eastern Mediterranean, and the resupply of their forces in North Africa, lay in the removal of British carrier air power. As a result the Luftwaffe made an all-out effort to destroy the carrier *Illustrious*. As the situation in Greece deteriorated, it was decided to attempt to send supplies to the Greek Army. Accordingly, a convoy organized under the code name Operation Excess entered the Mediterranean in January 1941, escorted by Force H under Admiral Somerville as far as the Sicilian Narrows. The convoy would then proceed with a small escort, dropping off a cargo ship with stores for Malta, before being met by Admiral Cunningham with units of the Mediterranean Fleet, including *Illustrious*, some 15 miles southeast of the island of Pantelleria.

The British forces were sighted, and on 9 January *Fliegerkorps X* began a series of heavy air raids against the ships. Seven hits and a number of near misses were recorded on the *Illustrious*, resulting in serious damage, but the carrier was saved by her armoured deck. She eventually limped into harbour at Malta, where she was again subjected to round-the-clock bombing by *Fliegerkorps X*. In spite of the ferocious attacks, emergency repairs were completed and *Illustrious* managed to slip unnoticed out of Malta under cover of darkness on 23 January and sail via the Suez Canal for the United States, where she underwent permanent repairs.

With *Illustrious* out of action, Admiral Cunningham was left with only the old carrier *Eagle*, and the Royal Navy's position in the middle Mediterranean became virtually untenable. However, until the loss of Greece and Crete and a further build-up of enemy land-based air power, British naval forces were able to continue aggressive patrolling through the Mediterranean.

In North Africa the Africa Korps under Rommel carried out a lightning advance eastward, which left the British with even fewer bases from which the Army could be supplied, although, by the very nature of their retreat, the British land-based lines of communication were shortened. Nevertheless, the situation in the Mediterranean rapidly turned critical. Fortunately the ability of the British to read German coded signals through the ULTRA set-up, together with their ability to read Italian coded signals, gave Admiral Cunningham prior warning of many movements planned by the Italian navy.

Following fast and accurate decrypts of German and Italian signals in one such operation, warning was given of impending moves by the Italian navy to prevent the passage of supply ships heading for British forces in Greece. As a result, Admiral Cunningham was able to despatch four cruisers, *Orion*, *Gloucester*, *Ajax* and *Perth*, escorted by nine destroyers, to a position 50 miles west of Crete, ready to meet the Italian fleet after it set sail. On the evening of 27 March Cunningham received the latest decrypts of signals from Bletchely Park, and he set sail with the Mediterranean Fleet, comprising the battleships *Warspite*, *Barham* and *Valiant*, the carrier *Formidable* (which had been sent to the Mediterranean to replace *Illustrious*) and nine destroyers, to intercept the Italian fleet.

During the 28th, while Admiral Cunningham raced to the area, aircraft from *Formidable* launched a series of air strikes in an attempt to cripple the battleship and slow her down, to enable the British battleships to catch up with her and complete her destruction. Meanwhile, the four cruisers had joined action with the Italian force, which comprised the battleship *Vittorio Veneto* and a number of cruisers and destroyers. Coming under fire from the Italians, the British cruisers disengaged and joined up with Cunninhgam's force. Despite intense anti-aircraft fire, *Formidable*'s aircraft pressed home their attacks and eventually recorded one hit on the Italian battleship. By this time the Italian fleet had already reversed course to head for home, and the single torpedo hit on the *Veneto* had little effect on her ability to make good speed.

As a result of the air strike and air reconnaissance, the composition and disposition of the Italian units was now known with some certainty. *Vittorio Veneto* was in the centre, screened by four destroyers, with three cruisers on either beam and an outer screen of three or four destroyers. With this information, a final air strike consisting of ten Swordfish and Albacores was prepared late in the day.

Again anti-aircraft fire was intense, and only one hit was achieved. This hit, however, was to spell disaster for the Italians. The ship struck was the cruiser *Pola*, which came to a complete stop. The Italian Admiral, Iachino, ordered two more cruisers, *Zara* and *Fiume*, and four destroyers to stand by the stricken *Pola*. Admiral Cunningham decided to carry out a night attack to prevent the Italians reaching the safety of their land-based air cover. Unbeknown to him, however, the damage to *Vittorio Veneto* was only slight, and she was soon able to make 19kts, taking her out of range of the British forces.

As Cunningham's destroyers raced ahead in an effort to carry out a night torpedo attack on the Italian fleet and slow it down, they gained a radar contact on a stopped Italian cruiser. On learning of this, Cunningham ordered *Formidable* to sail out of the danger area in case of torpedo attack, and pressed on to attack the radar contact with the battleships. The Italians were completely surprised, with even their main armament trained fore and aft. At the incredibly short range of only 3,000yd the cruisers *Zara* and *Fiume* were treated to a devastating hail of shells from the British battleships and sunk, while the stopped *Pola* was torpedoed by the destroyers *Nubian* and *Jervis* after most of her crew had been taken off. The covering Italian destroyers were found by the British destroyers *Stuart* and *Havock* and the *Alfieri* and *Carducci* sunk, the other two escaping. British losses in the action consisted of just one aircraft.

The success of the Battle of Matapan, and the tremendous boost to British morale which resulted, was soon to be followed by disaster in the eastern Mediterranean. Earlier in the year the Italians had invaded Greece, but had been held back by the Greek army. Hitler, however, was developing plans for the invasion of Russia, and, recalling how Churchill had developed his Balkan strategy in the First World War, albeit with disastrous results, Hitler was determined to secure his flanks before invading southern Russia. Consequently, in March, he embarked on the invasion of the Balkans. Fearing the political consequences of this move, Britain responded, sending troops to Greece early in March. In a *blitzkrieg* movement reminiscent of their invasion of France, the German army swept down into Greece in overwhelming strength on 6 April, supported by a thousand aircraft. The Greek and British forces were no match for the Germans, and within two weeks all resistance in Greece had collapsed.

Between 24-29 April Admiral Cunningham began evacuating from eight different ports and bases the 58,000 British troops in Greece. Yet again, much of the Army's equipment had to be left behind. Some 51,000 men were evacuated, of which 21,000 were sent to Crete to reinforce the garrison there.

There now developed just the sort of situation which had been feared. While the Royal Navy held overall superiority at sea, Germany held undisputed command in the air, together with complete control of the whole Balkan

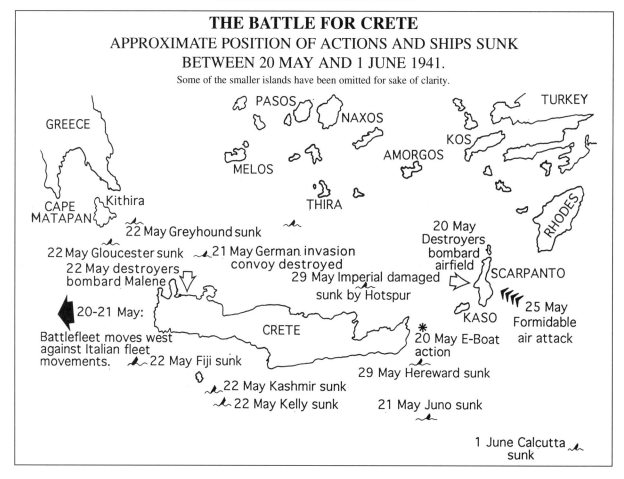

THE BATTLE FOR CRETE
APPROXIMATE POSITION OF ACTIONS AND SHIPS SUNK
BETWEEN 20 MAY AND 1 JUNE 1941.
Some of the smaller islands have been omitted for sake of clarity.

land region. In the face of such superiority, the eastern Mediterranean now became untenable for the Mediterranean Fleet based at Alexandria. With the situation becoming desperate it was decided to pass another convoy through the Mediterranean during the early part of May, to reinforce the British in North Africa and replace losses suffered in Greece. Codenamed Operation Tiger, the convoy was given protection by *Queen Elizabeth* and the cruisers *Naiad* and *Fiji*, which were to join Admiral Cunningham's forces at Alexandria. Air escort was to be provided by fighter aircraft from the carrier *Formidable*.

While the convoy managed to deliver 238 tanks and 43 Hurricanes to Alexandria, bad weather resulted in the loss of most of *Formidable's* aircraft, leaving her with just four Fulmar fighters. With Crete about to be evacuated, this was a tragic loss which was to have dire consequences for the navy's operations in the eastern Mediterranean.

The garrison on Crete now numbered some 32,000 men, but they lacked all but the very basic essentials for defence, except for a few very old tanks, the recently received tanks from the Tiger convoy all being desperately needed in North Africa. In such a situation there was very little that could be done other than evacuate the

forces from the island, for without adequate ground and air support they would have little to counter any German invasion. It would all be down to the navy, which would be forced to use light forces in the face of overwhelming enemy air superiority.

Anticipating the attack to come at any time after 15 May, Admiral Cunningham deployed his forces in four different sectors to carry out nightly sweeps around Crete, withdrawing beyond the range of enemy air power during the day. To the west of Crete a force comprising the battleships *Barham* and *Queen Elizabeth* and five destroyers was disposed to counter any moves by the Italian Fleet. Covering the northwestern approaches in the region of Cape Matapan were two cruisers, while towards the Greek mainland were two more cruisers and two destroyers. Covering the immediate northern part of Crete were two cruisers and four destroyers.

The German airborne assault on Crete began on the morning of 20 May. As soon as news of the assault came through, Cunningham ordered those of his forces that were near Crete to close the island, but to keep out of sight of land during daylight hours. The first ship to be lost was the destroyer *Juno* on 21 May, struck during an Italian high-level bombing attack.

One of the major problems in the succeeding days was the paucity of ammunition, for prodigious amounts were expended in the face of the heavy air attacks. On land, the Germans suffered heavy losses from which their airborne forces were never to recover. However, in spite of these losses the Germans slowly consolidated the gains of the first few days, and gradually they poured more and more troops into the island, forcing back the defenders. While this was going on, the Royal Navy continued to dominate the waters around the island by night, and many small caiques and other craft carrying German troops were intercepted and sunk. During the hours of daylight the British forces were forced to withdraw to beyond aircraft range. Gradually, however, the relentless air attacks began to take their toll. On 22 May the cruisers *Gloucester* and *Fiji* and the destroyer *Greyhound* were sunk and the battleship *Warspite* and cruiser *Perth* badly damaged, putting them out of action for seven and four and a half months respectively. The next day, following receipt of a corrupt signal, Admiral Cunningham ordered all forces to withdraw to Alexandria for replenishment, under the impression that the ships had no short-range AA ammunition left. This was unfortunate, as there was still enough ammunition on board the ships, though it was admittedly in short supply in view of the ferocity of the air attacks and the amount already expended in defence.

That same day, 23 May, two more destroyers were sunk, *Kashmir* and *Kelly*, while all five MTBs in Suda Bay were also sunk. On 26 May *Formidable* and the destroyer *Nubian* were severely damaged in an air raid, and the next day the battleship *Barham* was hit by bombs and the force recalled to Alexandria. Meanwhile, the defences on Crete had collapsed, and the evacuation of the island was ordered during the 27th. The evacuation started on 29 May, and during this operation the destroyers *Hereward* and *Imperial* were lost and the cruisers *Orion* and *Dido* badly damaged. Troops who managed to evade the German forces and reach beaches on the island continued to be evacuated throughout the next three days, with more ships being bombed and badly damaged. The last ship to be sunk was the AA cruiser *Calcutta*, which was dive bombed on 1 June.

If nothing else, Crete at last proved that surface ships could not operate close to enemy airfields unless adequate and timely air cover was provided. Without that cover Admiral Cunningham's forces suffered heavily in ships sunk and badly damaged and personnel killed. The end result of all this was to leave a greatly depleted Royal Navy in the Eastern Mediterranean, which imperilled the maintenance of sea power in that region. The only ships left fit for action were two battleships, two cruisers, nine destroyers and one minelayer. There was no aircraft carrier. This meant that the fleet at Alexandria could no longer sweep into the Mediterranean in support of convoys to Malta. Even more importantly, the navy could not support the Army in North Africa with supplies and shore bombardment, nor could it interrupt the constant flow of supplies from Italy to the Africa Korps in North Africa.

The only way in which supplies to the Axis forces in North Africa could be interrupted was by the submarines based at Malta. It was during this period that the famous 'U' boats (*Unbeaten, Unique, Upholder, Upright, Urge* and *Ursula*) inflicted heavy losses on the German and Italian supply convoys to North Africa. At the same time, from the western Mediterranean, the carriers *Ark Royal* and *Furious* were able to ferry some aircraft to the island to relieve the pressure of the relentless air attacks.

During the last three months of 1941 the decision was taken once again to station surface forces at Malta, for although the submarines were achieving sterling results, considerable supplies were still getting through to the Axis forces in North Africa. As a result Force K was formed comprising the cruisers *Penelope* and *Aurora* and two destroyers, *Lance* and *Lively*. Force K was soon in action, and on 8 November scored a resounding success when it intercepted a convoy of thirteen merchant ships escorted by six destroyers and with two cruisers in consort, bound for North Africa. During the night all thirteen merchant ships of 39,000 tons were sunk along with two destroyers, one of which was torpedoed by the submarine *Upholder*.

The success was short-lived, however, for it was now the turn of the German U-boats which had been ordered into the Mediterranean. On 23 November the battleship *Barham* was sunk by *U 331*. Force H from Gibraltar carried out two more operations to ferry aircraft to Malta, but on her return from the second, HMS *Ark Royal* was torpedoed

Below: On 25 November 1941 the battleship *Barham* was sunk in the Mediterranean. The battleship took a heavy list to port after being struck by three torpedoes fired at close range by *U 331*, and exploded as she sank, taking 862 of her crew with her. (Imperial War Museum)

by *U 81* and sunk. HMS *Galatea* was sunk by *U 557* on 15 December, while the battleship *Malaya* was damaged by a submarine. In a daring raid on Alexandria on 19 December, Italian human torpedoes penetrated the harbour at Alexandria and sank the battleships *Queen Elizabeth* and *Valiant* at their moorings. As the water was very shallow, both ships were refloated and repaired, but the blow to morale was heavy.

In the meantime, Force K was reinforced on 29 November when the cruisers *Ajax* and *Neptune* and the destroyers *Kimberley* and *Kingston* joined the force. Within a short time, however, disaster struck. On 18/19 December the Force ran into a minefield off Tripoli and the cruiser *Neptune* and destroyer *Kandahar* were sunk, the cruiser *Aurora* was severely damaged, and *Penelope* lightly damaged.

Intelligence gained via ULTRA led to many successful actions in the Mediterranean. This source resulted in a brilliant action on 13 December. Given advance warning of an Italian operation, four destroyers from Gibraltar (*Legion*, *Maori*, *Sikh*, and the Dutch *Isaac Sweers*) were in position to attack and sink the Italian cruisers *Alberto di Giussano* and *Alberico da Barbiano*, transporting petrol to North Africa. Escorted by the torpedo boat *Cigno*, the cruisers turned back after being sighted by air reconnaissance and were then intercepted by the British destroyers in what became known as the First Battle of Sirte.

By the end of the year more than 30 per cent of Italy's merchant tonnage had been destroyed, but the cost to the Royal Navy and other British forces had been high.

For the navy, the year 1942 opened relatively quietly in the Mediterranean, but this was not to last for long. In March the navy was again in action while escorting convoy MW.10, with the merchant ships *Breconshire*, *Clan Campbell*, *Pampas* and *Talabot* carrying 25,900 tons of supplies from Alexandria, bound for Malta. At 1424 on 22 March the convoy's cruiser covering force (*Cleopatra*, *Dido*, and *Euryalus*, and the destroyers *Jervis*, *Kelvin*, *Kingston* and *Kipling*) under Rear Admiral Vian sighted part of the Italian force comprising the cruisers *Bande Nere*, *Gorizia* and *Trento*, escorted by four destroyers. In heavy seas and a rising gale Admiral Vian turned towards the Italians and, under cover of smoke, opened fire in what became known as the Second Battle of Sirte. The Italians turned away in an attempt to draw the British ships on to the main Italian force.

At 1618 the main Italian force, with the battleship *Littorio* and six destroyers, was sighted approaching from the northeast. It soon became apparent that the Italians' intention was to work round and head off the convoy, forcing it to abandon its mission. Making smoke and weaving at high speed to avoid the Italian shells, Admiral Vian moved in to the attack. During the ensuing action the 15in guns of *Littorio* disabled the destroyers *Havock* and *Kingston* as they raced in, firing torpedoes at *Littorio*, none of which hit. As darkness began to fall the Italians

Above: In March 1942, British forces again clashed with the Italian Fleet at the Second Battle of Sirte. The picture shows the destroyer *Kipling* emerging from a smokescreen to fire torpedoes at the Italian battleship *Littorio* on 22 March. (Imperial War Museum)

turned away and headed for home having apparently achieved nothing.

The action had, however, so delayed the progress of the convoy that it did not arrive off Malta until after daybreak on 23 March. In this compromising position the ships were soon spotted and came under intense air attack by German aircraft, which sank *Clan Campbell* and seriously damaged *Breconshire*, which was beached. The two remaining merchant ships, *Pampas* and *Talabot*, entered harbour, but were sunk almost immediately, only 5,000 tons of their precious cargo having been landed.

These supplies were insufficient to sustain the island, and, as the situation in the Mediterranean continued to deteriorate, Malta came under the most intense siege. The navy was powerless to redress a situation which demanded its support in three different directions simultaneously: escorting convoys to Malta in the face of heavy attack from Italian ships and severe air attack by the German Luftwaffe, supplying the British Army in North Africa, and denying the Africa Korps access to supplies from the Italian mainland. On top of this, the situation in the Atlantic and Arctic also called for a superhuman effort from both the merchant and Royal navies, which meant that there was insufficient shipping available to send another relief convoy to Malta.

The air raids on the island increased in intensity, and the remaining light forces in the island were further reduced, three destroyers, a minesweeper, three submarines and a tanker, as well as several smaller ships, being sunk. In the face of these crippling attacks, Admiral Cunningham was forced to withdraw the submarines from Malta. The island was now totally besieged and alone, under constant air attack and with all approaches mined by Axis forces, reliant on just what remained on the island itself, and with no possibility of support from outside. Further disaster struck when six of the navy's submarines were lost to enemy action. Intelligence that an Italian convoy carrying reinforcements was bound for Benghazi led to the deployment of the destroyers *Jackal*, *Jervis*, *Kipling* and *Lively*. They were sighted before they could reach the convoy, and in ensuing German air attacks *Jackal*, *Kipling* and *Lively* were sunk. *Jervis* managed to survive and struggle back to Alexandria with 630 survivors.

In June it was decided once again to try and relieve Malta. This was a massive operation involving the despatch of two simultaneous convoys — Harpoon and Vigorous — from each end of the Mediterranean, with a total of 43,000 tons of supplies. Eleven ships sailed from Alexandria, while five merchant ships and the tanker *Kentucky* sailed from Gibraltar with escorts from Force H, supported by units of the Home Fleet.

The convoy from Gibraltar, with a covering escort comprising the battleship *Malaya*, the carriers *Eagle* and *Argus*, the cruisers *Kenya*, *Charybdis* and *Liverpool* and eight destroyers, came under intense air attack on 14 June, and the merchant ship *Tanimbar* was sunk and the cruiser *Liverpool* hit in the engine room, being forced to return to Gibraltar. On reaching the area of the Sicilian Narrows on the evening of 14 June, where it was within reach of the German air bases on the mainland, the covering force turned back, leaving the convoy with a close escort of the old cruiser *Cairo*, nine destroyers and four minesweepers. On 15 June, with the main escort force withdrawn, three Italian cruisers escorted by five destroyers moved in to try and finish off the convoy in the Sicil-

ian Narrows. The close escort turned to attack the Italian cruiser force, while at the same time the convoy came under heavy air attack by the Luftwaffe. The destroyers *Bedouin* and *Partridge* were severely damaged by the Italian cruiser force, the former subsequently being sunk in an air attack. The Italians were unable to penetrate the strong defence, however, and were driven off.

The air attacks on the convoy, which had been left without adequate AA cover, were pressed home, resulting in the loss of three merchant ships. The attacks had delayed the passage of the convoy, and in the turmoil the convoy and the destroyers arrived off Malta before the minesweepers. Unfortunately a new minefield had been laid in the route the ships were taking and, without the minesweepers to sweep the route ahead, the destroyer *Kujawiak* was sunk and the *Badsworth*, *Matchless*, *Hebe* and the merchant ship *Orari* were damaged. The only ship to enter Malta undamaged was *Troilus*. Together with *Orari*, *Troilus* unloaded 3,000 tons of desperately needed supplies.

The heavily escorted convoy from the eastern Mediterranean also came under intense attack. On the first day out, 12 June, an air raid damaged the merchant ship *City of Calcutta*, which had to put into Tobruk. The next day another merchant ship which suffered machinery problems was also forced to leave the convoy and sail for Tobruk, being sunk by aircraft a few miles outside harbour. In the afternoon the main convoy was attacked and another cargo ship sunk, while towards evening German E-boats sank the destroyer *Hasty* and damaged the cruiser *Newcastle*.

Meanwhile, another Italian force comprising the battleships *Littorio* and *Vittorio Veneto*, four cruisers and twelve destroyers had sortied to attack the convoy from Alexandria. On 15 June this force was attacked by aircraft from Malta and Egypt, but the only damage suffered was a bomb hit on *Littorio* and another on the cruiser *Trento*, which was disabled and later sunk by the submarine *Umbra*. Failing to approach the convoy, the main battle force turned for home when *Littorio* was again hit by a torpedo dropped by an aircraft from Malta, but damage

Right: In June 1942 the navy carried out a double convoy operation in an attempt to relieve Malta. Codenamed 'Vigorous/Harpoon', the convoy sailed from Alexandria and Gibraltar respectively. The flagship of Admiral Vian, HMS *Cleopatra*, which formed part of the covering force, is seen in action on 14 June when the convoy came under heavy air attack from Ju 87 and Ju 88 aircraft south of Crete. (Imperial War Museum)

Left: The light AA cruisers of the 'Dido' class with their heavy battery of ten 5.25in DP guns, proved extremely effective in helping to break up the heavy air attacks mounted against the convoys attempting to relieve Malta. The *Euryalus* is seen here in Malta, possibly in November 1942, after escorting one such convoy, Operation 'Stoneage'. With the arrival of this convoy the siege of Malta was finally and effectively lifted. (ACPL)

was only slight. However, the threat from the main Italian force had so delayed the progress of the convoy from Alexandria that it came under intense attack from both E-boats and aircraft. In the ensuing battles ammunition was expended at such a prodigious rate that eventually the C-in-C Eastern Mediterranean, Admiral Harwood, ordered Admiral Vian, in charge of the convoy escort, to abandon the effort to get the convoy through and return to Alexandria. During the day the destroyers *Airedale* and *Nestor* were sunk and the cruiser *Birmingham* damaged in air attacks, while on the following day, 16 June, the cruiser *Hermione* was sunk by *U 205*.

The limited supplies delivered as a result of Operation Vigorous, and subsequent high-speed runs to Malta by the minelayer *Welshman*, were insufficient to sustain the island, which desperately needed another supply convoy. It was now that the lack of carrier-borne aircraft really

made itself felt, for none would be available until August. In the meantime the Maltese would have to make do with the very limited supplies available on the island.

At last, in August, another convoy was ready to sail to Malta, Codenamed Operation Pedestal. The convoy consisted of thirteen cargo ships and the tanker *Ohio*, with a close escort of four cruisers (*Cairo*, *Kenya*, *Manchester* and *Nigeria*) and eleven destroyers which were to accompany it all the way to Malta, and a distant covering force comprising the battleships *Nelson* and *Rodney*, the carriers *Eagle*, *Furious*, *Indomitable* and *Victorious*, the cruisers *Charybdis*, *Phoebe* and *Sirius* and fourteen destroyers. This was the largest escort ever afforded a single convoy during the whole of the Second World War.

The convoy entered the Mediterranean on 10 August, and the following day *Furious* flew off 37 Spitfires for Malta, to provide air cover as the convoy entered the

Left: The submarine *Unruffled* seen leaving Malta for patrol in June 1943. She acted as a beacon submarine for the amphibious landings in Sicily – Operation 'Husky' – on 10 July 1943. Because of their size, the 'U' class submarines formed a major part of the Mediterranean Fleet's submarine force, many of them operating out of Malta and achieving considerable success against Italian supply convoys to North Africa. (ACPL)

Sicilian Narrows, when the majority of the surface ships would have left the convoy. *Furious* then returned to Gibraltar. In the meantime, the carrier *Eagle* was torpedoed and sunk by *U 73*. Air attacks on the convoy began on 12 June, and a transport was bombed and left behind with a destroyer escort, later being scuttled after being torpedoed by an aircraft. The enemy realized the threat posed by the convoy, and in particular the role of the carriers, which at once became the main targets for the air attacks. Fortunately the armoured flight deck of *Victorious* saved her from severe damage.

Simultaneously with the air attacks, Italian submarines and German U-boats concentrated to attack the convoy and its escorts. *Cobalto* was rammed and sunk by the destroyer *Ithuriel*, which herself was badly damaged by the ramming. In the afternoon *Indomitable* came under attack by German aircraft, and three hits were scored which started severe fires, destroying her ability to operate aircraft. This was a severe loss to the convoy's air cover. Aircraft also torpedoed the destroyer *Foresight*, which later had to be sunk by the destroyer *Tartar*. Late in the evening the distant covering force reached the Sicilian Narrows, the limit at which it could successfully operate without prejudicing its own defence, and turned back for Gibraltar.

The convoy was now left with just the close escort. With the main force gone, the submarines were able to penetrate closer to the convoy, and Italian submarines torpedoed the cruisers *Cairo* and *Nigeria* and the tanker *Ohio*. *Cairo* was abandoned, and *Nigeria* turned back for Gibraltar with an escort of three destroyers. The air attacks continued, and two more merchant ships were sunk, and one, *Brisbane Star*, brought to a stop. The Italian submarine *Alagi* torpedoed the cruiser *Kenya* and transport *Clan Ferguson*, which were both damaged, while shortly before midnight the Italian submarine *Bronzo* sank the wreck of another merchant ship. The next day, 13 August, Italian and German MTBs joined the fray and in successive attacks torpedoed the cruiser *Manchester*, which was later abandoned, torpedoed the wreck of another merchant ship, which sank, and torpedoed and sank three more merchant ships. During the night the sorely pressed convoy escort was reinforced by the cruiser *Charybdis* and two more destroyers, which were sent off to rescue survivors from the *Manchester*.

The next morning, 14 August, the air attacks continued with unabated ferocity in continuous relays as the convoy neared the air bases in Sicily and the Italian mainland. Another transport was sunk and two more merchant ships struck, and further hits were scored on the tanker *Ohio*. The attacks continued throughout the day. Eventually, in the evening, the cargo ship *Dorset* was finally sunk, having already suffered heavy damage in the air attacks. Minesweepers from Malta at long last reached the convoy and escorted the remaining merchant ships, *Melbourne Star*, *Port Chalmers*, and *Rochester Castle*, into the harbour. Later the badly damaged *Ohio*, barely afloat, reached Malta, accompanied by destroyers, while *Brisbane Star* arrived in damaged condition on 15 August. The close escort then returned to join the main covering force off the North African coast.

With the ships safely at berth, the work of unloading the 32,000 tons of cargo that survived could begin. Mercifully, the work was allowed to proceed uninterrupted, practically the whole island turning out to lend a hand. Malta was saved, and the Allies were in a strong position to regain the initiative in the Mediterranean. The way was again clear for convoys to transit the Mediterranean under escort and with some degree of immunity to air attack.

For the remainder of the war the navy was primarily involved in supporting amphibious operations in North Africa and up the Italian coast, as the Army slowly pushed the Germans back up the Italian mainland. On 24 October the Battle of El Alamein started, and the long-awaited offensive in North Africa began to push back the Africa Korps. On 8 November the Allies landed in Tunisia in Operation Torch. Escort for two of the amphibious task groups was provided by the Royal Navy, with Force H from Gibraltar providing cover. Sadly, French resistance to the landings resulted in heavy losses for the French navy. On 3 January 1943 Royal Navy chariots penetrated the harbour at Palermo and severely damaged the Italian cruiser *Ulpio Traiano* and the cargo ship *Viminale*. On 9 July 1943 the Allies landed in Sicily under Operation Husky, the covering forces again being provided mainly by the Royal Navy. On 3 September British troops crossed the Straits of Messina and landed on the Italian mainland. Five days later, on 9 September, Italy surrendered, and the following day the Italian fleet was escorted into Malta by units of the Royal Navy.

On 9 September, in another major amphibious operation, Operation Avalanche, troops were landed at Salerno. Although the major part of the operation was conducted by US warships, units of the Royal Navy provided distant cover and organic naval air support from the carrier *Unicorn* and four escort carriers. During the landings the cruiser *Uganda* was seriously damaged off the assault area on 14 September by wireless-controlled bombs, and the next day the battleship *Warspite* was badly damaged in a similar attack.

The last major operation in the Mediterranean was Operation Shingle, the amphibious landings at Anzio. As at Salerno, the Germans again used wireless-controlled bombs, but although a number of ships were damaged, no major losses were suffered by the Royal Navy. Operations in the Mediterranean continued until the end of the war, but mainly involved small units operating against German MTB forces or the occasional submarine, while submarines of the Royal Navy continued to operate against enemy shipping trying to supply the German Army as it retreated up the Italian mainland.

Chapter 30

The Battle of the Atlantic

Although nearly always referred to as the Battle of the Atlantic, this was in reality a campaign and not a battle. As such it is broken down into a number of phases and many individual battles. Furthermore, it was not a tactical campaign, but a strategic campaign on which hung the outcome of the war.

At the outset of the war, submarine operations formed part of the overall pattern of German naval operations, together with the surface-warship and armed-raider operations. All were designed to enforce a total blockade of Britain, denying the passage of merchant shipping to Britain and closing our vital trading links with the outside world — the importation of oil so necessary for the British war machine and on which military operations depended, the inflow of food and raw materials so vital to feeding and clothing the population and keeping industry working, the export of manufactured goods which would earn foreign currency, and the transport of troops and military equipment to sustain military operations overseas.

At the start of the war Hitler placed severe restrictions on the employment of his submarines; prize regulations were to be strictly adhered to and an unrestricted submarine campaign formed no part of German strategy. Admiral Dönitz, C-in-C of the U-boat arm had, however, been secretly preparing for a submarine campaign for many years.

On the outbreak of war the Admiralty at once assumed control over the movement of all British merchant shipping, and captains were given orders regarding the routes they were to follow. The convoy system, plans for which had been set up before the war, was instituted, the first coastal convoy sailing on 6 September, followed the next day by the first of the outward bound overseas convoys. These were given close surface and air escort out to about 150 to 200 miles west of Ireland. The ships then continued unescorted in convoy for two more days before dispersing to proceed independently to their destinations. Vessels bound for the Mediterranean and Africa formed into a separate convoy off the Scilly Isles, sailing under the protection of an ocean escort, usually a single sloop, until met by escort vessels from Gibraltar.

By the end of September 1939 a system of regular convoys was operating from Halifax, Gibraltar and Freetown homeward bound, and outward bound from Liverpool and around the coast of Britain. The convoys had, perforce, to sail at the speed of the slowest ship. Hence the Admiralty instituted a 'two-tier' system, consisting of fast convoys which took on average thirteen days to reach Britain from Newfoundland, and slow convoys with an average time of fifteen days. From Freetown the voyage took about nineteen days. Weather conditions, however, could seriously impair the passage of a convoy, slowing it down and scattering ships, or the convoy could be slowed down by persistent stragglers. This meant that the escorts were forced to wait at the mid-ocean rendezvous point. As a result they might be low on fuel when the convoy arrived, forcing some escorts to head for home to refuel and leaving the convoy escort considerably weakened. Owing to the lack of escorts available for convoy work, and because of the problems noted above, evasive routeing for the convoys had to be maintained.

By the end of 1939 a total of 5,756 ships had sailed in convoy, and of these only seventeen (five of which were stragglers) had been sunk, for the loss of nine U-boats. On the other hand, a total of 97 merchant ships sailing independently had been sunk by U-boats.

The figures completely vindicated the institution of the convoys, but there was still criticism of the system. There were those who claimed that it tied up vast tonnages of merchant shipping while waiting for suitable convoys, while others regarded the convoy as a purely defensive measure, and felt that a more offensive spirit was required. As a result 'hunting groups' of destroyers and aircraft carriers were formed (see above, page 145) to search for submarines, a method already proved to be ineffective during the First World War. The only merit in the scheme was that it did force submarines away from the areas that were being patrolled. Even so, there were some daring submariners who refused to be intimidated by such moves, and this resulted in the hunting groups suffering heavy losses (see above, page 146).

Carriers proved to be particularly vulnerable in these tactical operations. On 14 September *Ark Royal* was attacked by *U 39*, which was herself then sunk by the carrier's escort (the destroyers *Faulknor*, *Firedrake* and *Foxhound*), while three days later *Courageous* was sunk by *U 29*.

At the beginning of 1941 Churchill estimated that Germany would have between 200 and 300 U-boats operational by the summer, the number which Dönitz himself had stated before the war would be necessary for the successful conduct of a submarine campaign (Germany had entered the war with just 56 submarines operational). Present and future shipbuilding programmes for the Royal Navy showed that only 32 destroyers were under construction. Churchill noted that 'the type of destroyer constructed must aim at numbers and celerity of construction, rather than size and power'. At that time the

Above: The mainstay of the Atlantic convoy escort force was the small 'Flower' class corvette. Based on the design of a commercial whalecatcher, these escorts were built in large numbers. As the war progressed they were modernized to keep pace with new technological developments designed to counter the U-boats. The picture shows the modified 'Flower' class corvette HMS *Charlock*. At the rear of the bridge can be seen the massive lantern housing the Type 272 radar. Radar played a major role in defeating the U-boat in the Atlantic. (ACPL)

first of what was to become the largest escort class, the 56 'Flower' class corvettes, were under construction. In addition to these vessels, new classes of ocean escort were also required. At the start of the war 100 trawlers had been commandeered for anti-submarine patrol duties. As well as these, a large number of other trawlers were also requisitioned and organized into groups based at various ports.

During the Norwegian campaign, the German invasion of the Low Countries and the evacuation from Dunkirk, the navy suffered heavy losses and depletion of its already under-strength escort forces. The situation became so desperate that, on 15 May 1940, in his first message to President Roosevelt of the USA, Churchill was forced to ask for the loan of 40-50 old US destroyers to cover RN requirements until the new escorts then building entered service. The situation was further compounded by uncertainty as to whether Italy would enter the war on the side of Germany. If she did, then the meagre escort forces available to the Royal Navy would be stretched even further to counter the threat of a further 100 submarines in the Mediterranean.

In his reply, Roosevelt informed Churchill that the loan of the destroyers would require the authorization of Congress, and that this would not be forthcoming. On 11 June, the day after Italy entered the war, Churchill sent a second note to Roosevelt explaining the situation since Italy had entered the war, and the dire need for the loan of the destroyers. Further notes were sent on 15 June and

31 July. In spite of these repeated pleas from Churchill, Roosevelt could do nothing about releasing destroyers for use by the Royal Navy.

Fortunately for Britain, Italy did not embark on an unrestricted submarine campaign, although her submarines still constituted a grave threat (some were later sent to the German bases in the Biscay to take part in Atlantic operations). The Admiralty had, therefore, to institute the convoy system in the Mediterranean, with the necessary attendant escorts to counter submarine attacks. This further reduced the number of vessels available for escorting the Atlantic convoys. By the end of May 1940, however, the Royal Navy could feel reasonably well pleased with its ability to counter the submarine. The situation seemed under control and the continuous anti-submarine patrols by the navy and Coastal Command were forcing the U-boats away from coastal waters, deeper out into the Atlantic in the area of the South Western Approaches.

Fortunately the number of U-boats available for operations had fallen owing to losses, trials and training, and of the twenty or so larger boats available for ocean patrols at any one time, only about seven were on patrol, while seven were on their way home or in dock refitting and about seven on their way out to patrol. This, together with the fact that more and more ships were opting to sail in convoy, meant that losses were kept to a tolerable level and easily replaced by new construction.

However, one or two disturbing factors were beginning to give cause for concern. Owing to the lack of numbers, the escorts were constantly overworked, resulting in a steadily increasing incidence in the number of mechanical breakdowns and reduced numbers available for escort duties.

The most damaging factor, however, was the fall of France on 25 June. This had an immediate impact on German submarine operations. The capture of French bases and the Biscay ports opened up tremendous possibilities for the Germans. No longer was the limited range of the submarine an overriding factor, for the long and dangerous haul from Germany up the North Sea and out through the Denmark Straits was eliminated by the use of the Biscay ports. No longer were the U-boats forced to remain close to the British coast, where they were subject to almost continuous harassment by patrolling aircraft of Coastal Command and destroyers of the navy. At last Dönitz was in a position to implement plans for a submarine campaign which he had slowly been developing since the end of the First World War. The only thing lacking was a sizeable force of submarines. However, sufficient numbers were available to begin attacking convoys with packs of U-boats.

In July 1940, as the U-boats moved further out into the Atlantic in an effort to find escort-free areas, the Admiralty was forced to extend the limit to which convoys were escorted from 15°W to 17°W — 300 miles west of Ireland. This, together with the almost complete closure of the English Channel to shipping and the refusal by Southern Ireland to allow British forces to be based in the country, forced the Admiralty in July 1940 to reroute shipping. Instead of using the South Western Approaches, where the U-boats now gathered, convoys were routed round the North Western Approaches, nearer to ports in the north of England, shipping bound for the East Coast having to pass round the north of Scotland.

On 17 August Germany declared an area of unrestricted U-boat warfare around the coasts of Britain, bounded by the latitude and longitude 60°N 20°W. Within a very short time ships were being attacked out to 25°W, well beyond the limit where the escorts left the convoys and beyond the range of the current anti-submarine patrols. The navy and Coastal Command lacked both numbers of units and radius of action to reach these new limits. In the Western Atlantic, convoys were escorted out to about 350 miles east of Halifax by Canadian destroyers. After this they continued to Britain under the escort of an armed merchant cruiser until met by the escorts of Western Approaches Command. The U-boats soon began to congregate in the gap between these two limits and reap a vast harvest of merchant ships.

During the summer and autumn of 1940 Dönitz had been able to obtain spasmodic assistance from the Luftwaffe. Finally, on 7 January 1941, a bomber unit was placed under his command for the Battle of the Atlantic. The aircraft were used to locate convoys and then home U-boats on to them. The method proved successful, and resulted in ten ships of 52,874 tons being sunk without the loss of a single aircraft or submarine. In an effort to combat the aircraft menace, the Admiralty began to fit a number of merchant ships with a catapult over the foc's'le. Known as CAM (Catapult Aircraft Merchantman) ships, they carried a Hawker Hurricane on the catapult for launching when enemy reconnaissance aircraft were sighted.

The great upsurge in merchant losses in the area beyond where the escorts left the convoys reached a climax in September, and threatened an almost total breakdown in the flow of imports into Britain. In August 56 merchant ships totalling 267,618 tons had been sunk by U-boats in the Atlantic, while another 15 of 53,283 tons were sunk by aircraft of the Luftwaffe operating in support of the U-boats (a total of 71 ships of 320,901 tons). During September sinkings by aircraft and U-boats rose still further, to a total of 74 ships of 351,660 tons sunk (the total number of merchant ships sunk from all causes in all areas during September totalled 100 of 448,621 tons). In October the tonnage sunk in the Atlantic rose still further to 361,159 tons, but amounted to only 69 ships.

Below: While awaiting the delivery of the new escorts, a number of the old First World War 'V' and 'W' type destroyers were converted to escort duties. The after bank of torpedo tubes was removed and AA and anti-submarine armament augmented, while the removal of the after gun allowed depth charge stowage aft to be increased. In addition the forward boiler and funnel were removed and the space used for additional bunkerage and accommodation. One of the vessels so modified was the *Whitehall*, shown here in 1943. (ACPL)

Above: The Navy suffered heavy losses in the destroyer and light escort categories up to the fall of France in June 1940. To make up the the the number of escorts, the United States eventually agreed to loan the navy 50 old destroyers in return for a 99-year lease on British naval and air bases in the West Indies. One of the destroyers loaned was the *Ripley*, shown here in her camouflage markings and with the prominent radar housing on the bridge. A Hedgehog ahead-throwing anti-submarine mortar is mounted to port and starboard at the forward base of the bridge. (ACPL)

The heavy losses were mainly attributed to the fact that many of the escorts had been withdrawn from the Atlantic convoys during the summer to provide anti-invasion coverage on the south and east coasts should the German amphibious assault then being prepared (Operation Sealion) take place. As the long-awaited invasion failed to materialize the escorts were gradually returned to their duties in the North Atlantic and the crisis passed.

Finally, following assurances as to the future of the Royal Navy in the event of capitulation, and the offer of a 99-year lease on British naval and air bases in the West Indies, which was accepted, the US Congress agreed to loan the 50 destroyers requested by Churchill earlier. The deal was formally agreed on 2 September 1940, and the crews were immediately assembled and sent out to Halifax to take over the destroyers. The first eight vessels were commissioned on 6 September (the day Dönitz carried out his first pack attack against a convoy). The US destroyers certainly increased the numbers of escorts, but having been laid up for many years they unfortunately suffered from a number of defects which took time to rectify and delayed their deployment as convoy escorts. However, after refits and some modification these venerable vessels had sufficient endurance to accompany convoys right across the Atlantic.

Meanwhile, at the beginning of September 1940 U-boats conducted their first successful pack attack against the 53 ships of convoy SC2. Shortly after the escort of seven ships joined on 6 September, *U 65* made contact with the convoy. During the night she homed *U 47* on to the convoy, and this submarine then sank three ships. Aircraft forced the submarines away from the convoy the following day, but they again approached late on

8 September, when *U 47* sank another ship. Towards daylight on 9 September *U 28* and *U 99* came up and sank a fifth ship. Five vessels of 20,943 tons had been sunk without any loss to the U-boats.

Then, in October 1940, came the first major convoy battle involving two convoys — SC7 and HX79. SC7 was a slow convoy of 35 ships proceeding eastwards at a speed of about 7 knots. The convoy covered an area of about four square miles in eight columns of ships, three columns each of five ships being placed in the centre. However, four of the merchant ships had straggled, breaking the symmetry of the convoy and creating difficulties for the sole escort, the sloop *Scarborough*, which had joined the convoy at the ocean rendezvous point. No further escorts would be available until the local escort from Western Approaches Command joined.

However, the convoy was more fortunate than some, for on 16 October two more escorts joined at a position far out into the Atlantic beyond the normal local escort meeting point. The sea was smooth and calm, and a full moon was shining. In these ideal conditions *U 48* sighted the convoy and reported its position. Before waiting for other U-boats to form an intercept line across the path of the convoy, *U 48* attacked and sank two ships. The convoy executed an emergency turn and two of the escorts left to hunt the U-boat, leaving the convoy in the care of a single escort, the corvette *Bluebell*. *Bluebell* then stopped to rescue the crews from the sunken merchant ships, leaving the convoy without any escort. The sloop *Scarborough*, meanwhile, was left so far behind, hunting *U 48*, that she was never able to rejoin the convoy. This left the convoy with two escorts, the sloop *Fowey* and *Bluebell*. At this point two more welcome escorts arrived.

During the 17th *U 38* sighted the convoy and carried out two attacks early the next morning, sinking a ship before being driven off by three of the escorts, the convoy being left with just one escort. Then, at 2015 on the 17th, the convoy ran into the waiting Wolf Pack. In a short time all was confusion as ships were torpedoed and sunk and the escorts raced around the perimeter of the convoy searching for submarines and picking up survivors. At this point the weather deteriorated, and heavy rain reduced visibility to a few hundred yards. During the run-

Left: The design of the 'Flower' class corvette was developed into the 'River' class frigate and then the similar 'Castle' class corvette and finally into the 'Loch/Bay' design. Large numbers of these designs were ordered and built using prefabrication techniques. The 'River' design met to a very large degree the Naval Staff's concept for an ocean escort vessel, being larger and faster than the 'Flowers'. The 'Rivers' retained the same well tried commercial machinery fitted in the 'Flowers', but installed two sets driving two propellers. (ACPL)

ning battle and the bad weather the convoy finally scattered, 21 ships (including the four stragglers) of 79,592 tons being sunk while another was torpedoed. The following night *U 38* and *U 48* located convoy HX79, which had been joined by a powerful escort from Western Approaches Command after leaving outward-bound convoy OB229. During the night of 19-20 October five U-boats (*U 48*, *U 47*, *U 38*, *U 46* and *U 100*) carried out a series of attacks on HX79 (40 ships) in which 12 ships of 75,069 tons were sunk and a tanker torpedoed.

In October the Admiralty was forced to extend the convoy escort limit further out, to 19°W. With the limited radius of the escorts this meant that convoys had to follow a more direct route and refrain from zig-zagging and evasive alterations of course. Escorts were no longer permitted to engage in numerous bursts of high speed to catch U-boats. Submarines that were sighted would only be hunted long enough to prevent them from catching the convoy on the surface; they could no longer be hunted to destruction. The grave shortage of escorts meant that it was inadvisable for an escort to be away from the convoy screen for too long, for the gap left while a hunt was in progress invariably could not be covered.

During October the pocket battleship *Admiral Scheer* had broken out into the Atlantic undetected, tasked with attacking merchant shipping. On 5 November the homeward-bound convoy HX84 (37 ships), under the sole escort of the armed merchant cruiser *Jervis Bay* (Captain E.S.F. Fegen), sighted the *Scheer*. Fegen ordered the convoy to scatter under cover of a smoke screen as *Jervis Bay* moved out to attack the *Scheer*. In the ensuing unequal action *Scheer* sank *Jervis Bay* before going in pursuit of the convoy. By this time the convoy had become so scattered that *Scheer* could only intercept five ships of 33,331 tons, which she sank. *Scheer* then continued with her voyage, which finally accounted for sixteen merchant ships of 99,059 tons sunk, together with the AMC *Jervis Bay*.

The winter of 1940/41 highlighted another factor which previously had not been of consequence. The need to maintain convoys and to provide escorts for them through a succession of severe gales placed a heavy strain on the strength of Western Approaches Command. Weather damage accumulated, and there was serious risk of the navy being unable to find sufficient seaworthy vessels to escort convoys, even out to 19°W. By the beginning of 1941 50 per cent of the 146 escort vessels available to the escort command were out of action from weather and battle damage, mainly owing to lack of strategically sited repair yards. It became an urgent priority to develop fully equipped bases at Londonderry, Liverpool, Greenock, and Belfast, and at St Johns in Newfoundland.

One of the emergency measures used to combat submarines and raiders, introduced by the Admiralty at the start of the war, was a carbon copy of a device used during the First World War, the Q ship. Eight old tramp steamers were requisitioned, given a hidden armament and pressed into service around the coasts of Britain and in the Atlantic. They failed to sink or even decoy a single submarine, and as the navy could ill afford to waste highly trained men in abortive operations, the ships were paid off early in 1941.

Dönitz firmly believed that the best means of strangling the British war effort and starving the country into surrender was by the use of submarines. Following his experience in the First World War, he was firmly convinced that his submarines could exploit what he saw as the weakest link in Britain's armour – her dependence on seaborne trade for her continued fighting effort. Hitler, however, refused to sanction the total break-up of the surface fleet in favour of putting all shipbuilding effort into U-boat construction. Neither, in the face of considerable pressure from Goering, would he accede to Dönitz' requests for the building and allocation of long-range aircraft to support the attacks on convoys in the Atlantic.

Right: The final development of the Atlantic escort was the 'Loch/Bay' design. The picture shows the *Loch Insh* escorting the minelayer *Apollo*, from which the picture was taken. The frigates were fitted with a much improved radar, the Type 277, and the new 3-barrelled Squid mortar which had replaced the Hedgehog. Two Squids can be seen mounted on the superstructure forward of the bridge and just abaft the 4in gun, which is sited on a separate 'bandstand'. A quadruple 2pdr pom-pom is mounted aft, and in the small housing in front of the bridge a new sonar set is installed. (ACPL)

However, Dönitz had sufficient U-boats available during the winter of 1940-41 to develop his Wolf Pack tactics, first begun begun in September 1940.

To some extent the development of the Wolf Pack concept was forced on Dönitz. Ever since the beginning of the war the Germans had been able to decipher many of the British messages relating convoy movements. In August 1940 this invaluable intelligence was denied them when the Admiralty changed all of the ciphers. Henceforth, intelligence concerning convoy routes and shipping movements had to be obtained by other means until the codes could again be broken. With sufficient U-boats available, Dönitz was able to put into operation his plan for shore-based control of his submarines and their Wolf Pack tactics.

In essence, the Wolf Pack concept relied on a U-boat or aircraft locating a convoy and then shadowing it and reporting its position, composition and general pattern of steaming. While the convoy was shadowed, the shore-based HQ would assemble available U-boats in a patrol line across the anticipated path of the convoy. Once the U-boats were in position they were given the order to attack. Attacks would be carried out from the surface by night, the boats withdrawing submerged by day to a distance beyond which the escorts could safely leave the convoy. The submarines would then surface and race ahead of the convoy to be in position ready to attack it the following night. Using these methods the U-boats were able to achieve considerable success against the convoys. This was primarily because the escorts relied on their ASDIC sets to detect the U-boats. ASDIC, however, was only effective against submerged submarines, and as the boats attacked on the surface by night, they remained undetected, being invisible to any lookout on a ship at ranges greater than about half a mile. Even if U-boats were detected, they could often escape from the escorts, for the escorts lacked the speed necessary to catch a surfaced U-boat. The only way to combat the surfaced U-boat before it attacked was

with the aid of radar, but at the beginning of 1941 only a few escorts were fitted with the new centimetric radar, which was still primitive and unreliable.

On the other hand, Wolf Pack tactics demanded extensive use of wireless communication. From this a fairly accurate position could be determined using HF/DF, which was available initially from shore-based stations, and later on board the escorts themselves. By July 1941 HF/DF fixes were being given almost instantaneously with the start of a U-boat transmission. The introduction of HF/DF was followed shortly by centimetric radar, which gave the escorts a tremendous advantage against a surfaced U-boat.

Communications were also a problem until the winter of 1940. Normally, strict radio silence was imposed on all ships and aircraft, and any signalling was carried out by means of flags, Aldis lamps and sirens. Communications were further complicated by the difficulty of co-ordinating messages with escort aircraft circling round a convoy, a simple request sometimes taking hours to pass. From November 1940 this situation gradually eased as the escorts and aircraft began to fit radio telephone (R/T or Talk Between Ships — TBS). This high-frequency set had the advantage that its radius of reception was limited to horizon distance, and only submarines in the vicinity of a convoy could pick up the messages.

On 17 February 1941 a new area combined HQ for Western Approaches Command was opened at Liverpool. Soon after, Admiral Noble took over from Admiral Nasmith as C-in-C of the command. During March the plot at Derby House showed that the U-boats had moved even further out into the Atlantic, and that convoys were being attacked by larger numbers of submarines using the Wolf Pack tactics. The whole situation proved very worrying for a time, until an action around convoy HX122 in March gave a clear indication of the new tactics. This convoy (41 ships, 5th Escort Group — five destroyers and two corvettes) was sighted by *U 110* on 15 March 1941.

During the night of 15-16 March four other U-boats gathered round the convoy and attacked. Further attacks occurred on the night of 16-17th. At the height of the action the destroyer *Walker* (Commander Donald Macintyre) gained an ASDIC contact and attacked with the destroyer *Vanoc*, but the target surfaced and both ships lost contact. At about 0250 the 286 radar set on *Vanoc* picked up the unmistakable echo of a submarine at a range of 1,000yd. The destroyer closed the contact, and on visual sighting rammed *U 100*. While *Vanoc* was rescuing the crew of *U 100*, *Walker* gained another contact, which was attacked. *U 99* surfaced and surrendered, and, with her, Germany's most successful U-boat commander was captured. HX122 lost five ships of 34,505 tons, and two U-boats were sunk.

The crisis in the Atlantic caused Churchill to issue a Directive on the Battle of the Atlantic. The Battle of the Atlantic Committee was formed, and held its first meeting on 19 March. Topics covered all aspects of the fight against the U-boats.

With the projection of U-boat operations further out into the North Atlantic, it became imperative that some form of air cover be provided along the unescorted convoy routes between Iceland and Newfoundland. This was instituted, and together with the advanced fuelling base at Hvalfjord in Iceland, which had come into operation for the Royal Navy in June 1940, permitted an extension of the convoy escort to 35°W. To reduce the time the escort had to be away refuelling, the convoys were routed further to the north, nearer Iceland. However, there still remained a large gap between the west-bound escorts from the UK and the east-bound escorts from Canada.

During May a British-Canadian Conference laid down the future strategy of air co-operation, which arranged for air cover to be provided to a distance of 700 miles from Britain, 400 miles south of Iceland and up to 500 miles east from Newfoundland. A gap of some 300 miles still remained in the mid-Atlantic, however, and it was here that the next phase of the U-boat campaign took place.

Although it was possible to provide end-to-end escorts for the North Atlantic convoys, using the ex-American destroyers and a new base built at St Johns, Newfoundland (the first convoy to be escorted end-to-end was HX129, which sailed on 27 May 1941), it was still essential that long-range surface escorts be built as quickly as possible. The design for a new class of long-range escorts (the 'River' class frigates) had been drawn up in 1940, and the first of these was laid down in July 1941, under the 1940 Programme. However, many of the yards used to build the 'Flower' class corvettes were unable to undertake construction of the 'Rivers' because of the short length of their building slips.

This led to the design of another class of shorter escorts, the 'Castle' class corvettes, the first of which was also ordered under the 1942 Programme. The first units of the 'Castle' class were laid down in 1943. They retained the same machinery as the 'Flowers' but were fitted with two water-tube boilers. Because of the large number of aerials which had to be carried (radar, HF/DF, etc) they suffered from high windage which made them difficult to manoeuvre at slow speed. This apart, they were good sea boats and a great improvement on the 'Flowers'. They were well equipped for ASW, and the *Hadleigh Castle*,

Class/ Programme	1939	1939 War	1940	1941	1942	1943	Total
Planned							
Flower	56	60	25	10	4		211
River		27	19	17			63
Castle					10	17	27
Loch/Bay					5	25	30
Actual*							
Flower	60	50	25				135
River		27	19	11			57
Castle					11	15	26[1]
Loch/Bay					4	40	44[2]

TABLE X. ESCORT CONSTRUCTION 1939–43

* Numbers of these were handed over to other Allied navies or were manned by crews from other nations and operated under the white ensign
1. 51 Cancelled
2. 56 Cancelled

Right: In early 1941 the Germans drafted plans for a mass attack on merchant shipping in the Atlantic using all available surface ships combined with a major attack by U-boats. As part of this plan the battleship *Bismarck*, accompanied by the heavy cruiser *Prinz Eugen*, were to sortie. Forewarned of the operation, the Admiralty positioned units ready to intercept the two ships. As well as two radar-equipped cruisers, the newly-commissioned battleship *Prince of Wales* and the battlecruiser *Hood* were sent to keep a lookout for the German force. The picture shows the *Prince of Wales* shortly before departing for the Denmark Straits. (Imperial War Museum)

launched in June 1943, was the first to be fitted with a new ASW mortar, the Squid, which became standard equipment on later vessels.

On April 15 the Admiralty assumed operational direction of Coastal Command, when it was formally agreed that the Admiralty would be responsible for the strategic direction of the war at sea by all ships and aircraft. The navy laid down the tasks and their priority and the C-in-C Coastal Command, through the Group AOC, was responsible for carrying out these tasks. Aircraft were controlled exclusively from the Area Combined HQs by the Group AOC, except for local tactical control by an SOE, but even then the Group had overriding control to divert or recall aircraft.

During April 1941 Coastal Command stepped up its patrols under this new direction, but it became clear that aircraft numbers were inadequate to meet the task in hand. The need for very-long-range aircraft was paramount, but the majority of such aircraft – Liberators, which Coastal Command hoped to use – were already allocated to Bomber Command. The Admiralty and Air Ministry therefore drew up a plan to expand the Command's strength with aircraft suitable for anti-submarine duties. After a close examination of past operations, the Admiralty and Coastal Command felt that a large number of aircraft were being wasted on the close escort of convoys in areas which were relatively clear of U-boats, facts which were well known from ULTRA information. Such tactics did not take full advantage of an aircraft's great superiority in speed and radius of action over a surface escort. It was decided, therefore, to dispense with the close air escort to convoys which were not in any immediate danger, and to use the aircraft so released to reinforce areas where, from ULTRA information, U-boats were known to be congregating, and to cover their fairly well defined transit areas in the Bay of Biscay and North Sea.

The placing of aircraft in depth around threatened convoys and along the routes of convoys which could not be evasively routed was made possible by the explicit ULTRA information. The scheme was tried out during April and became operational on 9 May, but again lack of aircraft prevented full implementation of the plan.

The whole of Germany's maritime strategy was based on the concept of destroying Britain's ability to wage war by annihilating her merchant fleet. In pursuance of this goal, German naval operations were formulated on the basis of deploying surface units either singly or in very small groups of no more than two or three units to dislocate shipping movements and tie down as many Royal Navy units as possible in searching for them. A Jutland-style action was to be avoided at all costs. Apart from anything else, the composition of the German navy ruled out such an eventuality.

However, during the early part of 1941 plans had been drafted for a mass attack on shipping using all available surface units in conjunction with a major U-boat attack. The plan was impaired at a critical stage, however, when *Gneisenau* and *Scharnhorst* were badly damaged in air raids on Brest, *Hipper* was under refit in dry dock in Germany, and the battleship *Tirpitz* was still uncompleted. The only units available for the operation were the battleship *Bismarck* and the heavy cruiser *Prinz Eugen*.

On 18 May the two ships, under the command of Admiral Lütjens, left Gdynia bound for the North Atlantic. Already forewarned that an operation was pending, the Admiralty immediately put ships on alert. News of the departure reached the Admiralty on 21 May, the day that the ships were sighted in a Norwegian fjord. Knowing that their route to the North Atlantic lay through the Denmark Straits, the navy disposed its forces accordingly. Two cruisers, *Norfolk* and *Suffolk*, both fitted with radar, were sent to patrol the Straits, while the

C-in-C of the Home Fleet, Admiral Tovey, ordered the recently completed and not then fully worked-up battleship *Prince of Wales* and the unmodernized battlecruiser *Hood* (Admiral Holland), escorted by six destroyers, to leave Scapa and patrol the northern latitudes. The remaining units of the Home Fleet were held at short notice in Scapa to await further confirmation and more precise details regarding the passage of the German vessels.

On 22 May in atrocious weather conditions a reconnaissance aircraft sent to examine the fjords reported that the ships had sailed. At this the C-in-C gave orders for the Home Fleet in Scapa to sail.

At 1922 on 23 May the cruiser *Suffolk* sighted the German ships and began shadowing, staying out of sight in the mist. *Suffolk*'s report was received in *Hood*, then some 600 miles away and to the south of Iceland. Maintaining strict radio silence, Admiral Holland made full speed towards the reported position. Contact was lost during the night of 23 May, and when it was regained Admiral Holland had to turn his ships northward to intercept. This was a somewhat compromising position, as only the forward guns of the British ships would be able to bear, and their advantage of heavier firepower would be lost. At the time, however, the overriding requirement was to engage.

At 0532 the two forces sighted each other and opened fire at a range of 25,000yd. At once the Germans were able to bring their full broadside to bear on the British ships, which started to alter course in order to bring their own broadside to bear. At this point *Hood* was struck and fire broke out abaft the after funnel. A few moments later she disappeared in a cloud of smoke, leaving three survivors from a crew of 1,324. The British force was now in a very difficult situation. The command had devolved on the captain of *Prince of Wales*, and the fact that she was not fully worked up began to tell. Breakdowns were suffered in two of her main armament turrets, and she was forced to break off the engagement and turn away under cover of smoke.

Calamity was not all on the British side, however. During the action *Bismarck*, too, had suffered a hit, which although not in itself serious, was a harbinger of the catastrophe which was to befall the battleship. The damage to *Bismarck* resulted in an oil leak which her crew was unable to control, and which gave a clear indication of her movements on subsequent days, and to salt water contamination of her fuel supply. This was even more serious, for it seriously reduced her radius of action. At this point Admiral Lütjens decided to abandon the operation and sail for the safety of a French port to repair the damage.

The British cruisers, meanwhile, continued to shadow the German ships while the Admiralty ordered every available unit to converge on the anticipated scene of operations in an endeavour to head off the Germans and defeat them. All convoys due to sail across the Atlantic were cancelled and some were recalled, their escorts, including a number of battleships, being ordered to the scene. In addition, Force H from Gibraltar was ordered up to join the other forces converging on the area.

In the meantime, *Bismarck* was able to detach the *Prince Eugen*, which was ordered out into the Atlantic to continue the operation on her own.

In spite of the British efforts to confront the battleship, *Bismarck*, with her superior speed, could evade the Royal Navy and reach France before she could be engaged. It was essential, therefore, that she be slowed down. As a result an air raid was mounted by Fleet Air Arm aircraft from the carrier *Victorious*. *Victorious*, too, was a new ship and not fully worked up, and was in the process of transporting Hurricane fighters to the Mediterranean when she was diverted to take part in the *Bismarck* operation. Nevertheless, nine Swordfish of 825 Squadron took off at 2208 on 24 May to attack the battleship. Coming in at 2350, the Swordfish scored a single hit on *Bismarck*'s starboard side, just abreast the bridge. Although this did not affect the ship's combat capability, her violent manoeuvring to avoid the attack resulted in the leak suffered earlier being opened up still further, with further contamination to her fuel supply.

Shortly after this the cruiser *Suffolk*, radar-shadowing the zig-zagging battleship, lost contact when *Bismarck* made a sudden and unexpected alteration of course just out of radar range. During the 25th various aircraft were despatched from the carriers and from Britain to search for the battleship, but her whereabouts remained uncertain. However, Rear-Admiral Wake-Walker in the cruiser *Norfolk* was convinced that *Bismarck* would head for Brest. The Admiralty, too, concluded that the ship would head there, and orders to this effect were transmitted to the forces at sea. By the evening, many of the British ships were getting very low on fuel, which gave the C-in-C cause for serious concern. A number of ships were forced to sail for Iceland to refuel.

At daylight on 26 May *Ark Royal* launched ten Swordfish to search for *Bismarck*. With these aircraft in the air, six more Swordfish were readied for launching should the battleship be sighted. Meanwhile, a Coastal Command Catalina aircraft, already on patrol, sighted *Bismarck* at 1030. An hour later one of the Swordfish sighted the battleship. Shadowing then continued throughout the rest of the day, and at 1450 *Ark Royal* launched a strike of fifteen Swordfish to attack *Bismarck*. Meanwhile, *Sheffield* had been ordered ahead to shadow the battleship in the deteriorating weather. Unfortunately this information did not reach *Ark Royal*, and the Swordfish mistook *Sheffield* for *Bismarck* and attacked her. Fortunately none of the torpedoes launched struck the cruiser, but it meant yet a further delay in efforts to hinder the progress of *Bismarck* towards Brest. A second strike of fifteen Swordfish took off at 1910 and, attacking *Bismarck* from all directions against heavy

THE SINKING OF THE *BISMARCK*
THE NIGHT ACTION BY THE 4TH DESTROYER FLOTILLA, 2230 TO 2400, 26 MAY 1941.

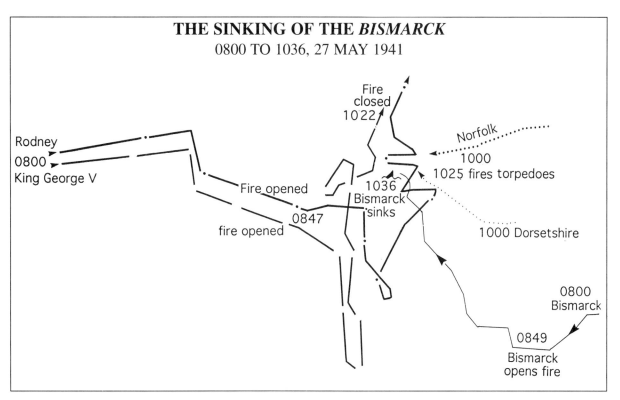

2230 Maori 2230 Piorn
2230 Cossack
2230 Sikh   2300
2230 Zulu
                2300
         Bismarck 2230
                    2300
2300
    2300

anti-aircraft fire, launched thirteen torpedoes, two of which struck the battleship. One of these was to seal the *Bismarck*'s fate, for it struck and jammed one of her rudders.

The battleship could no longer manoeuvre, and Admiral Lütjens at once concluded that the only option left was to stay and fight to the last against the forces now moving in for the kill. At 2248 Royal Navy destroyers took up shadowing positions around the battleship, and a little while later, at 2324, in heavy rain squalls, the destroyers were ordered in to carry out independent attacks. These continued throughout the night and a number of torpedoes were fired in the face of heavy fire, which included shells from her main armament. Eventually *Bismarck* came to a stop, but then got under way again, at a very slow speed.

By morning the main British forces were within range, and in a northwesterly gale in clear visibility the battleship *Rodney* opened fire at 0847, followed shortly after by the battleship *King George V*. *Bismarck* returned fire with remarkable accuracy. Then the cruiser *Norfolk* joined the action. The outcome was not in doubt, and eventually the fire from the British battleships began to tell. At 1010 the last of *Bismarck*'s guns fell silent. It was now just a matter of time before the great ship sank. As it was obvious that the guns would not hasten the ship's end, the British ships ceased fire, and the cruiser *Dorsetshire* came up and fired a number of torpedoes into the battleship, which turned over and sank at 1040.

THE SINKING OF THE *BISMARCK*
0800 TO 1036, 27 MAY 1941

Rodney
0800
King George V

Fire opened

fire opened

0847

Fire closed 1022

Norfolk

1000
1025 fires torpedoes

1036 Bismarck sinks

1000 Dorsetshire

0800 Bismarck

0849

Bismarck opens fire

During the spring of 1941 a number of U-boats were sent to the area around Freetown, Sierra Leone, where few escorts were available. During May six U-boats operating in the Freetown-Cape Verde Island area sank a total of 32 ships, many after they had left convoys to enter ports along the African coast. To prevent further such losses the Admiralty diverted three escort groups from Western Approaches Command during the late summer. That they were able to divert these escort resources from the North Atlantic was due to a slight easing of the escort situation in the Atlantic. This was a result of the resiting of the Mid Ocean Meeting Point (MOMP), where the escort forces changed over to 22°W. As a result, Royal Navy escorts no longer had to be detached to Iceland to refuel and could cover convoys from Ireland to the MOMP and back without refuelling.

During the early part of May there occurred one of the most significant events in the whole of the U-boat campaign. On 7 May convoy OB318 (3rd Escort Group) was attacked by *U 94*, which sank two ships. Just before midday on 9 May *U 201* and *U 110* attacked, sinking one and two ships respectively. The corvette *Aubretia* gained ASDIC contact on *U 110* and carried out two accurate attacks. She was being backed up by the destroyers *Broadway* and *Bulldog* when *U 110* surfaced about three-quarters of a mile away. *Bulldog* at once turned to ram, but on reflection her captain thought there might be a chance of capturing the U-boat and cancelled his order. As *Bulldog* headed towards *U 110* at 15kts, all guns that could bear opened fire. About a cable's length from the U-boat *Bulldog* stopped and sent a boarding party over. By this time the crew of *U 110* had abandoned their submarine.

Several loads of confidential books and papers were ferried over to *Bulldog*, along with the greatest prize of all, an ENIGMA coding machine complete with a signal set up ready for transmission, from which the British were able to reconstruct messages sent to the German submarines. The captured material gave the daily settings for the ENIGMA machine for the U-boats' intended three-month patrol. Data on all German naval units (except the armed merchant raiders) was also captured, as were charts with the marked positions of replenishment ships. After her survivors were rescued, *U 110* was taken in tow by *Bulldog*, but sank on 11 May.

The Germans were completely unaware that *U 110* had been captured, or that an ENIGMA machine and all the relevant ciphers were in the hands of British intelligence. The capture of the machine enabled the remaining gaps in ULTRA information dealing with U-boats to be filled in, and from then until February 1942 all German naval signals dealing with U-boats were made available to British naval intelligence. So complete was the knowledge gained, that the exact position of every U-boat, its operational status and its commanding officer were known.

The fear of compromising such valuable intelligence meant that it was not always possible to make use of the ULTRA information. Even so, there were occasions when the secret was in jeopardy of being compromised. The first of these occurred during June, when, as a result of the material captured from *U 110* and a weather ship, Royal Navy ships skilfully intercepted nine German naval supply ships in the Atlantic and Indian Oceans and destroyed them. Without these ships, German naval operations in the Atlantic and Indian Ocean had to be severely curtailed.

In August 1941 British forces achieved another major success against the U-boats and gained further vital knowledge as to their operational capabilities when *U 570* was captured. The events leading up to the capture began on 26 August. In bad weather, a patrolling Hudson aircraft of 269 Squadron Coastal Command sighted the U-boat on the surface about 80 miles south of Iceland. The U-boat, unaware of the presence of the aircraft, dived. Following normal procedure, the Hudson dropped a smoke float to mark the position and sent a sighting report. The first Hudson was relieved by a second, which sighted *U 570* when she surfaced at 1030. The aircraft immediately attacked, and neatly dropped four depth charges across the submarine. These caused some minor damage which led the inexperienced crew to panic, some jumping overboard. The captain surrendered *U 570* while

Left: Organic air protection for convoys had come to be seen as essential in the face of both long range German air patrols out over the Bay of Biscay, and as a means of intercepting U-boats gathering into Wolf Packs to attack convoys. In January 1941 work began on converting a captured German merchant ship, the *Hannover*, into an Auxiliary Fighter Carrier, which was renamed *Empire Audacity*, subsequently *Audacity*. The picture shows her just after conversion. (Imperial War Museum)

the Hudson continued to circle until relieved by a Catalina and further relays of aircraft. Finally, at 2300, the trawler *Northern Chief* arrived, followed shortly after midnight by the trawlers *Kingston Agate*, *Wastwater* and *Windermere*, and subsequently by the destroyers *Burwell* and *Niagara*. *U 570* was then taken in tow by *Northern Chief* and brought to Britain.

Following the success of the CAM ships, the Battle of the Atlantic Committee noted in May 1941, '... a great advance will have been made if our convoys can carry their own co-operation aircraft.' At the time this suggestion was being put forward, the ex-German cargo ship *Hannover* was already undergoing conversion to a Merchant Aircraft Carrier (MAC-Ship). The Admiralty had first discussed the possibility of using converted merchant ships as small carriers for trade protection as early as 1932. Plans were prepared, and three such vessels were provided for in the 1936 Estimates, but the need for fast Fleet carriers and financial stringencies led to the proposals being dropped. The idea was later resurrected, and conversion of *Hannover* began in January 1941. Her superstructure was razed and the upper deck rebuilt and topped with a wooden flight deck. She was fitted with the barest minimum of equipment necessary for flying operations — two arrester wires and a crash barrier being all that was provided on the flight deck. There was no hangar, and the aircraft had to be parked aft on the flight deck and maintained in the open. Accommodation for the aircrew was ample, their messdeck being sited aft, below the well deck.

Named *Empire Audacity*, she sailed with her first convoy, OG74 outward bound for Gibraltar, on 13 September, carrying four Martlet fighters. The convoy comprised 27 merchant ships covered by an Escort Group consisting of one sloop and five 'Flower' class corvettes. The convoy was sighted and reported on the 20th by *U 124*. *U 201* was directed to the convoy, but was forced to submerge by one of the Martlets. Meanwhile, *U 124* succeeded in sinking two ships. The next day the rescue ship *Walmer Castle* was sunk by a Focke-Wulf Fw 200 while rescuing survivors. A second Fw 200 was shot down by a Martlet. By this time four merchant ships were straggling from the convoy, and three escorts turned back to accompany them. Before they could arrive, however, U-boats had sunk three of the ships. *Empire Audacity* provided the convoy with continuous air cover during the hours of daylight, and her four Martlets succeeded in shooting down two Fw 200 reconnaissance aircraft.

Convoy HG76 (32 ships, 36th Escort Group under Commander F.J. Walker, together with the carrier *Audacity*, renamed after her first operation) sailed from Gibraltar on 14 December in nine columns, and was continuously under air and U-boat attack until 23 December. The 36th Escort Group (sloops *Stork* and *Deptford*, and seven 'Flower' class corvettes) was highly trained and had been well drilled in new anti-submarine

warfare tactics which Commander Walker was developing.

For the first few days, to help the convoy break through the U-boat patrol line, HG76 was provided with an additional escort of three destroyers, two sloops and three 'Flower' class corvettes from Gibraltar. On 17 December *U 131* sighted the convoy and shot down one of the Martlets from *Audacity*. She was then herself forced to scuttle when the escort came up. The next day the submarines closed in on the convoy and the Luftwaffe provided almost continuous air reconnaissance. During the day two Fw 200s were shot down by *Audacity*'s aircraft, and *U 434* was forced to the surface and sunk by the close escort. The next night a merchant ship and the sloop *Stanley* were sunk, the latter by *U 574*, which was then sunk by *Stork* when she rammed the U-boat. The next afternoon (the 19th) two more Fw 200s were shot down by Martlets and a U-boat ahead of the convoy was forced down by the presence of the carrier. During the next two days more U-boats closed in on the convoy, and during the night of 21 December the convoy carried out an evasive alteration of course. While this was in progress the escorts proceeded on their original course in an attempt to draw away the U-boats.

Unfortunately, Snowflake rockets fired by one of the escorts illuminated the convoy, and a merchant ship of 3,324 tons was sunk. During the action the carrier moved away from the scene of the action, but was then herself sunk by *U 751*. In the melée *U 567* was sunk by the escort. By dawn on 22 December the escort was exhausted after four days of continuous action which resulted in the loss of two merchant ships of 6,133 tons, the carrier *Audacity* and the destroyer *Stanley*. The sloops *Stork* and *Deptford* were damaged. For this meagre success an experienced Wolf Pack of ten U-boats suffered the loss of *U 131*, *U 434*, *U 567* and *U 574*, and four Fw 200s were shot down by aircraft from *Audacity*. The action around convoy HG76 was extremely significant, as it proved beyond any doubt the value of organic air cover to protect convoys, the need for highly trained and efficient escorts working as a cohesive group without the need for a continual flow of instructions and orders from the Group commander, and new tactics and equipment. The losses in U-boats and aircraft, and their inability to penetrate the screen of escorts and aircraft to sink large numbers of merchant ships, were proof enough of the success of the operation.

After the success of *Audacity*, the Battle of the Atlantic Committee suggested that five similar conversions be undertaken and that six more be ordered under Lend-Lease. These plans were put in hand, but it was many months before the first of the new escort carriers and MAC-ships entered service.

Following the opening of the British 8th Army's offensive in North Africa in November 1941, Hitler ordered Dönitz to transfer a number of U-boats from the Biscay bases to the Mediterranean. Forewarned of the impending operation by ULTRA information, the Admiralty ordered intensified anti-submarine patrols from Gibraltar. Fortunately at Gibraltar there were nine radar-equipped Swordfish of 812 Squadron which had flown off *Ark Royal* just before she had sailed for Britain and been sunk by *U 81* on 18 November. Equipped with ASV II radar, they were immediately pressed into service to assist the RAF, carrying out night anti-submarine patrols in the Straits to catch the U-boats which were transiting the narrow passage on the surface. On 1 December a Swordfish forced *U 96* to abandon an attempt to enter the Mediterranean, and during the next three weeks other aircraft from the squadron forced *U 558* (3 December), *U 432* and *U 569* (16-17 December), and *U 202* (20-21 December) to turn back in night attacks. Finally, on 21 December a Swordfish of 812 Squadron sank *U 451* in a night attack. This was the first night sinking of a submarine by an aircraft.

With corvettes completing at the rate of between six to eight a month, the strength of the groups in Western Approaches Command was increased to about nine, generally composed of about three destroyers and six corvettes. In addition, other groups of about five Fleet destroyers were formed, ready to reinforce any convoy which ran into trouble. These formed the forerunners of the Support Groups, but with the entry of Japan into the war in December 1941, and the need for America to transfer forces to the Pacific, escorts were urgently needed for other tasks, and the situation soon reverted to that prevailing in the early part of 1941.

On 7 December 1941 Japan attacked the US fleet in its base at Pearl Harbor, following which America entered the war. As a result of the transfer to the Mediterranean of a number of U-boats and the losses suffered in the Bay of Biscay, Dönitz had only five U-boats immediately available for operations off the US coast. During the first three months of 1942 about 60 tankers totalling 765,000 tons were sunk or damaged by U-boats, mostly in US waters where convoys were not in force and few escorts were available. There was a real threat that the reduced flow of oil to Britain would seriously jeopardize military operations. In view of the terrible losses being suffered off

the US east coast, and to make up for the grave shortage of anti-submarine vessels in the US Navy, the Royal Navy, on 10 February 1942, offered the US 240 ASDIC equipped anti-submarine trawlers and 10 'Flower' class corvettes together with their crews. These were gratefully accepted, and the first ships arrived in New York in early March. The gradual strengthening of the US defences forced the smaller Type VIIc U-boats to return to the North Atlantic convoy routes, where it was hoped that the lull in that area would have deceived the Admiralty into transferring its escorts to other more dangerous areas, a trap into which the Admiralty refused to be drawn.

To ease the strain of the attacks off the US east coast, the Admiralty and Coastal Command worked out a scheme to delay U-boats in transit across the Bay of Biscay, and reduced their time on station by carrying out continuous day and night patrols. The plan required additional aircraft which the Air Ministry refused to release to Coastal Command, as it would seriously detract from the strategic bombing operation against Germany.

While the controversy raged between the Air Ministry and the Admiralty over the allocation of aircraft, the Trade Division of the Admiralty took up the Battle of the Atlantic Committee's suggestion (see above) that, pending the entry into service of the escort carriers, the 300-mile gap in the mid-Atlantic could be covered by MAC-ships. This would involve fitting tankers and grain ships with flight decks to carry a few Swordfish aircraft. These ships, with their long, unobstructed deck areas, were particularly suitable for conversion to MAC ships. With such heavy merchant losses then being suffered,

Below: The success of the *Audacity* prompted Coastal Command to recommend in November 1941 that a carrier be provided for every convoy, which would require a total of 30 carriers. It was estimated that nine months would be required to convert a merchant ship to an improved *Audacity* design. By February 1942, however, it was obvious that the numbers forthcoming would not meet the demand. To make up the numbers it was decided to prepare a design for an even more austere conversion known as a MAC-ship (Merchant Aircraft Carrier). The plans aimed at using tramp steamers which would retain their cargo capacity, but upon which a flight deck would be mounted capable of operating three or four Swordfish anti-submarine aircraft. A small hangar was installed above the after hold, a feature not fitted on converted tankers. Contracts for the first two conversions were awarded in June 1942, the first completed being the *Empire MacAlpine*. A total of 30 were planned, but only nineteen were converted. The picture shows a tanker conversion: a Swordfish is preparing to land and two more are parked at the forward end of the flight deck. (ACPL)

however, the Ministry of War Transport was loath to release such valuable tonnage to undergo conversion, and the first MAC ships did not sail with a convoy until after the escort carriers had entered service.

During the early part of 1942 new weapons and equipment became available to the anti-submarine forces. In January the Hedgehog anti-submarine mortar entered service, while the following month the magnetic anomaly detector (MAD) became operational with US forces and was gradually fitted to Coastal Command aircraft. In June the Leigh Light entered service with Coastal Command. The first sortie was flown on 4 June, and resulted in the Italian submarine *Luigi Torelli* being attacked and severely damaged. The first kill was achieved on 5 July, when *U 502* was sunk. As a result of further operations and attacks, Dönitz, on 16 July, instructed all U-boats crossing the Bay of Biscay after that date to remain submerged at night, forcing them to surface by day to recharge their batteries.

In September 1942, Admiral Noble formed the first Support Group, the 20th Escort Group, under Captain Walker. The following month the Group took part in its first operation, in support of convoy ONS132. Unfortunately it had to be disbanded shortly after, as the ships were required for other duties. Many other Western Approaches escorts were also withdrawn from convoy duty at the time to prepare for Operation Torch — the Allied landings in North Africa. Likewise, the entry into service on convoy escort duty of the first of the new escort carriers was also delayed, as they were needed to provide fighter cover and anti-submarine patrols for the assault forces.

Coincidentally with Coastal Command's problems in finding sufficient numbers of aircraft to meet commitments, Admiral Horton, who had just taken over from Admiral Noble as C-in-C Western Approaches Command, encountered a similar problem viz-à-vis numbers of escorts. In a note to the Admiralty on 19 November he pointed out that so far during the war the winter months had shown a depletion in escort numbers, and that there was no reason to expect that 1942-43 would be any different. This critical situation was exacerbated by the fact that Western Approaches Command possessed no general reserve of escorts which could be drawn on in emergencies.

Admiral Horton repeated a request of Admiral Noble's that Support Groups be formed to reinforce convoys threatened by large numbers of U-boats. These Groups were to be able to remain in the Atlantic for long periods, and were to have sufficient speed to enable them to cover wide distances between threatened convoys rapidly. Together with Coastal Command aircraft, they would then hunt the U-boats to destruction, leaving the convoy escort to continue with its task of providing close escort to the convoy, rather than detaching units to hunt U-boats. The request was put forward again on 25 November, and Horton stressed the need for very-long-range aircraft. The Admiralty then informed him that, at a meeting of the Anti-U-boat Warfare Committee, the Chief of the Air Staff had stated that two squadrons of Halifaxes from Bomber Command would be lent to Coastal Command, and that more would follow.

At the end of October two convoys suffered heavy losses for very little credit against the U-boats. In a five-day battle starting on 27 October, convoy SL125 (37 ships with a small escort) was beset by nine U-boats and lost ten ships of 67,122 tons before further surface escorts and aircraft arrived to drive off the U-boats. Only *U 659* suffered damage, from a depth charge attack. On 30 October convoy SC107 (42 ships) with a strong surface escort suffered heavy losses in a six-day running battle with no fewer than fourteen U-boats, before the arrival of a strong air escort forced the U-boats to break off the action. A total of fifteen ships of 82,827 tons were sunk for the loss of just two U-boats – *U 520* sunk by an aircraft and *U 132*, which disappeared in the vicinity of the convoy.

By early November it was clear both from Intelligence and convoy reports that there was a considerable increase in the number of U-boats operating in the North Atlantic. At the beginning of December convoy HX217 was under attack by no fewer than seventeen U-boats. The convoy was saved by its strong escort (Escort Group B.6) and the timely arrival of a powerful air escort. Two U-boats were sunk — *U 254* after being rammed by another U-boat, and *U 611*, which was sunk by an aircraft. Only two merchant ships of 13,467 tons were sunk. Other convoys at sea during November and December also suffered severe losses.

By the end of the year the situation in Britain was becoming critical. Only 300,000 tons of commercial bunker fuel (not including the Admiralty's special reserve for emergency use) remained in the country, and this was being used at a rate of 130,000 tons a month, and food and raw materials were also at a desperately low level. During 1942 U-boats had sunk 1,160 ships of 6,266,215 tons in all areas. Throughout the year no fewer than 1,664 ships of 7,790,697 tons had been sunk. Against this, over seven million tons of new shipping had entered service, mostly Liberty ships built in the United States. Dönitz was almost succeeding in his task.

The year 1943 opened on a sombre note in the battle of the Atlantic. The situation was so critical that, at the Allied conference held at Casablanca in January, it was decided that the most important objective for 1943 should be the defeat of the U-boat.

On 30 January 1943 Raeder was replaced as head of the German navy by Admiral Dönitz, who at once set about putting Germany's major maritime effort into the submarine campaign.

During the early part of the year the Germans continued to achieved great success in decrypting Allied naval signals. With the knowledge of date of sailing, routes taken and ports of destination in their hands, they were able to place lines of U-boats across the anticipated course of convoys.

Great success was also being achieved by the British in decrypting German orders to U-boats. The voluminous ULTRA information, HF/DF bearings and fixes and general intelligence enabled Rodger Winn and Patrick Beesley in the Submarine Tracking Room of the Admiralty to inform Admiral Horton at Western Approaches Command of the exact position of U-boat concentrations. This enabled Horton to order convoys to make evasive alterations of course to avoid the Wolf Packs, or, if this was impractical, to request close air escort for extra protection.

To improve the situation further, much new equipment had entered service in vast quantities. Most escorts were fitted with 10cm radar, new and improved depth charges with deeper setting were in use, and the Hedgehog ahead-throwing mortar was in widespread service. Finally, escorts were able to refuel at sea, enabling them to remain with convoys much longer, though this to a very large degree depended on weather conditions.

Against these developments, new U-boats capable of diving much deeper to avoid damage from depth charges were at sea in much greater numbers. Far more patrol lines were being set up to intercept convoys. U-boats were also able to remain at sea longer, as they were supplied by new and very large U-boats specially built to carry additional fuel and supplies.

But it was the weather that was to cause the gravest problem. A succession of extremely fierce gales, the like of which had not been experienced for many years, raged throughout the early months of 1943. This resulted in large numbers of ships suffering severe damage, delays to convoys and damage to escorts, which had to be repaired before they could venture to sea again. To add to this problem, on 10 March the Germans changed their weather codes, and this vital stream of information via ULTRA was denied the Admiralty. As a result, it was much more difficult to assess where the Germans would site their U-boat patrol lines and decide what evasive routes could be followed by the convoys. In consequence, a number of convoys ran into very heavy concentrations of U-boats during the following two months and bitter battles took place, some of the heaviest losses being sustained. The crisis in the battle for the Atlantic was fast approaching, and the Royal Navy came close to losing the fight against the U-boats.

During March there occurred one of the greatest convoy battles of the war. The action developed around two convoys, HX229 (38 ships, Escort Group B.4 — four escorts and a destroyer from Western Approaches local escort which had to return because of fuel shortage) and SC122 (51 ships, Escort Group B.5 — nine escorts), a slow convoy some 120 miles ahead of the HX convoy.

During the next few days, as the action developed, the two convoys slowly converged until the ocean was filled with a huge mass of shipping. To avoid a U-boat patrol line already shadowing another convoy, these two convoys were evasively routed. However, the evasive routeing instructions were deciphered by the Germans, and on 15 March two Wolf Packs (eventually to total 26 U-boats) began to assemble to meet SC122, and another Pack (a total of 11 U-boats) gathered to intercept HX229. In a heavy storm SC122 passed one of the Packs, while HX229 was routed around the patrol line. HX229 was sighted on 16 March, and the U-boats began to establish contact in the afternoon, ready to attack during the night.

During the night of 16-17 March, HX229 was attacked and eight ships of 59,750 tons sunk, while SC122 lost four ships of 24,972 tons. Using HF/DF fixes, the escorts around SC122 were able drive off six U-boats, so preventing further losses. Further attacks were made the next day by the U-boats, and a ship of 4,071 tons was sunk from SC122 and two of 12,410 tons from HX 229. During the afternoon, escorting aircraft forced the shadowing U-boats under and they lost contact with the convoys. During the day many U-boats had gathered against SC122, but only two merchant ships of 13,045 tons were sunk, and that was after dark.

By the next day, of the 30 U-boats still operating against the convoys, only nine were in the immediate vicinity, and these were forced to remain submerged by the constant air patrols. Only two ships of 15,484 tons from HX229 were sunk during the day. The escort to HX229 was brought up to strength when two more destroyers of EG B.4 arrived after dark. Only one ship from SC122 was sunk during the night. The following day, the 19th, the U-boats were again driven off from both convoys, and a lone straggler from one of the convoys was sunk. During the night still more escorts joined to support HX229, and during the 20th yet more U-boats were driven off, *U 384* being sunk by an aircraft of Coastal Command. In view of the strong air and surface escort, Dönitz decided to break off the action and withdraw his U-boats. During the battle a total of 21 merchant ships of 140,842 tons had been sunk from the two convoys.

During the first ten days of March a total of 41 merchant ships had been sunk, followed by a further 56 during the next ten days, a total of over half a million tons (68 per cent of which was in convoy) for the loss of just sixteen U-boats. Losses were so catastrophic that a terrible strain was imposed on the escort groups, which were under-strength as a result of storm and action damage. A subsequent Admiralty anti-submarine report noted, 'the enemy never came so near to disrupting communications... as in the first 20 days of March...', and the losses sustained by SC122, HX229 and two other convoys gave rise to fears that the convoy system might have to be suspended.

The following month saw the turning point in the campaign against the U-boats. By careful rearrangement of escort groups it was possible to form the first of the roving Support Groups, and by the beginning of April five of these were operating in the North Atlantic, two of them including the first of the escort carriers — USS *Bogue* and HMS *Archer*. These Support Groups were composed of fast sloops or frigates and destroyers from the Home Fleet and Western Approaches Command. Their task was to provide additional support to convoy escorts as and when required. In addition, Coastal Command at long last received the first 30 of the new very-long-range Liberators, some of which had been used in the battles during the previous month.

The climax finally developed around convoy ONS5. A total of 51 submarines were deployed against the convoy and its seven escorts. The convoy (42 merchant ships and seven escorts under Commander P. Gretton — two destroyers, a new 'River' class frigate and four 'Flower' class corvettes) consisted in the main of lightly laden, very elderly tramp steamers which ploughed their way slowly westwards on a northerly route. Right from the start the weather was atrocious, the worst seen in the North Atlantic for some time. The speed of the convoy was slowed right down, and by 27 April two of the merchant ships had been sent back to harbour, one damaged in a collision and the other having proved far too slow, even for a convoy as slow as ONS5.

The convoy was reported on 28 April, and the Admiralty Tracking Room kept Commander Gretton and the convoy Commodore appraised of the developing situation, the shadowing U-boat being detected by the escorts' HF/DF. In the twilight a U-boat was spotted and kept down by the frigate *Tay*. During the night the Wolf Pack closed in, but was chased off by the vigilant escort. The weather was so foul, however, that the encounters proved inconclusive, although all the attempted attacks by the U-boats were foiled. The following day, the 29th, a lone U-boat which had stayed behind while the others raced ahead to a new waiting position penetrated the escort screen and sank a merchant ship.

By 30 April a full southwesterly gale was raging with hurricane force winds and mountainous seas, which reduced visibility to a few hundred yards. In the heavy seas the convoy gradually lost all semblance of order, some ships heaving to, others wallowing all over the place, and the ships were gradually scattered over an immense area. Fortunately the weather was so bad that it also prevented the U-boats from operating against the convoy, and they were called off to form a new patrol line. By 2 May the weather had abated somewhat, and the convoy gradually began to reassemble into three groups; a main group of about twenty ships with the main escort, a second group of about ten ships under the escort of *Tay*, and, some 50 miles astern, another group of about six ships escorted by the 'Flower' class corvette *Pink*. During the day the 3rd Support Group joined the escort. Although the weather had abated, it was still too rough for the escorts to refuel, and the leader, *Duncan*, suffering from an acute shortage of fuel, was forced to leave the convoy on 3 May and race ahead to Newfoundland to refuel. On the following day, 4 May, three of the destroyers from the 3rd Support Group also had to leave to refuel in harbour.

By now the convoy had re-formed into a group of 30 ships, with the small group of six ships under the escort of *Pink* still some way behind. The convoy was warned by the Admiralty Tracking Room of the concentration of U-boats ahead, but in its still somewhat disorganized state was unable to carry out an evasive manoeuvre to avoid the Pack. During the day (4 May) HF/DF intercepts warned of the approach of the U-boats, and air escorts were called up, one sinking *U 630*, lying in wait ahead of the convoy. During the day the weather continued to abate and about 30 U-boats began to congregate around the convoy. The attack began that night, when a straggler from the convoy was sunk. During the night a further six ships were sunk.

Right: By late 1943 the escort carriers were beginning to enter service in increasing numbers. The picture shows HMS *Tracker* escorting a convoy, with Avenger anti-submarine aircraft ranged on the deck aft. (Imperial War Museum)

The following day (5 May) the *Pink*, still some way behind, sank *U 192*, but lost one of the ships in her group to a U-boat attack. During the day the main group lost another four merchant ships to U-boat attack. As the weather abated, a thick bank of fog descended over the convoy, blotting out all visibility right down to a few hundred yards. During the night of 5-6 May the U-boats made a concentrated effort to annihilate the convoy. Twenty-four attacks were mounted, but were all frustrated by the well-trained escorts using radar to its full advantage in the thick fog. During these attacks *U 638* was sunk, and Lieutenant R. Hart in *Vidette* sank *U 125* with her Hedgehog. *U 531* was rammed and sunk by the destroyer *Oribi* from the 3rd Support Group, while *Pelican* from the 1st Support Group, which was coming up to join the escort, sank *U 438*. By daylight on 6 May Dönitz had called off the U-boats, the battle having constituted a defeat for his forces. He ordered them to regroup to attack convoys HX237 and SC129, but they showed great reluctance to attack.

As many as 60 U-boats had been directed to the battle against ONS5, which resulted in the loss of twelve merchant ships. Dönitz lost six U-boats sunk by the air and surface escorts nearby or around the convoy, while two more had collided and been sunk. Additionally, a number of others were severely damaged.

The major success achieved in checking the U-boats led Admiral Horton to issue a message to the air and naval units of Western Approaches Command, in which he noted, 'the tide of the battle has been checked ... the enemy is showing signs of strain...'. And the Admiralty noted, 'Historians ... are likely to single out ... April and May 1943 as the critical period during which strength began to ebb away from the German U-boat offensive ... because for the first time U-boats failed to press home attacks on convoys when favourably situated to do so. There is ground for confident estimate that the enemy's peak effort is passed.'

The months of March-June 1943 signalled the peak in the Battle of the Atlantic. In those months the war was

nearly lost, and won, by both sides. The period March to May 1943 proved to be a turning point in the fight against the U-boats. Shipping losses due to U-boats dropped to 50 ships of a quarter of a million tons in May, for the loss of 41 U-boats (39 per cent of the total then at sea), 25 of which were sunk in the North Atlantic.

There were three major reasons for the reversal in U-boat fortunes during the late spring of 1943. First, with the return of many escorts after operation Torch, and with the delay in sailing two Russian convoys, Admiral Horton was able to form five Support Groups (the benefit of which was felt by convoy ONS5), one of which included an escort carrier, *Biter*. Second, although German Intelligence on Allied convoy movements enabled them to assemble large Wolf Packs (averaging about twenty boats) to attack convoys, they were hampered in their operations by a number of factors, of which the Allied possession of ULTRA information revealing the position of Wolf Packs and the areas in mid-Atlantic designated as U-boat refuelling points was the most important. Furthermore, ULTRA information on U-boats, shipborne HF/DF bearings, radar contacts and, finally, the new tactics developed by Captain Walker, enabled the convoy escort and support groups to deal effectively with U-boat attacks. Thirdly, the decision of the Casablanca Conference to make the defeat of the U-boat a strategic priority led to the convening of the Atlantic Convoy Conference in March 1943, at which it was decided to pool all Allied anti-submarine resources. The Convoy Conference also decided that the newly forming US escort carrier groups should be stationed in mid-Atlantic to deal with the information on roving supply U-boats derived from ULTRA.

After June 1943 the U-boats never again posed the threat to Britain's lifeline that they had. New escorts were entering service in increasing numbers with new and more sophisticated weapons and electronics, while merchant ship construction was at last outstripping losses. Although U-boats were still being built at a rate that

Left: A Swordfish is seen taking off on an anti-submarine patrol from a MAC ship. The objects beneath the wing are anti-submarine rockets. In the background are ships of the convoy. (ACPL)

could keep pace with losses, the quality of the crews was not the same as it had been in the early days of the war. The aces and their crews from the early days had all been lost or captured, and the new crews were never trained to the same degree, and never had the opportunity to gain experience before they were pitted against the highly trained Allied escort crews. Never again did the German submarines prove a deadly menace to the convoys, although there were still many losses to be suffered before the war ended.

With the reduction in U-boat activity in the North Atlantic, Coastal Command was able to withdraw some of its aircraft from convoy escort duties and reinforce its patrols in the Bay of Biscay. Here the offensive reached a climax during July 1943, when eleven U-boats were sunk. The U-boats countered by sailing in groups on the surface, armed with heavy AA weapons, determined to fight it out with the aircraft. To support the aircraft the navy stationed Support Groups in the Bay of Biscay which were homed on to the groups of U-boats. The U-boats were loath to submerge, for they then lost their mutual support and became vulnerable to attacks by the aircraft and easy detection by the Support Group.

The stationing of the Support Groups in the Bay led to a spectacular action on 30 July, when seven aircraft and the 2nd Support Group sank three U-boats, including a supply submarine. Early in the day a Liberator sighted *U 562*, *U 462* and *U 504* crossing the Bay. Other aircraft were directed to the scene, and the 2nd Support Group was homed on to the position. In the meantime, relays of aircraft carried out attacks on the group of submarines, one aircraft sinking *U 461* and damaging *U 462*. The 2nd Support Group then arrived and opened fire on *U 504*. *U 462* was severely damaged by gunfire and sank. *U 504* submerged, but was detected by ASDIC, and in difficult conditions the ships carried out a number of creeping attacks. After two hours evidence came to the surface indicating that *U 504* had been sunk.

To counter the Support Groups in the Bay the Germans used radio-controlled glider bombs launched from high altitude. The first such attack occurred on 25 August, when the sloop *Landguard* was damaged. On 28 August the 1st Support Group, which was sailing in a loose formation to counter the standoff attacks, was attacked by a number of glider bombs which severely damaged the destroyer *Athabaskan*. The sloop *Egret* was hit amidships and disappeared in a great explosion. As the smoke cleared she twisted on her side, rolled back, and slid stern first slowly under the surface. As a result of these attacks the Support Groups were withdrawn beyond the range of the German aircraft, and Coastal Command was left to continue its offensive in the Bay on its own.

During September 1943 the U-boats returned to the North Atlantic armed with the new German naval acoustic torpedo (Gnat) and heavy AA armament. In a series of attacks on convoys ONS18/ON202 during 18-23 September they achieved a degree of success. Following ULTRA information indicating the presence of a Wolf Pack (twenty U-boats), the Admiralty ordered the 9th Support Group RCN (six escorts), heading for the Bay of Biscay, to the support of ONS18 (27 ships and ten escorts, including the MAC ship *Empire MacAlpine*). By midday on 19 September ON202 (38 ships and six escorts) was 120 miles astern of ONS18. During the afternoon of the 18th ULTRA again noted the presence of U-boats, and ONS18 was rerouted to the northwest. At dawn on the 19th, aircraft from Newfoundland provided air escort, sinking *U 341*. During the night of 19-20 September the U-boats attacked ONS18, but were frustrated in their attempts by the escorts. By daylight ON202 was only 30 miles to the northeast of ONS18, and was reported by *U 270*, which was located by HF/DF and attacked by *Lagan*. Just as *Lagan* lost ASDIC contact and prepared to drop depth charges, she was struck by a Gnat and lost way. The *Gatineau* turned to support, and *U 270* disengaged. During the attack two ships were sunk and Gnats were fired at *Gatineau* and *Polyanthus*. At dawn on 20 September aircraft again provided air support and sank *U 338*.

By this time the two convoys were so close that they were ordered to combine. During the afternoon the 9th Support Group arrived, and in the ensuing action *U 305* sank *St Croix*. As *Itchen* came up in support, another Gnat exploded in her wake. During the night other Gnats were fired and missed, but *U 952* succeeded in sinking *Polyanthus*. During the 21st thick fog descended, and in the gaps the MAC ship flew off air patrols. Early on the 22nd the destroyer *Keppel* sank *U 229*, and during the afternoon the fog lifted, allowing the MAC ship to fly off air patrols, while shore-based aircraft gave additional cover. In further U-boat attacks during the night, *U 666* sank *Itchen* with a Gnat. *Itchen* had on board all the survivors from *St Croix* and *Polyanthus*, and of all the crews, tragically only three men were picked up. During the action *U 238* managed to penetrate the escort screen and sink three ships.

With increasing air support from shore-based aircraft during the 23rd, the attack died away and the U-boats withdrew from the area. During six days of almost continuous action the twenty U-boats had succeeded in sinking only six ships of 36,422 tons and three escorts, for the loss of *U 229*, *U 338* and *U 341*. They had fired a total of 24 Gnats, and claimed to have sunk twelve escorts.

Further attempts at Wolf Pack attacks, using Gnats, had not proved the success that Dönitz had hoped, and with the changing of the Allied codes in the summer of 1943, and the consequent lack of intelligence concerning convoy movements, the U-boats were withdrawn from the outer convoy routes further towards Britain and the English Channel, around the focal areas through which all convoys had to pass before entering or leaving ports in Britain. Finally, in April 1944, the U-boat campaign in the Atlantic was suspended.

Chapter 31

Arctic Operations

On 22 June 1941 Hitler invaded Russia and the German Army began its lightning *blitzkrieg*, rolling across eastern Europe right up to gates of Moscow, where it was finally halted. Stalin was caught unprepared, and with an obsolescent army and limited and outmoded resources he could not hope to halt the German advance. However, if Stalin could be sustained and aided to keep on fighting, it was argued in the West, there was every reason to think that Hitler would eventually be defeated. At the time Britain was the only country still fighting Hitler, and could not hope to sustain the mighty Russian military machine from her own meagre resources. Russia desper-

ately needed tanks, aircraft, ammunition and oil, and in an effort to support her it was decided that a convoy supply system should be started to give Stalin every possible assistance.

While the Arctic convoys were in many ways regarded as a side show, the operation nevertheless meant that the Royal Navy, already stretched to breaking point, was called upon to provide escorts for yet another operation which was to continue until the end of the war. The task facing the navy was to open and protect a new shipping route to Russia which, for the greater part of its length, ran past enemy-held Norwegian territory. The escorts for

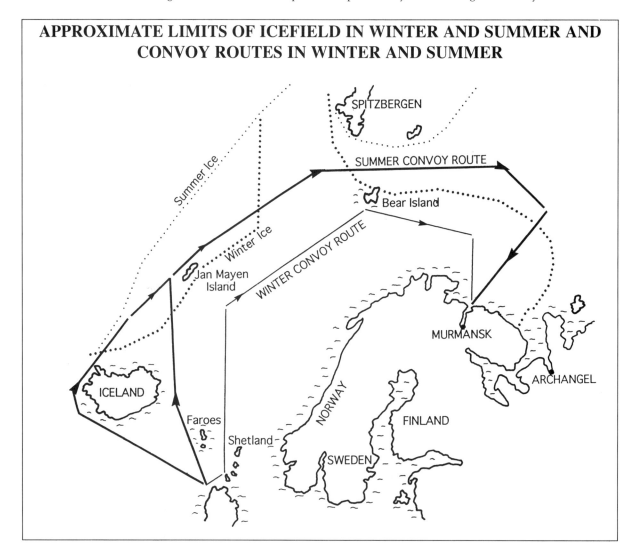

APPROXIMATE LIMITS OF ICEFIELD IN WINTER AND SUMMER AND CONVOY ROUTES IN WINTER AND SUMMER

the convoys were drawn mainly from the Home Fleet with, on occasions, ships crewed by refugees from Poland and Norway, and other allied navies. The convoys were mainly composed of British and American merchant ships, the latter often outnumbering the former.

The route was noted for the unequalled hardships faced by both the seamen and the ships, all of which left a legacy of damage and distress. The convoy route ran through the most inhospitable climate in the world, characterized by tremendous gales, far worse than those seen in the North Atlantic, and seas with tremendous swells which frequently hid even columns of ships from one another. During the winter months the ships sailed through perpetual darkness, with raging gales and bitter snowstorms frequently battering the convoys. Because of the nearness of German forces, they were forced to sail right up to the edge of the ice pack, with all the attendant risks of damage from pack ice. As a result the ships were often encrusted with ice which had to be chipped away by hand from the superstructure and fittings to prevent the vessels becoming top heavy and capsizing. The work was treacherous, and anyone unlucky enough to fall into the sea could expect to last for no more than a minute at the most before the freezing cold numbed all senses and the person drowned. Even below decks, icicles hung from bulkheads and deckheads. Warships were not immune from these hardships either, one 'Town' class cruiser even having the armoured top of her 6in gun turret ripped off by the sea in a heavy gale.

On top of this came relentless attacks by German aircraft and submarines based in Northern Norway. Ships that became scattered in gales stood no chance against the determined Germans. It was a constant battle to keep the orderly arrangement of the convoy together for its own mutual protection and safety of the crews. During the summer months there was perpetual light in the northern latitudes, which made continuous attack from the air almost inevitable.

Less than two months after Hitler invaded Russia, the first convoy of seven ships sailed for Archangel. When America joined the war six months later, she, too, joined the operation and many American merchant ships made a hazardous journey across the Atlantic, followed by an even more terrifying journey to Russia. From then until the end of the war convoys were fought through to Archangel and Murmansk with tremendous determination, with only a short pause during the summer months. In these conditions it was far too dangerous to send the convoys, for they risked losses so heavy that they would far outweigh any benefit the Russians might derive from the few ships that arrived.

The task of the Home Fleet was to defend the convoys against attack by submarines; the high-altitude bombers, dive bombers and torpedo aeroplanes of the Luftwaffe; and even the heavy units of the German fleet. Not only had convoys to be given adequate escorts to fight off sub-

marine and air attack, but they also had to be provided with heavy close and distant cover, as far north as was practicable. Defence had to be provided against any possible foray by the German surface fleet with the battleships *Tirpitz*, *Scharnhorst*, *Gneisenau* and *Lützow*, and heavy cruisers such as *Hipper* and *Prinz Eugen*, which could sortie from their hideout in northern Norway and be on a convoy within a matter of hours. The entry into Russia was via the Kola Inlet, just a bare 30 miles from German-held territory.

The safety of the convoys depended on the covering forces being available at the right time and in the right place, ready to repulse the heavy units. On occasions they were not, which resulted in gallant destroyers speeding out to harry German surface units, while cruisers came under attack from U-boats and aircraft because they were retained as close escort for the convoys against surface attack.

As the Germans swept forward into Russia they destroyed large numbers of obsolete Russian aircraft. The need for aircraft to defend cities and strategic centres was vital, and on 21 August the veteran carrier *Argus* with 24 Hurricane fighters, together with six merchant ships loaded with 15 crated Hurricanes and raw materials, sailed for Russia. The convoy was escorted by six destroyers, and distant cover was provided by the carrier *Victorious* and the cruisers *Devonshire* and *Suffolk* under the command of Rear-Admiral Wake-Walker.

So keen were the Allies to help Russia that, on 6 October, Churchill informed Stalin that Britain would run a continuous cycle of convoys leaving every ten days. The Admiralty, however, had planned to run the convoys on a 40-day cycle. On 28 September, the day a party of British and American delegates arrived in Moscow to discuss the arrangements for providing aid to Russia, the first of the PQ convoys sailed from Iceland for Archangel. The convoy consisted of ten merchant ships escorted by the cruiser *Suffolk* and two destroyers. Among the cargo were 193 fighter aircraft and about twenty tanks.

The Germans were slow to react to the Arctic convoys, and by the end of the year a total of 53 ships had arrived in Russia, while 34 had returned, with no loss. Deliveries included 750 tanks, 800 fighters, 1,400 vehicles and more than 100,000 tons of general cargo. Escorts normally consisted of a cruiser, a couple of destroyers, a minesweeper and two anti-submarine trawlers. Air cover could only be provided for a short distance out from Iceland; thereafter the convoys had to rely on whatever could be provided by CAM-ships until they came within range of Russian aircraft bases, but air cover from that quarter was noticeable by its absence.

While convoys had sailed unimpeded to Russia during 1941, the same would not be so for 1942. On 15 January the new battleship *Tirpitz* arrived at the Norwegian port of Trondheim, where her sheer presence became the single most important influence on the Arctic operation.

Although she remained in port for most of her life, *Tirpitz* continued to pose a very considerable threat to the Arctic convoys until she was finally sunk. Immediately on learning of her presence, the Admiralty delayed the sailing of an outward bound convoy, PQ9. Previously, convoy PQ8 had been the first to come under attack. The convoy had left Iceland on 8 January, and just in sight of the Kola Inlet *U 454* sank the commodore's flagship and the destroyer *Matabele*, all but two of whose crew froze to death in the icy water.

The first serious attempt to interfere with the convoys came early in March, when *Tirpitz*, escorted by three destroyers, sortied to intercept convoy PQ12. At sea covering PQ12 were the battleship *King George V* and the carrier *Victorious*. When *Tirpitz* was sighted by the submarine *Seawolf*, the convoy carried out an evasive alteration of course, but bad weather then prevented the opposing forces from sighting each other. Admiralty intelligence kept Admiral Tovey on *King George V* informed of the state of affairs and, finally, after *Tirpitz* had given up trying to locate the convoy and was nearing her home base, *Victorious* was able to launch a strike of twelve Albacores of 817 Squadron FAA, armed with torpedoes. In the morning light the aircraft attacked from all directions, two aircraft being shot down. *Tirpitz* sailed on undamaged, but Admiral Ciliax believed that she had been struck by one or possibly two torpedoes which had failed to detonate.

The first of 32 U-boats to be sunk in action against the Russian convoys was *U 655*, which was sunk by the minesweeper *Sharpshooter* on 24 March during an attack on the homeward-bound QP9. The parallel outward bound convoy, PQ13, was not quite so lucky. The convoy was first scattered by a fierce gale four days out from Iceland. On 28 March it was sighted by a German reconnaissance aircraft, and soon after came under high-altitude bombing attack, which continued on and off for the rest of the day, two merchant ships being sunk. Three German destroyers were ordered to sea to intercept

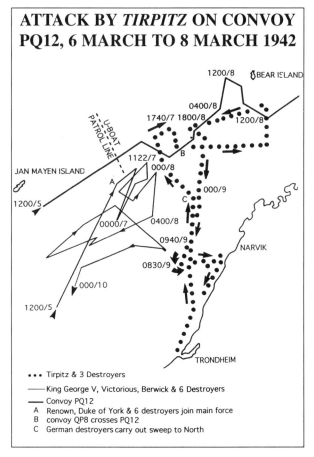

ATTACK BY *TIRPITZ* ON CONVOY PQ12, 6 MARCH TO 8 MARCH 1942

1200/8   BEAR ISLAND
0400/8
1740/7 1800/8   1200/8
U-BOAT PATROL LINE
1122/7
B
JAN MAYEN ISLAND
000/8
A
000/9
1200/5
C
0000/7   0400/8
0940/9
NARVIK
0830/9
000/10
1200/5
TRONDHEIM

••• Tirpitz & 3 Destroyers
—— King George V, Victorious, Berwick & 6 Destroyers
—— Convoy PQ12
A   Renown, Duke of York & 6 destroyers join main force
B   convoy QP8 crosses PQ12
C   German destroyers carry out sweep to North

the convoy, and on the evening of 28 March they sank a straggler, from which they gained details of the convoy's composition and escort. The destroyers sighted the convoy the next day and attacked. During their run-in they came under fire from the cruiser *Trinidad*, which also fired torpedoes, one of which ran amuck and torpedoed the cruiser herself. All of this occurred in deteriorating weather conditions with a snow storm and bad visibility.

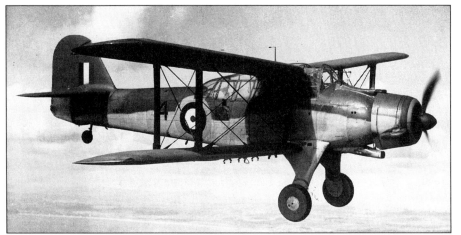

Left: The first Arctic convoy to Russia to come under determined attack from German forces stationed in Norway, was PQ12. The convoy was protected by a strong distant screening force including the carrier *Victorious* and the battleship *King George V*. The *Victorious* was able to launch a strike of twelve Albacore torpedo-bombers of 817 squadron against the German battleship *Tirpitz*, which had sortied to attack the convoy. Unfortunately none of the torpedoes struck the *Tirpitz*. The photograph shows Albacore N4257 of the third production batch. (ACPL)

Right: The next convoy, PQ13, also came under attack. She had been provided with a weak escort of two destroyers (*Fury* and *Eclipse*) and two trawlers, with the cruiser *Trinidad* (shown here) for close cover. The convoy was scattered by a severe gale on 24 March and, although some ships managed to gather together, the remainder were spread out over 150 miles of ocean. German destroyers sailed to intercept the convoy, and in a subsequent mêlée, the *Trinidad* was struck by a rogue torpedo she had fired. (Imperial War Museum)

In the mêlée *Trinidad* had managed to hit the destroyer *Z 26*, which later sank. The damaged *Trinidad* finally reached the Kola Inlet on 30 March. Off the entrance to the inlet a pack of four U-boats waited for the merchant ships to arrive, and two were sunk. The convoy had lost a total of five of its nineteen merchant ships.

On 28 May convoy QP11 (thirteen ships) left Murmansk for Iceland, escorted by four destroyers, four corvettes, and an anti-submarine trawler. Close escort was provided by the cruiser *Edinburgh* and two destroyers, *Foresight* and *Forester*. On 29 April the Germans made contact with convoy and *Edinburgh* was struck by two torpedoes from *U 456*. Three German destroyers sent to intercept the convoy were repeatedly driven off by the convoy escort, but managed to sink one freighter, a straggler. The destroyers then found and attacked the cruiser *Edinburgh*, which returned fire and severely damaged the *Hermann Schoemann*, which later sank. During the action the destroyers *Forester* and *Foresight* were badly damaged by gunfire, while *Edinburgh* was again struck by a torpedo from one of the German destroyers, subsequently having to be scuttled by a torpedo from *Foresight*. The defence of QP11 had proved to be so determined that never again did the German destroyers venture out to attack a convoy on their own, only sailing as escort to larger ships.

On 13 May the damaged *Trinidad*, which had been patched up by steel plates shipped to Russia aboard *Edinburgh*, sailed for Iceland. The damaged cruiser was given a close escort of four destroyers, while further cover to the west of Bear Island was provided by the cruisers *Kent*, *Liverpool*, *Nigeria* and *Norfolk*, screened by four destroyers. Distant cover was provided by Admiral Tovey aboard the battleship *Duke of York*, the carrier *Victorious*, the American battleship *Washington* and the cruiser *Tuscaloosa*, and eleven destroyers. The Russians were asked to provide air cover out to a distance of 200 miles, but only three Hurricane fighters made a brief appearance before returning to base. *Trinidad* was located by the Germans on the evening of the second day out, and a bombing attack quickly followed. Soon after there followed a low-level torpedo attack, during which a lone bomber dived to place an accurate stick of bombs on the cruiser's starboard side. Fire broke out and spread rapidly.

Although the cruiser took on a list, she managed to keep steaming at 20kts, but was forced to slow down to reduce the flow of air fanning the fire. In this compromising state, and being only 170 miles from enemy-held coast, it was decided that *Trinidad* would have to be scuttled. Rear-Admiral S.S. Bonham-Carter, who had flown his flag in *Edinburgh* and then transferred to *Trinidad* for the passage home, commented, 'Until the aerodromes in north Norway are neutralized and there are some hours of darkness, the continuation of these convoys should be stopped. If they must continue for political reasons, very serious and heavy losses must be expected.' Admiral Tovey concurred with these views, and even Churchill himself accepted them to some degree. But it was felt that such would be the political opprobrium that might accompany the cessation of the convoys that the risk of heavy losses must be accepted. Churchill felt that it was Britain's moral duty to continue supporting the Russian cause. But Admiral Bonham-Carter's views were soon to be proved horribly true.

In view of what had recently happened, Admiral Tovey considered that the greatest threat the convoys faced was that of air attack. The most effective defence was provided by the cruisers with their heavy AA armament, but unfortunately Admiral Tovey had only four of these cruisers available. To ensure their safety and make the most effective use of their AA capability, he decided to keep them concentrated to provide cover for the next convoy to sail, PQ16, until they met the homeward bound QP12, to which they would then transfer. For cover beyond the changeover point, all ships in PQ16 were provided with kite balloons, while the convoy's AA defence was bolstered by the AA ship *Alynbank* and the CAM ship *Empire Lawrence*, which carried a Hurricane fighter. In addition, two submarines accompanied the convoy to operate against any German surface ships which might attempt to interfere with the convoy's passage.

The convoy of 35 ships sailed on 21 May and was detected on 25 May. Heavy air attacks followed, during which two bombers were shot down by the convoy's AA defences, while the Hurricane fighter from the CAM ship shot down a torpedo bomber. During the night of 25-26 May *U 763* sank a freighter of 1,691 tons. Apart from this, the U-boats assembled against the convoy failed to achieve any success, and a number were damaged in depth-charge attacks. As a result of the U-boats' failure to interfere with the convoy, Dönitz decided against using them in heavy concentrations during the summer months, considering that the convoys could best be attacked by the Luftwaffe. However, the U-boats had achieved some success, for their presence led to the convoy's close escort being withdrawn on 26 May. Further air attacks took place during the day and became almost continuous, and in varying strength. The Luftwaffe achieved its greatest success on the following day, 27 May, when six ships of 36,963 tons were sunk. The convoy finally arrived at its destination on 31 May and 1 June, having suffered a total loss of 43,205 tons.

With the next convoy which sailed, PQ17, the worst fears of many who doubted the wisdom of continuing with the Russian convoys were realized. PQ17, consisting of 36 merchant ships (two ships were forced to return to Iceland as a result of damage sustained in a collision and from ice), a fleet tanker and, for the first time on a Russian convoy, three specially fitted-out rescue ships, with a close escort of six destroyers, four corvettes, seven smaller vessels, two special AA ships and two submarines, left Iceland on 26 June. Close cover was provided by four cruisers and three destroyers, while distant cover was provided by the Royal Navy battleship *Duke of York* and the American battleship *Washington*, the carrier *Victorious*, two cruisers and fourteen destroyers.

The convoy was located on 1 July by the German radio location service B-Dienst, and subsequently by two U-boats, *U 255* and *U 408*. With this intelligence ten U-boats were directed to attack the convoy. The next day, 2 July, the U-boats began their attack but were driven off by the strong escort. In the afternoon the battleship *Tirpitz*, the cruiser *Hipper* and six escorts left Trondheim for Altenfjord, near the North Cape. During the afternoon the convoy came under air attack, but no ships were hit. On 3 July another group of German ships, comprising the *Scheer*, *Lützow*, and six destroyers, left Narvik for Altenfjord. Air reconnaissance reported that Trondheim was clear of German ships, and Admiral Tovey and PQ17's escort were informed accordingly.

During 4 July further air attacks were mounted against the convoy, which resulted in one freighter being sunk, another torpedoed and later scuttled, and another damaged and subsequently sunk by *U 334*.

Following the experience of the previous convoy, PQ16, the Admiralty had been most reluctant to sail PQ17, considering it a very unsound decision, but their objections were politically overruled. With the knowledge that the German ships had left Trondheim, and as their exact whereabouts were unknown, Admiral Pound, the First Sea Lord, felt that he had no alternative but to order the convoy to disperse, as it was considered most likely that it would come under attack from the surface fleet which might soon be within striking range. Orders were therefore despatched ordering the close escort and convoy escort to return and the convoy to scatter in anticipation of a surface attack.

The following day, 5 July, German reconnaissance aircraft detected the break-up of the convoy and the departure of its close cover. With this knowledge *Tirpitz*, *Hipper*, *Scheer* and nine escorts were ordered to sortie and destroy the now unprotected ships. The German force was first sighted by the Russian submarine *K21*, which carried out an unsuccessful attack, and then by air reconnaissance and the submarines *Unshaken* and *Trident*. Knowing that they had been detected, and with Hitler's strict orders following the loss of *Bismarck* that surface ships were not to be involved in any action which might result in their destruction, the force reversed course and returned to port.

During the 5th the convoy, which had dispersed in all directions singly or in groups of two or three for mutual support, came under heavy air attack. Five freighters of 28,573 tons and the rescue ship *Zaafaran* were sunk, and two others of 13,840 tons were damaged, later being sunk by *U 334* and *U 703*. Four more ships of 24,760 tons were sunk by *U 88*, *U 456* and *U 703*. The air attacks continued the following day, and a freighter was sunk, while *U 255* sank another ship of 7,191 tons. With the ships widely dispersed it was now the turn of the U-boats, and on 7 July three ships were sunk by *U 255*, *U 355* and *U 457*, another being sunk by *U 255* the next day. By then, 8 July, some of the convoy were at last beginning to reach the relative safety of Russian waters. One such group consisted of five ships together with the two AA ships and a rescue vessel. On 9 July two more vessels and the other rescue ship reached the safety of Archangel. On 10 July combined air and U-boat attacks resulted in another two freighters being sunk, but the following day another section of the convoy arrived safely at Archangel. The last of the survivors from the ill-fated PQ17 finally reached safety between 20-24 July. Of the 34 ships which made up the convoy, 23 of 143,977 tons had been sunk for the loss of just five aircraft. Only 11 freighters survived to unload their cargo in Russia.

With the massacre of PQ17 fresh in their minds, and the withdrawal of a number of escorts for duty in the Mediterranean in support of Operation Pedestal, a supply convoy to Malta, the Admiralty decided to postpone the August convoy until September.

Consequently, PQ18 left Iceland for Russia on 2 September. The convoy, which consisted of 40 ships, was escorted by 18 destroyers, the cruiser *Scylla*, eight corvettes and trawlers and two AA ships. Close cover was provided by three cruisers, but there was no distant cover.

In the light of the disastrous losses suffered by PQ17, Admiral Tovey was determined to develop new tactics to counter the German air, surface and sub-surface threats to which the convoys were now subject. He felt that the convoy escort should be so constituted that it would be strong enough to counter not just attacks from U-boats and aircraft, but attacks by surface ships as well. He further believed that the large battleships were no longer required in the Barents Sea. As a result of these deliberations Admiral Tovey formed the Fighting Destroyer Escort (FDE), which consisted of twelve to sixteen destroyers. These were to accompany the convoy and reinforce the close escort of corvettes and trawlers. In the event of a surface attack, the destroyers would leave the convoy to engage the enemy, but would otherwise remain with the convoy to provide additional ASW and AA protection.

Admiral Tovey also recognized that the best counter to the air threat was to engage and break up enemy air formations long before they reached the vicinity of the convoy. For this it was essential to provide organic air cover. With the advent of the new escort carriers this was now possible, and for the first time an Arctic convoy included an escort carrier, *Avenger*. Carrying twelve Sea Hurricanes of Nos 802 and 833 Squadrons, FAA, and three anti-submarine Swordfish, *Avenger* was to provide the much-needed air cover to counter the heavy air attacks which were now anticipated.

PQ18 was first located by air reconnaissance on 8 September, but in poor weather the Germans lost track of the convoy. It was relocated on 12 September, and two U-boats which approached were kept under by the Swordfish from *Avenger*. The real attacks began the next day, and during the morning two ships were sunk. One U-boat was also destroyed. The main air attacks started at 1530, when 85 aircraft carried out a classic dual high/low-altitude bombing/torpedo attack. In perfect formation, all of the torpedo aircraft dropped their 110 weapons simultaneously. Faced by the threat of the massed torpedo attack, the convoy's commodore ordered an emergency 45° turn to starboard. In the two outer starboard columns there was some confusion, and six ships were sunk. Two more ships, in the centre of the convoy, succumbed to torpedoes. Of the attackers, only eight aircraft were shot down. Further fierce air attacks followed. Realizing that the escort carrier posed the greatest threat to their operations, the Luftwaffe concentrated their attacks on *Avenger*. She came under severe attack at midday on the 14th, and continued to be the prime target for the rest of the day.

In all, PQ18 lost thirteen ships, while the Germans lost a total of 38 aircraft, five of which were shot down by *Avenger*'s Sea Hurricanes, while a further 17 were damaged; four Sea Hurricanes were lost. Three U-boats were sunk; *U 88*, *U 457* and *U 589*. The official Luftwaffe account of its operation against PQ18 acknowledged the effect of Admiral

Right: The tragedy to PQ17 led to a major reappraisal of the Arctic convoy operations. The next convoy to sail, PQ18, was given considerably enhanced air defence as well as an additional twelve to sixteen destroyers, which were formed into the Fighting Destroyer Escort (FDE). The role of the FDE was to reinforce the ASW and AA screen of a convoy in the event of a major attack by German surface ships. The photograph shows the destroyer *Fury* leading the *Ashanti* and the *Mahratta* (at the rear) of the FDE, while carrying out exercises prior to sailing with PQ18. (Imperial War Museum)

Tovey's new tactics and the importance of the escort carrier, 'It was found that not only was it impossible to approach the carrier to launch an effective attack on account of the fighters, but that a wide screen of warships made the launching of torpedoes against the inner merchant vessels an extremely hazardous undertaking'.

During October the Arctic convoys were again temporarily suspended, this time because large numbers of ships were required for the landings in North Africa — Operation Torch. By mid-December the escort strength had again been built up with the return of ships from North Africa, and the Arctic convoys could again be resumed. There was, however, a difference of view between the Admiralty and Admiral Tovey, C-in-C Home Fleet, as to how best to run and escort the convoys. The perpetual hours of darkness during the winter months considerably restricted the efforts of air reconnaissance, but this affected both sides equally. Admiral Tovey favoured sending smaller, lightly escorted convoys more frequently, while the Admiralty considered it better to send a larger convoy with a strong escort. The Admiralty finally agreed to sending the next convoy in two sections, to sail at an interval of one week. In addition, and again contrary to Admiral Tovey's advice, the Admiralty insisted that two 6in-gun cruisers from the Home Fleet should provide cover for the convoy well into the Barents Sea. As events were soon to prove, this was a wise decision. So it came about that future Arctic convoys, now renumbered in the JW and RA series, were frequently sent in two sections, A and B.

The first of the new series of convoys to sail was JW51, the A section leaving Loch Ewe on 15 December, followed by the B section on 22 December. JW51B consisted of fourteen freighters escorted by six destroyers (Achates, Onslow, Obdurate, Obedient, Orwell and Oribi — the latter losing touch with the convoy through gyrocompass failure) and five smaller vessels. The cruisers Sheffield and Jamaica, which had escorted the A portion of JW51 to Russia, left the Kola Inlet on 29 December to cover the approaching B portion of the convoy.

JW51B was first located by air reconnaissance and then by U 354 on 24 December. The U-boat continued to shadow the convoy, and on 30 December reported it to be weakly protected. On this information Admiral Raeder ordered the battleship Lützow, the cruiser Admiral Hipper and six destroyers to sortie and head for the area of U 354. The orders given to the German commander, Vice-Admiral Kummetz, laid down guidelines that, if he should come up against equal or superior forces, he was to avoid action. On the other hand, he was to make every attempt to destroy the convoy.

By 0830 on 30 December the convoy was steadily ploughing its way eastwards in reasonable visibility (range 7-10 miles) with occasional snow squalls which blotted out everything. The ships were covered in a mantle of ice and snow, as the temperature was well below

freezing. In these conditions the destroyer Obdurate, on the starboard bow side of the convoy, sighted two German destroyers, and left to investigate. The opening moves of what became known as the Battle of the Barents Sea had begun.

At 0930 the German destroyers opened fire on Obdurate, at which Captain R. Sherbrooke in Onslow, together with Orwell, Obedient and Obdurate, formed up to attack the enemy. This left the convoy with the destroyer Achates and three smaller escorts, which were ordered to lay a smokescreen between the convoy and the enemy, allowing the convoy to carry out an evasive alteration of course. At this point the two cruisers from Russia had not yet arrived. The four British destroyers then sighted the cruiser Hipper, which opened fire on them. The action continued for half an hour in poor visibility in which the sea and sky merged into a murky grey. During this part of the action the British destroyers weaved in and out of smokescreens, controlling their gunfire by radar. The sea was calm, but the spray thrown up by the destroyers as they raced about froze in the air and made operating the forward guns extremely difficult. At this point Captain Sherbrooke detached Obedient and Obdurate to close the German destroyers which had become separated from

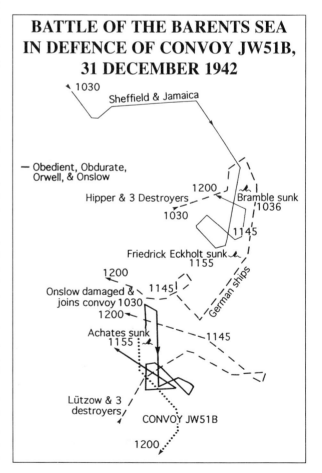

BATTLE OF THE BARENTS SEA IN DEFENCE OF CONVOY JW51B, 31 DECEMBER 1942

1030
Sheffield & Jamaica

Obedient, Obdurate, Orwell, & Onslow

Hipper & 3 Destroyers
1200
Bramble sunk
1036
1030
1145

Friedrick Eckholt sunk
1155
1200
German ships
1145

Onslow damaged & joins convoy 1030
1200
1145

Achates sunk
1155
1145

Lützow & 3 destroyers
CONVOY JW51B
1200

Hipper, while *Onslow* and *Orwell* continued to threaten *Hipper* with feint torpedo attacks.

At about 1013 *Onslow* was struck by four shells from *Hipper* and set on fire. A snowstorm now descended over the scene, reducing visibility to about two miles. *Sheffield* and *Jamaica*, meanwhile, had intercepted signals from the area of the convoy, and raced southeast in support, though they were uncertain of the convoy's exact position. In the poor visibility the two British cruisers at first were unable to distinguish friend from foe. News was then received of a second German force, comprising the battleship *Lützow* and more destroyers. At this point a snowstorm blotted out all visibility. At 1100 the weather cleared and the *Lützow* force was sighted and engaged by the British destroyers, which laid a smokescreen to hide the convoy. *Lützow* opened fire, damaging *Obdurate* and hitting one merchant ship. *Hipper*, meanwhile, had reappeared at 1115 and concentrated her fire on the luckless *Achates*, which was quickly reduced to a smoking shambles. She then shifted fire to *Obedient*, which was also hit, but torpedoes fired by *Obdurate* forced *Hipper* to break off the action. Visibility then deteriorated severely, and was further reduced by the remains of the numerous smoke screens which hung over the battle.

At 1130 *Jamaica* and *Sheffield* opened fire and scored three hits on *Hipper*, which turned away making smoke and with her speed reduced. Two destroyers were then sighted, and *Sheffield* sank the destroyer *Friedrich Eckoldt* at point-blank range. At 1137 Vice-Admiral Kummetz ordered the German forces to break off the action and return to base. *Achates* continued to cover the convoy with smoke until the end of the action, when she at last called for assistance. Before it could arrive, however, the gallant ship capsized and sank in the growing darkness. The convoy finally arrived safely in Russia on 3 January 1943.

Hitler was furious at the outcome of the action, and decreed that all the heavy ships should be decommissioned. Raeder failed to change Hitler's mind and was forced to resign, being replaced by Admiral Dönitz.

In spite of the decree, Admiral Dönitz managed to get Hitler to agree to keeping the big ships in commission in Northern Norway, and even to reinforcing the squadron with the battleship *Scharnhorst*. There the squadron continued to pose a considerable threat to the passage of the Arctic convoys — the classic stratagem of a 'Fleet in being'. But the convoys continued to sail, by and large with relatively few losses. The approach of the summer months and perpetual daylight, however, led to a further suspension in the convoy cycle.

The navy was all too well aware of the threat posed by the German heavy squadron, and intense efforts were made to reduce its potential. On 22 September 1943, in a carefully prepared and rehearsed operation, midget submarines which had been towed behind submarines to a launch point off the Norwegian coast penetrated Altenfjord, where *Tirpitz* lay at anchor. Six midget submarines had left Britain to take part in the raid; *X 9* was lost during the passage, and another which suffered mechanical troubles had to be scuttled. *X 10* was forced to abort her mission, which left just *X 5*, *X 6* and *X 7* to make the attack. These laid charges under the hull of the mighty ship, and the resulting explosion severely damaged *Tirpitz* and put her out of action until the following March.

Following the summer suspension, as the days shortened and became darker, the convoys resumed sailing again in October 1943. They were again run in two sections of about twenty ships each, with cruisers providing close cover through the most dangerous section of the passage between Bear Island and the Kola Inlet. Distant cover was again provided by a battleship force cruising in

Left: After a lull the next convoy to sail was JW51B. Again the Germans made a determined effort to interfere with the passage of the convoy, the cruisers *Hipper*, *Lützow* and six destroyers sailing to attack. As the German force approached the convoy the close escort of *Onslow* (Captain R Sherbrooke), *Obdurate*, *Obedient* and *Orwell* moved out to intercept the Germans. In a running action with the *Hipper* the *Onslow* was severely damaged. The picture shows the damaged destroyer on her return. (Imperial War Museum)

an area to the southwest of Bear Island. JW55A (nineteen freighters) left Loch Ewe on 12 December and reached the Kola Inlet without loss on 20 December.

The Germans were well aware that the convoys had resumed sailing, but made only a half-hearted effort to interfere with them. The German Naval Staff considered that British superiority in radar made it inadvisable to risk sending *Scharnhorst* out on what might well develop into a night action. However, Admiral Dönitz could only justify retaining the large ships in commission if they were to conduct some sort of operation. Thus it came about that JW55B was to witness the last action in northern waters in the Second World War between opposing major surface ships.

On 20 December JW55B (nineteen ships) sailed from Loch Ewe escorted by ten destroyers and three smaller vessels. Close cover east of Bear Island was to be provided by the cruisers *Belfast*, *Norfolk* and *Sheffield*, which had accompanied the A portion of the convoy to Kola Inlet. The cruisers sailed from the Inlet on 23 December. Distant cover was provided by the battleship *Duke of York*, the cruiser *Jamaica* and four destroyers.

On 18 December Dönitz gained Hitler's approval to carry out a surface-ship operation against the next convoy to sail, and when JW55B was located by air reconnaissance on 22 December a group of seven U-boats was directed to the area while the Battle Group was put on alert. Late on 23 December two U-boats made contact with the convoy, but were driven off by the escorts.

The next day German aircraft began shadowing the convoy, which was then about to enter the most dangerous part of its passage. At this point the distant covering force was still some 400 miles astern of the convoy, its speed of advance being restricted by the need to conserve fuel in the escorting destroyers. To close the gap between the two forces, the convoy was ordered to reverse course for three hours to allow the battleship group to catch up. This was an extremely complicated manoeuvre, and as JW55B had only just resumed its orderly formation after being scattered in a gale the previous day, it was decided it would be better if it merely reduced speed. At this juncture four more destroyers from the homeward-bound convoy RA55A, passing to the south, were detached to join JW55B.

Late on 25 December *Scharnhorst*, accompanied by five destroyers, sortied from Altenfjord and headed north at 25kts into a force 7 southerly gale with heavy rain which reduced visibility to about two miles. At this time the Germans were unaware that the battleship force was heading east to catch up with the convoy. According to their intelligence, *Scharnhorst* would be more than a match for the convoy escort.

In the early hours of 26 December the British forces at sea were warned by the Admiralty from ULTRA decrypts that the *Scharnhorst* and destroyers were at sea. Just after 0830 the radar sets on the cruisers *Norfolk* and *Belfast* picked up the *Scharnhorst*, opening fire at 0939. Hits were immediately scored on the German ship, destroying her radar and high-angle director. Caught completely unawares, and now blind as well, *Scharnhorst* increased speed and moved out of range before moving round to attack the convoy from another direction. The British cruisers turned back to cover the convoy, ready to head off the Germans.

On receipt of the 'enemy sighted' report, the C-in-C Home Fleet, Admiral Fraser, ordered the convoy to alter course to keep clear of the battle area, and the four destroyers from RA55A were ordered to join the cruisers.

Left: The operation to sail convoy JW55B to Russia led to the destruction of the German battlecruiser *Scharnhorst*. In the action the destroyer *Saumarez* was struck by one of the battlecruiser's 11in shells, which passed through the director control tower (shown here after the action) killing all but one of the crew. (Imperial War Museum)

Radar contact was lost at 1025, and the cruisers formed a scouting screen some 10 miles ahead of the convoy, with the destroyers in front of the cruisers forming an anti-submarine screen. At 1205 *Belfast* regained contact with *Scharnhorst*, and at 1220 the destroyers moved in to attack with torpedoes while the cruisers opened broadside fire at a range of 10,500yd. *Scharnhorst* returned fire

and *Norfolk* was hit, losing her radars and X turret. The range gradually opened, and at 1241 the German ship disappeared from view.

Through the dark afternoon, from a position some 7 miles astern, the British cruisers continued to track *Scharnhorst* on their radars. At 1617 *Duke of York* gained radar contact, and at 1647 the German ship was illumi-

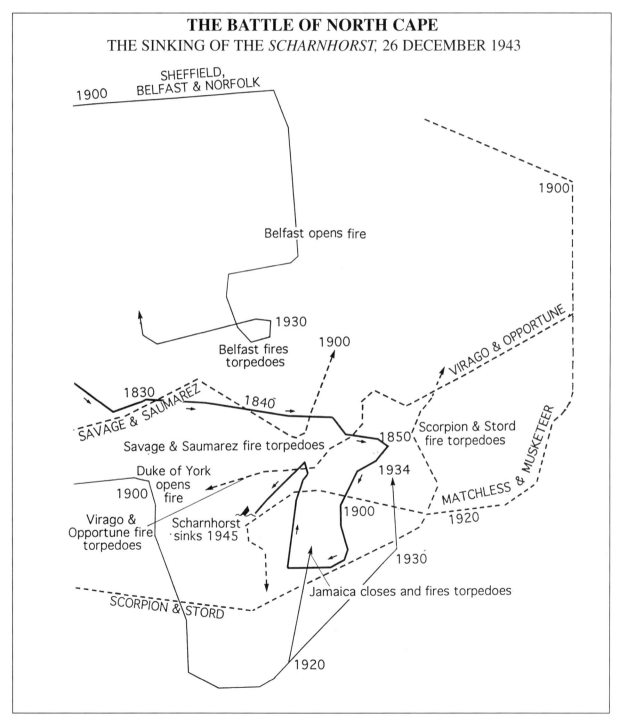

THE BATTLE OF NORTH CAPE
THE SINKING OF THE *SCHARNHORST*, 26 DECEMBER 1943

nated with starshell. Yet again she was taken completely by surprise, with her guns still trained fore and aft. At 1650 *Duke of York* opened fire at a range of 12,000yd, and *Scharnhorst* replied. The action now settled down into a long chase, the gap between the opposing forces gradually opening out. Just after 1820, however, a 14in shell from *Duke of York* struck *Scharnhorst* in her machinery compartment and she began to lose speed. At 1859 the four destroyers closed in and fired torpedoes, a number of which struck, further reducing *Scharnhorst*'s speed. With the range down to 10,400yd, *Duke of York*, *Jamaica*, *Belfast* and *Norfolk* opened a steady fire on *Scharnhorst*, and at 1945 she rolled over and sank after being struck by a torpedo from *Jamaica*. Although many of the crew managed to jump into the water, only 36 from a total of some 2,000 were picked up alive.

With *Scharnhorst* sunk and *Tirpitz* out of action, the threat of surface attack had virtually disappeared. The main threat, however, remained the U-boat, with aircraft proving a particular menace, mainly because of their reconnaissance reports which gave vital intelligence as to the composition and courses of convoys, enabling U-boats to be directed to the area for attack. Finally, there remained that old foe against which there was no protection or security, the weather.

As the days lengthened and lightened, Admiral Fraser introduced a change in convoy tactics, sending the convoys in a single large concentration of ships with a heavy escort which included an escort carrier. This was possible because the battle in the Atlantic had now been virtually won, and Western Approaches Command was able to release some of its assets. Thus convoy JW57, with 52

freighters, was escorted by an AA cruiser (*Black Prince*, armed with eight 5.25in dual-purpose guns), the escort carrier *Chaser* and thirteen destroyers, as well as a Western Approaches Command escort group of four vessels. In addition, three cruisers provided close cover. Fourteen U-boats were directed to attack the convoy, *U 713* being sunk by the destroyer *Keppel* and *U 601* by a Coastal Command aircraft. *U 990* sank the destroyer *Mahratta* with a Gnat. All 52 ships reached the Kola Inlet safely.

Convoy JW57 set the pattern of the Arctic convoys for the rest of the war, and although the Germans introduced new weapons and tactics which led to some sad losses in warships, the majority of convoys got through relatively unscathed.

Tirpitz, however, still posed a threat, and in the light of intelligence which revealed that the damage sustained in the midget submarine attack had been repaired, it was decided to carry out further attacks to immobilize the great battleship. On 3 April 1944 two strikes each of 21 Barracuda bombers from the carriers *Victorious* (Nos 827, 829 and 830 Squadrons, FAA) and *Furious* (No 831 Squadron, FAA) attacked the ship in her anchorage, causing severe damage which put her out of action for another three months. Other raids were carried out, but *Tirpitz* was finally sunk by the RAF on 12 November 1944.

During the war the Arctic route carried about a quarter of the total amount of supplies sent to Russia. It was much the shortest route, but by far the most vulnerable. The loss rate among merchant ships was 7.5 per cent, higher than on any other route, including the Atlantic. A total of 82 merchant ships was lost at sea, six of them sailing independently, while another five were sunk in Russian ports.

Losses suffered by the Royal Navy amounted to two cruisers, six destroyers, two sloops, a frigate, two corvettes and four minesweepers, while the Germans lost two major warships, *Tirpitz* and *Scharnhorst*, three destroyers, 32 U-boats and a large number of aircraft.

It has to be argued that the Arctic convoys were more a visible sign of the political display of Allied solidarity than real quantitative material assistance. If such was the case, the price paid was extremely high, and it must be questioned as to whether, in the end, it was worth it.

Opposite page: In April 1944 the navy mounted Operation 'Tungsten', a carrier raid on the *Tirpitz* designed to further impede any possibility of her carrying out another sortie to attack the Russian convoys following completion of repairs after the midget submarine raid. The picture shows Hellcat fighters on the deck of an escort carrier, with the carriers *Furious* and *Victorious*, the battleship *Anson* and cruiser *Belfast* (behind from left to right) during the raid. (Imperial War Museum)

Above: Operation 'Tungsten' was the first operation in which the Fairey Barracuda sprang into prominence. The Barracudas achieved fifteen direct hits

on the *Tirpitz* and put her out of action for a further three months. The picture shows a Barracuda II nearest the camera, with a Mk III behind, with ASV Mk X radar in a radome under the rear fuselage. (ACPL)

Below: The destroyer *Scorpion* runs down the side of convoy RA64 in February 1945. RA64 lost a freighter and two escorts to U-boat attack, and was the last convoy attacked by German aircraft, which sank one straggler, the freighter *Henry Bacon*. She was the last ship in the Second World War to be sunk by German aircraft. (Imperial War Museum)

Chapter 32

Operations in Home Waters

Following the evacuation from Dunkirk, and with Germany in possession of the entire north European coast and all its bases, Royal Navy operations in the Channel dwindled away and the Channel convoys virtually ceased. Because of the danger the navy retained only light forces in the Channel ports.

The first major action involving British naval forces following Dunkirk concerned the infamous Channel dash of *Gneisenau*, *Scharnhorst* and *Prinz Eugen*. Following the sinking of *Bismarck* in May 1941, all three ships had remained bottled up in Brest on the Atlantic coast, where they suffered bomb damage in numerous RAF raids. With damage mounting, and with all their supply ships in the Atlantic sunk, it was decided that the ships should be brought back to Germany for a thorough refit before deploying them against the Arctic convoys. It was essential that the plans for their voyage to Germany should be developed in the utmost secrecy.

To the British, it was obvious that at some time in the near future the ships would be ready to put to sea, and that some kind of operation should be anticipated. Uppermost in the minds of some was the probability that the ships might sortie to operate against the Atlantic convoys, in spite of the fact that their supply ships in the Atlantic had been sunk. But credence was given to the fact that the ships might return to Germany, particularly by the head of the Admiralty's Operational Intelligence Centre. Furthermore, the Centre considered it most likely that the Germans would attempt to pass the ships up the Channel.

Having decided to bring the ships back, the Germans then had to decide the route they should take. Hitler, too, favoured bringing the ships back through the Channel, and refused to accept any other proposal. Such a move would have a double advantage in that, if the details of the operation could be kept secret, there was a much better chance of the ships getting through, for only light forces covered the Channel and therefore it was possibly a safer route than up through the Denmark Strait. Furthermore, the route through the Channel was quicker. Given a heavy air and surface escort, and with increased AA armament, the ships might well be able to force their way up the Channel relatively undamaged. To conceal their intended operation further, the Germans gradually increased shipping movements in the Channel along the intended route the ships would take.

On the British side, the problem of how to intercept the three ships was compounded by the fact that the U-boat ciphers had been changed at a critical moment, and had not been broken at the time of the break-out. As a consequence, intelligence had to rely on spies in France, who nevertheless gave extremely accurate intelligence, and general signal traffic, from which it could be interpreted that a move was imminent, though its exact date or time was unknown.

Left: As the Germans overran France, convoys in the English Channel came under increasing air attack until eventually they had to be stopped altogether The picture shows a convoy in the Channel under air attack on 14 July 1940. During the month of July a total of 40 Allied merchant ships totalling 75,698 tons were sunk together with four destroyers. (Imperial War Museum)

Right: With the withdrawal of all major units from the Channel ports, it was left to coastal forces to carry on the fight. At the forefront of maritime operations were the motor torpedo boats and motor gunboats of the Royal Navy. The picture shows *MTB 631* off the Norwegian coast in March 1943. (ACPL)

A detailed pattern of reconnaissance was set up, covering all possible routes the ships might take for a break-out, and included continuous air surveillance of the English Channel as well as monitoring of the South Western Approaches and the area of Brest itself. However, the 'need to know' rule was so strictly applied that those responsible for organizing the reconnaissance and surveillance missions were not provided with the general details of the ULTRA decrypts which would have given them some indication of the urgency and vital importance of the task. Further complications arose on the day the break-out was made, when aircraft suffered vital equipment breakdowns in radar etc, which meant that there were gaps in vital parts of the cover.

The German squadron slipped out of Brest at 2345 on 11 February 1942. The Royal Navy submarine *Sealion* had been stationed to monitor the approaches to Brest, but at the time of the break-out she had withdrawn seaward to surface and recharge her batteries. In this compromising position she was attacked by a German aircraft at 2100 and forced to dive and move further out to seaward. By 0130 the ships were off Ushant and steaming at 30kts. Surveillance over the next sector was provided by an RAF Hudson. However, as the aircraft approached its patrol sector it was engaged by a German night fighter. The Hudson evaded the enemy and returned to its patrol sector, but it suffered a radar malfunction and had to return to base. By the time a replacement aircraft reached the sector, the German squadron had passed into the next sector. This sector, too, was uncovered because the aircraft suffered a radar malfunction and returned to base, no replacement being provided.

The aircraft detailed to cover the third sector, between Le Havre and Boulogne, was recalled when thick fog descended over its home base just as the ships approached its patrol area. The squadron was then over halfway through the most dangerous part of its voyage. At 0720 German fighters provided vital air cover, and extra surface escorts arrived at 0915. By now the ships had had to reduce speed to pass through a newly swept channel in a minefield laid the previous night. As the ships passed beyond Boulogne a British shore radar sta-

tion at last picked up their echo some 27 miles southwest of Cap Gris Nez. Forces in southern England were alerted, and a Spitfire reconnaissance was flown off to confirm the radar report. Meanwhile, six Swordfish of 825 Squadron FAA, based at Manston, were armed with torpedoes and made ready to fly. The Spitfires, under the strict orders of Fighter Command to maintain radio silence, did not land and report their sighting until 1109, by which time the weather was closing in. As the squadron headed for the Straits of Dover, coastal forces at Dover were ordered out to attack the ships, while the coastal battery at Dover was given permission to open fire on the target. As they approached the heavily escorted squadron, the five MTBs came under heavy fire. Two of them broke down, but every effort was made to fire torpedoes. In the event none reached their target.

In the meantime, the Swordfish at Manston were awaiting a promised strong escort of RAF fighters. By 1228 only ten Spitfires had arrived at the rendezvous, and as the slow Swordfish could wait no longer because they would not get to the target, the small and completely inadequate force set off to carry out an attack. Some 10 miles out from Ramsgate and about 12 miles from the German force the aircraft came under heavy attack from the German escort fighters. The Spitfires became heavily involved in a dogfight and were unable to cover the Swordfish any longer. The obsolete Swordfish continued on their suicide mission, and as they approached the squadron they came under the most intense AA barrage. Gradually all the aircraft were shot out of the sky; not a single torpedo dropped reached its target.

This raid was followed by further raids by the RAF, all equally unsuccessful. One more attack was mounted by the navy. At the time a force of six old First World War vintage destroyers was exercising off Harwich, and they were ordered to intercept the German squadron. *Walpole* soon developed machinery problems and was forced to return to base, leaving five destroyers. The rest pressed on and picked up the German force on radar at 1517. The weather had deteriorated, and in the poor light, low visibility and heavy seas they mounted their attack. The ships were bombed and strafed by both the RAF and

Luftwaffe as they pressed in towards their target, which was visually sighted at 1542. Torpedoes were fired under a hail of shellfire from the German ships and aircraft, but none found their targets and *Worcester* was badly damaged. Thus ended the Channel dash, as far as the British were concerned. The ships finally reached Germany, but only after both *Scharnhorst* and *Gneisenau* had suffered damage from newly laid mines.

Much of the naval involvement in home waters during 1941-43 concerned small units and raiding parties. In October 1941 Lord Louis Mountbatten was appointed to take over command of Combined Operations, an inter-service unit formed specifically for the task of raiding. One of the potential targets originally examined by Mountbatten's predecessor, Admiral Sir Roger Keyes, was the port of St Nazaire, some 150 miles south of Brest. St Nazaire was considered a worthy target for a Combined Operations raid because of its dock gates and the U-boat pens which the Germans had built there on the collapse of France in 1940. Between October 1941 and the end of January 1942, the strategic importance of the port in the wider context of the war had grown enormously. The Battle of the Atlantic had become the major focus of attention, and was seen as critical to the survival of Britain. Because of this, the fact that St Nazaire possessed the only dry dock outside Germany capable of taking the battleship *Tirpitz* had become of vital importance. To forestall any plans for basing the battleship on the Atlantic ports, from where she could menace the Atlantic convoys, it was decided to mount a raid to destroy the dock, and at the same time endeavour to put the U-boat basin out of operation.

After some deliberation it was planned that an expendable destroyer, packed with explosive, would ram the southern caisson of the dock. Troops carried by the destroyer would then land and attach portable explosive charges to the lock gates leading into the submarine basin adjacent to the dock, which would severely hamper U-boat operations. Other targets to be attacked by the Commandos included the pumping house and two winding houses. On completion of the raid the Commandos would be re-embarked on a second destroyer. It was found during the planning stage, however, that no other destroyer would be available, so a flotilla of small motor launches was substituted. As St Nazaire lay some way up the estuary of the river Loire, it was essential that surprise be maintained until the last possible moment. To achieve this it was proposed to mount a diversionary raid from the air, Bomber Command being asked to lay on a raid on the docks as the raiding squadron steamed up the river.

The men selected for the raid were No 2 Commando, one of a group of twelve newly constituted units which formed the Special Service Brigade. The old ex-American destroyer *Campbeltown* was stripped of all unnecessary armament and equipment and lightened so that her reduced draught would enable her to navigate the Loire at high speed at high tide. Her upperworks were drastically altered and numerous light AA weapons added so that she looked remarkably like a German torpedo boat. The compartment underneath the forward gun mount position was packed with 4¼ tons of high explosive in the form of 24 depth charges. The plan was for *Campbeltown* to ram the dock gates at high speed. There she would be left with a waterproof delayed time fuze which linked all the depth charges.

The raiding force left Falmouth at 1400 on 26 March 1942; *Campbeltown*, with commandos on board, towing the *MTB 74* and surrounded by four torpedo-armed MLs and twelve other MLs carrying further Commandos. The command headquarters was carried on board *MGB 314*,

Left: As part of the training to invade Europe, a reconnaissance in strength was planned against Dieppe for August 1942. Special assault craft were developed and built. Here troops are seen loading LCMs with Bren Gun Carriers ready for the raid. (Imperial War Museum).

while escort for the crossing was provided by the 'Hunt' class destroyers *Atherstone* and *Tynedale*. Additional reinforcement was furnished by the 'Hunt' class destroyers *Cleveland* and *Brocklesby*.

The air raid started at 2330 on 27 March as the raiding force steamed up the Loire. About two miles from the gate the Germans detected the flotilla, and the full force of the German defences was turned on the ships speeding up towards St Nazaire.

At 0134 *Campbeltown* crashed into the dock gates at a speed of about 18kts, her forward end buckling back for 36ft. Immediately the Commandos poured over her bows to carry out their mission. Behind the destroyer came two lines of MLs. Everywhere was chaos and apparent confusion, with searchlights playing over a scene from Dante's *Inferno* as every gun available to the Germans fired at anything and everything, seen and unseen.

With great precision the Commandos from the destroyer set about the task of laying demolition charges in the winding gear that opened and closed the lock gates. Meanwhile, the MLs attempted to land their Commandos under a hail of heavy fire. Most were hit and damaged, but enough Commandos were landed to try and silence the German guns. In the meantime, the MTB had fired two torpedoes with delayed time fuzes at the lock gates of the old entrance.

With the main mission accomplished, the MLs began to re-embark survivors. Of the 611 Commandos who left Falmouth, 169 were killed and 200 taken prisoner. At 1030 on 28 March the explosive in the destroyer detonated in a tremendous explosion which rendered the dock unserviceable for the remainder of the war.

As part of the training and planning for the eventual return to Europe it was decided to carry out a small-scale assault — or, as it was termed, a reconnaissance in strength — against Dieppe. The aim was to carry out a frontal assault on a defended seaside town and withdraw. To implement such a plan against a defended position it was essential that the utmost secrecy and surprise was maintained.   To carry out the assault it was first necessary to secure the flanks on either side of Dieppe and to capture the coastal defence guns sited there. Once this objective had been attained, the main assault could go in over the beach in front of the town. The force was to comprise 4,961 Canadian troops and 1,057 Commandos (including a small number of US Rangers), assisted by 58 Churchill tanks which were to be landed across the beach. The assault was to be directed from the 'Hunt' class destroyer *Calpe*.

Originally planned for July 1942, the raid had to be postponed because of high winds which prevented the paratroops from carrying out their intended drop to seize coastal batteries to the east and west of the town. The assault was finally mounted on 19 August 1942, but with a major departure from the original plan. With more assault craft available, the paratroop role was reassigned to Nos 3 and 4 Commando. To maintain secrecy and surprise there was no pre-assault bombardment from the sea or air. The assault was planned for first light, and the landing ships arrived in their prearranged zones 10 miles

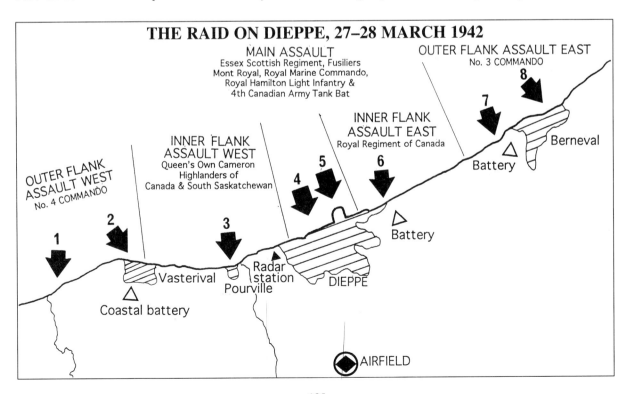

THE RAID ON DIEPPE, 27–28 MARCH 1942

MAIN ASSAULT
Essex Scottish Regiment, Fusiliers Mont Royal, Royal Marine Commando, Royal Hamilton Light Infantry & 4th Canadian Army Tank Bat

OUTER FLANK ASSAULT EAST
No. 3 COMMANDO

INNER FLANK ASSAULT EAST
Royal Regiment of Canada

INNER FLANK ASSAULT WEST
Queen's Own Cameron Highlanders of Canada & South Saskatchewan

OUTER FLANK ASSAULT WEST
No. 4 COMMANDO

Berneval

Battery

Battery

Vasterival

Radar station

Pourville

DIEPPE

Coastal battery

AIRFIELD

offshore. By 0320 the troops had transferred to their assault craft. Unfortunately, the outer eastern assault force with No 3 Commando ran into a German convoy at 0347 and a sharp action ensued in which 16 of the 23 assault craft were scattered. When the surviving craft eventually reached their landing zone it was daylight, and vital surprise had been lost. Surprise on the inner eastern flank was also lost, and the force was unable to destroy the coastal battery.

On the outer western flank No 4 Commando fared much better and captured all of its objectives, including the coastal battery in that sector. The inner western flank assault force also captured their objective, but in the face of stiffening resistance which ultimately prevented the main assault force from the town joining up with them. The forces on the western flank thus remained effectively isolated from the rest of the forces on the beach. This left the German forces in control of the inner defences of the town as the main assault went in.

The destroyers lifted their bombardment as the main assault went in, allowing the Germans to open a withering fire with concealed weapons as the troops scrambled ashore from the landing craft. In this state they were at their most vulnerable. The tanks were not much help, for

Above: Codenamed Operation 'Jubilee', the Dieppe raid, which involved two Commando units, turned out to be a major rebuff. Here assault craft are seen racing for the shore through the smokescreen laid by the covering force. (Imperial War Museum)

they were all stopped by road blocks at the exits from the beach and destroyed. Without the tanks there was nothing the lightly-armed infantry could achieve against the heavily-armed German defences. Gradually all the reserve forces, including No 40 (Royal Marine) Commando, were funnelled into the increasingly congested beach, which, contrary to reports, was crisscrossed by a heavy and concentrated fire from the defences. Noting the state of the beach and the situation as they approached, the Colonel of 40 Commando made the signal to withdraw, thereby ensuring that some 200 of his troops were saved from being wiped out.

With the realization towards midday that the operation could not succeed, and that heavy losses had been sustained, it was decided to withdraw. The destroyers moved in to provide gunfire support while the evacuation began. Of the original 6,100 men landed, 1,179 were killed and 2,190 taken prisoner, while 30 tanks were

Left: Among the losses was the 'Hunt' class destroyer Berkeley seen here severely damaged after being bombed by German aircraft. She was scuttled by torpedoes from another 'Hunt' class destroyer, the Albrighton. (Imperial War Museum)

destroyed. The destroyer *Berkeley* was sunk and *Calpe* was damaged, and 33 landing craft and small vessels were also lost. In spite of the disaster (23 per cent of the Commandos were casualties), many vital lessons were learnt which proved invaluable when the Normandy landings took place in June 1944.

From mid-1942 until the Normandy Landings in June 1944, much of the activity in home waters consisted of a series of hard-fought actions in which the navy's coastal forces, comprising MTBs and MGBs, sought to impede the passage of heavily armed and escorted German coastal traffic along the North European coast, and the passage of heavily escorted armed merchant cruisers. The Germans countered these forays with their own attacks on British convoys sailing along the southwest and east coasts of Britain with their high speed, heavily armed coastal forces and torpedo boats. Most of these actions occurred at night, with the small craft chasing each other across the sea at high speed, the darkness lit by criss-crossing tracers and explosions as torpedoes and shells struck home on the merchant ships. Apart from the losses suffered by coastal forces, the navy also lost a number of small destroyers and some larger vessels.

In the spring of 1943, and from then until the end of the war, the Germans carried out a large number of extensive minelaying operations using their coastal forces. The minefields, laid in the southern North Sea and the Channel, led to a number of sharp engagements between the opposing forces.

On 22 October 1943 the cruiser *Charybdis*, with the destroyers *Grenville*, *Limbourne*, *Rocket*, *Stevenstone*, *Talybont*, and *Wensleydale*, sortied from Plymouth to intercept a blockade runner. The next day they ran into a German convoy off the north Brittany coast, and during the ensuing action *Charybdis* was hit by a number of torpedoes fired by the torpedo boats *T23* and *T27*, and sank. The *T22* sank the *Limbourne*.

In preparation for the invasion of Normandy, the Admiralty laid a number of deep minefields in the Channel and Western Approaches. Apart from protecting the invasion forces from the Biscay-based U-boats, the minefields were designed to counter the Schnorkel-fitted U-boats which the Admiralty surmised would be used in the near future. The mines were laid by the high-speed minelayers of the 'Abdiel' class, which sailed unescorted from Milford Haven. In the area of the lay, the minelayer rendezvoused with an escort detailed to cover the vessels against U-boat attack. This was necessary because the mines were laid at a speed of 12kts on a steady course and speed.

Since the fall of France in June 1940, the entire war had been devoted to the destruction of Hitler and his armed forces. To this end, all efforts had been aimed at building up and preparing for a Second Front — albeit with some secondary campaigns such as North Africa, Italy, etc — to be opened in France. Normandy was finally selected as the place where the assault, Operation Overlord, would take place. The safe and timely arrival of the assault forces at the appointed beaches, their protection, and the subsequent protection, support and maintenance of the rapid build-up of the forces ashore was the entire responsibility of the naval forces under Operation Neptune.

The assault called for a preliminary landing by two airborne divisions, to be followed at first light by five divisions and Commandos and Rangers landing on a 50-mile front between Caen and the start of the Cherbourg Peninsula. The succeeding build-up was to consist of a seaborne landing by $1^1/_3$ divisions on each succeeding day.

Admiral Sir Bertram Ramsay was put in overall command of the naval forces, and at sea all military forces came under his command. The assault was divided principally into two main landings — the British landing the 2nd Army on a 30-mile front to the east on Sword, Juno and Gold beaches, and the Americans to the west. Each main landing was to be covered by a massive naval force, providing both close escort for the assault forces and naval gunfire support from battleships, cruisers and monitors offshore. To the west and east of the assault zone the navy provided covering forces against attacks by surface craft, a number of which were mounted. In command of the eastern landings was Admiral Vian.

To counter any invasion, the Germans had available 25 U-boats, a large number of small warships such as minesweepers and torpedo boats, five destroyers and 39 E-boats. To protect the landing forces the Allies assembled 286 destroyers, sloops, frigates, corvettes and trawlers, 79 per cent of which were provided by the Royal Navy. During the initial assault 1,213 warships were involved, including seven battleships, two monitors, 23 cruisers, 100 destroyers, 130 frigates and corvettes and 4,126 landing ships and craft of all types. Ships involved in the assault were assembled in every port and anchorage along the south coast of Britain, and massive air support was to be provided over all the assault routes across the Channel.

Before the assault, the approaches to the landing beaches were swept, and channels for the convoys were marked by a force of 287 minesweepers and small craft, a number of which were provided by the Royal Navy.

At 0530 on 6 June 1944 the bombarding force opened fire in what was the largest amphibious assault in history, Operation Neptune. As the first assault waves reached the beaches, special landing craft blanketed the beaches with rockets, providing a wall of explosive behind which the troops could storm ashore. In spite of the choppy sea, the majority of landing craft in the British sector managed to negotiate the vast array of beach obstacles and safely land their troops, tanks and equipment. By the end of the day most of the objectives laid down by the planners had been attained with lower losses than anticipated.

At nightfall the naval forces moved in to defend the landing zones against possible attack. The main problem

Left: Many types of special landing craft were built for the invasion, designed to destroy or nullify the many ingenious anti-invasion devices planted by Rommel's forces on the beaches. Here a landing craft rocket (LCR) has just discharged her load in an attempt to destroy barbed wire and anti-shipping traps on the shore. (Imperial War Museum)

Left: A very heavy bombardment of German positions went on for a number of days until the Allied troops had reached the limit of the warships guns. Here the battleship Warspite is seen opening fire on gun positions at Villerville which flanked the British 'Sword' beach. (Imperial War Museum)

Left: On 25 June a joint US/British Task Force commenced a bombardment of German positions near Cherbourg, on the Cotentin Peninsula. The port was under attack by the US Army from the south. German coastal batteries returned fire, and the cruiser Glasgow received a a direct hit, fortunately not serious, and she was able to continue her bombardment. (Imperial War Museum)

THE BOMBARDMENT OF THE NORMANDY INVASION BEACHES, 6 JUNE 1944

For sake of clarity only major Royal Navy units have been shown. Although a number of batteries are shown as not being engaged, these were in fact allocated to US, French and Dutch naval units, and all were targeted during the day.

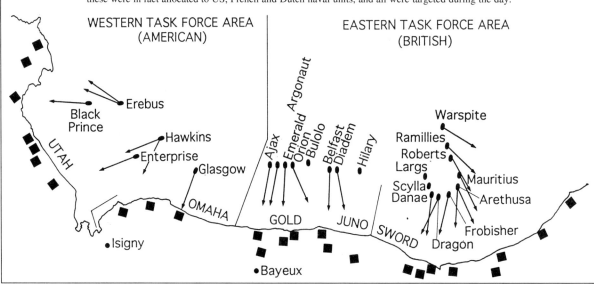

encountered by the naval forces, apart from the beach obstacles, was the pressure mine, but countermeasures were instigated during the first few days after D-day and the problem, although not overcome, was at least neutralized. Attacks by E-boats were also countered, and a destroyer action took place off Le Havre. The main threat, however, remained the U-boat, and Dönitz had a number of schnorkel-equipped boats available.

Once the initial assault had been successfully concluded, the Allies were able to set about providing facilities for handling the vast flow of supplies that would be required to sustain the armies as they moved forward into France. As the assault areas boasted no harbours or associated cargo handling facilities, two massive breakwaters were prefabricated and towed across the Channel to each of the main landing sectors. Together with a large number of blockships and floating pontoons, these were assembled during the course of the next ten days to form two massive artificial harbours through which the vital supplies could be channelled.

By the end of June the Allied armies were firmly established ashore, and on 26 June the port of Cherbourg was at last captured. With this facility available, the main task of the Allied naval forces in Operation Overlord was completed and the naval forces could be withdrawn, leaving smaller warships to continue escorting the troop and supply convoys across the Channel. Total British losses during the invasion amounted to four destroyers and a number of MTBs and MGBs, as well as a large number of landing craft and ships.

With the opening of the Allied Second Front in Normandy, Admiral Dönitz ordered all available U-boats into the English Channel area to attack shipping crossing to France. To cover the Channel and its western approaches, the Admiralty stationed ten escort groups and three escort carriers in the area, supported by aircraft from Coastal Command. Twenty-five U-boats were ordered into the Channel area to attack invasion shipping, but by the end of June only four of these had reached their patrol area. Of the remainder, five had been forced to return to base, three had to return after being damaged on patrol, and seven others had been sunk. Six other U-boats were still trying to penetrate the strong anti-submarine patrols. The use of the schnorkel boats led to a rapid decline in the effectiveness of Coastal Command's anti-submarine patrols, radar being unable to detect the small head of the schnorkel except under the most favourable circumstances. Air patrols were forced to rely on visual sighting of the small head, or puffs of smoke which might indicate a U-boat.

The uncertainty surrounding the sighting of a U-boat led to a number of missed opportunities, as well as numerous false alarms. The U-boats that were sunk nearly all fell victim to surface forces, usually after an attempt to attack an escort and an ensuing lengthy hunt. This was due to difficulties experienced in detecting submarines.

The majority of escorts were used to operating in the deep waters of the Atlantic, and many experienced wartime trained operators had never had the opportunity to conduct ASDIC searches in shallow water.

As the Allied Armies moved up the coast of Europe, the Germans despatched a number of small midget submarines from bases in Holland to attack shipping off the east coast of England and in the Channel. While on anti-E-boat patrol during the night of 11 March 1945, the frigate *Torrington* picked up a radar contact at about 30 miles which appeared to be a buoy. The contact disappeared, and *Torrington* headed for the position and dropped three patterns of about 30 depth charges. As the explosion from the third pattern subsided, a midget submarine surfaced. *Torrington* opened fire, and the two-man crew surrendered just before their craft sank. Two days later *Torrington*, following up a sighting report of a submarine one mile to the south of the Goodwin Sands, carried out a search in the reported position. She failed to make contact, but as a precautionary measure to scare off any U-boat in the area she dropped a depth charge pattern. As the explosions subsided a midget surfaced, the crew scrambling clear just before it sank. The midgets were so small that they were almost invisible on the surface, exceedingly difficult to detect with radar, and virtually undetectable by ASDIC.

From papers taken from the crews of the midget submarines, the Admiralty were appraised of midget operations, and as these attacks grew in intensity Coastal Command was asked to provide special air patrols to intercept the craft. The patrols were mainly flown by Albacore and Swordfish aircraft, which, being slow, were ideal for countering small, slow speed targets. By the end of the war surface escorts had accounted for about 50 midget submarines and aircraft for 16, with another possible 10 to their credit.

The problems being experienced in detecting schnorkelling U-boats, and the strong probability that the high speed Type XXI and Type XXIII boats might soon enter service, raised grave anxieties in the Admiralty. Even if a faster escort were designed to deal with the new submarines, there was still the problem of ASDIC, which could not be used at speeds above 20kts. The high speed schnorkel-equipped boats would completely outmanoeuvre the highly efficient Allied anti-submarine forces. The only possible tactical counter would be to have four escorts in contact with one U-boat, but at high speeds this entailed a grave risk of collision. The U-boat had only to drop speed to 15kts, fire a Gnat and then escape at high speed in the ensuing confusion. The long-term solution, following the failure of the Strategic Bombing Policy to halt production of the U-boats, was to capture the building yards and factories. Fortunately the Allied Armies managed to do this before the high speed U-boats were able to enter service in large numbers.

Chapter 33

Pacific Operations

In January 1941 Britain and America had agreed that their overriding priority must remain the defeat of Germany and Italy. This was to be adhered to at all costs, even at the expense of denuding naval forces in the Far East. Indeed, this had already happened to Britain's naval forces in the Far East. As the situation in the region continued to deteriorate during 1941, strenuous efforts were made to bolster British defences, but such was the danger of the situation in Europe and the Mediterranean that only a very small trickle of forces could be spared for despatch to the Far East.

The Eastern Fleet, which comprised the majority of British naval forces in the Far East, was based at Trincomalee in Ceylon (the East Indies Station), with further units based at Singapore (the China Station). The Admiralty was well aware of the threat posed by the Japanese navy, but the navy at home was so stretched that it was impossible to spare anything like the forces that would be required to bring the Eastern Fleet up to an effective war strength. Most of the battleships available were required nearer home to counter the threat posed by the German capital ships, and to counter the Italian Fleet in the Mediterranean. The new 'King George V' class battleships were at last beginning to enter service, the lead ship and *Prince of Wales* having already been commissioned, and one more due to be operational by the end of the year. The remaining two vessels, however, would not be available before the summer of 1942, while the latest battleship, *Vanguard*, had only just been laid down.

The only units available for deployment to the Far East were either *Barham* or *Valiant*, which the First Sea Lord, Admiral Pound, and the Vice-Chief of the Naval Staff, Admiral Sir Tom Phillips, recommended should be sent to the Far East in September, followed by the four obsolete 'R' class battleships at the end of the year. The desperate need for modern aircraft carriers in home waters meant that only the old *Eagle* could be spared to accompany the battleships east. None of these ships could be expected to be put up against the First 15 fielded by the Japanese; they were not even a Second 15! It was felt, however, that this force would be sufficient to secure the Indian Ocean until the middle of the following year, when it ought to be possible to send out three more modern battleships and a modern fleet carrier.

However, not even the initial part of this proposal was implemented. *Barham* was sunk in the Mediterranean in November, while *Queen Elizabeth* and *Valiant* were immobilized in Alexandria by Italian frogmen (see pages 158).

Churchill, however, was not at all impressed by the proposal. He considered that nothing less than one of the most modern battleships was what was required in the Far East, and believed that this alone would deter Japan from any further hostile actions against Malaya. The Admiralty was horrified by Churchill's idea, and put forward an alternative proposal. On 3 October the battlecruiser *Repulse* had arrived at Durban, South Africa, having completed escorting a convoy to the Middle East. On arrival in Durban, Admiral Pound transferred the battlecruiser to the East Indies Station, and she sailed immediately.

This plan did not satisfy Churchill, and on 17 October he ordered Admiral Pound to reinforce *Repulse* with *Prince of Wales* and a modern carrier, all three to be based at Singapore. Admiral Phillips, and later Admiral Pound, strongly objected to what they rightly saw as a terrible misuse of major units of the Fleet. To them it was inconceivable that such a small force would have any impact on Japanese strategic thinking or objectives. Admiral Pound therefore proposed to send *Nelson*, *Rodney* and four 'R' class battleships to the Far East in the New Year. Churchill again countered this plan by stating that he did not think that the Japanese would risk a war with Britain by invading Malaya. To Churchill it seemed far more probable that the Japanese would carry out raids against British trade in the Indian Ocean using their fast, powerful units. This view was endorsed by the Foreign Secretary, Anthony Eden, who argued that a single 'King George V' class battleship would be more profitably employed as a political deterrent in the Far East than awaiting a possible attack by the *Tirpitz* on an Atlantic convoy.

The inevitable outcome of such wrangling was a dangerous compromise. Against his better judgement, Admiral Pound agreed that the *Prince of Wales* should be despatched as soon as possible to South Africa, where she was to await further instructions. On 25 October the battleship left the Clyde accompanied by two fleet destroyers, *Electra* and *Express*, all that could be spared for escort duty.

However, Admirals Pound and Phillips were fully aware, from war experience so far, that any surface unit was completely at the mercy of air attack, particularly from shore-based aircraft, unless it was provided with some form of organic air cover. They therefore planned that, as soon as she had completed her work-up, the new armoured carrier *Indomitable* should be sent to the Far East instead of the old *Eagle*, which lacked speed. Unfortunately *Indomitable* ran aground in the West Indies during her work-up, and it was subsequently decided that no other carrier could be spared to replace her, a decision that was to have tragic consequences. Meanwhile, it was clear to the Admiralty, in spite of the War Cabinet's decision to hold *Prince of Wales* in South Africa, that her ultimate destination, as far as Churchill was concerned, was the Far East. Accordingly, on 11 November, while Force Z (as the battleship group was known) was still in the Atlantic, the Admiralty ordered Admiral Phillips, who had been designated C-in-C Eastern Fleet, to join up with *Repulse* in Ceylon and proceed to Singapore.

The *Prince of Wales* and the two destroyers reached Colombo on 28 November, where they joined *Repulse*. Together, Force Z, which had then been joined by two more destroyers, *Encounter* and *Jupiter*, sailed for Singapore, where it arrived on 2 December.

Two days later, on 4 December, a Japanese assault force set out for Malaya. The force was located by British air reconnaissance on 6 December and its position reported, but in the poor weather conditions contact was lost. The Japanese went ashore during the night of 7-8 December and news of the assault was received the following morning, at about the same time as an air raid on Singapore took place. With news of the Japanese raid on Pearl Harbor, and rightly assuming that only light Japanese forces would be protecting the assault landings, but unaware of the formidable Japanese shore-based naval air forces, Admiral Phillips decided to sortie with Force Z in an attempt to intercept the landing force at Kota Bharu. Accordingly, *Prince of Wales* and *Repulse*, together with the destroyers *Electra*, *Express*, *Tenedos* and the Australian *Vampire*, set sail from Singapore at 1735 on 8 December, and headed north for the Gulf of Siam.

The success of the operation depended on the doubtful policy of surprise, and on fighter cover flown by the RAF to head off any attacks by the Japanese air force. This was a very forlorn hope, as the RAF had no aircraft available, everything that could fly being committed to the land battle. Besides, the aircraft that were operational were completely outclassed by their Japanese opponents. Furthermore, the Gulf of Siam was under constant surveillance by the Japanese, and the timing of the operation was too late. By the time *Prince of Wales* arrived, the Japanese would have completed their landing and the transports would be on their way back.

Unfortunately for Admiral Phillips, and unbeknown to him, Force Z had been sighted at about 1400 on 9 December and its position reported by the Japanese submarine *I 65*. Then, just before 1800, Force Z sighted three floatplanes low down on the horizon. As darkness would soon fall, Admiral Phillips held his northward course until dark, detaching *Tenedos* to return to Singapore at 1835, with instructions to break radio silence at 0800 the next morning to warn Singapore that Force Z was abandoning its mission. At 1900 Force Z altered course to the west and increased speed to 26kts as if to reach the landing zone as planned. However, during the night Singapore signalled

Admiral Phillips, warning him about Japanese air strength and saying that the Japanese advance could not be stemmed. With surprise lost and no fighter cover available it was folly to continue with the mission, so Force Z turned southwards at 2015 when it was no longer being shadowed.

However, some four hours later Admiral Phillips received a signal from Singapore informing him that further landings were taking place at Kuantan. As Kuantan was much further south (in fact Force Z had not then reached the area as it headed south), Admiral Phillips was in a good position to make a surprise attack on this new invasion and fall on it during the crucial disembarkation phase. With speed increased to 24kts it would be possible for Force Z to reach the landing zone just after dawn on 10 December. So at 0100 Force Z altered course for Kuantan. Sadly, Admiral Phillips was not to know that this was a false alarm.

In the fog of war there now unfolded a terrible tragedy. Phillips maintained strict radio silence, and assumed that as the information came from Singapore it must be accurate. He also assumed, incorrectly, that air cover would be provided, as Kuantan was much closer to Singapore. At Singapore nobody assumed that Admiral Phillips would act on the signal referring to Kuantan, and as he did not inform Singapore of his intentions, nobody knew what was happening to Force Z.

In the meantime, the Japanese submarine *I 58* had sighted Force Z, and carried out an unsuccessful torpedo attack before reporting the position and course of the Force. Once this report had been received, a powerful force of Japanese naval bombers and torpedo aircraft were

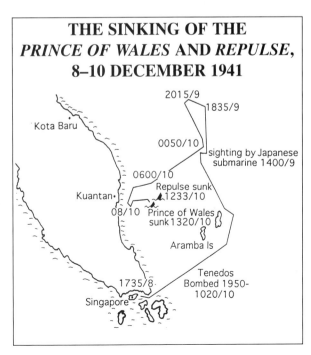

THE SINKING OF THE
PRINCE OF WALES **AND** *REPULSE*,
8–10 DECEMBER 1941

armed and flown off to attack Force Z. On nearing Kuantan, Force Z at last found that the landing report was a false alarm. At about 1030 Force Z picked up a report from *Tenedos* that she was being bombed, and, with his ships in an extremely vulnerable situation, Admiral Phillips resumed course for Singapore at 25kts, with the crews at action stations.

At 1100 *Repulse*'s radar detected an incoming air raid. The first attack began at 1115, with high altitude bombers pressing on in the face of a heavy AA barrage put up by 5.25in and 4in guns. In spite of the heavy AA fire the attack was very accurate and *Repulse* was hit amidships, but the damage did not affect the battlecruiser's fighting efficiency. At about 1130 another raid was picked up on *Prince of Wales*'s radar, and at 1140 two groups of sixteen torpedo aircraft dived down on the battleship. *Repulse* managed to comb the tracks of the torpedoes, but *Prince of Wales*, having less time in which to manoeuvre, was struck aft by two torpedoes which hit the rudder and port shaft, which was jammed. Her speed at once dropped to 15kts and the battleship listed to port, with power lost to half of her secondary armament, considerably reducing her AA defences.

Just before midday the Japanese attacked *Repulse* again, in a perfectly co-ordinated mission in which high-altitude bombers dropped their bombs simultaneously with a torpedo attack by nine aircraft. Again *Repulse* managed to avoid the bombs and torpedoes. At 1220 another torpedo attack came in, six aircraft aiming for *Prince of Wales* and three for *Repulse*. At the last moment three of those heading for *Prince of Wales*, probably realizing that she was already crippled, veered away to join the other

three aircraft heading for *Repulse*. The tracks of the first three torpedoes were successfully combed by *Repulse*, but in avoiding them she could not avoid those from the three aircraft which had turned away from *Prince of Wales*, and a torpedo struck her on her bulge. *Prince of Wales*, no longer able to manoeuvre, was struck by three torpedoes which left her wallowing very low in the water.

At 1225 another attack concentrated on *Repulse*, aircraft diving on the ship from all directions. Unable to evade so many bombs and torpedoes, the battlecruiser was struck by four torpedoes and sank at 1233. *Encounter* and *Vampire* rescued the survivors just before another attack was mounted against *Prince of Wales*. More bombs added to the damage already caused in the previous attacks, and at 1305 Admiral Phillips ordered *Express* to come alongside and take off the wounded, while the rest abandoned ship just before she rolled over and sank at 1318.

On 3 January 1942 the ABDA (American, British, Dutch, Australian) Command was set up under General Wavell, covering the area of the Dutch East Indies and southwest Pacific. Throughout January and into February Japanese assault forces carried out numerous landings on islands in the Dutch East Indies, and eventually Sumatra fell. On 15 February Singapore fell, and the way was open for the Japanese to concentrate all their efforts on capturing Java and the important oilfields. Following reports of the Japanese assault forces, the Eastern force of the ABDA Command under Rear Admiral Doorman (the cruisers *De Ruyter*, *Java*, *Houston*, *Exeter* and *Perth*, and nine destroyers) sortied from its base at Surabaya. Short of fuel and ammunition and completely lacking any form of

Left: Personnel from the sinking *Prince of Wales* transferring to the destroyer *Express*, 10 December 1941. (Imperial War Museum).

THE BATTLE OF THE JAVA SEA, 27 FEBRUARY 1942

Tracks have been simplified for clarity, and sinkings other than Royal Navy ships have not been marked.

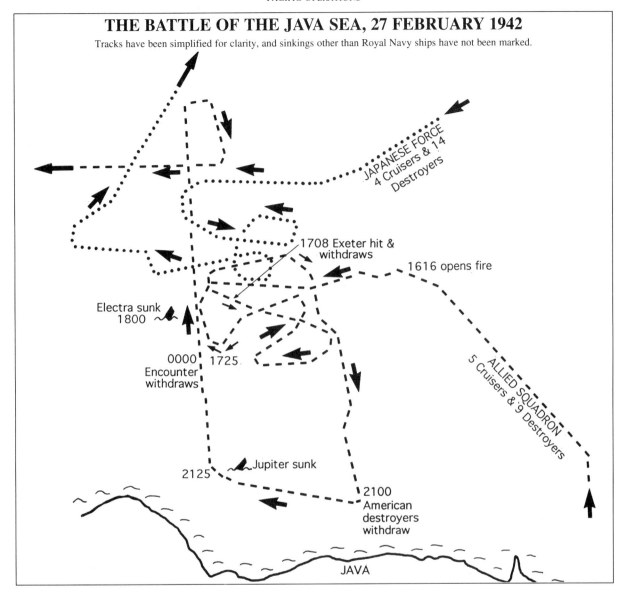

air cover, the force headed for the reported position of the Japanese force.

The squadron was sighted by the Japanese 5th Cruiser Squadron (the cruisers *Haguro* and *Nachi*, together with the light cruisers *Jintsu* and *Naka* and fourteen destroyers) under Rear-Admiral Takagi in the afternoon of 27 February. In what became known as the Battle of the Java Sea, the Japanese heavy cruisers opened fire at 1616 at a range of 28,000yd, while the light cruisers and destroyers closed and delivered a massed torpedo attack of 43 weapons. Of the torpedoes fired, a number exploded or sank before reaching their targets. Only one of those which reached the Allied Squadron found a target, striking the Dutch destroyer *Kortenaer*, which sank. The remainder all missed.

Just after the torpedo attack, at 1708, *Exeter* was struck by a shell from one of the Japanese heavy cruisers and fell

out of line, being followed by the rest of the squadron. The British destroyers were ordered to make smoke, and under cover of this to attack the Japanese while the Dutch destroyer *Witte de With* escorted *Exeter* out of the battle zone and back to Surabaya. The British destroyers engaged *Jintsu* and her destroyers at close range, and *Electra* was hit and sank at 1710. A second torpedo attack began just before 1800 and a total of 92 weapons were fired, but all missed.

As darkness fell, the Allied squadron headed south, but was shadowed by Japanese aircraft. During the night *Jupiter* struck a mine and sank. In a night action the squadron was decimated, but *Exeter* managed to reach Surabaya without further damage.

During the night of 28 February the damaged *Exeter*, escorted by the destroyer *Encounter* and the US destroyer

Left: The cruiser *Cornwall* sinking after being struck by 53 dive-bombers from the Japanese 1st Carrier Fleet in the Indian Ocean, 5 April 1942. (Imperial War Museum)

Pope, left Surabaya to slip away to the west for Ceylon. The following morning the group was spotted, and a powerful Japanese squadron consisting of the heavy cruisers *Ashigara*, *Myoko*, *Nachi* and *Haguro*, escorted by five destroyers and accompanied by aircraft, closed to attack. At 1115 *Exeter* was hit again in the boiler room and the ship was abandoned. She sank at about 1200, followed soon after by *Encounter* and *Pope*, which succumbed to bombs.

After Japan had consolidated her gains and cleared the southwest Pacific region of Allied naval units, the Japanese carrier Task Group which attacked Pearl Harbor sortied into the Indian Ocean at the end of March 1942 to raid Ceylon. The force comprised five large carriers, four battleships, two heavy cruisers, one light cruiser and nine destroyers and a supply train.

News of the intended Japanese attack reached Admiral Somerville, C-in-C Eastern Fleet, on 29 March. The Admiral divided his forces into two groups; Group A, consisting of the battleship *Warspite*, the carriers *Indomitable* and *Formidable*, the cruisers *Cornwall*, *Dorsetshire*, *Emerald* and *Enterprise* and six destroyers; and Group B, comprising the old battleships *Resolution*, *Ramillies*, *Royal Sovereign* and

Revenge, the carrier *Hermes*, the cruisers *Caledon*, *Dragon* and *Jacob van Heemskerck* (Dutch) and eight destroyers.

Having sighted nothing by 2 April, the two groups sailed to Addu Atoll in the Indian Ocean to replenish. The cruisers *Cornwall* and *Dorsetshire* were detached to return to Colombo, while *Hermes* and the destroyer *Vampire* headed for Trincomalee. The Japanese carriers were finally spotted by air reconnaissance on 4 April, and all operational ships sortied from Colombo to avoid the impending air raid. *Cornwall* and *Dorsetshire* were ordered to join up with Group A, which had sortied from Adu Atoll just after midnight. The Japanese launched their air raid against Colombo during the morning of 5 April. On their way in, the Japanese aircraft clashed with Fulmars (803 Squadron FAA), Hurricanes and Swordfish providing air defence over Ceylon. At midday Japanese air reconnaissance sighted *Cornwall* and *Dorsetshire*, and an ensuing raid sank both ships.

The Japanese continued their raiding operation against merchant shipping in the Indian Ocean, and on 9 April launched another raid on Ceylon, this time concentrating on Trincomalee. As before, Admiral Somerville ordered all shipping in the port to sea, but *Hermes*, *Vampire*, the

Left: The carrier *Hermes* sinking after being attacked by aircraft from the Japanese 1st Carrier Fleet off the coast of Ceylon, 9 April 1942. (Imperial War Museum).

corvette *Hollyhock* and two tankers were sighted withdrawing southwards along the coast. All five ships were sunk.

As a result of these raids the Eastern Fleet was forced to remain in the western half of the Indian Ocean or in East African waters until the tide turned against Japan. Having forced the Royal Navy away from the area of the East Indies and the Eastern Indian Ocean, and secured the flanks of the Japanese invasion of the East Indies, the Japanese carrier force withdrew .

There now followed a period of relative inactivity in maritime operations in this region until the early 1944, when the Royal Navy at last found itself in a position to release units from home waters for the Far East. During late 1943 and early 1944 German U-boats and Japanese submarines operating in the Indian Ocean inflicted a number of losses on merchant ships sailing independently and in convoy. Until then the situation in home waters, and the general shortage of escorts, had meant that convoys in the Indian Ocean were generally provided with only a weak escort. However, as the situation in the Atlantic eased and the threat from German surface forces abated, it became possible to release a number of units for deployment to the Eastern Fleet.

However, it was found that warships already under construction and which could be released to help build up the Royal Navy in the Far East were not altogether suitable for the tasks envisaged, so far exemplified by US Naval operations in that theatre. Escorts currently under construction were designed primarily for the Battle of the Atlantic, concentrating on anti-submarine capability and with reduced emphasis on anti-aircraft capability. Hence they were too lightly armed to cope with the heavy air attacks mounted by the Japanese. On the other hand, Japanese submarine operations had not been developed on the same scale and with the same precision as those mounted by U-boats in the Atlantic. Consequently, escorts under construction to meet the requirements of the Battle of the Atlantic but now destined for the Far East were modified. To meet the needs of the Far East theatre about half of the 'Loch' class were altered to carry a

heavier gun armament and reclassified as the 'Bay' class. The only escorts immediately available and suitable for Far East operations and which possessed a heavy AA armament were the 'Black Swan' class sloops, but they lacked sufficient speed for the main task force, although they were eminently suitable for escorting the fleet train.

In October 1943 the escort carrier *Battler* arrived in the Far East, and at the end of January 1943 Vice-Admiral Somerville received reinforcements in the shape of the battleships *Queen Elizabeth* and *Valiant*, the battlecruiser *Renown*, the carriers *Illustrious* and *Unicorn*, the cruisers *Sussex* and *Tromp* (Dutch) and fourteen destroyers. Six more destroyers followed in March. The destroyers were units of the the the 'P' 'R' and 'Q' classes, recently commissioned into the Royal Navy as part of the war construction programmes. The new forces joined the battleship *Ramillies*, the carrier *Battler*, the cruisers *Ceylon*, *Danae*, *Emerald*, *Frobisher*, *Hawkins*, *Kenya*, *Newcastle* and *Suffolk* plus eleven destroyers and thirteen frigates, sloops and corvettes. In April more escort carriers (*Atheling*, *Begum* and *Shah*) arrived at Trincomalee to spend a period in the Indian Ocean before continuing east to join the newly formed British Pacific Fleet.

In July the Eastern Fleet was further strengthened by the arrival of the carriers *Illustrious* and *Victorious*, while the battleship *Howe* joined in August. With these latest additions the Eastern Fleet was now the most powerful fleet in the navy, and contained the bulk of the navy's carrier assets.

There had, however, been tremendous obstacles to the formation of a powerful British fleet in the Far East, not least from the Americans, who were extremely suspicious of British intentions in that region. Many Americans felt that behind the British insistence on building up a Far East Fleet was the wish at least to regain, if not expand, her former colonial territories. The Americans were determined that this should not be allowed to happen. Churchill, on the other hand, was equally determined that Britain would play a part in the defeat of Japan.

American military officials were extremely sceptical as to the role which a British Pacific Fleet could play and,

Right: The progress of the Allied armies in Europe reduced German naval operations to a minimum, except for those of the U-boats, which continued to demand extra vigilance from convoy escorts. However, many ships were freed from the European theatre and sent out to the Far East, including the large Fleet carriers such as the *Illustrious*, seen here operating with the Eastern Fleet in 1944. (ACPL)

Above: Many escort carriers were also sent out east. The *Shah* is seen here being used to ferry aircraft while on her way out to India. (ACPL)

apart from any strategic misgivings, were determined that the appearance of British forces in the region should not hinder their efforts by drawing away vital supplies and support from their own forces to support the British effort. Nonetheless, when the Pacific Fleet was forced to call on the Americans for support on a number of occasions, it was always forthcoming. At an operational level there was always enthusiasm on both sides for the mutual benefits to be gained by working together. This was never better displayed than when the Japanese began their Kamikaze attacks, from which the American carriers with their unarmoured decks suffered so much, being out of action for weeks and months, while the British carriers, with their armoured decks, were back in operation within a few hours of being struck.

With his force up to strength, Admiral Somerville was at last able to begin carrying out a series of carrier raids against Japanese positions and bases in the East Indies, raids which continued until the end of the year. On 23 August Somerville was succeeded by Admiral Sir Bruce Fraser, and towards the end of November 1944 the East-

ern Fleet underwent a reorganization. The Fleet was divided into two new fleets: the British East Indies Fleet (Vice-Admiral Power) with the battleship *Queen Elizabeth*, the battlecruiser *Renown*, five escort carriers, eight cruisers and 24 destroyers; and the British Pacific Fleet (Admiral Fraser) with the remainder, consisting of all the most modern units including the battleships *King George V* and *Howe*, the carriers *Indefatigable*, *Illustrious*, *Victorious* and *Indomitable*, the cruisers *Argonaut*, *Black Prince*, *Ceylon*, *Newfoundland*, *Swiftsure* and the New Zealand *Gambia* and *Achilles*, and three destroyer flotillas of the 'Q', 'U' and 'W' classes.

During January 1945 the large carriers were again involved in raids against Japanese bases in the Dutch East Indies, while the escort carriers and other units of the East Indies Fleet were involved in supporting British Army

Left: New aircraft were also joining the fleet in large numbers. The Grumman Avenger was manufactured in large numbers in the USA during the Second World War, and almost 1,000 were transferred to the Fleet Air Arm. The picture shows an Avenger of 851 NAS from the escort carrier *Shah* on patrol in the Pacific. (ACPL)

operations in Burma. On 16 January a Task Force (TF 63) formed from the Pacific Fleet and comprising the four carriers *Indomitable*, *Illustrious*, *Indefatigable* and *Victorious*, the battleship *King George V*, the cruisers *Argonaut*, *Black Prince* and *Euryalus* and two destroyer flotillas left Trincomalee for the Pacific to carry out raids on oil refineries in Sumatra. Because of the steaming distances involved and the logistics, it was decided to make the Task Force self-sufficient, so it was accompanied by its own fleet train of tankers for refuelling at sea, which enabled it to remain on station for an extended period of time.

Raids on the oil refineries were carried out on 24 January and again on 29 January. After this the force carried on to Australia, and on 16 March it at last came under the overall command of the American Admiral Nimitz in the Pacific for operations in support of the American assault on Okinawa. For this the the British Pacific Fleet was renamed TF 57.

Operating out of its main base in Sydney, TF 57's task was to attack Japanese staging airfields between Formosa and Okinawa, supported by a very extensive fleet train which the navy had built up and which would provide the Task Force with food, fuel and ammunition while it remained on station. On 14 March the Task Force was at sea off Manus Island, carrying out final exercises before heading north under command of Vice-Admiral Sir Bernard Rawlings to join Admiral Nimitz's force on 16 March. TF 57 comprised the battleships *King George V* (flag) and *Howe*, the carriers *Indomitable*, *Victorious*, *Illustrious* and *Indefatigable*, five cruisers and eleven destroyers. On board were 142 fighters and 65 torpedo bombers.

The Task Force began daily strikes against the Japanese airfields on 26 March. On 2 April a Kamikaze struck *Indefatigable* at the base of her island, which put the flight deck temporarily out of action. However, she was very soon back in action, having been saved by her armoured flight deck. The American liaison officers aboard were astounded at the ability of the carrier to retain her fighting efficiency in the face of such an attack, when their wooden-decked carriers suffered horrendous damage in similar circumstances. The air strikes were sent out nearly every day for the rest of the month, apart from short withdrawal periods from the battle zone to replenish at sea. On 20 April the Task Force withdrew from the battle zone and headed for Leyte for rest and recuperation.

With some slight changes (*Formidable* had replaced *Illustrious*), the Task Force put to sea again on 1 May and headed back for the Japanese airfields on the islands to the south of Okinawa. Strikes were mounted on 3 and 4 May, and the Task Force was again attacked by Kamikazes. Just after 1130 on 4 May a Zero dived on *Formidable* and crashed into the carrier abreast the island. Considerable damage was caused, aircraft parked on deck being set on fire and all but one of the carrier's radars being put out of action. By 1254 the fires were under control, and by 1700 the carrier was able to recover aircraft on the repaired flight deck. Once again a carrier had been saved by her armoured deck.

Simultaneously with this attack, another Kamikaze had dived on *Indomitable*, which suffered minor damage. Air strikes continued to be mounted, but the Kamikazes returned on 9 May and this time the carrier *Victorious* was the main target for the leading attackers. At about 1700 one aircraft struck the carrier on the flight deck near the forward lift, holing the flight deck, jamming the lift and destroying the catapult and a 4.5in turret. As the damage control parties raced to deal with the damage, a second Kamikaze hit the carrier, slid across the flight deck, destroyed some aircraft in the deck park and caused sundry other minor damage before crashing into the sea alongside. The damage to the aircraft lift proved a major handicap, greatly reducing the carrier's effectiveness.

While *Victorious* was dealing with her Kamikaze attacks, others were aiming at *Formidable*. One of these struck the carrier right in the middle of a full deck park of aircraft. The explosion set off a major fire which destroyed seven aircraft, but again the bomb did not penetrate the armoured flight deck. By about 1800 both carriers were back in operational condition, although with

Right: Task Group 57 was formed to operate in the Pacific and carried out numerous raids against Japanese forces and bases. While operating in the Pacific the Task Group came under heavy attack from Japanese Kamikazes. Here the *Formidable* is seen just after a Kamikaze has crashed onto the after flight deck among parked aircraft which have just returned from a bombing raid on Myako on 9 May 1945. (Imperial War Museum)

reduced capability. The interesting factor in all of these attacks was that the 20mm cannon proved completely incapable of breaking up or diverting the incoming aircraft. The 40mm guns, large numbers of which were being acquired for mounting on ships bound for the Far East, proved much better for dealing with this type of attack.

These attacks proved to be the last in which the Pacific Fleet suffered any major damage, although the air strikes continued to be mounted, including some on the mainland itself, until the day the Japanese finally surrendered, 2 September.

Meanwhile, in the Indian Ocean, the Japanese cruiser *Haguro* and the destroyer *Kamikaze* had sailed from Singapore on 10 May to evacuate Japanese troops from the Nicobar and Andaman Islands. The ships were sighted by the British submarines *Statesman* and *Subtle*, and Task Force 61 (the battleships *Queen Elizabeth* and *Richelieu* (French), the cruisers *Cumberland*, *Royalist* and *Tromp* (Dutch), and the escort carriers *Emperor*, *Hunter*, *Khedive* and *Shah* and eight destroyers) sortied from Trincomalee

to intercept the Japanese. On 14 May the cruiser *Cumberland* and the 26th Destroyer Flotilla (the destroyers *Saumarez*, *Venus*, *Verulam*, *Vigilant* and *Virago*) were detached to intercept the Japanese, who, realizing they had been detected, had returned to Singapore.

They sailed again on 15 May, a decrypted message informing the navy that they were at sea. They were spotted by an aircraft from *Shah* but again turned back, but it was considered that they could be intercepted in the Malacca Straits before they reached port. The two ships were at last trapped by the 26th Destroyer Flotilla during the night of 15-16 May. *Haguro* was picked up on radar at 68,000yd and the destroyers moved in and took up positions round the cruiser and her escorting destroyer. *Haguro* opened fire and *Saumarez* was hit by three shells. In the darkness *Haguro* was unable to detect the British destroyers, which closed in and fired torpedoes. Three struck the cruiser, which finally rolled over and sank.

On 30 July two midget submarines, *XE 1* and *XE 3*, penetrated Singapore and laid charges under the damaged cruiser *Takao*, which settled on the seabed.

Left: Many of the later destroyers of the 'P', 'Q', 'R', 'U', 'V' and 'W' classes were also dispatched to the Pacific theatre. The 'S' class in particular had proved to be a most successful design, and succeeding classes were all based on it. Typical of these was the *Ulysses* of the 'U' class. (ACPL)

Left: In the Pacific Theatre the armoured decks of the fleet carriers proved their value, the British carriers returning to duty almost within days, whereas the American carriers with their wooden flight decks suffered very severe damage in the Kamikaze attacks. These are the remains of a Japanese Kamikaze on the after flight deck of the *Formidable* on 9 May 1945. (Imperial War Museum)

Chapter 34

The Cold War Era

On 7 May 1945 the guns in Europe fell silent as Germany signed the terms of an unconditional surrender. This was followed on 2 September by the Japanese surrender on board the US battleship *Missouri*. After six long, hard years the war was over, and Britain could at last settle down to resume life where it had been left off in 1939. But, as in 1918, things would never be the same again.

By the end of the war the Royal Navy had reached its zenith: it was the strongest it had ever been and, after the US Navy, the most powerful in the world. The total number of vessels on the Navy List amounted to 8,940 warships of all types, 4,500 merchant ships and 1,200 fishing craft which had been requisitioned for war duties, 1,336 front line aircraft and a manpower strength of 864,000, of which 74,000 were Wrens. With the end of the war the large numbers of men and women called up for hostilities were demobbed, while the merchant ships and fishing craft taken up from trade (STUFT) had to be decommissioned and returned to their owners.

The navy now had to set about redefining its mission in the post-war era, a mission which in all probability would be much the same as in the post-Napoleonic era; securing the freedom of the seas and all that that entailed. The future, however, was extremely uncertain, and it soon became apparent that many of the navy's peacetime tasks would involve dealing with an increasing number of incidents of law-breaking at sea, as well as international incidents between opposing nations, which threatened world peace and stability. Whatever the future might hold, however, certain factors were inescapable; the navy would not need anywhere near the number of ships and men then in service, and, with the country bankrupted by the war, Britain could no longer afford to retain her navy at even its pre-war strength, let alone the current strength. All the ships acquired under Lend-Lease were returned, while vast numbers of small craft and older ships laid up in ports and rivers all around the coasts, awaiting a decision as to their fate. Many of these were worn out from their wartime duties, and no longer worth even keeping in reserve, let alone in commission. By the end of 1946 some 840 warships had been stricken from the Fleet List and orders for 700 new ships cancelled.

Almost as soon as the war ended the Royal Navy began to get a taste of what its peacetime missions might involve. The Mediterranean became the focus of attention, and for a time friction between Greece and Albania posed a considerable threat to the region. To restore a balance of power in the region it was decided to re-form the Mediterranean Fleet, which was built up so that it became the main concentration of the navy's strength. The Mediterranean Fleet had been severely run down towards the end of the war, when many of its ships were transferred to the Far East for the build-up of the Royal Navy in that theatre. As re-formed the Fleet exhibited a very mixed capability, with many of its vessels worn out from war service, others designed for different theatres, and the majority all in need of urgent refits, long-delayed because of the war.

While it was still in this state, on 15 May 1946, the navy became embroiled in its first peacetime action. A force of destroyers transiting the Corfu Channel was fired on by Albanian shore batteries. Undeterred, the British Government resolved to maintain the right of free passage, and in October sent the destroyers *Saumarez* and *Volage* through the Channel. Both struck mines, and 43 sailors were killed. *Saumarez* was so badly damaged that she had to be scrapped, while *Volage* had her bows blown off.

In the southeastern part of the Mediterranean, along the coast of Palestine, the navy became involved in a very distasteful task. Here the ships of the Mediterranean Fleet were required to board ships carrying illegal Jewish immigrants, many of them survivors from the Holocaust, to Palestine, where they hoped to settle. In all some 78 ships were intercepted and 70,000 illegal immigrants sent back to Cyprus.

Nearer home, in the North Sea, a force of 1,900 minesweepers, 513 of them from the Royal Navy, began the enormous task of sweeping the whole area for the mines laid in prodigious quantities by both sides during the war, as well as mines still left over from the First World War. Between May 1945 and March 1946 20,000 mines were swept, and the dangerous work continued for some years, both at home and overseas, before the right of free passage for merchant ships could be safely guaranteed.

Lastly, a Fishery Protection Flotilla was formed to carry out patrols in coastal and near-ocean waters.

In spite of the post-war run-down of the Royal Navy, many inventions and new technologies were being developed for introduction into the Fleet. But although considerable effort was devoted to research and development, it was many years before the results of these endeavours reached the Fleet, some being nearly obsolete before they entered service.

Propulsion was one area in which considerable effort was being devoted to developing new technologies. In

Left: The end of the Second World War saw large numbers of ships laid up and eventually scrapped. Of the wartime programmes, only limited numbers of the latest types of warship were eventually commissioned into the fleet. The most pressing need was for destroyers and frigates to replace the units worn out by wartime service. The 'Battle' class was designed in 1942 and developed as a result of experience in the Mediterranean theatre, with emphasis on AA capability. A number were completed at the end of the war, some being converted later into radar picket vessels as the need for long range warning increased. The picture shows the *Corunna* in 1954 as originally completed. She was the first ship to be operationally fitted with the Seacat surface-to-air guided missile in 1962. (ACPL)

Left: Another new design which entered service just after the war was the 'Weapon' class. The *Broadsword* is seen here as converted to a radar picket ship. (ACPL)

1947 a gunboat, *MGB 2009*, went to sea to test a revolutionary propulsion system, the gas turbine. The trials proved most successful, and it was decided to develop the concept. However, it was to be nearly twenty years before the first ship powered by gas turbines was commissioned into the navy. After that, marine gas turbines gradually began to enter the Fleet in increasing numbers, eventually entirely replacing the reciprocating steam engine as the prime propulsion system in the Royal Navy.

Trials were also undertaken with Hydrogen Test Peroxide (HTP), a fuel which the Germans had used in the U-boat designs which they began to commission during the closing stages of the war. The *U-3017* had been handed over to Britain at the end of the war, later being renamed HMS *Meteorite*. Trials were carried out with her propulsion system, and it was considered that HTP fuel offered a major way forward for submarine propulsion. As a consequence two submarines, *Excalibur* and *Explorer*, were built to carry out further investigations of the potential of HTP as a fuel. It was also planned that HTP should be used to fuel a new torpedo. But HTP required absolute standards of cleanliness in handling, as it was very volatile. HMS *Meteorite* suffered from a number of minor fires, but fortunately none of them were very serious.

In 1948 development of a new anti-aircraft missile began, the first for the Royal Navy. Later called Seaslug, it finally went to sea in 1962.

As well as new weapons and equipment, new ships were also entering the fleet. In 1946 the last battleship to be built for the Royal Navy, *Vanguard*, finally entered service. Originally designed in 1938, *Vanguard* had suffered continual delays owing to the war. She had originally been designed to counter the new Japanese battleships, but by 1940 it was realized that, with the then current war situation and emergencies, no triple 16in gun could be built before 1944 at the earliest. Consequently, the Director of Ordnance put forward an alternative suggestion to install the excellent 15in guns which had been removed from *Courageous* and *Glorious* when they were converted to carriers. By 1950 *Vanguard* was the only battleship still operational, the four remaining 'King George V' class being laid up and the remainder scrapped.

Other new ships completed just after the war included the light fleet carrier *Triumph*, sixteen destroyers (the 'Battle' and 'Weapon' classes), six 'A' class submarines and a number of smaller vessels.

On 3 December 1945 a Sea Vampire jet aircraft landed on the carrier *Ocean* and heralded in a new era of carrier air power for the Fleet Air Arm, which by 1946 had been renamed Naval Aviation. Other developments allied to carrier aviation which were pioneered and tested soon after the war included the flexible deck (fitted to the light fleet carrier *Warrior* in 1948-9), the steam catapult (which began trials on the carrier *Perseus* in 1949), the mirror landing sight and the angled flight deck.

Right: The last battleship to be built for the Royal Navy was the *Vanguard*, designed to use the mountings from the *Courageous* and *Glorious*, which were landed when they were converted to carriers, in order to reduce construction time, allowing the ship to be completed before the projected '*Lion*' class, which were never built. The design was similar to the '*King George V*' class, but lengthened to accommodate the four smaller turrets mounting the 15in guns. (ACPL)

Right: The urgent war need for carriers led to the design of the smaller light fleet carrier with an unarmoured deck, capable of operating aircraft up to 20,000lb in weight, which could be rapidly constructed to build up the fleet's organic air capability. Sixteen carriers in two classes were planned, a number being eventually sold to other navies, some still being in service. The photograph shows the *Theseus*. (ACPL)

By 1947 a number of far-sighted officers considered that the future power of the navy lay not in the battleship but in the carrier. These men advocated the formation of carrier task groups such as Task Force 57, which had performed so well in the Far East in the war against Japan. The 1947 Defence Estimates noted; 'The aircraft carrier is now second to none among fighting ships of the Royal Navy', and concluded that carrier air power was 'an integral part of the Royal Navy'. Together with the modern force of destroyers and frigates only recently completed for war service, and a modern fleet of submarines, these carriers would henceforth form the backbone of the Royal Navy as it emerged from a long hard war.

In the Far East the navy was engaged in the age-old tradition of gunboat diplomacy. In China the Communists and Nationalists were engaged in a bitter civil war which posed a serious threat to foreigners in the country. To the Royal Navy fell the task of deploying ships to carry out emergency evacuations of British nationals from threatened areas. As part of this operation a frigate or destroyer

Right: To meet the developing need for faster, better equipped aircraft, a number of inventions were formulated and adopted in carrier design. The first major post-war development was the steam catapult, shown here undergoing trials on the light fleet carrier *Perseus* in 1951. The aircraft sitting on the catapult is a Sea Hornet, the navy's first single-seat twin-engined fighter. The development of the catapult enabled much heavier aircraft to be launched and with much heavier payloads. (ACPL)

Above: As the war ended, a new class of submarine, the 'A' class, began to enter service. Basically an improved 'T' design, but with increased surface radius of action and speed for operations in the Far East, the 'A' class (the *Andrew* is illustrated) carried six torpedo tubes in the bow and two at the stern. The large tube seen running along the deck by the conning tower is the schnorkel mast in the lowered position. (ACPL)

was stationed at Nanking. Matters came to a head on 21 April 1949, and the frigate *Amethyst* was ordered up the river Yangtse to Nanking from Shanghai to relieve the destroyer *Consort*. On her way up-river on 22 April *Amethyst* was fired on and severely damaged by Communist gun batteries hidden along the river bank. In the complex channels of the river the frigate ran aground and became a sitting target for the Chinese guns. There now developed a major incident, in which *Consort* attempted to reach *Amethyst* and was herself damaged, losing ten men killed and being forced to retreat down-river. On the 23rd the cruiser *London* and the frigate *Black Swan* attempted to reach *Amethyst*, but they too were forced back by the shelling, with the loss of fifteen men. Finally, on 30 July, *Amethyst* managed to break out and reach safety, seventeen of her crew having been killed in the initial bombardment.

On 12 January 1950 the navy suffered a tragic loss when the submarine *Truculent* was rammed by a small Swedish vessel in the Thames estuary. The loss was doubly tragic, for the submarine was carrying an increased complement which included a number of civilian dockyard workers who were overseeing post-refit trials of the submarine. A total of 64 men lost their lives.

While events in the Far East were rapidly deteriorating, nearer to home another threat loomed. In 1948 the so-called 'Iron Curtain' came down along the divide between the Soviet Union-controlled part of east Germany and the part of west Germany administered by the British, French and Americans. A new era, the Cold War, had dawned, the tyranny of Hitler being exchanged for the iron hand of Stalin, Communism and the Warsaw Pact.

It soon became evident that the Soviet Union was embarking on a massive arms build-up to make good the losses suffered during the war. Part of this build-up included a major programme of submarine construction. With the lessons of the Second World War still fresh in their minds, the Admiralty considered it imperative to ensure that the navy's anti-submarine capability be kept up to date, and that a sufficient number of ASW vessels be kept in service. As an emergency measure it was

decided that a number of wartime-built destroyers of the more recent classes (the 'R' and 'W' classes, etc), which were now considered to be obsolescent, should be rebuilt as anti-submarine frigates. The conversion entailed a complete rebuilding of the upper deck, with the foc's'le being extended right aft; a new anti-submarine mortar, the Limbo, being fitted; a reduction in the gun armament and the installation of a much improved ASDIC set (soon to be called Sonar); plus updated radar and communications. Work on the conversions began in 1949, and eventually 23 of these destroyers were converted to Type 15 anti-submarine frigates, while another 10 underwent a limited conversion which entailed giving them an anti-submarine armament but making no structural changes. These were referred to as Type 16 frigates.

During the war (1944), plans had been drawn up for a frigate with a hull that could be mass-produced by many yards around the country. It was planned that the common hull would then be outfitted with weapons and electronics compatible with whatever role the frigate would perform, e.g. anti-submarine warfare, air defence, general patrol, etc. By 1950 the concept had developed to the stage where orders could be placed, and in the 1950 Estimates it was announced that a new type of frigate for anti-submarine warfare, the Type 12 (subsequently called the '*Whitby*' class), would be ordered during the year, while a simpler, and hence cheaper, version, the Type 14 (later known as the '*Blackwood*' class), would also be considered. These vessels were to incorporate the basic ASW capabilities of the Type 12 in the smallest possible hull, retaining the same steam plant but having only one shaft instead of the two of the Type 12, and developing a lower maximum speed.

Using the basic hull of the Type 12, two other versions were subsequently developed, the Type 41 anti-aircraft

Right: To improve the Fleet's anti-submarine capability a number of wartime destroyers of the 'R', 'T', 'U', 'V' and 'W' classes were rebuilt as ASW frigates, referred to as the Type 15s. The reconstruction, commencing with the 'R' class, involved stripping the ships down to the bare hull, extending the forecastle deck well aft, building a new bridge super-structure – much of it in aluminium – adding a short lattice foremast for the radar and communications aerials, and completely re-arming the vessels, a new Limbo anti-submarine mortar being added aft in later conversions. Shown here is HMS *Venus*. (ACPL)

Right: The first post-war frigate programme provided for three specialised types – the Type 12 ASW, Type 41 AA and Type 61 air-direction – it not being possible to combine all three roles into one hull. The ASW frigates of the '*Whitby*' class were planned for the 1950 Programme, but the *Whitby* was not laid down until September 1952. The picture is of the *Tenby* as originally completed. (ACPL)

Right: Four Type 41 AA frigates were completed, again the first, the *Leopard*, not being laid down until until March 1952. The picture shows her as modernized with new radar on the foremast and mainmast. (ACPL)

Right: Almost identical to the Type 41s were the Type 61s, differing in that the after 4.5in turret was replaced by additional radar, and an enlarged operations room fitted. Again the first unit, the *Salisbury*, was not laid down until 1952. The picture shows the *Chichester* modernized with new radars in 1969. (ACPL)

Left: The Type 14 'Blackwood' class ASW utility frigates were a cheaper, simpler version of the Type 14. Built at the same time as the 'Whitby' class, they proved good sea boats and considerably boosted the navy's frigate strength. The picture shows the *Dundas* as completed. (ACPL)

Left: The last wartime-designed destroyer class to be completed for the navy was the 'Daring' class, provisional orders being placed in March 1945. During the late 1950s the class was extensively refitted, the after set of quintuple torpedo tubes being removed and the deckhouse extended. The picture shows the *Diamond* in 1969, shortly before she decommissioned for the last time. (ACPL)

frigate and the Type 61 aircraft direction frigate. These were fitted with diesel propulsion systems, as no suitable steam plant was available. Only a few units of each type were built.

Also under the 1950 Estimates it was announced that a number of submarines would have their underwater performance and capabilities improved. This resulted in the 'Guppy' conversions of a number of wartime-built 'T' class and post-war 'A' class vessels. The modernization included fitting a new streamlined fin, removing the 4in gun mounted on the deck casing, and increasing the length of the 'T's to accommodate an extra section of new, higher-powered batteries. In addition, a new generation of torpedoes was planned, using HTP fuel.

In June 1950 the Soviet-equipped and supported North Korean communists launched a massive attack across the 38th Parallel into South Korea, sweeping the defending forces right down to the southeastern corner of the Peninsula and leaving South Korea with just one port, at Pusan, through which supplies and reinforcements could be funnelled. In desperation the United Nations sought the formation of an international force to help the South Koreans, and in response a Commonwealth Task Force was formed. This eventually included six light fleet carriers (the successors to the wartime escort carriers), seven cruisers, eight destroyers, fourteen frigates, two submarines and two depot ships from the Royal Navy, together with a Fleet Train of twelve tankers and a hospital ship.

The Korean war was primarily a land war which dragged on for three long years. The main effort by the Royal Navy involved providing ground support for the troops ashore, air reconnaissance and patrols, and interdiction of enemy air strikes by the navy's new aircraft – Hawker Sea Furies and Fairey Fireflies – while the cruisers, destroyers and frigates provided naval gunfire support.

At the start of the war the Far Eastern Fleet was in a parlous state, having suffered from post-war cutbacks in order that the Mediterranean Fleet could be built up. To bring the Fleet's ships up to their wartime complements, Reservists had to be called up and men about to retire from the Service were kept on for the duration of the emergency. Others due to return home because their tour of duty was about to end were retained for a time.

By August 1950 the Commonwealth Task Force comprised the light fleet carrier *Triumph* and the aircraft repair ship *Unicorn*, with the carrier *Ocean* on her way out from Britain. She was shortly followed by *Warrior* and *Theseus*, the cruisers *Belfast*, *Jamaica* and *Kenya*, eleven destroyers (including one Australian and three Canadian), eleven frigates (including one Australian and two New Zealand) and a hospital ship, *Maine*.

The war in North Korea highlighted the important role that air power would play in naval operations in the future. Aircraft from *Triumph* carried out daily strikes against coastal and inland targets, while *Jamaica* and the destroyers *Charity*, *Consort* and the Canadian *Sioux* carried out shore bombardment to support the troops. A number of ships (including *Jamaica* and *Comus*) suffered slight damage from enemy air strikes, and a number of aircraft were lost to North Korean Russian-built MiG-15 jet fighters. On paper these aircraft completely outclassed the navy's piston-engined aircraft, but the consummate skill of the navy pilots frequently enabled them to outmanoeuvre their faster but less skilful opponents. In one incident, in August 1952, four Sea Furies bounced by a force of MiG-15s managed to destroy one and damage two others.

The North Koreans' extensive minelaying campaign led to the urgent need to build up the Royal Navy's minesweeping capabilities. Many of the ships held in reserve were old wooden vessels from the Second World War, and on inspection were found to be beyond repair. As a result an emergency programme of construction of a new design, the 'Ton' class, was instigated, together with new inshore minesweepers of the 'Ham' and 'Ley' classes. However, serious delays were experienced in completing the new ships, and they did not finally enter service until the late 1950s, long after the Korean War had ended. The sudden demand for vessels and equipment occasioned by the Korean War placed a severe strain on the British defence industry, which was only just recovering from the ravages of the Second World War, and was not geared up to embark on another emergency war construction programme. However, the delays did have one unforeseen benefit, in that the completion of a number of ships over a greater period of time overcame any potential problem that might arise from block obsolescence of many units in the 1970s.

Like the Royal Navy, the US Navy was also woefully short of minesweepers with which to counter the North Korean mining campaign. To make up the shortfall, they formed helicopter units dedicated to searching for mines from the air. Late in 1950 one of these units was flown on to HMS *Theseus* to carry out minehunting operations. This was the first time that helicopters had flown operationally from a British warship.

The impact of the air war over Korea on naval thinking can be gauged from views held by the then 5th Sea Lord, who was responsible for naval aviation. He set out, in order of priority, what he considered would be the future roles of air power in the navy. The most important role, as he saw it, would be anti-submarine warfare, followed by air defence of the Fleet and merchant convoys and, lastly, air strike against enemy warships and shore targets. Three prototype aircraft were already under development to meet the proposed anti-submarine requirement, the Blackburn Y.A.5 and Y.B.1 and the Fairey Q. The last, a prototype of which had been ordered in 1946, was first flown in 1949, and made its first carrier landing

Right: In 1950 the Korean War erupted. The navy was mainly involved in carrier operations, and its latest aircraft played a prominent role. The Hawker Sea Fury entered service in 1947 and was the last piston-engined fighter in front line service. A total of six squadrons of Sea Furys was engaged in the Korean War, operating from the light fleet carriers *Ocean*, *Theseus*, *Glory* and *Sydney*. On a number of occasions Sea Furys were pitted against Russian MiG jet fighters, with a number of kills to their credit. The aircraft illustrated is a FB.11 version from the carrier *Theseus*, carrying Korean War markings. (ACPL)

Right: During the Korean War it was realized that the navy was woefully inadequate in mine warfare vessels. This led to the design and ordering of a large number of wooden-hulled ocean minesweepers of the 'Ton'-class. These remained in service for many years, a number subsequently being completely modernized and fitted with sonars to become minehunters. The picture shows the *Thames* (ex-*Alverton*) as originally built. (ACPL)

in June 1950. Quantity production of the new aircraft, the unique double-turboprop Gannet, was ordered in March 1951.

For air defence, two fighters were developed; the two-seat all-weather de Havilland Sea Venom (developed from the Vampire) and the Supermarine Attacker. Only a relatively few examples of the latter were built (first entering service in 1951), it soon being superseded by the Hawker Sea Hawk. For the strike role no suitable jet was under development, and as an interim measure the twin-turboprop Westland Wyvern, the prototype of which had flown in 1946, was produced, becoming operational in May 1953. To operate these new aircraft, in particular the high speed jets, the carriers were modified with strengthened flight decks and arrester wires, and lifts capable of handling the heavier aircraft.

By early 1951 the potential of the helicopter had been recognized, and following the success achieved by the Americans in operating helicopters from carriers in the search and rescue role, the navy carried out trials with a Sikorsky Dragonfly helicopter on board the RFA stores ship *Fort Duquesne*. It was also realized that, in the future, helicopters might play a major role in anti-submarine warfare.

On 16 April 1951 the navy suffered another submarine tragedy when *Affray* sank off the Isle of Wight with the loss of 75 men. The wreck was finally located by the diving vessel *Reclaim*, and it was found that the submarine's

schnorkel mast had broken off at the bottom, said to be due to faulty materials, but the real cause for the loss was never revealed.

During 1951 a number of new ships joined the fleet, showing the promise of things to come. The carrier *Eagle* and the first of the Second World War destroyer-frigate conversions, *Relentless*, commissioned, while the first of the new 'Daring' class destroyers started contractor's trials and two new gunboats, *Bold Pathfinder* and *Bold Pioneer*, were launched. These were to be powered by the new gas turbine, but initially were completed with petrol engines.

The Korean war dragged on, with the navy continuing to provide naval air and gunfire support. In another part of the Far East, Malaysia, another crisis developed, with communist forces trying to overthrow the ruling party. It was in Malaya that another application for the helicopter began to be developed. Westland Whirlwinds of No 848 Squadron were sent to support the security forces engaged in combatting the Communists, providing air lift for troops and dropping supplies. It presaged their role in support of Commando operations.

In June 1953, following the Coronation of Her Majesty Queen Elizabeth II, an enormous review of the Fleet was held at Spithead. Comprising some 197 warships of the Royal Navy, this was the largest Review to have been held since long before the Second World War; even larger than the 1937 Coronation Review, in which only 145 ships took part. The Queen reviewed the fleet from the

Left: The first jet fighter to be standardized in first-line service was the Supermarine Attacker. Carrier trials were concluded aboard the carrier *Illustrious* in October 1947 and the aircraft entered service in August 1951. (ACPL)

Lower left: Only 60 Attackers were built, and in 1953 the aircraft began to be replaced in first line service by the Hawker Sea Hawk. A total of 434 Sea Hawks were built, remaining in service until 1960. The first squadron to be equipped with the Sea Hawk was No 806 NAS, which later embarked in HMS *Eagle*. Sea Hawks provided close support for Operation 'Musketeer', the Anglo-French amphibious assault on Egypt in November 1956, operating with Nos 800, 802, 804, 810, 897 and 899 NAS on the carriers *Albion*, *Bulwark* and *Eagle*. (ACPL)

Right: In early 1942 a new carrier design was prepared, the first unit being laid down in October 1942. Little progress was made with the ship, the *Audacious*, and construction was suspended at the end of the war. The design was then updated to incorporate war experience and work on the *Audacious* resumed, the ship being renamed *Eagle*. When completed she differed little from the wartime design. She was finally commissioned into service in 1951 and is seen here in the early 1950s. *Eagle* was also the first carrier in the navy to operate jet fighters, the Attackers of 800 NAS. (ACPL).

Right: The second helicopter to enter service with the Royal Navy (the first being the Sikorsky Dragonfly) was the Westland Whirlwind, an indigenous-built helicopter. An earlier version, the HAR.21, was supplied to the navy in 1952 under MDAP (Mutual Defence Aid Programme), forming the Navy's first operational helicopter squadron, No 848 NAS. (ACPL)

despatch vessel *Surprise*, which served as the Royal Yacht. The review highlighted the considerable changes that had taken place in the power structure of the navy since 1937. Then the battleship reigned supreme, eleven vessels of this category being present, while only four carriers were reviewed. In addition, the 1937 Review boasted a total of fifteen cruisers. At the 1953 Review air power was the new strength on which the navy relied. Seven carriers were present, while squadron upon squadron of new aircraft, totalling over 300 aeroplanes, flew over the ships lined up for the Queen's inspection. Apart from the carriers there was just one battleship, *Vanguard*, and only eight cruisers. Of other categories there were 28 destroyers, including four of the new 'Daring' class, 38 frigates, 28 submarines and 31 minesweepers.

On 27 July 1953 the war in Korea ended, but it left the navy with a dangerous legacy. By the following year the navy was suffering from a serious manpower problem. Men were leaving the Service faster than they were being recruited, and this resulted in many men having to spend longer at sea, away from their families, leading to discontent among the lower ranks. A number of cases of wanton damage to ships occurred, committed by sailors in a vain effort to prevent their vessels sailing, often on long overseas deployments.

By 1954 the general state of affairs in the Royal Navy had reached such a low ebb that three former Admirals of

the Fleet were moved to draw attention to the situation in the House of Lords, during the debate on the Queen's speech at the opening of Parliament. The speech had not made any reference to a new building programme for the navy, and the Admirals felt that it was time the matter was brought to the attention of the public. Lord Chatfield, who had been Staff Captain to Admiral Beatty at the Battle of Jutland in 1916, made the point that 'We have neither the ships nor the men, nor the aircraft that we need to fulfil our responsibilities.'

But all was not doom and gloom. In March the first anti-submarine-warfare helicopter squadron had been formed, No 845, equipped with the S.55 helicopter (later called the Whirlwind). The previous month the first squadron of Hawker Sea Hawk jet fighters had embarked on HMS *Eagle*, and the light fleet carrier *Centaur* was being fitted with an angled deck to enable her to embark the new jet aircraft about to enter service. The mirror landing aid was also introduced into the Fleet's carriers during the year. This equipment considerably eased the problems encountered in landing jet aircraft on the flight deck.

On 16 June 1955 there occurred another tragic accident to a navy submarine. This involved *Sidon*, which was loading torpedoes from the depot ship *Maidstone* in Portland harbour. An internal explosion occurred in the forward torpedo compartment, and thirteen crew members

Left: During the middle to late 1950s a number of new inventions to improve aircraft operations from carriers were introduced into the fleet. One of the most important was the angled deck. HMS *Centaur* (seen here) was the first to have the new angled deck (at 5.5º) which was modified during 1954. The angled deck offered increased deck parking area forward and enabled an aircraft that failed to catch the arrestor wire to take off again for another try without having to run into a crash barrier, with attendant damage to the aircraft. (ACPL)

died. The accident was attributed to a torpedo's volatile HTP fuel coming into contact with a material in the weapon (a Second World War converted Mk 8 torpedo) which caused it to ignite. The disaster led to the abandonment of HTP as a fuel.

By 1956 trouble was again looming in the Middle East. At the end of July, President Nasser of Egypt nationalized the Suez Canal. From a commercial point of view this created considerable disquiet among some European countries, in particular Britain and France. The Middle East was Britain's source of oil, and the main route from the oilfields was through the Suez Canal. Previously, Britain had maintained a large force of troops in Egypt, but under a treaty concluded in 1954 British forces were to be withdrawn from the Canal Zone by June 1956, although Britain was to retain the use of a vital supply base at Ismailia. Having concluded a military supply agreement with Russia, Nasser felt suitably strengthened to counter the highly active Israeli stance which was then being adopted, particularly in the Gaza region.

Then, in July, Britain withdrew from the Aswan dam project, while the Russians publicly denied that they had offered any financial assistance to complete the dam. As the Aswan dam was at the heart of Nasser's home policy, and vital for the economy of the country, it would have been disastrous not to proceed with its construction. In order to finance the massive venture, the only other source of revenue open to Nasser was the Suez Canal. So late on 26 July 1956, in a public speech in the centre of Alexandria, Nasser told the waiting crowds that the Suez Canal was to be nationalized. There was no turning back now. Within a few hours martial law had been declared on the Canal Zone and the Egyptians were in complete control of the Canal's operations.

The following day the British Cabinet and Chiefs of Staff decided on military action to secure the freedom of

Below: Another new invention was the gyro-stabilized mirror landing sight. This was a large mirror mounted on the deckside of the carrier which showed the pilot of an approaching aircraft by means of coloured lights on either side of the mirror whether he was approaching at too high or low an angle or too far to port or starboard. An audio tone gave indication of the approach speed. This development proved to be essential with the new generation of high-performance jet aircraft. (ACPL)

the Suez Canal. The Foreign Secretary, however, was cautious, and adamant that American support should be secured before any precipitate action was taken. The Americans were not in favour of any military action, as it might have imperilled their own overtures to various other Arab nations currently then in progress. Instead they preferred to pursue the possibility of a conference on the issue.

It was only when the British and French decided to settle the issue by military force that they discovered that their forces were outclassed by the Russian equipment which Nasser had received, in particular the MiG-15 aircraft. Two French carriers in the Mediterranean had only piston-engined aircraft on board, and although HMS *Eagle* carried the more modern Sea Venom and Sea Hawk jets, these were no match for the MiG-15s either. Then there was the question of a suitable base from which to launch an invasion to secure the Suez Canal. Any assault would have to be mounted from Cyprus, but on Cyprus Greek separatist EOKA terrorists were causing considerable trouble, operations against the EOKA seriously interfering with the training of both paratroops and marines on the island. The nearest amphibious squadron was based at Malta. This consisted of two LSTs, each capable of carrying eight assault landing craft and two LCTs; nowhere near sufficient transport for an operation such as that envisaged against Egypt. Furthermore, very little assault equipment remained in the UK armed forces inventory, most of that left over from the Second World War having been sold overseas or scrapped.

On 2 August a Royal Proclamation announced the calling up of the reserves, while all regular troops due for discharge were retained. Precautionary emergency measures were instituted which included putting all ships on alert, and a notice was sent to all the shipping companies, warning of the possible need to requisition ships. The cruiser *Jamaica* and the fast minelayer *Manxman* were retained in the eastern Mediterranean, while in the UK all carriers at sea returned to port and *Bulwark* embarked her air group of three squadrons of Sea Hawks. The training carriers *Theseus* and *Ocean* had no aircraft facilities, so, as there was a shortage of suitable transports, they were pressed into service as troopships, sailing for the Mediterranean at the end of July. During August the carrier *Albion* was also despatched to the Mediterranean, with Sea Venoms and Sea Hawks embarked.

In the meantime, *Theseus* and *Ocean* had returned home and were hurriedly being equipped with more permanent accommodation for troops, *Ocean* also being fitted out with an operating theatre and extensive hospital facilities. During the planning which had continued since the crisis first broke, it was found that the amphibious forces available to the navy and, indeed, the troop transports of the RAF, were completely inadequate for an opposed invasion of Egypt.

In any assault the primary need is to get as many assault troops as possible ashore as quickly as possible, to secure a bridgehead to enable follow-up forces to land in strength. The forces allocated included 45,000 British troops, 12,000 vehicles, 300 aircraft and warships, while the French provided the remainder of the forces. It was found that, of the 32 tank landing ships available to transport troops and equipment to the Mediterranean, only two were actually in service. The remainder had been mothballed, and only twelve could be made ready in time. The logistics problems were horrendous.

In spite of all the deficiencies, preparations for the invasion continued. The main landing was scheduled to take place at Alexandria. The basic plan was to secure total air superiority before carrying out an airborne assault to secure initial objectives. This would be followed by a seaborne invasion to consolidate and secure a beachhead for the main assault, in which troops and material would land under cover of naval gunfire support. The landings were scheduled to take place on 15 September, after two weeks of air strikes. On 10 September a political decision was made to change the objective from Alexandria to Port Said, and the landings were postponed first to 1 October and then to an undetermined date.

Before the work of converting *Theseus* and *Ocean* to troop transports could be completed, however, it was decided to assign them a new role. In part this was dictated by the need to provide extra transport for the initial seaborne assault, to ensure that sufficient numbers of troops were put ahsore in the first few hours. It was decided that troops should be landed by helicopter, and, to achieve this, plans were rapidly drawn up to convert *Theseus* and *Ocean* into helicopter carriers. *Ocean* eventually embarked a mixed force of Whirlwind and Sycamore helicopters from the Joint Experimental Helicopter Unit, while *Theseus* carried the Whirlwinds of No 845 Squadron. After carrying out exercises, the two carriers sailed for the Mediterranean in mid-October.

On 29 October the Israelis launched an offensive against the Egyptians in the Sinai. This was followed later in the day by an Anglo-French ultimatum calling for both countries to withdraw their forces to 10 miles either side of the canal. Meanwhile, in Malta, HMS *Ocean* embarked No 45 Commando, while the LST *Lofoten* took on board their equipment and heavy stores. On 2 November the two ships, with an escort of destroyers and frigates, headed out into the Mediterranean.

Hostilities commenced on 31 October. During the night the cruiser *Newfoundland*, on patrol at the southern end of the Canal, picked up a contact on her radar. On being challenged, the target opened fire on the cruiser, causing minor damage. The cruiser's 6in guns replied, and after six minutes the Egyptian frigate *Domiat* was sunk, 69 of her crew being rescued. Shortly after this the frigate *Crane* was attacked by four Israeli aircraft, and in the ensuing gunfight shot down one of the jets.

During the night of 31 October / 1 November the RAF began air raids against targets in Egypt. These were followed in the morning by air raids on Egyptian airfields by carrier-borne Wyverns, Sea Hawks and Sea Venoms. The Egyptians were caught completely by surprise, many of their aircraft being destroyed on the ground. By nightfall on 2 November the Egyptian air force had virtually ceased to exist. The carrier air strikes continued for the next three days, and on 5 November the first paratroops were landed on the airfield at Gamil, on the outskirts of Port Said. As the troops consolidated their position ashore, Whirlwind helicopters from *Albion* and *Bulwark*, stationed offshore, landed with urgent supplies and ferried out wounded troops.

Left: In 1956 the Fleet Air Arm and the Royal Marine Commandos played a major role in Operation 'Musketeer', the Anglo-French amphibious assault on the Suez Canal. This was the first major helicopter-borne assault in history. The Wyverns, Sea Hawks and Sea Venoms of the Fleet Air Arm, together with aircraft from the RAF and French Air Force, virtually destroyed the Egyptian Air Force. Here a Sea Venom of 893 NAS, damaged by anti-aircraft fire, lands on the carrier *Eagle* with no undercarriage. Note the mirror landing sight behind the aircraft. (Imperial War Museum)

The next day, 6 November, Sea Hawks and Sea Venoms carried out pre-assault bombardments of enemy positions on the beaches where the troops were to go ashore. As the helicopters lifted off from the decks of the carriers with the Commandos, the landing craft headed for the beaches. At 0430 precisely the doors of the LSTs opened and the initial wave of LVTs (landing vehicle tracked), each with 30 troops of Nos 40 and 42 Royal Marine Commando and their equipment, slid into the water and headed for the beach. As the Commandos fanned out across the beaches to secure their initial objectives they were supported by a number of Centurion tanks.

With the beachhead secure and the first objectives in Commando hands, the way was clear for the first helicopter-borne assault in history. The first wave of Whirlwinds of No 845 Squadron lifted off from the decks of *Albion* and *Bulwark* at 0540 and headed towards the secured beach areas, carrying troops of No 45 Commando. The helicopters approached the landing zone in waves and orbited the area, going in singly to land their complement of Commandos and pick up any wounded men before taking off and allowing the next helicopter to land its troops. The helicopters then returned to the carriers to reload, taking only one minute to get Marines aboard. They refuelled after every second trip, an operation which took just four minutes. By nightfall most of the objectives had been secured, and the following day, 6 November, the first LST was able to berth in Port Said and unload its cargo of Centurion tanks. By nightfall, fourteen LSTs had unloaded full cargoes of troops, vehicles and stores in the port, while more troops came ashore from troopships anchored in the harbour.

While the British and French were consolidating their position ashore, the United Nations was bringing strong pressure to bear on the two governments to order a ceasefire. At 2345 on 6 November a ceasefire came into effect, and the short operation was over as far as the Royal Navy was concerned. The evacuation of most of the British troops began on 7 December, and the last troops left on 22 December.

One immediate outcome of the affair was that emphasis was placed on the rapid movement of troops to any part of the world in a fire-fighting role. The value of the helicopter in the assault role had been proven, and, together with the rapid transportation requirement, led to the decision that *Albion* and *Bulwark* should be permanently converted to Commando Carriers. As such they were subsequently able to render invaluable support to operations in Kuwait, Malaysia and the states of the Arabian Gulf.

In 1957 Duncan Sandys, who was appointed Minister of Defence in the Conservative Government of Harold Macmillan, was instructed by the Prime Minister to carry out a major review of the armed services with a view to instigating far-reaching reductions in expenditure and manpower. To carry out the reforms considered necessary to achieve the cuts, Sandys was given extensive authority, far greater than any previous Minister of Defence. To aid him in carrying out his brief he was given authority over force structure, size and organization, equipment, pay, administration, and even military appointments.

As part of the review the Minister set out to address three major questions relating to naval policy:

1 Should the navy's carrier-borne aircraft contribute towards the nuclear deterrent?

2 What magnitude of naval forces were required which did not contribute to the deterrent?

3 For operations out of area, what sort of naval forces were required?

However, Sandys answered only the last of these questions in the 1957 Defence White Paper. The paper also noted that the future role of naval forces was 'uncertain', and that there was no future for manned military aircraft, it being presumed that any future war would be nuclear and would be against Russia under the umbrella of NATO. Hence, there would be no requirement for aircraft carriers in the North Atlantic, which cast a major shadow over the future of the carriers. It seemed to many that there was really no role at all for the navy, particularly as no

Right: In 1958 the Second World War carrier *Victorious* emerged from a complete rebuild equipped with an angled deck, steam catapult, mirror landing sight and massive Type 984 fighter control radar antenna mounted atop her superstructure. (ACPL)

mention was made concerning a contribution towards the deterrent.

On one aspect there was no confusion or uncertainty — naval manpower over the next five years was to be dramatically reduced by 75,000 officers and men, the Reserve Fleet of some 550 ships was to be scrapped or sold, and over 100 shore establishments closed, in what became known as the Sandys Axe. Included in the ships of the Reserve Fleet that were to be scrapped were the four '*King George V*' class battleships and 21 cruisers, while the three '*Tiger*' class cruisers were to be replaced by a missile-armed, improved '*Daring*'-type vessel. In addition, a new missile cruiser that had been planned was cancelled. Finally, all research and development on guns was stopped, and some of the funds released from this and other cuts were transferred to new construction and other new weapons, in particular missiles. In effect, the late 1950s could be said to be the dawn of the missile age for the Royal Navy.

There was a small crumb of comfort, however, in that much greater emphasis was to be placed on afloat support tankers and supply ships, it being considered that all shore bases would be destroyed in a nuclear war. It was also stated that the navy would be organized around a number of carrier task groups, one of which would be based at Singapore. So there did seem to be some sort of future for the aircraft carrier after all, though nobody was quite certain what it might be.

In the debate following publication of the White Paper, details were released of the navy's nuclear submarine programme, which was to be speeded up. Although it was not revealed at the time, there was a body of opinion which regarded the nuclear-powered submarine as the new capital ship of the fleet. With emphasis veering towards nuclear propulsion for submarines, all work on the HTP programme was quietly dropped. This was not too difficult a decision to take, for many problems had been experienced with the volatile fuel.

In August an order was placed for the first of the new fleet missile-armed escorts, *Devonshire*, which was to be powered by a mix of steam and gas turbine. During the autumn of 1957 further progress was made with integrating the helicopter into naval operations when flight trials with a Fairey Ultra Light helicopter took place on HMS *Grenville*. The success of these, and succeeding trials with the Saunders-Roe P.531 private venture helicopter (eventually developed into the ubiquitous Wasp, designed specifically for operations from small warships) in 1959, led to the concept of extending the ASW range of frigates by arming the helicopters with depth charges or homing torpedoes. By the early 1960s all Royal Navy frigates and destroyers were being equipped to carry helicopters.

Seeking to forestall any trouble following the previous year's defence cuts, the Prime Minister decided to make an announcement before the publication of the 1958 Defence White Paper. In his statement, Macmillan said that a balanced fleet would no longer be maintained in home waters, as emphasis in this area would be on ASW. However, outside Europe, balanced naval forces would be retained. When published, the White Paper laid down three primary roles for the navy. These were:

1 To protect shipping in peacetime.
2 To protect shipping in areas where limited war broke out.
3 To provide an effective contribution to the com bined naval forces of the Western Alliance.

Stress was laid on ASW. Two carriers, one each based in the Mediterranean and North Atlantic, were to operate predominantly in the ASW role, but would retain some fighter and strike aircraft capability. However, even on this subject there was confusion, for the fixed-wing Gannet ASW aircraft was about to be phased out of service in favour of ASW helicopters. The announcement raised the question of whether Britain still needed large fixed-wing carriers.

In 1958 Iceland introduced a 12-mile fishing limit around her coast which British trawlers refused to recognize, this being one of their richest fishing grounds. During the autumn the disagreement between British

fishermen and the Icelanders spilled over into a number of ugly incidents, and the navy was called in to help protect the British fishing vessels, augmenting the small vessels of the Fishery Protection Squadron with frigates. In attempting to protect their rights, Icelandic gunboats clashed with the navy's frigates in a number of increasingly acrimonious exchanges in which shots were frequently fired at British trawlers. The incidents were a great test of seamanship, with frigates and gunboats manoeuvring at speed around the trawlers at very close quarters, collisions often being avoided by a hair's breadth as the frigates endeavoured to prevent the Icelanders from boarding and attempting to 'capture' British trawlers.

The 'Cod War', as it came to be known, continued on and off until 1960, when the British fishermen finally and reluctantly agreed that they would no longer fish in the disputed waters. In return, Iceland agreed not to pursue claims for the island of Rockall off the northwest Scottish coast, an area which the UK Government had reason to believe would be extremely rich in undersea oil reserves. But the 'war' in the harsh environment of Icelandic waters had taken its toll on the navy's new frigates. As a consequence all the 'Blackwood' Type 14 frigates had to be docked so that their hulls could be strengthened.

In 1959 the keel of the navy's first nuclear-powered submarine, HMS *Dreadnought*, was laid down at the Vickers yard in Barrow. The main machinery was provided by America, who also assisted Vickers in the construction of the boat. Even so, it was to be four years before *Dreadnought* completed.

Above: In the late 1950s the navy became embroiled in a series of incidents with Icelandic gunboats over fishing rights, which was referred to as the Cod War. Much close sailing was involved and a number of warships suffered damage from close encounters. To prevent serious damage while interposing warships between the Icelandic gunboats and fishing boats they were attempting to board, a number of navy ships were fitted with extra protection around the bows. Here the frigate *Lincoln* is seen at Chatham with wood sheathing to her bows. (ACPL)

Left: During the mid-1950s the Navy began to commission a new generation of ASW aircraft into service. The Fairey Gannet (aircraft from 825 NAS from HMS *Eagle* are illustrated) was the world's first aircraft to fly with a double airscrew turbine unit – a twin-engined aircraft in a single engine configuration. It featured a large weapons bay, aft of which was a radar scanner housed in a retractable radome. (Imperial War Museum)

Left: In 1952 the standard AEW aircraft of the Fleet Air Arm was the American Douglas Skyraider. In 1959 this venerable aircraft began to be replaced in front-line service by the Gannet AEW.3, derived from the earlier ASW Gannet. The Gannet AEW was tasked with providing early warning of low-flying hostile aircraft as well as strike coordination, ASW and SAR. (ACPL)

Chapter 35

The High-Tech Navy of the Nuclear Age

The turn of the decade saw a number of new ships laid down for the navy. Nuclear power was about to be introduced into the Fleet with *Dreadnought*, while in January 1962 the first UK-built nuclear-powered submarine, *Valiant*, was laid down. Following the lessons learned from the Suez operation of 1956, the Fleet's amphibious warfare capability was to be considerably augmented by the laying down in 1962 of two purpose-designed assault ships, *Fearless* and *Intrepid*.

Computerization was also about to enter the Fleet, the carrier *Eagle* undergoing modernization with a new Action Data Automation system to speed up the handling and display of radar data. In the frigate category the Type 12 'Rothesay' class had been developed from the original 'Whitby' class, and was now itself being developed into the ubiquitous 'Leander' class which was to become the mainstay of the navy's frigate force into the 1980s. In addition, a new frigate class, the Type 81 general purpose 'Tribal', was under construction. This design, developed primarily for service in the Persian Gulf to replace the obsolete 'Loch' class, introduced a revolutionary machinery arrangement — a combination of steam and gas turbine, or COSAG (combined steam and gas). This arrangement was also being installed in the new guided-missile destroyers, the lead ship of which, *Devonshire*, had been laid down in March 1959. The 'Tribals' were also the first frigates designed from the outset to operate helicopters.

In June 1961 further trouble broke out in the Middle East, when military movements in Iraq indicated that she was about to invade Kuwait, with whom Britain had recently concluded a defence agreement. The ruler of Kuwait invited British forces to come to his aid, and on 1 July 750 men of 42 Royal Marine Commando from *Bulwark* (which fortuitously happened to be visiting Pakistan at the time) were landed by helicopters of 848 Squadron. Already in the Persian Gulf were the frigate *Loch Alvie* and the Landing Ship Tank (LST) *Striker*, the latter having on board a squadron of Centurion tanks which were landed to support the Commandos. Two more frigates, *Loch Ruthven* and *Loch Fyne*, in the Indian Ocean area, were also ordered into the Gulf to support the operation. Other units in the Far East which were ordered to the Gulf were the carrier *Victorious*, the destroyer *Cassandra*, and frigate *Lincoln*, while the carrier *Centaur*, three 'Battle' class destroyers (*Camperdown*, *Finnistere* and *Saintes*), the

Right: The navy's first swept-wing two-seat all-weather fighter, designed to replace the Sea Venom, was the Sea Vixen. This aircraft became operational with 892 NAS aboard the carrier *Ark Royal* in March 1960. The Sea Vixen was the first aircraft in the Navy to operate with guided missiles instead of guns. Armed with Firestreak missiles, the aircraft provided the Fleet Air Arm with a powerful defence system. The aircraft illustrated is seen firing rockets. (ACPL)

frigates *Yarmouth* and *Llandaff*, the LST *Messina*, the minesweepers *Ashton* and *Rodington*, and the fleet tanker RFA *Olna* were also despatched to the Gulf. The minesweepers were ordered to join the force in anticipation that Iraq might lay mines off the Kuwaiti coast.

On 2 July No 45 Commando from Aden flew in, and by 11 June British forces in Kuwait totalled 5,700 men, including the 2nd battalion of the Coldstream Guards and the light armoured reconnaissance vehicles of the 3rd Carabiniers from the Army. Offshore, the amphibious command ship HMS *Meon* acted as command and communications centre for the landing, while *Bulwark* provided air warning cover with her radar until the arrival of *Victorious*. On her arrival *Victorious* took over command of all air operations, including the tasking of RAF Hunter jets, while numerous sorties were flown by her own de Havilland Sea Vixens and Supermarine Scimitars. *Bulwark*, meanwhile, was used as an accommodation and recreation base for the troops ashore. Gradually the crisis eased, and the ships were able to return to their normal duties.

Yet again the presence of a carrier with indigenous air power, together with support from the amphibious assault ship *Bulwark*, had proved its value in containing a situation that might have developed into a major threat to stability and peace in a volatile region of the world.

Among the vital lessons learned were the importance of commando ships and their helicopters in maintaining and supplying troops ashore in a hostile situation, while the extensive communications, command and control (C^3) facilities and the early warning radar on the carrier proved invaluable until bases could be set up ashore.

Apart from problems in the Middle East during the 1960s, trouble was also brewing in the Far East. In Indonesia the communist-led Government was seeking to expand its influence over an increasingly extensive part of the region. Malaya, Borneo and Brunei in particular became prime targets for communist infiltration and agitation. To counter the developing threat, British forces in the Far East were augmented by the aircraft carrier *Ark Royal*, the commando carrier *Bulwark*, the cruiser *Tiger*, a destroyer, three frigate squadrons, a division of submarines, a minesweeper and various fleet support vessels. Also included in the Order of Battle were two Royal Marine Commando units and the headquarters of 3 Commando Brigade, based at Singapore.

At the beginning of December 1962 No 42 Commando was airlifted from Singapore to Brunei to help the local forces flush out communist rebels operating in the state. Forces in the immediate vicinity were gradually built up to contain what was considered might be a major Indonesian-supported insurrection. Towards the latter part of December 1962 the Commando carrier *Albion* ferried 700 men of No 40 Commando to the State, while the minesweepers *Wilkieston* and *Woolaston* conducted sea patrols around the island, being supported by the *Woodbridge Haven* and the RFA *Gold Ranger*. As the situation deteriorated, units moved from place to place to interdict communist infiltrators from Indonesia. Helicopters proved invaluable in the work, rapidly transporting troops to trouble spots and supporting them in their missions.

At the end of 1962 the Government announced that an agreement had been reached for Britain to acquire the Polaris submarine-launched intercontinental ballistic missile (ICBM) from America in lieu of the Skybolt air-launched missile. Hitherto, the RAF had had complete responsibility for deploying Britain's nuclear deterrent, in the form of the Blue Steel bomb. Plans had been drawn up to replace Blue Steel with a new weapon, Blue Streak, but the British Government had cancelled this, deciding instead to acquire the American Skybolt, which itself was then cancelled by the Americans. By the end of 1962 details were beginning to emerge concerning the deployment of the Polaris missiles by the navy. It was revealed that a new submarine would be built, equipped with sixteen tubes for launching the missiles. In addition, the

Left: Following the success at Suez in 1956 of the helicopter assault from the light fleet carriers, the Navy converted the *Albion* and *Bulwark* into commando assault carriers between 1959 and 1962. The *Albion* is seen here with Royal Marines boarding their helicopters in a practice assault. (ACPL)

Right: In 1962 the navy's first missile-armed ship entered service – HMS *Devonshire*. Armed with the Seaslug surface-to-air missile, the launcher for which can be seen on the quarterdeck, this class also featured gas-turbine propulsion in combination with a steam plant. Two twin 4.5in turrets were mounted forward, but B turret was later replaced by four launchers for Exocet surface-to-surface missiles. At the stern can be seen two noise-makers for decoying acoustic homing torpedoes. (ACPL)

Right: In 1963 the navy entered the nuclear age when its first nuclear-powered submarine, HMS *Dreadnought*, was commissioned. Powered by an American reactor, she featured a whale-shaped hull and distinctive fin-shaped conning tower designed to reduce underwater drag to a minimum, as she was designed for purely underwater navigation. (Mike Lennon)

Right: The 'Rothesay' class (a direct descendant of the 'Whitby' class) was developed into the general purpose 'Leander' class frigates. The picture shows the *Ajax* as completed with twin 4.5in turret forward, two single 40mm at the rear of the superstructure, a hangar for the Wasp helicopter and a Limbo anti-submarine mortar in a well aft. Many of the ships in the class were substantially modified for various specific roles during their lives. (L. van Ginderen)

Right: During the late 1960s the cruisers *Tiger* and *Blake* underwent conversion to helicopter command ships, the after 6in gun being removed and replaced by a flight deck and hangar capable of housing four Sea King ASW helicopters. In addition the 3in guns amidships were replaced by two quadruple Seacat surface-to-air missile launchers. The cruisers were also equipped to carry a company of Royal Marines which could be put ashore by helicopters. (ACPL)

Left: In 1968 the navy's first nuclear-powered ballistic missile submarine launched her first Polaris missile. The picture shows HMS *Repulse* paying off for her third two-year refit in 1984. The boats deploy Polaris missiles armed with the British designed and built Chevaline MRV (multiple re-entry vehicle) warhead. (ACPL)

boats would be fitted with six torpedo tubes. It was announced that the first Polaris submarine would be in service by mid-1968.

On 30 July 1963 the Minister of Defence announced that a new 50,000-ton carrier would be built to replace *Victorious*. It was to deploy both conventional and vertical-take-off aircraft, the latter being the Hawker P.1154, the forerunner of which, the P.1127, had carried out deck landing and vertical-take-off trials in *Ark Royal* on 8 February. No mention, however, was made of further orders to replace *Ark Royal* and *Eagle*. *Ark Royal* was due to reach the end of her operational life by the early 1970s, leaving just *Eagle* and *Hermes* to sail on into the 1980s. Although it was not stated at the time, it was evident that both *Eagle* and *Hermes* would have to be extensively modernized for them to remain in service until the 1980s. Nor was anything said about the obsolete light carrier *Centaur*; presumably she would not be replaced. This would leave the navy with only three effective carriers. If such was the case, then the concept of developing a number of carrier task forces for duty around the world was now dead. Furthermore, it would be impossible to keep more than one fully operational carrier East of Suez at any one time because of refits and training.

The beginning of 1964 saw the Royal Navy engaged in further operations against dissident and rebel forces in the Far East and Indian Ocean regions. The Indonesian confrontation worsened, and further forces were despatched east, including the carrier *Centaur*. While in the Indian Ocean, *Centaur* was diverted to stand by off Zanzibar, where the Sultan had been deposed. Troubles then broke out in Tanzania, Uganda and Kenya, while men of 45 Commando Royal Marines were engaged in containing trouble in the Radfan Mountains in Aden. The Indonesian confrontation in the Far East, however, remained predominant and was to last for another year, with numerous clashes between the opposing forces, principally involving the small 'Ton' class minesweepers of the navy.

The end of a 336-year-old establishment in the political history of England came on 1 April 1964, when the Board of Admiralty was dissolved and a unified Ministry of Defence formally established.

A General Election in September 1964 brought to power a Labour Government under Harold Wilson, with Dennis Healey as Secretary of State for Defence. Shortly after taking office the new Defence Minister initiated a complete overhaul of Britain's defence commitments and priorities, based on the Government's political objectives and the economic situation. Already the seeds were being sown which would result in a total reordering of the nation's overseas commitments, and of the perceived military requirements to meet those commitments. In the debate on the 1965 Defence Estimates the Conservative opposition gave a hint of what the future might hold for the Fleet Air Arm. During the debate the opposition stated that it was doubtful whether a British presence East of Suez could be maintained with only three carriers, suggesting that two new carriers would therefore be required to keep three in commission. The Conservatives themselves had conveniently forgotten this fact when in office, considering the cost of three carriers beyond the financial capability of the nation when combined with its committed expenditure on the Polaris project.

But the Labour Government was carrying out a complete reappraisal of its foreign policy, one aim of which was eventually to withdraw completely from all commitments East of Suez, thus abrogating the need for replacement carriers and new conventional fixed-wing aircraft for the navy. The Labour Government covered its tracks, rightly claiming that it had considered purchasing an 'Essex' class carrier from the USA as a stopgap measure. Nevertheless, they were determined to cancel the new carrier and destroy the navy's ability to provide its own organic air cover — a task that was to be fulfilled by the RAF.

Towards the end of 1965, following Ian Smith's announcement of the Unilateral Declaration of Independence in Rhodesia, the navy became involved in the economic blockade of that country. In what became known as the Beira Patrol, a steady succession of ships were sent out to the Indian Ocean to prevent any contraband, and particularly oil supplies from South Africa, reaching the country through the Mozambique port of Beira.

On 22 February 1966 the Government published its long-awaited Defence Review. In what became known as the Healey Axe, the review proposed the abolition of the navy's carriers and the Fleet Air Arm. In future, the Fleet's air defence would be provided by guided missiles, while helicopters would provide screening and limited strike capability. Overall air defence would be provided by RAF aircraft flying from the United Kingdom and island bases overseas; bases which had still to be built (and which, if the Government proceeded with its well-hidden plans, would never be built, as most overseas commitments were to be abrogated). Such a policy, it was claimed, would be more cost-effective. The review also claimed that, in the light of new developments in missile technology, carriers would be vulnerable to long-range missiles. On closer inspection it was found that the costings for the new policy were grossly inaccurate, the island bases alone being double the cost of a new carrier. It was later discovered that the cost comparisons presented to Parliament had been worked out on the basis not of one carrier but of two, and also included the cost of four new missile-armed destroyers to act as escorts to the carriers.

Even before the review was presented, the top echelons of the navy knew that the new carrier, CVA 01, was to be cancelled. A furious row developed over the cancellation, it being claimed that the project was to be dropped in favour of purchasing 50 American General Dynamics F.111 aircraft for the RAF, some of which would be used to provide strike cover for the navy. In addition, McDonnell Douglas Phantoms were to be purchased from the USA, and some of these would be used for air defence for the Fleet. The Minister of Defence for the Navy, Mr Mayhew, together with the First Sea Lord, Admiral Sir David Luce, and the Deputy Chief of Naval Staff, Vice-Admiral Sir Frank Hopkins (responsible for the Fleet Air Arm), had all threatened to resign if the carrier was cancelled. The carrier protagonists justly claimed that the RAF would be unable to provide adequate air support either for the Fleet or for transatlantic resupply convoys in the event of war. The Cabinet was undeterred, and went ahead with its decision to cancel CVA 01. Before the news was published in the Defence Review, Mr Mayhew and Admiral Sir David Luce resigned.

The cancellation of CVA 01 was a blow from which the Royal Navy has not yet fully recovered. The post-CVA 01 era was characterized by the higher echelons of the navy constantly looking over their shoulder, wondering if there would be more similar reviews and cuts — and not without a great deal of justification, as future events were to demonstrate.

In April 1966 the new First Sea Lord, Admiral of the Fleet Sir Varyl Begg, set up a working party under Rear-Admiral J.H. Adams in the specially created post of Assistant Chief Naval Staff (Policy) (ACNS(P)). The purpose of the working party was to produce a future plan for the navy, based on the cancellation of CVA 01.

However, within the higher realms of the Admiralty the controversy over the carrier issue continued. The Working Party's Report was due to be presented in October 1966, and would result in a complete and fundamental reassessment of the navy's role and structure. Adams's working party came to the inescapable conclusion that some form of 'big ship' would be required to deploy helicopters and vertical/short take-off and landing (V/STOL) aircraft to perform three vital functions which they felt the RAF would be unable to provide – AEW, ASW and strike – in support of the Fleet and merchant convoys, together with a major integrated command and control capability for ASW task group operations.

This was felt to be particularly necessary as the previous Conservative Government had so procrastinated over the ordering of CVA 01 that they had been voted out of office before the carrier could be finally ordered. A period of some two years had elapsed since they had first committed themselves to acquiring the new carrier.

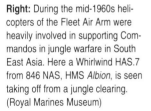

Right: During the mid-1960s helicopters of the Fleet Air Arm were heavily involved in supporting Commandos in jungle warfare in South East Asia. Here a Whirlwind HAS.7 from 846 NAS, HMS *Albion*, is seen taking off from a jungle clearing. (Royal Marines Museum)

The First Sea Lord was implacably opposed to any suggestion of resurrecting the carrier and told the Naval Staff under Adams that the report of the Working Party would be shelved and not presented to the Admiralty Board, while Adams was told he would not be recommended for further service. As a result, when Adams's term of service as ACNS(P) came to an end he left the navy — a sad loss.

With the cancellation of CVA 01 the navy lost its dependance on the carrier as its primary capital ship for the future, and its image and role was apparently severely diminished. As a result, and with the Government's reappraisal of the nation's future commitments under way, emphasis came to be placed on the nuclear-powered attack submarine (SSN). Fortunately Adams's report was not totally ignored and filed away to gather dust on a shelf. In the event it formed the basis of a plan for the future, the main outcome of which was the decision to design a 'through deck cruiser' to operate helicopters and possibly V/STOL aircraft, and to provide a command and control capability for ASW. In other words, the vessel would concentrate on ASW — no mention was made of any AEW or strike capability.

But all this was in the future. As for the present and the rest of the navy's carrier force, this would be gradually run down and not replaced. The Government considered that the existing carriers would continue to be required until the mid-1970s, to cover the withdrawal of British forces from overseas bases and commitments while they were being run down. This was a singularly inept understanding of the role of maritime power, and of organic naval air power in particular. If the carriers were needed for peacetime operations such as these, when no direct major threat was posed which required ASW, strike or AEW capabilities, then surely the provision of adequate, balanced and suitable maritime forces in a time of conflict would require some form of organic air capability using carrier-type ships. This, in fact, proved to be the case in 1982 in the South Atlantic.

Apart from the Governments's stated intention to withdraw from the bulk of its commitments 'east of Suez', further run-downs in other areas were also pushed forward. In April 1967 it was announced that the naval base at Aden would be closed by 1968, and on 5 June 1967 the Mediterranean Fleet ceased to exist when the C-in-C Mediterranean, Admiral Sir John Hamilton, hauled down the flag for the last time.

The news that the navy was to withdraw from Aden led to further troubles in the Colony, and eventually the British-backed independent Government collapsed. Ashore, men of 45 Commando, Royal Marines, carried out vigorous patrols to keep order, and in the late summer and autumn of 1967 a powerful naval task force was assembled offshore, eventually comprising some 25 ships. It included the carriers *Eagle* and *Victorious*, the Commando carrier *Bulwark* with 42 Commando, Royal Marines (who were disembarked ashore), the assault ship

Above: Between 1967 and 1969 the carrier *Ark Royal* underwent a major refit, which enabled her to operate American Phantom fighters. These were being acquired for the navy in lieu of a new fixed-wing fighter, it being intended that the *Ark Royal* should remain in service until the late 1970s, when some form of new helicopter carrying ship would be commissioned to replace the fixed-wing carriers. All her guns were removed and she was armed with quadruple Seacat surface-to-air missile launchers, while a lattice mast replaced the former tripod mast. Improved steam catapults, mirror landing aids and new arrester gear was fitted to handle the new, very much heavier Phantom aircraft. (ACPL)

Fearless (which was to co-ordinate the withdrawal), and later *Albion*, *Hermes* and *Intrepid*. The last British forces left the former colony on 29 November 1967.

At home, the range of major cutbacks introduced by the Government had little effect on the worsening economic situation and the resulting devaluation of sterling. In view of the situation the Government announced further cuts in the defence budget, the immediate effect of which was to pay off the carrier *Victorious*, currently undergoing a major refit. The reason given for the decision to pay off the carrier was that she had suffered a fire, the damage from which would be uneconomic to repair. This gave rise to a scandal when it was found that the fire was a small one, and that the damage would cost only a few thousand pounds to put right.

Unabashed, the Minister of Defence, Mr Healey, claimed that the navy would still have one and frequently two carriers available for service anywhere in the world (in fact, the navy now had just three carriers — *Eagle*, *Ark Royal* and *Hermes*). It was said that *Eagle* would be too expensive to convert to operate the Phantom aircraft that the navy was to acquire, so it was realized that she, too, would soon be decommissioned. The unmodernized *Ark Royal* was to be left to serve until 1972 as the navy's only strike carrier. *Albion* and *Bulwark* had already been converted to commando assault ships, and plans were drawn up to carry out a similar conversion of *Hermes*. To ensure that no carrier would be reincarnated by a future government, *Eagle* was stripped of her catapults and arrester gear, while an order came from very high up to destroy all the plans for CVA 01.

The final blow to any hopes the navy might have had of retaining a carrier force came on 1 September 1967, when the appointment of Flag Officer Aircraft Carriers was abolished and replaced by Flag Officer Carriers and Amphibious Ships.

However, the Government was forced to admit that a carrier was still required, and *Ark Royal* was retained in service until 1978, when it was hoped that she might be replaced by some form of aircraft-carrying ship — not to be called a carrier.

In spite of all the gloom, the navy did manage to achieve some credibility during those dark years. On 15 February 1968 the submarine *Resolution* launched the navy's first Polaris missile off Cape Kennedy, Florida, and began her first operational patrol at the end of June. The navy had at long last taken over complete responsibility for deployment of Britain's nuclear deterrent. Towards the end of the year the first of the new air defence destroyers, HMS *Sheffield*, armed with the new Sea Dart surface-to-air missile, was ordered. The ships were to be equipped with a new computer-controlled command centre, the Action Data Automation Weapons System (ADAWS).

Above: In 1971 the carrier *Hermes* was taken in hand for a two-year conversion to a commando carrier to replace the *Albion*. All fixed-wing equipment (catapults, arrestor gear, barriers, landing light system, etc.) was removed, but the angled deck and deck edge lift were retained. The enormous Type 984 radar was removed and replaced by a much smaller Type 965. In addition she was fitted to carry four LCVPs (Landing Craft Vehicle and Personnel) and a complete Royal Marine Commando of about 750 men and their equipment, vehicles, stores, etc. Helicopter complement normally comprised sixteen Wessex V troop-carrying helicopters, together with four Sea King ASW helicopters.

Right: In 1975 the first of a new class of destroyer, the Type 42, was commissioned into the Navy. The lead ship, HMS *Sheffield*, later to be sunk in the Falklands, featured a new 4.5in gun, the new Sea Dart surface-to-air missile, a large air warning radar antenna and was powered by a COGOG (Combined Gas or Gas) installation. Apart from the '*Leander*' class, the Type 42s are the largest class of warship built for the Royal Navy since the Second World War, a total of fourteen having been completed, of which two were sunk in the Falkland Islands conflict. (ACPL)

By early 1970 *Hermes* had been withdrawn from service to be converted into a commando carrier, leaving the navy with just the *Ark Royal* and *Eagle*. It was now becoming clear that the row over whether the navy should have carriers or not had arisen not so much because of the poor financial state of the country, although that was indeed a major concern, but over the Labour Government's 'hidden agenda' — its undeclared intention to withdraw from all overseas bases and commitments. In other words, the whole question of defence cuts devolved from the Government's plans with regard to its future foreign policy.

Although the Government was to be fully committed to NATO, Britain was no longer to view herself as a major international power. Hence the armed forces were to be severely pruned and reorganized to meet their NATO commitment. Under the umbrella of the powerful US forces in Europe, Britain could afford to reduce the strength of her armed forces, and as far as the navy was concerned her ASW capability would be developed to meet this NATO commitment. This, it was argued, was a logical development, for ASW was an expertise in which the navy had excelled since the Second World War, and in which it was considered to be a world leader. In future, therefore, the navy would devote its major effort to developing the nuclear attack submarine — its new capital ship. In meeting its obligation to NATO, the navy's main operational areas would henceforth be confined to the eastern Atlantic and the Iceland-Faroes gap, and to providing ASW support to US Carrier Task Groups operating into the Arctic. Furthermore, the navy's amphibious capability would be committed to supporting NATO forces in Northern Norway. The navy, in fact, would be in the front line facing the growing might of the Soviet navy.

Integral with this new policy was the decision to continue with the design for a replacement for the '*Tiger*' class cruisers, which were being converted to incorporate an ASW capability, deploying helicopters from a large flight deck aft. Meanwhile, development of the V/STOL aircraft which was to emerge as the Harrier was proceeding apace. In the light of this new technology it was considered advisable to make some provision in the new design for V/STOL aircraft, in case they eventually entered service. However, V/STOL aircraft required a runway for take-off in order to increase payload and endurance. Hence, the new vessel would have to have some form of flight deck if she were to be able to operate V/STOL aircraft. So it came about that the new design featured an unobstructed length of flight deck which led to the design being referred to as a 'Through Deck Cruiser' – a carrier in all but name.

Meanwhile, on 25 February 1970 the conventional carrier *Ark Royal* recommissioned following her major refit, which enabled her to operate Phantoms. The refit involved fitting new catapults and arrester gear, a new flight deck, new radars, and other major refurbishments.

In July 1970 a Conservative Government was returned to power, and soon after taking office the new Secretary of State for Defence, Lord Carrington, presented a Supplementary Statement on Defence Policy. In this the Minister noted that Britain would continue to maintain a contribution east of Suez (although this was not to last for long), and that *Ark Royal* would be retained in service until towards the end of the decade, when it was hoped that the new 'Through Deck Cruiser' would enter service. The first these, HMS *Invincible*, was laid down in 1973. In the meantime the Fleet's offensive capability, hitherto vested in strike aircraft, was to be

Left: Coincident with the entry into service of the new destroyers, was a new helicopter for the Fleet Air Arm, developed specifically for operation from the navy's small ships and designed to replace the ubiquitous Wasp. The Lynx has since been developed to undertake a wide variety of roles including anti-submarine and anti-surface vessel. Armed with the Sea Skua anti-ship missile in the latter role, it proved an extremely potent weapon in the recent war with Iraq. The photograph shows a Lynx HAS.3 armed with Stingray lightweight torpedo, two Sea Skua missiles and MAD (Magnetic Anomaly Detection) pod on the outer stub-wing station. (ACPL)

Right: The Sea Harrier VSTOL air-craft first became operational in 1980 with 800 NAS. The Sea Harrier traces its lineage back to 1960 and the first VSTOL aircraft, the P.1127. The first vertical landing of a VSTOL aircraft took place on the previous *Ark Royal* in February 1963. (ACPL)

improved by the purchase of the French Exocet sur-face-to-surface missile.

In 1974 the Conservative Government was again defeated in a general election, and a Labour Government returned to power. Once more the poor financial state of the country had resulted in a change of government. In an attempt to redress the deficit, the Labour Govern-ment instigated another Defence Review aimed at reduc-ing the defence budget still further. Presented in the 1975-76 Defence White Paper, this spelt further shrink-age for the navy. Under the new plans, the numbers of destroyers/frigates and mine countermeasures vessels were to be cut by a seventh, the number of submarines reduced by a quarter, no navy ships would be allocated to NATO in the Mediterranean, and the ships on the Caribbean station would be withdrawn. Plans to build a number of new ships were scrapped, including nine destroyers and frigates, some mine countermeasures ves-sels and five support vessels. The amphibious ships *Bul-wark*, *Hermes*, *Fearless* and *Intrepid* were not to be replaced.

In 1975 Iceland imposed a 200-mile Extended Eco-nomic Zone around the island. Once again this led to bit-ter recriminations between British fishermen and the Icelanders, the 1975-76 'Cod War'. To help police the sit-uation some old frigates were brought forward from the Standby Squadron and given special wooden strengthen-ing in the bows and stern. It was considered that, thus reinforced, they would be able to withstand any colli-sions with Icelandic gunboats in a confrontation. Fortu-nately the dispute ended the following summer without any major incidents.

Late in 1978 *Ark Royal* returned to Devonport to decommission for the last time, marking the end of con-ventional fixed-wing flying in the navy.

The following year the Conservatives were once again returned to power, and at once set about implementing some major changes. The decision was taken to replace the Polaris missile with the Trident, for which a new subma-rine would have to be designed and built, together with new docking and maintenance facilities. In November 1979 full-scale production of a new lightweight torpedo,

Right: Originally planned to replace the '*Leander*' class, the fourteen ships of the Type 22 '*Broadsword*' class (the lead ship is illustrated) are designed as fleet escorts, providing an ocean-going ASW capability, but with a very extensive general pur-pose capability. For their main ASW role the ships are fitted with exten-sive sonar systems, including a towed array sonar, and two triple lightweight torpedo launchers. For general purpose duties the ships are equipped with the short range Sea Wolf anti-air missile (two 6-tube launchers are mounted), and four Exocet anti-ship missile launchers. Extended range ASW and surface attack capability is provide by the two Lynx helicopters that can be car-ried. (ACPL)

the Sting Ray, began, and the Harpoon surface-to-surface missile was ordered.

In June 1979 the first Sea Harrier V/STOL aircraft was delivered to the Fleet Air Arm, and in July 1980 the first of the new 'Through Deck Cruisers', *Invincible*, was commissioned. Just before this, in early 1980, the commando carrier *Hermes* had entered Portsmouth dockyard to undergo conversion to operate the Sea Harrier, re-emerging in June 1981. The carriers were fitted with a new invention, the 'ski-jump' ramp, which allowed the Sea

Harrier to achieve an increase in take-off speed without the need to increase engine power.

The unstable political situation in the near East following the Iranian Revolution led to the decision to re-establish a naval force in the Gulf of Oman. Constituted in October 1980, the Squadron comprised four destroyers or frigates, two of which remained on patrol in the Gulf while the other two underwent rest and basic refit work at a base in Kenya. Support was provided by a tanker of the Royal Fleet Auxiliary.

Above: In July 1980 the navy commissioned the first of a new generation of carriers. The new ships heralded a totally new concept of organic maritime air operations. Their operational capability is centered around the vertical/short take off and landing aircraft, the Sea Harrier, which is intended to provide the fleet's ASW task groups with improved air defence capabilities. Apart from the Sea Harrier, the other main component of the carrier is the long range ASW Sea King. With their Sea Kings, the 'Invincible' class carriers formed the core of the navy's ASW Task Group contribution to the NATO

Alliance until the ending of the Cold War. The illustration shows the second two units of the class, HMSs *Illustrious* (foreground) and *Ark Royal*. (ACPL)

Below: In 1981 the carrier *Hermes* emerged from yet another major reconstruction during which she was given a ski-jump and converted to operate Sea Harrier VSTOL aircraft. She is pictured here leaving Portsmouth for a major NATO exercise at the beginning of January 1983. (ACPL)

Chapter 36

War in the South Atlantic and 'The Way Forward'

During the summer of 1980 the Prime Minister, Margaret Thatcher, had told senior naval officers that the Government intended to redefine the country's defence policy, which would result in greater emphasis being placed on the nation's maritime capability. However, there was a problem in that strong forces had to be maintained in Europe to ensure that the USA did not withdraw her forces from the region.

Then, in January 1981, Mr John Nott was appointed Secretary of State for Defence. It was not long before rumours began to circulate that the navy was to suffer major cuts in its strength. It was said that the destroyer/frigate force would be reduced from 50 to 32 by the end of the decade, one of the new 'Invincible' class carriers would be sold and the other two mothballed on completion, the amphibious fleet would be scrapped, the Royal Marines disbanded, and personnel reduced from 66,400 to 47,000.

The rumours were strenuously denied, but on 25 June 1981 Mr Nott published his defence review *The Way Forward*. The document revealed that the destroyer/frigate force would be reduced from 59 to about 50, of which eight would be in long-term preservation; one of the carriers would be sold and *Hermes* phased out of service as soon as the second 'Invincible' class carrier was commissioned; and during 1982-84 the two amphibious assault ships *Fearless* and *Intrepid* would be phased out and not replaced. It was also stated that plans to carry out half-life modernizations of destroyers and frigates were to be abandoned. However, it was revealed that a new frigate, the Type 23, would be ordered to replace the aging *'Leander'* class, new minesweepers were to be acquired for the RNR, the nuclear submarine attack fleet was to be increased from twelve to seventeen, and a new diesel-electric submarine was to be constructed.

Although not revealed at the time, it was also planned to reduce the destroyer force by a further ten units by the end of the decade. Manpower was to undergo further reduction by almost 20,000 by the end of the decade, leaving a strength of 46,000. No further mention was made of the total disbandment of the Royal Marines, although one Commando unit, No 41 Commando RM, had been disbanded earlier in the year.

The Parliamentary Under Secretary of Defence for the Royal Navy, Mr Keith Speed, spoke out against any proposals to downgrade the navy's capability, and was dismissed. At this the Government took the opportunity to reorganize the political framework of the Ministry of Defence, and replaced all three Service Ministers by a single Minister of State for the Armed Forces. This was major blow to the navy's policymakers, for they no longer had their own political voice to represent their case to Parliament and the public.

Gradually, as the last decade has passed, and particularly in the present stringent financial climate, in which defence is yet again facing heavy cuts, it has become evident that the Government is determined, come what may, to reduce its financial commitments (in other words, is Britain bankrupt?); even to the extent of severely compromising national security. But this perception did not become clear until the beginning of the 1990s.

Right: During the 1980s the navy began to commission a new class of mine warfare vessels the GRP-hulled 'Hunt' class. Although only a few units were operational by the end of the Falklands War, these (then untested) ships sailed south under their own steam and carried out very hazardous operations in extremely environmentally hostile waters, clearing areas of large numbers of mines laid by the Argentine navy. The picture shows three 'Hunt' class MCMVs involved in yet another conflict situation, carrying out operations in the Gulf in support of merchant shipping during the Iraq-Iran war in 1987. (ACPL)

Much was to happen in the interim to lessen the effect of *The Way Forward*. However, that document was to form the basis of yet another review, *Options for Change*, at the beginning of the 1990s. But in 1980-82 much of the political thinking with regard to maritime power appears to have been very disjointed. Although it is not absolutely clear, even some ten years later, it seems that at the time many people confused the role and need for the emerging Trident submarine-based nuclear deterrent with a coherent, balanced, maritime-based policy. At the time the Soviets were just beginning to commission their latest and most powerful nuclear-powered ballistic missile submarine, the *Typhoon*.

It now appears that, for many politicians and policymakers, the main threat was posed by massive nuclear forces, and that in the overriding need to counter this threat conventional forces would have a very minor role to play. In the face of such a threat it was considered that any future war would most probably be nuclear, and would be over within a matter of days, long before any conventional naval forces could be brought into play to influence the situation. There were those, however, who saw through this fallacy and perceived the dangerous waters into which the navy was being forced to steam.

One such voice was that of Admiral Sir James Eberle, C-in-C Naval Home Command. In a lecture to the Royal United Services Institute in October 1981, Admiral Eberle referred to the fact that '... twice in less than twenty years the Government of an island nation has appeared to turn its back on the concepts of maritime power; firstly in 1966 in its withdrawal from east of Suez, and now in the latest decision on the Defence Programme where the reduction of capability falls most heavily on the Navy.' He continued: 'If too many of our warships become too large and too expensive [a veiled reference to the distortions that would be caused by the Trident programme], we breed a defensive mentality, we lose the initiative, we suppress boldness and we rapidly find ourselves bogged down at sea solely in defensive concepts of blockade, by submarine or surface or air barriers, concepts not far from a form of Maginot Line thinking ...'.

Admiral Eberle could not then have foreseen how accurate his prognostication was to be, for towards the end of the 1980s and into the 1990s the Royal Navy has, in fact, become involved in just such a role — maintaining blockades in the Persian Gulf and Adriatic with just the sort of outcome that the politicians failed to foresee; long-drawn-out operations which have created such a major drain on the navy's limited resources. Resources limited by continual piecemeal cuts and reductions, forced on the navy by an ever more restrictive budget.

At the time, the country's leading naval correspondent, Desmond Wettern, commented: 'By the end of the decade the Navy's ability to conduct a war of any duration at sea, or even to maintain the existing level of peacetime commitments, must be doubtful'. Fortunately,

before any further cuts could be implemented, there occurred just the sort of contingency that many had feared might happen, for which the navy would find it difficult to provide the necessary resources.

Early in 1982 events in the South Atlantic began to unfold which would involve the navy in its first full-scale war since Suez in 1956. On 18 March an Argentine navy transport, the *Bahia Buen Suceso*, landed a party of 42 'civilians', some of whom were Marines, on the small island of South Georgia to dismantle a derelict whaling station. In contravention of all legal requirements, the party ran up the Argentine flag on the island. Later, when the transport came to pick up the party, some twelve of them were left behind with their flag still flying. At this, the ice patrol ship HMS *Endurance* landed a party of 22 Royal Marines on the island to 'keep watch' on the party.

On 28 March an Argentine naval task force, including the carrier *Veinticinco de Mayo*, the British-built Type 42 destroyer *Hercules*, two other destroyers, a landing ship and three transports, sailed, so it was claimed, to take part in exercises with the Uruguayan navy. Simultaneously, two French-built missile-armed corvettes sailed for South Georgia to support the Argentine party on the island there. But the main task force, instead of sailing for Uruguay, headed southeast for the Falkland Islands, where they arrived after dark on 1 April. Although the party of Royal Marines on the Falkland Islands put up a spirited resistance, they were no match for the major amphibious assault mounted by the Argentines, and within a day more than 4,000 Argentine troops had landed and captured the islands. Similarly, the small British force on South Georgia was soon overwhelmed, but not before it had inflicted serious damage on an Argentine corvette, *Granville*, and shot down two helicopters. There was little *Endurance* could do, apart from carry out general surveillance and keep out of the way of the Argentine naval forces.

While strenuous diplomatic efforts were entrained to resolve the situation, including the imposition of economic sanctions against Argentina, the British Parliament on 3 April almost unanimously agreed to the despatch of a naval task force some 8,000 miles south to restore the situation.

Meanwhile, Argentina continued to build up her forces on the Falklands. In the UK *Hermes* and *Invincible*, the only two carriers in the navy (construction of the second '*Invincible*' was far advanced, but she would not be ready in time to take part in the operation), were made ready for sea in just three days, sailing for the Falkland Islands on 5 April. The logistic ship *Sir Geraint*, loaded with stores, sailed from Plymouth on the evening of 2 April, within hours of the news of the invasion, and was quickly followed by the fleet oilers *Tidespring*, *Olmeda*, *Appleleaf* and *Pearleaf* and the fleet replenishment ships *Fort Austin*, *Resource* and *Stromness*. *Stromness* was fitted out as a troop transport in a matter of days, and

Right: In April-May 1982 the Royal Navy became involved in its first major 'hot-war' operation since the invasion of Suez in 1956. Again it was up to the navy to land British troops against an enemy well entrenched in an amphibious operation. Never before had the armed services had to respond so quickly and over such a great distance, some 8,000 miles, against an enemy within a very short striking distance of his own home bases. Inevitably, there were losses. One of the most tragic was that of the destroyer HMS *Sheffield*, struck by an Argentine air-launched Exocet missile. The picture shows the burnt-out hulk of the *Sheffield* which was taken in tow but which had to be scuttled subsequently when the weather turned bad. (ACPL)

embarked men of 45 Commando, Royal Marines. The old oiler *Tidepool*, which had been sold to Chile two months earlier but temporarily released by that country, rehoisted the blue ensign to join the growing fleet.

Other ships making up the task force included the destroyers *Antrim*, *Glamorgan*, *Coventry*, *Glasgow* and *Sheffield*, and the frigates *Battleaxe*, *Brilliant*, *Broadsword*, *Ariadne*, *Plymouth* and *Yarmouth*. The assault ship *Intrepid*, already decommissioned and awaiting disposal, was rapidly brought back into service and joined the logistic landing ships *Sir Bedivere*, *Sir Galahad*, *Sir Lancelot*, *Sir Percival* and *Sir Tristram*. The Task Force eventually included 44 warships, 22 RFAs and 45 merchant ships.

By 4 April contingency plans had been put in hand to requisition a number of merchant ships to carry additional troops and equipment. The first to be taken over was the cruise ship *Canberra*, which docked at Southampton on 7 April. She was rapidly converted into a troopship and embarked men of 40 and 42 Commando, Royal Marines, and the 3rd Parachute Battalion. She was followed by the container ship *Elk*, which loaded two troops of the Royal Horse Guards with their Scorpion and Scimitar tracked vehicles and heavy bridging gear of the Royal Engineers. The ferries *Europic* and *Norland* embarked the 2nd Parachute Battalion, while the container ship *Atlantic Conveyor* was converted into a makeshift aircraft carrier to transport 20 Harriers. In the Mediterranean the educational cruise ship *Uganda* disembarked 1,000 school children at Gibraltar and was rapidly fitted out as a hospital ship, subsequently being joined by the converted survey vessels *Hecla*, *Herald* and *Hydra*.

On 12 April a 200-mile Maritime Exclusion Zone came into operation around the Falklands, this being changed to a Total Exclusion Zone (TEZ) on 30 April. Any Argentine vessels found within the zone were liable to be sunk without warning.

On 22 April the destroyer *Antrim*, the frigates *Brilliant* and *Plymouth* and the oiler *Tidespring* left the Task Force

and headed towards South Georgia. On 26 April the first action at sea occurred when helicopters from the warships attacked the Argentine submarine *Santa Fe* on the surface near South Georgia. The submarine was severely damaged, and beached on the island. Later that day Royal Marines and Special Forces (including members of the SBS) recaptured the island.

On 2 May the nuclear-powered submarine *Conqueror* detected the Argentine cruiser *General Belgrano* sailing near the TEZ. Considering that *Belgrano* posed a major threat to the Task Force, the submarine torpedoed her. After this major loss the Argentine navy remained well out of the way of the Task Force, taking no further part in the campaign, although Argentine submarines continued to pose a serious threat to naval operations.

On 4 May the navy suffered its first serious loss when Argentine aircraft carried out a long-range air-launched-missile attack against ships on forward radar picket duty. An Exocet missile fired by an Argentine Super Etendard aircraft struck the destroyer *Sheffield* and started serious fires. In spite of assistance rendered by the frigate *Arrow*, the fires could not be contained, and after some four hours the order was given to abandon ship, twenty of her crew having died in the attack.

By the middle of May the Task Force had established control of the waters around the islands and safely transported the bulk of the troops to the vicinity of the Falklands ready for an amphibious assault. The carriers had proved crucial in establishing sea control, providing essential air defence for the Task Force and attacking enemy shipping and ground forces, while the helicopters on board carried out continuous anti-submarine patrols at a distance from the Task Force, providing early warning of any impending Argentine underwater attack. Meanwhile, men of the SAS and SBS had been inserted by helicopter and submarine to gather intelligence and attack and destroy enemy outposts and aircraft.

On 20 May the main amphibious assault forces began to move towards the islands, the first ashore being men of 3 Commando Brigade, who quickly established a beachhead at San Carlos. The assault was covered by the guns of the Task Force, while Special Forces ashore carried out a series of diversionary raids on various Argentine outposts around East Falkland island. The assault was carried out at four separate points, landing craft ferrying the troops ashore in a continuous stream while helicopters transported an ever-growing mountain of supplies. Complete tactical surprise was achieved, and within a short time more than 5,000 men had been landed in the face of minor opposition. On landing, one of the first tasks was to install well sited anti-aircraft missile units, for it was anticipated that the Argentines would mount heavy air attacks against the mass of vulnerable amphibious shipping concentrated in San Carlos water — shipping which included the great white *Canberra* and the liner *Queen Elizabeth*.

At about midday a series of intense air raids began, and continued for the next few days as the Argentines tried strenuously to interfere with the build-up of the troops ashore. On 21 May the frigate *Ardent* was sunk on the 'gun line' in San Carlos water, followed on 24 May by the frigate *Antelope*, while another six ships were damaged. But heavy losses were also inflicted on the attacking Argentine aircraft, a total of 43 being shot down between 21 and 24 May. An all-out effort was mounted on 25 May, Argentina's National Day, and the destroyer *Coventry* was sunk. This was to be the last major raid against the assault forces in San Carlos waters.

The Argentines now turned their attention to the Task Force operating off the islands. At sea, *Atlantic Conveyor*, carrying vital supplies including replacement helicopters, was struck by two Exocets, set on fire and abandoned. While the troops ashore began the long march towards Port Stanley, at sea the Task Force continued to cover the islands and prevent any further attempt by Argentina to reinforce her troops ashore. The Royal Marine Comman-

dos played a major role, No 45 Commando, with 3rd Parachute Battalion, carrying out a remarkable 50-mile march over extremely inhospitable country, carrying everything on their backs. Using helicopters, 42 Commando Royal Marines leap-frogged forward to secure Mount Kent and Mount Challenger on the western approaches to the capital of the Falkland Islands, Port Stanley.

When it was found that the Argentines had evacuated Fitzroy settlement, it was decided to secure the area as rapidly as possible. It was at this point that the loss of the large Chinook troop transport helicopters carried aboard *Atlantic Conveyor* was most tragically felt. It was for just such a purpose that they had been sent south, and in this instance they would have been used to airlift the bulk of 5 Brigade to the area. As a consequence, to get as many troops as far forward as possible it became necessary to mount another amphibious landing. For this the 2nd Battalion Scots Guards and the 1st Battalion Welsh Guards were transported to Fitzroy aboard the assault ships *Fearless* and *Intrepid*. The bulk of the troops were landed during the nights of 5-6 and 6-7 June. Bad weather then descended, and the remainder of the Welsh Guards were transported to Bluff Cove, just beyond Fitzroy, aboard the logistic landing ships *Sir Galahad* and *Sir Tristram*. Unfortunately the cloud lifted on 8 June, before the last of the troops were able to disembark from the landing ships. The Argentine air force found the ships in this exposed and vulnerable position, and carried out a devastating air raid which resulted in *Sir Galahad* being set on fire and burned out with the loss of 50 men, 32 of them Welsh Guards, and *Sir Tristram* being severely damaged. Many lives were saved by the heroic efforts of helicopter pilots who flew into the thick, acrid smoke to tow liferafts clear of the stricken vessel and lift men off the burning deck.

Ashore, the troops began the hard battle for Mount Longdon, preparatory to investing Port Stanley. At sea, naval vessels carried out long-range bombardment of

Left: The assault ship *Fearless* in San Carlos Sound – referred to by all who were there as 'bomb alley' – suffers a near miss from a bomb dropped by an Argentine Dagger (Mirage) aircraft. (ACPL)

other Argentine targets ashore. During the night of 11-12 June, as the destroyer *Glamorgan* was withdrawing from bombarding shore positions around Port Stanley, she was struck aft by an Exocet missile launched from a shore battery. A severe fire started, which was quickly put out by the crew, but thirteen men died in the attack. This was the last attack suffered by the Task Force. The following night the Argentine forces ashore surrendered. Although the campaign had ended, there was still much work to do, and the navy's minehunters were busily engaged for some months afterwards, sweeping the waters around the Falklands.

In his book *The Decline of British Seapower*, published in the middle of the South Atlantic campaign (Operation Corporate), Desmond Wettern commented; '... there can be no one in Britain who does not now realize that the navy remains vital for a nation dependent upon the seas to uphold her interests and, indeed, in time of war to ensure her very survival'. Telling words indeed, at a time when all seemed set for the navy to be severely pruned in the interests of the national economy and on what would now appear to have been misguided foreign policy motives. Indeed, the South Atlantic conflict could not have occurred at a more apposite moment for the navy, for it gave a very clear demonstration of the importance of sea power to Britain. To transport two fully armed and equipped brigades across 8,000 miles of sea, carry out an opposed landing, and then continue to support those troops until they had secured all of their objectives, and completely to deny the enemy the use of the sea after sinking one of its major units, while containing a very major threat from an heroic air force and suffering heavy losses in the process, more than vindicated those who advocated the maintenance of a well balanced, well armed, and well equipped and trained navy. But within a few the years the dissenters were once again making their views known, voicing the opinion that the Falklands conflict was a one-off scenario that was unlikely to be repeated, and that the main effort should continue to be concentrated on dealing with the Soviet nuclear-powered ballistic missile submarine threat.

How wrong these assessments were to prove some ten years later, when the navy was once again called upon, this time in concert with other navies at the behest of the UN, to oppose the Iraqi invasion of Kuwait. This was followed shortly after by the fall of the communist governments in Eastern Europe and a complete realignment of military power in the region. But again, all this was in the future and could not be foreseen.

In the intervening years much effort was devoted to absorbing the lessons from the South Atlantic conflict. By the end of 1982 the Government had published a Supplementary Defence White Paper, *The Falklands Campaign: The Lessons*. The opening paragraph of the section entitled 'The Lessons' at once struck a discord as far as the navy's future was concerned, noting that the campaign

was unique and that any lessons drawn must be set against the nation's main defence priority of operating within NATO together with our allies to counter the Soviet threat. However, this was frequently ignored in the years to come, as the navy set about implementing its own lessons from the campaign.

The first, and most important lesson was that the navy now had first-hand experience of war at sea in the missile age — an experience which no other navy could at that time claim. Secondly, it was the first time since 1956 that the navy had had to undertake large-scale amphibious operations using purpose-built assault ships supported by suitably converted merchant ships to supplement the other landing ships. Examining the maritime operations, the White Paper concentrated on the amphibious aspect and the role played by the nuclear-powered submarines. The emphasis placed on the sinking of the obsolete cruiser *General Belgrano* by *Conqueror*, and the subsequent reluctance of the Argentine navy to venture outside its bases, might now be seen to have created a somewhat distorted view of the role that SSNs might play in a future maritime conflict. This may, perhaps, have played a part in the subsequent discussions concerning the need to build up the SSN fleet, even at the expense of the surface fleet. This is not to say that other aspects of the campaign were ignored or completely played down, but the part played by the SSNs does, in retrospect, seem to have been somewhat overstated.

Many lessons were learned from the campaign. Some of the most important related to damage control and the need to counter the rapid spread of fire and smoke; the need to update electronic warfare systems and fully integrate them with the whole command and control function of the ship to counter anti-ship missiles; the need to improve air defence capabilities and update existing surface-to-air missiles and their control systems; the value of airborne early warning and the need to introduce new close-in air defence systems; the value of organic air support to provide not just air cover for the fleet, but also strike capabilities in support of ground troops; the value of the helicopter and the need for a good, modern, medium-sized helicopter troop transport; the importance of naval gunfire support to troops ashore and in amphibious operations; and, finally, the need to improve shallow water anti-submarine warfare capabilities. A number of weapons systems were proved, including the Sea Wolf and Sea Dart surface-to-air missiles and the Sea Skua anti-ship missile.

Many of the recommendations were to be introduced into the fleet over the next ten years, and in addition the Government approved, after some discussion, the need to replace vessels lost during the campaign. In doing this, the opportunity was taken to improve existing designs such as the Type 42 air defence destroyer and Type 22 anti-submarine frigate along the lines suggested in the White Paper, while a larger and improved landing ship logistic was also ordered and plans were drawn up for substantial modernization of the remaining vessels.

The value of converting merchant ships into auxiliary warships and for supporting maritime operations was also noted, but little was done in the succeeding years to ensure that the nation possessed the right types of ship for similar conversions, should the need arise again.

On the question of the future, the White Paper noted that the amphibious capability of 3 Commando Brigade offered a greatly improved ability to respond rapidly to unexpected crises in a flexible way. That that would be so depended primarily on the navy's amphibious shipping capability, which was then invested in the two old assault ships *Fearless* and *Intrepid*, supported by a number of landing ships logistic. The value of *Fearless* and *Intrepid* was highlighted in the White Paper, which announced that the two assault ships were to be retained in service and would remain an important element in the country's amphibious capability. Nothing, however, was mentioned about their replacement, which was becoming a matter of some urgency. The Paper also noted that, although the Government would have liked to have achieved more in the amphibious area, there was little that could have been achieved given the limited margin in the defence budget for such additions over recent years.

In view of the necessity to ensure that two carriers were always available for deployment at short notice, a requirement shown up by Operation Corporate, the Government announced that it would not go ahead with the sale of HMS *Invincible*. The Paper also announced that ships lost in the campaign would be replaced by new orders, the two Type 42 destroyers and two Type 21 frigates being replaced by four Type 22 frigates, three of which were to be of the Batch III design, fitted with a 4.5in gun and close-in weapons systems which the campaign had shown to be necessary. The landing ship logistic *Sir Galahad*, sunk at Bluff Cove, was also to be replaced by a new and larger design, while *Sir Tristram* was to be brought back to the UK and repaired and enlarged. In addition, all aircraft losses were to be made good. Even more important was a note to the effect that the front-line strength of the navy was to be maintained at a level of 55 frigates and destroyers, at least until 1984, previous plans to put four ships in the Standby Squadron being dropped.

In general terms, the Paper emphasized that in future the navy, although retaining its role in the Eastern Atlantic and Channel as its primary objective, would nevertheless postulate a major capability for 'out of area' operations.

These were ambitious plans, but unfortunately a worsening economic situation began to play havoc with the programme, and seriously delayed or prevented important parts of it being implemented. The first signs that all was not well financially appeared in 1983, when £230 million was slashed off the defence budget, in spite of the commitment to 3 per cent growth in real terms in defence, made in the aftermath of the Falklands Campaign.

In spite of financial problems, however, the navy was determined to take to heart the Government's note in the White Paper about 'out of area' operations. Almost imperceptibly it began to evolve a new 'out of area' role for itself, attempting to maintain a balanced fleet to meet this concept for its future. In a remarkably accurate forecast of what was to happen in the early part of the next decade, the Vice-Chief of Naval Staff, Vice-Admiral Sir Peter Stanford, at a Conference in the autumn of 1983, stated; 'Did not the Falklands Campaign teach you something about the need to react to the contingent circumstances of an uncertain and violent world, outside the

Below: In July 1981 the first of a new class of much quieter nuclear-powered attack submarines, the *Trafalgar*, was launched, being commissioned in May 1983. The '*Trafalgar*' class have had their hulls coated with sound-absorbing acoustic tiles to reduce their sound signature. The picture shows HMS *Tireless*, which was commissioned in October 1985. (ACPL)

institutionalized Euro-Atlantic situation, in areas where conflict is still endemic?' Then, in July 1985, the magazine *Navy International* published an interview between this author and the First Sea Lord, Admiral Fieldhouse, in which the Admiral noted that the role of the navy had not changed much over the years, stating; 'It has always been one of defence of British interests, and deterrence to potential enemies, world-wide'. The Admiral concluded; '... this has increased many fold'. Both Admirals were emphatic that a balanced fleet, including nuclear submarines, organic air, mine warfare forces, anti-aircraft and anti-submarine surface forces and an amphibious capability were essential to the future security of the nation.

As if to prove the point, soon after the ending of the Falklands Campaign the navy became more heavily embroiled in yet another region of conflict. This time it was the Persian Gulf, where Iraq and Iran were at war, massive air strikes using air-to-surface missiles being mounted against oil installations and tankers. To counter the threat, and ensure the safety of British-flagged tankers in the area, the Armilla Patrol was strengthened.

But while the navy was busy establishing its case for 'out of area' operations and the need to maintain a relatively strong, balanced fleet to meet those commitments, the national economy was running into severe difficulties. With inflation starting to rise at an alarming rate, the 1985 White Paper made it clear that no more money would be made available for defence, and the planned 3 per cent growth in the defence budget was abandoned.

Along with it went many plans and projects. As the economic situation worsened during 1985, fears were expressed that defence decisions were beginning to be based on short-term financial considerations, instead of on the preparation a long-term defence plan for the nation's security. This became apparent in a major slowing down in the rate of ordering new ships which were urgently needed to rejuvenate an ageing fleet. Also alarming was the rising cost of modernizations, refits and maintenance, which resulted in yet more cuts and a consequent downgrading in effectiveness.

To replace the obsolescent frigates/destroyers, it was necessary to order at least three such ships each year. In fact only nine ships had been ordered since 1979, of which four were specially ordered to replace the losses suffered during Falklands Campaign. Only one of the nine was a new design, HMS *Norfolk*, the first Type 23, which was ordered in October 1984. Orders for more Type 23s were not placed until July 1986, and this against an ever-increasing number of older vessels which were being set aside for sale or scrap. It was becoming increasingly difficult to maintain the number of operational destroyers/frigates at the level of 55 planned in the White Paper on the Falklands, and the commitment to maintaining a sizeable force of frigates and destroyers withered. The old frigates reprieved as a result of the Falklands Campaign were eventually withdrawn from service by 1985, by which time the frigate/destroyer force strength stood at 40. By 1986 this had slumped to 34, and continued to decline gradually throughout the decade, although in part redressed in the early 1990s as the Type 23s began to come on stream.

Apart from the last of the 'County' class destroyers and Type 12 frigates which were decommissioned, a number of '*Leanders*' and '*Ton*' class mine countermeasures vessels were relegated to the Standby Squadron. The submarine fleet, on the other hand, received a major boost to its strength with the ordering of the seventh '*Trafalgar*' class nuclear attack submarine and three more '*Upholder*' class

Below: HMS *Norfolk*, the first of the new 'Duke' class Type 23 frigates, was commissioned in 1990. The class features extensive stealth technology designed to reduce acoustic, radar and infra red signatures. The vessels carry a powerful armament including Harpoon surface-to-surface missiles, a 4.5in gun, vertical launch Sea Wolf anti-air missiles, and Stingray light-weight torpedoes. Problems in developing a comprehensive command and control suite led to the first seven vessels of the class to be completed without a fully automated weapon and sensor coordinating system, to be retro-fitted at refit stage. The ships are capable of carrying the large Merlin helicopter. (ACPL)

Above: By the late 1970s it had become necessary to consider a replacement for the 'Oberon' class diesel electric submarines. The outcome of these deliberations was the four boats of the 'Upholder' class, the first of which, HMS Upholder (illustrated here) was commissioned in June 1990. Later that year the need to reduce defence expenditure resulted in plans for further orders for the class being dropped, and in 1993, in the wake of the end of the Cold War, and with further defence cuts necessary, it was announced that the four 'Upholders' were to be put up for sale or lease and disposed of by 1995. (ACPL)

ward Defence' the navy would be required to deploy ASW forces far up into the Arctic Circle, hundreds of miles in advance of the main US carrier strike fleet. That this was, in effect, a suicide mission in the face of the might of the Soviet naval air arm, against which the navy had very, very limited anti-aircraft capability, was conveniently forgotten.

Gradually, however, some of the improvements forecast as a result of the Falklands Campaign began to filter through to the Fleet during the mid- to late 1980s. Most of the major surface units eventually received close-in weapon systems for point defence (Phalanx and subsequently Goalkeeper, which became the preferred fit), the Harpoon long-range anti-ship missile for both surface ship and submarine deployment, large flight decks in new frigate/destroyer construction to accommodate a new ASW helicopter to replace the ageing Sea King, towed array sonar, and a new command system.

Concerning the last of these, however, the Falklands experience, together with the vast improvements in target detection then being offered by the new towed-array sonar and advanced signal processing, led to demands for a much improved command system (Computer Assisted Command System – CACS 4) with very high capability. In the event, industry found itself unable to develop a sufficiently advanced and reliable system to meet the navy's demands. Working at the very limits of technology, the system as developed failed to achieve the capabilities the navy had specified. As a result the project was cancelled in 1987, and a new specification drawn up for which new tenders were invited. The whole argument over the command system developed into a major scandal, and even at the time of writing the new system, Surface Ship Command System (SSCS), has still not entered service with the Fleet, and a number of the navy's latest frigates, the Type 23, are in operational service without an integrated command and control suite, which is still under development.

Apart from the debacle which developed over the command system, the question mark over the navy's amphibious capability remained unresolved. One of the main features of flexibility in amphibious operations highlighted by the Falklands Campaign was the need for some form of vessel with a helicopter capability to embark and transport commandos rapidly. The other major requirement was to replace Fearless and Intrepid with a new landing platform dock (LPD) design. Studies for a new LPD began in 1984, but were soon overshadowed by the need for a new helicopter assault ship (Hermes had been converted from such a role before the Falklands – see above, page 232), and no decision was made concerning replacements for Fearless and Intrepid. With two major programmes competing for an ever-diminishing defence budget, the MoD procrastinated further, unable to decide whether to embark on a merchant ship conversion for the helicopter assault ship or opt for a new design.

diesel electric submarines, while the 'Oberon' class conventional boats had their capabilities considerably improved by a new sonar suite and fire control system.

The Government, however, refused to be 'rushed' into a review of defence policies and commitments because of the worsening economic situation. As a result there was a constant 'nibbling away' of the navy's assets, and its aspirations for an 'out of area' role began to look increasingly hopeless. If the 'out of area' role were to be abrogated, then the whole concept of a 'balanced' fleet might be called into question, for within the NATO context the main role of the navy was anti-submarine warfare, with a secondary amphibious capability to support the Northern Flank in Norway. But under the new US concept of 'For-

Eventually, in 1986, it was announced that £450 million was being set aside in the long term costings budget to provide for two container ship conversions for the helicopter assault ship and two replacements for *Fearless* and *Intrepid*, with, in addition, a feasibility study into carrying out a service-life extension refit for the two assault ships. At the end of 1986 it was announced that the amphibious capability was to be retained, and once again the threat of disbandment of the Royal Marines receded. But no final decision was made concerning the amphibious ships.

In the meantime, a new *Sir Galahad* had been built and *Sir Tristram* repaired, and by the turn of the decade it had been decided to give the remaining landing ships logistic a service life extension refit although here too financial difficulties are currently playing havoc with the timescale. But the concept of Ships Taken Up From Trade (STUFT) for amphibious operations was quietly shelved and left to gather dust as the country's registered merchant tonnage continued its dramatic decline.

Progress, however, was made in the field of mine warfare, although by the latter part of the decade this, too,

fell on hard times. A new class of minesweeper was designed and built to be manned by the RNR, while work began on the design of a new single-role minehunter. In fact, it was planned that the mine warfare forces would be given a major boost, the planned strength being twelve new minesweepers, fifteen 'Hunt' class mine countermeasures vessels and twenty of the new single-role minehunters.

It was also intended to purchase a new OPV design for general purpose duties to meet the 'out of area' requirement. However, with the increasingly heavy cuts being demanded in the defence budget, and with the Trident ballistic missile submarine programme beginning to devour an ever larger portion of the navy's defence budget, the OPV project was quietly shelved in spite of many protestations. In April 1986 the first of the new Trident submarines, HMS *Vanguard*, was ordered.

Another programme to fall victim to increasing pressures on the defence budget was the single-role minehunter project, which suffered a major delay. The first unit, HMS *Sandown*, was ordered in August 1985, and was followed by an order for four more vessels in July 1987. It

Right: During the early to mid-1980s the navy began to commission a class of steel-hulled minesweepers for deep-team sweeping. Known as the 'River' class, these small vessels were designed to clear deep water passages to the major bases. The illustration shows the first of class to be commissioned, the *Waveney*. (ACPL)

Right: The 'Sandown' class single role minehunters (HMS *Sandown*, commissioned in June 1989, is illustrated) were designed to hunt and destroy mines in deep water. The hulls are of GRP, and the vessels carry a large variable depth mine-hunting sonar housed in a well in the hull, and a remote controlled underwater vehicle for mine destruction. (ACPL)

was planned to order a second batch of minehunters in July 1990, but at the time of writing no order has yet been placed for these vessels, although they are expected to be ordered in 1994; a slippage of some four years.

The ending of the Cold War, the collapse of the Soviet Union and the decline in the threat from the Warsaw Pact, coupled with the major economic threat of inflation, led the Treasury to demand that £650 million be slashed from the defence budget. This was £300 million more than the Ministry of Defence had anticipated. Responding to the critical economic situation and Treasury demands for a 'Peace Dividend' and reduction in defence spending, the Defence Secretary, Tom King, carried out a Review of defence priorities in the Spring of 1990. This resulted in the publication in the summer of a defence review entitled *Options for Change*. The review promulgated cuts for all three services which were to be implemented over a five-year period.

For the navy the immediate effect was to result in the paying-off for disposal by the end of 1990 of a *'Leander'* class frigate, one nuclear and two diesel electric submarines, two reserve *'Ton'* class minehunters, two patrol craft and the seabed operations vessel *Challenger*. It was also planned that the destroyer/frigate force would be reduced from 47 to about 40, while the submarine fleet would be cut from 17 nuclear and 11 diesel electric boats to 12 nuclear and 4 diesel electric by 1995. Other categories (the carriers, mine countermeasures vessels and the Fleet Air Arm), however, would remain more or less intact. The Westland Lynx helicopter would remain in service until well into the next century, following its major mid-life upgrade. The Defence Secretary also stated unequivocally that it was the intention to retain an amphibious capability 'in the longer term', which was merely repeating what a previous Defence Secretary had stated in December 1986. He also repeated comments he made in the 1990 Defence Estimates that it was hoped to place an order for the LPH, with studies continuing into replacements for *Fearless* and *Intrepid*.

But all defence planning was soon to be thrown into complete confusion. The chill 'wind of change' which began to blow in the late 1980s under Soviet President Gorbachev, with his twin concepts of *Glasnost* and *Perestroika*, suddenly became a roaring Russian gale as the decade turned and the whole communist edifice in the east crumbled and was swept away, and with it the Cold War concept of the Warsaw Pact confronting NATO. Amid these mind-blowing changes there arose yet another international crisis in the Middle East, when Iraq invaded the tiny sheikhdom of Kuwait. In the confusion over the collapse of Soviet-style communism it seemed as if the concept of 'out of area' operations for the navy was being vindicated yet once more. As if these problems were not enough, the recession which had slowly been eating away at the British economy now began to be felt with increasing severity.

In the face of increasing difficulties with the defence budget the navy was once again being called upon to intervene in a major way in 'out of area' operations. Throughout the latter part of 1990 considerable effort was devoted to building up the land and air forces in Saudi Arabia in support of UN resolutions designed to force Iraq to withdraw from Kuwait. These resolutions relied on a military and economic blockade of Iraq to achieve their objective, and in this the Royal Navy played a leading role, intercepting shipping bound to and from Iraq and inspecting their cargoes. Yet again there was an implied, if not direct, threat to maritime trade, in particular to the transport of oil through a very sensitive region of the world. The reality and potential effects of a maritime economic blockade was one in which Britain had considerable experience, having twice this century been virtually brought to a point of surrender by such a strategy. But maritime blockade takes time to become effective, and time is not always on the side of the nation imposing it. However, it would be misleading to draw any long-term conclusions from maritime blockade operations in the Gulf in 1990, because, according to some observers the entire scenario, both strategically and geographically, was unique. But every crisis is, in its own way, unique, and it is for just this sort of contingency that a balanced naval force is required, as was argued by Admirals Stanford and Fieldhouse in the early 1980s.

As in so many cases, time and patience ran out, and before the full effect of the maritime blockade could be tested in a modern scenario, the Coalition forces were at war with Iraq. Naval forces now had a much more important role to play than merely enforcing a maritime blockade. At once the difficulties of operating large naval forces in a closed sea such as the Persian Gulf became apparent. Previous experience during the Iran-Iraq war dictated that surface forces would face a major threat from air-launched anti-ship missiles. In addition, Iraq was known to have a large stockpile of naval mines, experience in the Iran-Iraq war having given clear indication of such a capability. The mine threat, combined with the air threat, in confined shallow waters near the head of the Persian Gulf, caused major problems for the naval planners and was to dominate naval tactics, and even strategy to some extent, during the very short war.

Air defence was obviously a major priority, together with some form of mine countermeasures capability. The Americans were also keen to project their amphibious capability, offering the option of landing a major force behind enemy lines to the north of Kuwait City while the bulk of the Iraqi army in Kuwait faced the Coalition forces to the south, the classic manoeuvre of cutting the enemy's lines of communication with his home bases and supplies. But it was not to be. Two US Navy ships, one of them an amphibious assault ship, were badly damaged by mines in the Gulf. At this, all thought of carrying out an amphibious operation was abandoned, although

Right: A vertical launch Sea Wolf missile being fired from one of the tubes in HMS *Norfolk*. The Harpoon launcher can be seen behind. The vertical launch system offers a very rapid response at short range to an incoming missile or aircraft threat.

the possibility was kept alive in order to tie down Iraqi forces, and prevent their forces in the main defensive line facing south from being strengthened.

In the meantime, 'Hunt' class mine countermeasures vessels of the Royal Navy were hard at work, spearheading naval operations at the head of the Gulf, sweeping channels clear of mines to enable major surface units of the Coalition to carry out long-range bombardment of Iraqi positions ashore from a position of relative safety. The minehunting operations also allowed the Royal Navy to operate surface ships far ahead of the other naval forces, to provide an advanced air defence and surface warning barrier. In a series of brilliant operations, Lynx helicopters of the Fleet Air Arm carried out a series of devastating attacks on Iraqi naval units, using Sea Skua anti-ship missiles. Almost at the end of the short conflict Iraqi troops fired two Chinese-manufactured Silkworm anti-ship missiles at HMS *Gloucester*, operating in the northern Gulf. Fortunately the missiles were detected in time for Sea Dart missiles to be fired from *Gloucester* to intercept the incoming missiles. One was destroyed, and the other disappeared off the radar screen.

With the conclusion of the Gulf War the navy was back to fighting its corner for whatever slice of a continually diminishing defence budget it could command, while at the same time trying to nullify the effects of the *Options for Change* review. As far as policy was concerned, the navy still held the view that 'out of area' operations might well be its *raison d'être* in the future. This was a concept that was gaining increasing credence in the light of the collapse of the Warsaw Pact. In January 1991 Admiral Benjamin Bathurst, in a briefing to journalists just before taking up his post as Vice-Chief of the Defence Staff, spoke about the maritime aspects of NATO's future in the light of the collapse of the Warsaw Pact. NATO's major maritime commitments had been maintenance of

the integrity of the sea lines of communication, protection of NATO's seaborne nuclear deterrent, and sea control. For the future the Admiral noted that NATO strategy must continue to contribute to enhancing stability. In pursuance of this objective the Alliance's maritime strategy would have to reflect increased emphasis on flexibility, mobility and crisis management. The Admiral also noted, significantly, that Western lifelines stretched beyond the Alliance's boundaries, and that these would assume increasing importance. According to the Admiral, mobility and logistics would be key items in the future. The Admiral also noted that areas of instability were of vital interest to NATO members and impacted significantly on Western European security. He commented; 'Naval forces provided presence, visibility and the overt capability to ensure the integrity of vital trade routes. They have also provided power projection or defensive escort service.'

Sadly, his views fell on deaf ears. The combined effects of a bitter recession, clamourings for a greater 'Peace Dividend' in the wake of the collapse of the Warsaw Pact, and indecision within political circles right across Europe as to what their future foreign policies should be now that the threat from the Warsaw Pact had virtually disappeared, rapidly led to a massive downturn in defence spending, and hence a reduction in capabilities. For the Royal Navy further swingeing cuts were planned, orders for new ships delayed yet again, and large cuts in manpower planned.

In the midst of all this, the politicians yet again called on the navy to pursue a major foreign policy objective, this time in concert with other NATO and Western European Union allies. The new assignment was to help enforce another naval blockade in support of economic sanctions, this time against the former states of Yugoslavia, where a bitter civil war raged.

The 1992 Defence Estimates picked up on Admiral Bathurst's point regarding mobility and flexibility, the message being that in the future Britain's armed forces would be smaller but more mobile, flexible and better equipped. What no one has so far pointed out is that there comes a point when small forces become so small that they are no longer mobile or flexible. Since 1992 this has become increasingly apparent in the Royal Navy, where more and more ships, including vital fleet support units, are being decommissioned without being replaced. It is true that a smaller fleet requires less logistic support, but if that, too, becomes too small, then the few warships available can no longer be adequately supported at sea.

Emphasis continues to be placed, rightly, on an adequate anti-submarine warfare capability, but the means to prosecute that capability continue to be eroded. The navy still relies on its aged Westland Sea King helicopters for ASW, and the new EH 101 Merlin helicopter will not be operational until at least the middle of the decade. A new nuclear attack submarine project was abandoned and replaced by a Batch II 'Trafalgar' design, but there was no indication as to when orders for these would be placed. It is uncertain for how long the 'Swiftsure' boats can be kept in commission, although the 1992 Estimates noted that they would be updated and kept in service for the rest of the decade, by which time most of them would have been in service for well over twenty years.

Nor has there been any major comment in either the 1992 or 1993 Defence Estimates regarding a replacement carrier design for the three 'Invincibles', the first of which will be twenty years old at the turn of the century. Furthermore, no decision has been taken regarding a follow-on to the Sea Harrier, currently being given a major mid-life upgrade. The strength of the destroyer/frigate force was quoted as being 40, but it was noted that a new air-defence frigate design was under consideration, in a joint venture with France, to replace the Type 42 air-defence destroyer at the turn of the century.

While emphasis was placed on mobility and flexibility incorporating logistic support, the 1992 Estimates had to admit that the first of the new one-stop replenishment ships was still under construction, some 5½ years after having been laid down.

If the 1992 Defence Estimates were complacent regarding the state of the navy and its future, the 1993 Estimates were devastating in their effect. The continuing decline in the country's economic fortunes finally struck home. All of the armed forces faced severe cuts, the heaviest falling on the navy. Paradoxically entitled *Defending our Future*, the 1993 Estimates announced that all four 'Upholder' class conventional submarines would be withdrawn from service and put up for sale or lease (the last of them having only just been commissioned), together with some five destroyers and frigates, the latter being the remaining three Type 21s and two 'Leanders'.

The Estimates stated that part of the defence policy was to contribute to the promotion of the UK's wider security interests through the maintenance of international peace and stability in concert with our Allies. Such tasks have, in the past, fallen firstly and often primarily on the Royal Navy. Comment was also made regarding 'out of area' operations. However, the Defence Ministry now considered that there was no distinction between 'in' and 'out' of area. What would count in future crises was the degree to which British and Allied interests were involved, and the implications for international peace and stability.

As a rationale for the cuts, the paper noted that, as a result of the demise of the Warsaw Pact, a major external threat of Cold War dimensions was '... even more unlikely to re-emerge in the forseeable future than seemed to be the case in 1991'. The Estimates went on to

Left: Currently undergoing trials is the navy's next generation helicopter, the Merlin. The Merlin will operate primarily in the ASW role but will have a secondary anti-surface ship capability. (ACPL)

Right: The newest ship currently under construction for the Royal Navy is HMS *Ocean*, a helicopter assault ship. Its primary role is to carry and support a squadron of helicopters for an amphibious assault operation with Royal Marine Commandos. The ship will have capacity to carry and offload the Marines' vehicles and heavy equipment. (ACPL)

note that previous planning assumptions could therefore be changed, with increased reliance being placed on forces held at a lower state of readiness and a number of selective reductions being made in force levels beyond those provided for under *Options for Change*.

One of the areas considered suitable for reduction concerned the likely scale of ASW operations required in the North Atlantic, for which only twelve active submarines would be required, rather than the sixteen previously planned; hence the four brand new 'Upholder' class conventional submarines could be withdrawn from service. The Paper also noted that, although sophisticated ASW capability remained important, future emphasis would be on modern, high capability, versatile vessels which could be deployed worldwide 'to undertake a broad range of operations'. The Paper then commented that such operations could be undertaken by a force of some 35 destroyers and frigates — a further reduction of five units in the numbers planned. However, the paper did note that further orders for Type 23 frigates were planned. But what is always omitted in discussions concerning numbers is the fact that, at any one time, three or more units will always be under short- or long-term refit, while another three or so will be working up or on training, and yet more will be in transit to their area of operations. Hence, the actual number available for immediate despatch to any area will be very much less than the 35 stated, probably only about 25.

On the question of mine countermeasures forces, the Estimates did note that further single-role minehunters would be procured, although it did not say when, and also noted that the 'Hunt' class would be given a mid-life update. On the other hand, the twelve 'River' class minesweepers were to be paid off, as they were no longer considered cost-effective.

In pursuance of flexibility and mobility discussed in the 1992 Estimates, the 1993 Estimates noted that a contract had been awarded for the design and construction of a new helicopter carrier, HMS *Ocean*, while project definition studies to replace the assault ships *Intrepid* and *Fearless* were to continue. Yet further delays in replacing these already very over-age vessels.

To conclude, at the end of November 1993 the Chancellor of the Exchequer presented a new form of all-in-one budget, addressing both income and expenditure. His aim was to reduce the nation's £50 billion deficit. Not surprisingly, defence was yet again the target for cuts. These will amount to about £1.3 billion over the three years 1994-97, some £500 million less than anticipated. Nevertheless the cuts will undoubtedly result in significant reductions in the navy's capability, in spite of the Defence Secretary's comment that the main cuts would be concentrated on the support services and not the front line. As if to emphasis this point, he also announced that up to seven minehunters were to be procured, four firm orders being placed shortly, with options on another three.

There was an immediate cut of £110 million in the current financial year's budget, while £230 million would be cut from the 1994 budget and £520 million from the 1995 budget — about £200 million more than expected. Planned cuts proposed for 1996 would seem to be about £250 million, much less than the £700 million anticipated, but a lot can happen in three years. The net outcome of these latest cuts will be yet further reductions in the procurement of equipment and systems, and cancellation of some projects. Against what appears to be a less savage cut than anticipated, considerable fears remain that, towards the end of the decade, further major cuts in the defence budget will have to be made, in which the navy will have to take its share, with yet further reductions in its capability and capacity to respond to international crises which may threaten the security of the nation.

Appendixes

APPENDIX 1: COMPARISON OF MAIN ARMAMENT OF 1880

Ship	Calibre	Length	Wt	Wt of shell lb	Muzzle vel ft/sec	Muzzle energy ft-tons	Penetration of compound armour at 20,000yds
Inflexible	16in ML	18cal	81 tons	1,684	1,590	29,530	15in
Benbow	16.25in BL	30cal	110 tons	1,800	2,148	57,580	19in
Anson	13.5in BL	30cal	67 tons	1,250	2,025	35,560	17in
Majestic	12in BL	35cal	46 tons	850	2,367	33,940	
Colossus	12in BL	25cal	45 tons	714	2,000	18,060	12.5in
Imperieuse	9.2in BL	25cal	22 tons	380	1,809	8,622	10in

APPENDIX 2: THE BOARD OF ADMIRALTY

First Lord	MP	In overall charge of the Admiralty
First Sea Lord	Naval post	Responsible for fighting and sea-going efficiency of the Fleet. Chief professional advisor of the First Lord
Second Sea Lord	Naval post	Responsible for the manning and training of RN personnel
Third Sea Lord ships,	Naval post	Responsible for the design of all (also Controller) aircraft and airships
Fourth Sea Lord	Naval post	Responsible for naval transport and stores
First Civil Lord	MP	Responsible for all shore works and buildings and the Royal Hospital at Greenwich
Second Civil Lord	MP	Responsible for handling contracts (Post created 1912, and dockyard business abolished 1917)
Parliamentary and (Abolished 1959 and duties absorbed by Civil Lord)	MP	Responsible for the Service Financial Secretary Estimates
Permanent Secretary	Civil servant	Responsible for general office organisaiton, procedure, precedent, etc

APPENDIX 3: REORGANISATION OF THE HOME FLEET, 1909

Nore Division	First Division	Based at the Nore
Channel Fleet	Second Division	Based at Portland
Nucleus Crew Vessels	Third Division	Based at Portsmouth & Devonport
Special Reserve Ships	Fourth Division	Based at Portsmouth & Devonport
Atlantic Fleet		Extension of Home Fleet and based on new port at Dover

The Home Fleet was made up of sixteen fully-manned and eight nucleus crew battleships, ten fully-manned and ten nucleus crew armoured cruisers (including three battlecruisers). The Atlantic Fleet was made up of six battleships and four armoured cruisers.

APPENDIX 4: STRENGTH AND DISPOSITION, AUGUST 1914

Home Waters
Grand Fleet

Battle Squadrons	(5)
Dreadnoughts	21
PreDreadnoughts	12
Battlecruiser Squadrons	(1)
Battlecruisers	4
Cruiser Squadrons	(4)
Armoured cruisers	8
Light cruisers	6
Destroyer Flotillas	(4)
Light cruisers (attached)	5
Destroyers	76
Miscellaneous Forces	
Cruisers	8
Destroyers	16
Torpedo gunboats	10
Armed yachts	1
Armed boarding steamer	2

Forces in British Waters

Battle Squadrons	(4)
PreDreadnoughts	26
Light cruisers (attached)	4
Cruiser Squadrons	(7)
Armoured cruisers	10
Cruisers	23
Destroyer Flotillas	(4)
Cruisers (attached)	7
Destroyers	98
Submarine Flotillas	(7)
Destroyers (attached)	3
Submarines	59
Miscellaneous Flotillas	(7)
Destroyers	8
Torpedo boats	45
Torpedo gunboats	2
Submarines	4
Armed tugs	6
Trawlers Admiralty	13
Chartered	13
Fitting out in Britain	
Dreadnoughts	1
Armoured cruisers	2
Cruisers	6
Armed merchant cruisers	5
Seaplane carriers	4

Overseas Forces
Mediterranean

Battlecruiser squadrons	(1)
Battlecruisers	3
Cruiser Squadrons	(1)
Armoured cruisers	4
Attached forces	
Cruisers	4
Destroyers	16
Torpedo gunboats	1
Armed merchant cruisers	1
West Atlantic	
Armoured cruisers	3
Cruisers	4
Armed merchant cruisers	1
South Atlantic	
Cruisers	1
South Africa	
Cruisers	3
Gunboat	1
Pacific	
Cruisers	2
Sloops	2
New Zealand	
Cruisers	3
Sloops	1
Australia	
Battlecruisers	1
Cruisers	4
Destroyers	3
Submarines	2
East Indies	
PreDreadnoughts	1
Cruisers	2
Sloops	3
China	
PreDreadnought	1
Armoured cruisers	2
Cruisers	1
Destroyers	8
Torpedo boats	4
Submarines	3
Sloops	6
Armed merchant cruisers	4 (fitting out)

APPENDIX 5: INTERWAR DEFENCE ESTIMATES

Year	Expenditure (in millions[1])		Construction[2] Ordered					Completed					Manpower (thousands)	
	Estimate	net	BB	CV	C	DD	SM	BB	CV	C	DD	SM	Voted	Average serving
1919	157.5	154								6	10		280	176
1920	84.25	92.5						1*		2			136	124
1921	82.5	75.75					1			1			123.75	127
1922	64.75	57.5	2		1					3	1		118.5	107.75
1923	58	54									1		99.5	99
1924	55.75	55.5			5	2			1	1	3		100.5	99.5
1925	60.5	60			4					1	1		102.5	100.25
1926	58	57.25			3		6			2	2	1	102.5	100.75
1927	58	58.25			1	9	6	2		1		2	102.25	102
1928	57.25	57.25				9	4			5			101.75	100.5
1929	55.75	56			1	9	3			4		6	99.75	99.3
1930	51.75	52.25			3	9	3			3	8	7	97	95
1931	51.5	51			3	9	3			1	10	1	93.5	92.5
1932	50.5	50.25			3	9	3				5	3	91.5	89.5
1933	53.5	53.5			3	9	3			2	5	3	90.3	89.75
1934	56.5	56.5		1	4	9	3			2	10	2	92.3	91.3
1935	60	64.75			3	9	3			3	8	4	101	94.25
1936	81.25	81	2	2	7	18	8			1	17	3	99	99.75
1937	78	78.25	3	2	7	16	7			5	9	3	112	107
1938	96.25	96.5			1	2	16		1	2	11	6	146.5	118.25
1939	63.5**	99.5			1	2	16			3	22	5	130	120
Total	1435	1461.5	7	7	52	149	53	3	3	46	125	46		

1 To nearest quarter

2 Does not include conversions

* Battlecruiser *Hood*

** In addition, 20 destroyer escorts and 56 corvettes were ordered under these Estimates

APPENDIX 6: PRINCIPAL POLITICAL AND NAVAL APPOINTMENTS, 1914–39

Year	Government	Prime Minister	First Lord	First Sea Lord
1914	Liberal	H. Asquith	W.S. Churchill A. Balfour (26/5/15)	L. Battenburg Fisher (29/10/14)
10/6/15	Coalition	,,	,,	Jackson Jellicoe (3/12/16)
7/12/16	,,	L. George	Sir E. Carson Sir E. Geddes (20/7/17) W.H. Long (14/1/19) Lord Lee (14/2/21)	,, Wemyss (27/12/17) Beatty (1/11/19)
23/10/22	Conservative	B. Law	L. Amery	,,
22/5/23	,,	S. Baldwin	,,	,,
22/1/24	Labour	R. Macdonald	Lord Chelmsford	,,
4/11/24	Conservative	S. Baldwin	W. Bridgeman	,, Madden (30/7/27)
8/6/29	Labour	R. Macdonald	A. Alexander	,, Field (30/7/30)
25/8/31	Labour	,,	Sir A. Chamberlain Sir B. Monsell (9/11/31)	,, Chatfield (21/6/32)
7/6/35	Conservative	S. Baldwin	,,	,,
22/11/35	,,	,,	,, Sir S. Hoare (12/6/36)	,,

Year	Government	Prime Minister	First Lord	First Sea Lord
28/5/37	,,	N. Chamberlain	A. Duff Cooper	
			Lord Stanhope (27/10/38)	Backhouse (7/9/38)
				Pound (15/7/39)
3/9/39	,,	,,	W.S. Churchill	,,

APPENDIX 7: PRINCIPLE AIRCRAFT OF THE FAA, 1919–39

Aircraft	Role	Crew	In service
Avro Bison	Spotter/Recce	3–4	1921–29
Blackburn Dart	Torpedo	1	1921–33
Blackburn Blackburn	Spotter/Recce	3–4	1923–31
Fairey Flycatcher	Fighter	1	1923–24
Fairey IIID	Spotter/Recce	3	1924–31
Fariey IIIF	Spotter/Recce	3	1928–36
Blackburn Ripon	Torpedo/Bomber/Recce	2	1929–34
Hawker Nimrod	Fighter	1	1932–39
Hawker Osprey	Fighter/Recce	2	1932–39
Fariey Seal	Spotter/Recce	3	1933–38
Blackburn Baffin	Torpedo/Bomber	2	1934–36
Blackburn Shark	Torpedo/Spotter	2–3	1935–39
Supermarine Walrus	Spotter/Recce	3	1935–45
Fariey Swordfish	Torpedo/Spotter/Recce	2–3	1936–45
Fariey Seafox	Spotter/Recce	2	1937–43
Blackburn Skua	Dive bomber/Fighter	2	1938–41
Gloster Gladiator	Fighter	1	1939–41

APPENDIX 8: FLEET AIR ARM STRENGTH

Date	No in service	Organisation
1/24	78	13 Flights
10/24	128	18 Flights
10/30	144	24 Flights
9/32	156	26 Flights
5/35	175	15 Squadrons
3/36	217	18 Squadrons
9/39	340*	20 Squadrons

*225 aircraft were based on carriers, the remainder being formed into catapult flights for service on battleships and cruisers

Glossary

AA	Anti-aircraft	HTP	Hydrogen Test Peroxide	RFA	Royal Fleet Auxiliary
ABDA	American, British, Dutch, Australian Command	ICBM	Intercontinental ballistic missile	RFC	Royal Flying Corps
				RM	Royal Marine
AEW	Airborne early warning	ihp	Indicated horsepower	RNAS	Royal Naval Air Service
AOC	Air Officer Commanding	in	Inches	RNR	Royal Naval Reserve
ACNS(P)	Assistant Chief Naval Staff (Policy)	KCB	Knight Commander of the Bath	SAS	Special Air Service
				SBS	Special Boat Service
ASV	Air-to-surface-vessel	kts	Knots	sec	Seconds
ASW	Anti-submarine warfare			SB	Smooth bore
		lb	Pounds	SOE	Senior officer escort
		LCT	Landing craft tank	SS	Steam ship
BEF	British Expeditionary Force	LPD	Landing platform dock	SSCS	Surface Ship Command System
BL	Breech-loading	LPH	Landing platform - helicopter	SSN	Nuclear-powered attack submarine
BLR	Breech-loading rifled	LST	Landing ship tank	
		LVT	Landing vehicle tracked	STUFT	Ships taken up from trade
CAAIS	Computed Assisted Action Information System	m	million	TB	Torpedo boat
CACS	Computer Assisted Command System	MAC	Merchant Aircraft Carrier	TBD	Torpedo boat destroyer
cal	Calibre	MAD	Magnetic Anomaly Detector	TBS	Talk Between Ships
CAM	Catapult Aircraft Merchant			TEZ	Total Exclusion Zone
		MGB	Motor gunboat	TF	Task Force
CID	Committee of Imperial Defence	ML	Motor launch	
		MLR	Muzzle loading rifled	VC	Victoria Cross
C-in-C	Commander-in-Chief	MoD	Ministry of Defence	VLR	Very Long Range
cm	Centimetre	MOMP	Mid Ocean Meeting Point	VSTOL	Vertical/Short Take-Off and Landing
COSAG	Combined Steam and Gas	MP	Member of Parliament	
cwt	Hundredweight	mph	Miles per hour	yds	Yards
		MTB	Motor torpedo boat	
FAA	Fleet Air Arm			
FDE	Fighting Destroyer Escort	NAS	Naval Air Squadron	
ft	Feet	NATO	North Atlantic Treaty Organisation	
		nhp	Nominal horsepower	
GNAT	German Naval Acoustic Torpedo	nm	Nautical mile	
grt	Gross registered tons	OPV	Offshore patrol vessel	
HF/DF	High frequency direction finding	pdr	Pounder	
HMS	His/Her Majesty's Ship	QF	Quick firer	
Hon	Honourable			
hp	Horsepower	RAF	Royal Air Force	
HQ	Headquarters	RCN	Royal Canadian Navy	

Indexes

INDEX OF WARS, BATTLES AND ACTIONS

254